MODERNITY
AND
THE AFRICAN
CINEMA

Femi Okiremuete Shaka

Africa World Press, Inc.

P.O. Box 1892
Trenton, NJ 08607

P.O. Box 48
Asmara, ERITREA

Africa World Press, Inc.

P.O. Box 1892
Trenton, NJ 08607

P.O. Box 48
Asmara, ERITREA

Book Cover: Roger Dormann
Book Design: Getahun Alemayehu and Sam Saverance
Cover Photo by Vincent Head and with the kind permission of California Newsreel

Library of Congress Cataloging-in-Publication Data

Shaka, Femi Okiremuete.
Modernity and the African cinema : a study in colonial discourse, postcoloniality, and modern African identities / Femi Okiremuete Shaka.
  p. cm.
Includes bibliographical references.
  ISBN 1-59221-085-6 (cloth) — ISBN 1-59221-086-4 (pbk.)
  1. Motion pictures—Africa. 2. Motion pictures in education—Africa.
3. Africa—In motion pictures. I. Title.

PN1993.5.A35S45 2003
791.43'096—dc22
                    2003025108

TABLE OF CONTENTS

ACKNOWLEDGEMENTS

This study was made possible by the Commonwealth Scholarship Commission, UK, which provided the grant for my graduate studies at the University of Warwick, Coventry, England, and the Fulbright Scholarship Commission, USA, which provided grant for additional research under its Fulbright African Senior Research Scholar Program. My profound gratitude goes to both bodies for funding my research.

Next, I should like to thank my supervisor, Professor Richard Dyer, who supervised my doctorate degree thesis, and the following Faculty staff under whom I studied, Ginette Vicendeau, Charlotte Brunsdon, Victor Perkins, and Allison Butler, of the Department of Film and Television, and David Dabydeen and Benita Parry of the (Post)Colonial Studies Program, University of Warwick.

My year's stay at the Africana Studies Program, New York University, was extremely rewarding. It afforded me the opportunity of getting under the tutelage of Manthia Diawara, Guy Martin, Clyde Taylor, and Awam Amkpa, and of meeting movie stars and participating in the lively cultural exchanges and debates being stimulated by the Program. I should like to thank Laura G. Rice, Barbara Lewis, Robert Hinton, and the entire staff of the entire staff of the Africana Studies Program, NYU, for the wonderful job they are doing.

Here, at the University of Port Harcourt, I owe a debt of gratitude to Professor Charles Nnolim, a seminal scholar of many parts, and former Dean, Faculty of Humanities, and the following Faculty members who read and engaged in enlightened debates on aspects of my work, G. Anke Nutsukpo, Onyemaechi Udumukwu, Acho Akakuru, Denis Ekpo and Frank Ugiomoh.

I have also enjoyed the goodwill and friendship of the following people at one time or the other, Onookome Okome, Kingsley Owete, Isaac Okonny and Emman Oga. I want to thank them for their camaraderie and moral support.

Finally, my expressed gratitude goes to my lovely wife, Esther, and my son, Brian, for enduring and tolerating my regular absence from home.

Femi Okiremuete Shaka
February, 2003

1 Introduction

In one of his earliest works, *Borom Sârret*, Sembène Ousmane, a pioneer African filmmaker, opens his film with an image of a horse-drawn cart with modern tyres. This symbolic contraption is a fitting image of the sort of creative grafting that has been going on since the encounter between Europeans and Africans, in the 15th century. The image appropriately symbolizes the concept of hybridity that underlies modern African identity. The horse is a traditional means of fast transport in Africa, but the motorcar is an introduction from Europe. In this film, Sembène seems to suggest that modern African experience is characterized by the need to creatively adjust to the concept of modernity. Of course, issues of race, nationality, ethnicity, class, gender and sexuality determine such creative adjustments. But generally speaking, the survival of continental and diasporic Africans has been predicated on this power of creative adaptation in often very difficult conditions. For the cart driver and people in his class who cannot afford a modern vehicle, the need to keep up with the times is met by creative grafting of a horse to a cart with modern wheels.

Modernity and the African Cinema sets out to explore the historical and cultural consequences of the contact between Europe and Africa, from the 15th century to the present era of globalization. The main argument pursued is that the construction of modern African identities, in all spheres of life, including that of the cinematic institution, is very much a product of the Euro-African contact, the patterns of discourses and institutional practices it has produced, and Africans' responses to them. The field of African cinema, like its scholarly, literary and artistic counterparts, is regarded as a product of the Euro-African contact, and *Modernity and the African Cinema* argues for a thorough archaeological analysis of the discursive practices, which have overlaid that contact. There is an urgent need for such a close interrogation of these archival discursive practices in order to understand their institutional and disciplinary contexts, what they teach us about the changing nature of the consequences of the contact, and strategies for reconstructing and reinventing modern African identities in the light of the globalization of the world.

This study is regarded as part of the soul-searching process which has produced insightful works such as Chinweizu's *The West and the Rest of Us*, Mudimbe's *The Invention of Africa*, Anthony Appiah's *In My Father's House*, Manthia Diawara's *In Search of Africa*, and Abiola Irele's *The African Imagination*, on the crises facing post-colonial modern African nations, as new institutions reflecting the emergence of the continent into modernity impose new identities which require coming to terms with the consequences of running a modern economy. *Modernity and the African Cinema*, is therefore, part of this ongoing self-examination, by Africans and people of African descent, to understand the pitfalls of traditional African institutional practices, which made and continues to make Africans vulnerable in their dealings with other races. The urgency of such a soul-searching process cannot be over-emphasized in the light of the borderless fierce competition of the global world in which there still exists the potentials for a replay of our historical experiences as a conquered, enslaved and marginalized race.

This writer is aware of the tendency of studies such as this to create discomfiture in our former colonial overlords who would wish that the historical antecedents of our current impoverished state should be laid to rest. But at whose expense are we now being asked to forget the history of our conquest and impoverishment? To forget such a horrendous experience, indeed, to be historically complacent, is to open us, once more, to a perpetual life of racial servitude. Rather than do that, this study has undertaken an archaeological analysis of the discursive practices underlying the Euro-African contact, as both products and producers of the uneven power relations between both continents, which is best understood within the context of the emergent experiences of the trans-Atlantic slave trade, colonialism, postcoloniality, and the continuing experiences of neo -colonialism and globalization. The argument is that we should undertake a constant critical self-examination in the light of this checkered history, to continue to use that history to guide and arm ourselves, and to avoid the pitfalls of traditional African institutional practices which made and continues to make us less competitive and vulnerable before our competitors and enemies alike.

One of the things, which struck one in the process of carrying out research for this book, is that the subjugation of Africans has been largely due to our susceptibility to easy, blind, trust in our dealings with strangers. Such blind trust, sometimes, borders on naiveté and is constantly exploited by our enemies. In order to overcome this shortcoming, there is an urgent need to develop a much more cynical and skeptical frame of mind in our dealings with people, even our so-called trusted friends. Anything short of this will leave us constantly vulnerable.

With respect to the cinematic institution, this study attempts to provide a theoretical framework for the criticism of both colonial and post-colonial African cinema. Emphasis is placed on the extent to which the nature of colonial cinematic policies and practices have influenced post-colonial African cinema, with reference to Africa's emergence into modernity, and the forms of subjectivity constructed through cinematic representation. The basic argument is that the cinematic practices of colonial Africa, and post-colonial texts located in that period, have not been given the serious attention they deserve compared, for instance, to the literature of the period, or post-colonial literary texts situated in the era. In literature, works such as Dorothy Hammond and Alta Jablow's *The Myth of Africa*, M.M. Mahmood's *The Colonial Encounter: A Reading of Six Novels*, and Abdul R. JanMohamed's *Manichean Aesthetics*, have given a detailed study of colonial and post-colonial literary texts situated within colonial Africa. The lack of a detailed study of the equivalent cinematic practices has resulted, when passing remarks are made to it, in generalizing arguments that lump uncritically together the two divergent cinematic practices that emerged in Africa during this period: colonial African instructional cinema and colonialist African cinema. The former is sponsored by governmental and non-governmental agencies, while the latter is produced for commercial reasons.

Though African cinematic studies such as Manthia Diawara's African Cinema, Françoise Pfaff's Twenty-five Black African

Filmmakers and The Cinema of Ousmane Sembène: A Pioneer
Filmmaker, Angela Martin's African Films: The Context of
Production, Lizbeth Malkmus and Roy Armes's Arab and African
Filmmaking, and Frank Ukadike's Black African Cinema, have all
helped in charting and clarifying the field of African cinema, in
terms of its history, they have often neglected to provide a
theoretical framework for the criticism of African cinema. For
instance, these works have paid very little attention to specifying
and accounting for the two divergent cinematic practices, which
co-existed in colonial Africa, i.e., colonialist African cinema and
colonial instructional cinema. As a result of this oversight,
historians and critics of African cinema have failed to account for
the cinematic practice, which inspired post-colonial African
historical texts, and the tradition of colonialist counter-discourse in
African cinema. The studies also neglect to give a proper definition
of African cinema and its nature. This current study attempts to fill
in these gaps.

Some of the major issues, which *Modernity and the African
Cinema* sets out to explicate, include the relation between traditional
African institutional practices and the legacy of European colonial
institutions. For instance, how have Africans been negotiating the
dual or, sometimes, the triple heritage [for those with the additional
burden of Arabized cultural influences], as represented through the
cinematic institutions of Africa? The crisis of identity in most
modern African societies can be traced to the problem of creative
adaptability, which Africans face in their daily lives with respect to
choices made in institutional practices, which are expected to yield
optimal social development. These choices affect who we are, and
the way we perceive the world around us. Since *Modernity and the
African Cinema* examines questions of subjectivity and agency, and
the relation between them and a modern institution such as the
cinema, a theoretical framework was deemed inevitable. Also
examined is the relation between the cinema and operational
concepts such as "Africanness," "Subjectivity," and "Modernity."
Within this framework, the question of how Africans negotiate the
complex issue of loyalty to constituted authorities with respect to
the Old State, signified by the authority of the traditional African
kingdom, and the Modern State, signified by the authority of
inherited European colonial institutions, is examined. Quite often,
Africans find themselves caught in the demand for loyalty by both

the ethnically configured old African kingdom and the modern secular state inherited from European colonialism. This study reveals that the cinematic institution, especially the discursive tradition of colonialist cinema which were canonized in works such as D.W. Griffith's *The Birth of a Nation* (1915) in America, and Alexander Korda's *Sanders of the River* (1935), in Britain, have traditionally demonized traditional African institutional practices in order to legitimize the authority of European colonialism in Africa.

The terms "colonialist African discourse/cinema" have been used in this work to designate continental and diasporic European representations of Africans/people of African descent, which use European metaphysical concepts, moral values, ethics and aesthetics, to judge and represent the broad spectrum of traditional African institutional practices as pathological or inferior imitations of European originals. The terms "colonialist African discourse/ cinema" are not tied exclusively to the debate surrounding the era of European colonialism in Africa, because, as argued in this work, the canonical authority of colonialist African discourse goes as far back as the classical era, and this history needs to be examined in conjunction with the nature of the popular images of "blackness" in the European imagination. To tie the debate to only the era of European colonialism in Africa is to overlook the relevance of the canonical authority of the discursive tradition under consideration. Hence terms such as "colonialist African discourse," "colonialist African literature," and "colonialist African cinema," respectively, have been used in this work to refer to the body of works produced within the tradition of colonialist discourse before, during, and after colonialism in Africa. Moreover, the term "African cinema" is used in this work to refer to the totality of the institutional practices of the film industry in Africa. It, therefore, covers aspects of the industry, ranging from film laboratories, production companies and film studios, distribution companies and exhibition theaters, trained manpower comprising producers, directors, writers, film texts, actors and actresses, cinemato- graphers, sound engineers and production recordists, light designers and technicians, editors, production and costume designers, stunts personnel, and the financial and advertising sub- sectors of the industry. The term "African cinema," therefore, refers to the totality of the institutional practices of the industry, while "African film" refers to the textual product of the industry.

In other respects, this study is concerned with providing a proper definition and theoretical framework for the criticism of African cinema. The main thrust is the examination of the nature of colonial and post-colonial African cinema, with emphasis on how the cinematic practices of the colonial period and post-colonial texts, situated in that era, have constructed African subjectivity and culture, in contrast to European subjectivity and culture in Africa in the same period. The selection of texts is based on content, that is, the presence of both Africans and Europeans in films set in the colonial period, and easy accessibility.

With respect to colonialist African cinema, only Richard Maynard's *Africa on Film: Myth and Reality* has attempted a study of how Africa and Africans are represented in colonialist cinema. This collection of anthropological and historical essays and film reviews is, however, a basic study of very limited scope, since it covers few colonialist African film texts, and does not offer any detailed textual analysis, nor does it explain how colonialist thoughts are articulated in the cinema. Besides, most of the assertions made in the book seem to equate cinematic representation with reality. Robert Stam and Louise Spence have, long ago, questioned the validity of such a methodological approach when they argued that

> studies of filmic colonialism and racism tend to focus on certain dimensions of film — social portrayal, plot and character. While posing legitimate questions concerning narrative plausibility and mimetic accuracy, negative stereotypes and positive images, the emphasis on realism has often betrayed an exaggerated faith in the possibilities of verisimilitude in art in general and the cinema in particular, avoiding the fact that films are inevitably constructs, fabrications, representations. (Stam and Spence, 1983: 3)

As a result of the problems involved in approaching the study of colonialist discourse in cinema from the perspective of realism and verisimilitude, this study specifically investigates the organizing thoughts and regime of authority, both contextual and intertextual, underlying colonialist African cinema. This choice of approach is informed by the fact that one considers colonialist African cinema as part of a larger discursive tradition within European scholarly and artistic works. This practice dates as far back as classical times, though it has become common practice to locate its roots within the ambit of the trans-Atlantic slave trade, European nineteenth century racial theories, and colonialism in Africa. The main argument pursued is that the uneven power structure, which underlies much of the Euro-African relationship, since classical times, should be taken into consideration in the analysis of colonialist African discourse and its cinematic practice. In specific terms, the study examines how the uneven relation of power and knowledge between the two continents has contributed to the constitution of African subjectivity and culture in colonialist African cinema. In this study, the analysis of colonialist African cinema is informed by Michel Foucault's argument that there is an underlying relation between power and knowledge in the constitution of any field of study:

> we should admit rather that power produces knowledge (and not simply by encouraging it because it serves power or by applying it because it is useful); that power and knowledge directly imply one another; that there is no power relation without the correlative constitution of a field of knowledge, nor any knowledge that does not presuppose and constitute at the same time power relations. (Foucault, 1977: 27)

In this analysis of colonialist African cinema, however, particular attention is paid to the visible exteriority of the texts and how they construct both Africans and Europeans, and not to what lies hidden in them, or in relation to reality. This is in keeping with Said's theoretical injunction that it is the exteriority of the colonialist text that describes. As he puts it,

> the things to look at are styles, figure of speech, setting, narrative devices, historical and social circumstances, not the correctness of the representation nor its fidelity to some great original. The exteriority of the representation is always governed by some version of truism that if the [Other] could represent itself, it would; since it cannot, the representation does the job, for the West, and *faute de mieux* for the poor [Other]. (Said, 1978: 21)

In this regard, the study has set out to investigate how European texts have constructed the African through the ages, in order to place in proper perspective the juncture at which the cinema picked up the practice. This work is, therefore, not very different from Donald Bogle's *Toms, Coons, Mammies and Mulattoes*, Henry T. Sampson's *Blacks in Black and White*, and Charlene Regester's work, with respect to accounting for Oscar Micheux's heroic efforts to produce a counter-discursive cinematic tradition to that of

Hollywood's representation of people of African descent. An exceptional representative impulse, in this regard, has been the recent work on Oscar Micheaux and his contemporaries, titled, *Oscar Micheaux and his Circle*, edited by Pearl Bowser, Jane Gaines and Charles Musser. This work gives a detailed account of the attempt by the pioneer African-American filmmaker, Oscar Micheaux, to cultivate an alternative cinematic representation of people of African descent, in contrast to that of Hollywood cinema of his era. For filmmakers in continental Africa, serious cinematic engagement with colonialist African cinema did not begin in earnest until the 1960s.

As regards post-colonial African cinema, the study examines the scope and limitations of works already done in the field, and proposes a theoretical framework, including a general cinematic reading theory, based on the concept of "subjectivity" for the criticism of African cinema. Also examined are both colonial and post-colonial film production structures and sponsorship policies in Anglophone and Francophone African countries, with emphasis on how these policies have affected film production in countries within both linguistic blocs.

Chapter One undertakes an assessment of modern African identity in all spheres of life, including that of the cinematic institution, with a view to placing, in proper historical context, the framework within which the cinematic institution emerged in Africa. This is followed with an account of how the institution has been mobilized by both Europeans and Africans in the construction of modern African social identity and history.

Chapter Two deals with methodological problems in the criticism of African cinema and colonialist African discourse. With respect to colonial African cinema, the near neglect of the study of the cinematic practices of the era is noted, and it is argued that this has resulted in generalizations that tend to lump uncritically together the two divergent cinematic practices of the period. To avoid this kind of generalization, the necessary distinctions are made in order to account for the practice, which inspired the tradition of colonialist counter-discourse in African cinema. As regards post-colonial African cinema, a tendency favoring the study of the history of the film industry, at the expense of textual analysis, has also been noted. When textual analyses are undertaken, the emphasis is on narrative, but, since narrative is trans-media, the specificity of the nature of narration within the cinematic medium is not responded to. As a result, such studies are indistinguishable from other forms of narrative-based analysis in other media. The study also attempts to explain the concept of African cinema in relation to theories of "Third Cinema." The literature on colonialist discourse is approached in this study through examination of the various critical perspectives on colonialist African discourse. This is followed by a genealogical study of the roots and scope of the practice. In

Chapter Three, a definition of African cinema is attempted. Also addressed, is the issue of the nature of African cinema, with respect to emerging generic forms, as well as how issues of African identity and subjectivity, belief-systems and culture, and the problem of tradition versus modernity are addressed by African filmmakers. This is followed by a proposed theoretical framework, including a general cinematic reading theory based on the concept of subjectivity, for the criticism of African cinema.

In Chapter Four, the roots of colonialist African cinema are traced to both colonialist African literature and an existing canon of colonialist African discourse in European archives. The main argument here is that to understand the resilience of the colonialist African mode of representation, one need to take cognizance of the uneven power and knowledge relations which underlay the contact between Europe and Africa, and the subsequent slave trade and colonialism which followed. Though Brian Street and some scholars seem to overlook both the canonical authority and the contextual influence of colonialist discourse in their studies of the novels of empire, as is evident in this study, there are sufficient grounds in acknowledging that value judgments made in the novels of empire have canonical authority behind them that stretch as far back as the classical era.

In Chapter Five, the historical context within which the practice of colonial African instructional cinema was instituted in Africa during the colonial era is examined. This is done by tracing the origin of instructional film practice in Africa, and by examining how it was institutionalized through projects such as the Bantu Educational Cinema Experiment, and those which followed, such as the instructional film practices of the Colonial Film Unit (CFU), the Film and Photo Bureau of the Belgian Congo, and the Congolese Center for Catholic Action Cinema (C.C.C.A.C.) of the same territory. This background information is intended to establish the context within which the practices of instructional cinema emerged in Africa during the colonial period. The argument in this chapter is that the practices of colonial instructional cinema instituted a different regime of representation of Africa and Africans that stands in direct contrast to that of films of colonialist African cinema.

Chapter Six investigates the historical background of colonialist African cinema by tracing its roots to colonialist African discourse in general and colonialist African literature in particular. The chapter also presents various types of films, which constitute the practice, and gives a general tabulation of its conventions and modes of representation. The main argument in this chapter is that colonialist African cinema draws upon various metaphors of savagery and bestiality already canonized in popular European culture and colonialist African discourse in its representation of Africans. These metaphors draw associations between Africans and animals in both the articulations of their physical outlooks and social attitudes. Furthermore, the practice attempts to legitimize European colonialism by setting up Africans as people incapable of sustaining modern democratic self-governance, social development, justice and equity. In relation to the general concept of African subjectivity, one has argued that colonialist African cinema devalues the humanity of Africans, and it should be distinguished from colonial African instructional cinema. Space and time in the genre are defined mostly by the presence and actions of white characters, with Africans acting as the background against which European adventurers and colonial administrators play out their fantasies, fears, anxieties and desires.

Chapter Seven deals with the nature of film production structures and sponsorship policies of both Anglophone and Francophone African countries. Also examined is the impact of both British and French colonial and post-colonial policies on post-colonial film production in Africa. This is done in response to some of the generalizations used to explain the relative high output and quality of film production in Francophone Africa, in contrast to those of Anglophone African countries.

In Chapter Eight, the historical background to the response of post-colonial African cinema to colonialism and colonialist African discourse/cinema is examined. The main argument in this chapter is that, though post-colonial African historical texts situated within the colonial period respond to the whole colonial enterprise, they are inspired, first and foremost, by the desire to construct alternative cinematic representations of Africans, African history and culture, in contrast to that of the discursive tradition of colonialist African cinema. In this regard, these texts present an African version of history and historical events that are essentially counter-discursive in nature. In this cinematic tradition, space and time are democratized in relation to the construction of African and European subjectivities. The representation of European colonial enterprise in Africa is, however, revealed through an African perspective of that history.

Chapter Nine concludes the study with a comparative analysis of the narrative strategies of the cinematic practices of the colonial era and that of post-colonial African historical texts.

2 MODERNITY AND THE AFRICAN CINEMA

Introduction

My basic argument is that the construction of modern African identity in all spheres of life, including that of the cinematic institution, is a product of the Euro-African contact that started in the 15th century. That contact transformed traditional African institutional practices by overlaying them with European substitutes during the period of colonialism. The post-colonial period, especially its early period, with its politics of cultural reawakening attempted to romanticize traditional African institutional practices but, as the years went by, this practice was abandoned in favor of a pragmatic marriage of the institutional practices of both continents in such a manner that the new institutional practices which have emerged can be considered hybrid in nature. These hybrid modern institutional practices have been represented through the cinema, which is one of the modern institutions inherited from European colonialism.

The cinematic institution started out quite early as a form of entertainment in Africa, promoted by smart businessmen out to make money. Exhibitions were held in city and small town halls and school compounds, even before movie theatres were built. As the popularity of the medium grew, missionaries out to convert Africans to Christianity used the cinema as an instrument for proselytization. Later on, government agencies such as Film Censorship Boards and Film Divisions within Ministries of Information began to be established to regulate the industry as well as to build some rudimentary infrastructure for the production of documentaries. During the Second World War, the cinematic institution was to become an invaluable propaganda tool for the British colonial government in its effort to mobilize the population of its colonies towards the successful prosecution of the war. The post-war years again witnessed the transformation of the medium into an institution for social mobilization for purposes of instruction in modern institutional practices by the colonial state.

Within the cinematic institutions of Africa, there were three competing institutional practices vying for the patronage of African spectators right from the earliest period of the industry's emergence on the continent. These were (i) the commercial interests whose productions and exhibition practices alarmed colonial authorities and therefore necessitated the establishment of Film Censorship Boards, (ii) missionary sponsored productions, and (iii) government sponsored productions. Each of these production practices had its formal regime of representation with respect to the constitution of African subjectivities and identities. Overall however, the documentary practices of the missionaries and those of government agencies seemed to carry certain affinities in the sense that they were out to teach Africans modern methods of doing things aimed at promoting colonial government developmental policies. In a sense, therefore, there was always a certain propagandistic or didactic orientation about these films. They always showed Africans enthusiastically embracing the new religious practices or colonial government developmental models.

The differences in goals, therefore, set films of both institutional practices apart, in comparison to those of the commercial cinematic practice whose audiences were essentially in Europe and North America, and which used the continent as an ethnographic space for rehashing popular European images of Africa as a frontier site full of barbarous natives engaged in cannibalism, paganism, perennial inter-tribal warfare, and other forms of bestialities, which were cinematically projected upon the continent and its people. The institutional practices and regime of representation of commercial cinema, therefore, stands in contrast to that of films sponsored by the missionaries and government agencies. What one has found out however is that because of the obvious paternalistic statements by officials of both the missionaries and government agencies that produced the films, historians and critics of African cinema seem to have conflated their views with their products. But since my concern is with differences in regimes of representation of Africa and Africans in instructional films compared to those of colonialist film practice, there is need for such distinctions to be made. These theoretical explanations are required because film scholarship involves a scholarly dialogue among film scholars, between them and students aspiring to scholarship in the field, and between them and the general reading public.

In this chapter, an attempt is made to define the cinematic institutions of Africa and to argue that their nature as a pluralistic institutional practice covering the broad spectrum of the people of the continent needs to be properly explained. In addition, the nature of modern African subjectivity and social experience as they manifest in institutional practices, especially that of the cinema, should be placed in proper perspective. The chapter examines these issues and concludes with an analysis of Ousmane Sembène's two earliest films, *Borom Sârret* (1963) and *Mandabi/The Money Order* (1968), to see how one of Africa's pioneers of the cinematic institution deals with the issue of modern African subjectivity and social experience in the early years of post-colonial rule in Africa.

Methodological Problems in the Theory and Criticism of African Cinema

Much of what has been written so far on African cinema has failed to make the kind of distinctions that I am talking about. In a sense, the cinematic practices of colonial Africa and post-colonial texts situated within the period by European and North American [especially Hollywood] cinematic practices, and Africans' counter-discursive rereading of the history of the period, are not adequately accounted for. For instance, when one analyzes film texts from the colonial period or post-colonial texts located within the era, there is arguably a clear indication that the cinematic practice, which has inspired Africans' rereading of their history with Europe, is that identifiable with colonialist African discourse/cinema. Lack of detailed study of the cinematic practices of colonial Africa has, therefore, resulted in generalizing arguments that lump uncritically together the two divergent cinematic practices that emerged in Africa during this period, i.e., colonial African instructional cinema and colonialist African cinema.

   This tendency is obvious in the works of historians and critics of African cinema such as Manthia Diawara's *African Cinema*, Françoise Pfaff's *Twenty-five Black African Filmmakers* and *The Cinema of Ousmane Sembène: A Pioneer Filmmaker*, Angela Martin's *African Films: The Context of Production*, Lizbeth Malkmus and Roy Armes's *Arab and African Filmmaking*, and Frank Ukadike's *Black African Cinema*. While these works have helped immensely in charting and elucidating the field of African cinema, in terms of its history, they have taken for granted the need to provide a proper theoretical framework for the criticism of African cinema. This theoretical oversight can be adduced as one of the reasons for lumping together several inter-related but distinct strands of the cinematic practices of both colonial and post-colonial Africa. Theoretical oversight may also explain why the problematic term "African cinema" is not conceptualized in the works in question. These scholarly works tend to homogenize and mask distinct issues, which require proper clarification before the term, can be used to qualify cinematic practices and institutions of Africa. To correct this theoretical oversight, this work uses three key concepts to anchor the issue of modernity and African cinema. The key concepts are: the notions of "Africanness," "modernity" and "subjectivity." These terms will also be contextualized to establish the order of knowledge that they yield.

   The concept of "Africanness," which is central to pan-Africanism as conceived by pioneer pan-Africanists like Kwame Nkrumah, Gamal Abdel Nasser, Sekou Toure, Nnamdi Azikiwe, Jomo Kenyatta, and Julius Nyerere, was a social secular concept of the continental unity of people of all races, religion, class, ethnicity and gender, inspired by the revolutionary anti-colonial political movement which climaxed in the post-Second World War years and continues to serve as a source of inspiration in the neo-colonial era of globalization and consumer capitalism. My usage of the term here is informed by its original sense as a social secular concept for the empowerment of people of the African continent. By the same token, the term, "African cinema" requires explication because not everybody on the continent wants to be identified as an "African" nor subscribes to the notion of "modern African culture" as a transitory and hybrid construct. Therefore, the scope and limit of the cinematic practices included in such a definition should be properly defined. Partly to respond to issues such as these, Ali

Mazrui poses the question of who an "African" is in the following manner:

> But what is an "African"? There are two main types - those who are "African" in a continental sense (like Egyptians and Algerians) and those who are "African" in a racial sense (like Nigerians, Ugandans and Senegalese). Egyptians and Algerians are Africa's children of the soil. Sub-Saharan Blacks are Africa's children of the blood. In reality all those who are natives of Africa are children of the soil (called *wana-nchi* in Swahili language). But sub-Saharan Blacks are in addition Africa's children by racial blood. (Mazrui, 2002: 12)

From the foregoing one can see the difficulty in qualifying who an "African" is. For one thing, Mazrui's definition has characterized the concept of pan-Africanism in terms of geographic and racial orientation. As should be expected, such essentialist characterization is not without its own problematic since it doesn't seem to account for European-Africans: white Kenyans, Zimbabweans, and Namibians, not to mention the only group of Europeans on the continent who claim Afrikaner as their tribal identity. These are factors of history, products of the Euro-African contact which nobody can wish way. Because of such difficulties, the term, "African," is used in this work in all its plural connotations.

The next notion is that of "modernity." The concept of "modernity" is historically determined and located in European Enlightenment and the industrial revolution. The historical ferment of the post-Medieval era with its secularization of thought and knowledge propelled Europe and subsequently the rest of the world into modernity. Within this historical specificity, one has come to understand the notion to mean human relations governed by social secular thoughts of science, rationality, logic, and state institutions conceived as liberal democratic institutions answerable to the people who have voluntarily elected to suspend some of their personal liberties to the state as a representative social institution which has the obligations to protect its citizens and their civil liberties. Among the rights granted citizens in the modern state is the right to freedom of association, ownership of personal properties, freedom of worship and religious faith, and to free speech. These rights are legislatively actualized and enshrined in the personal identity cards issued to citizens by the state. Finally, citizens in such a modern state are subject to the rule of law, which gives every citizen the right to a fair hearing, legal representation, equality before the law, and justice in judicial matters.

As an inherited concept therefore, "modernity" is conceived in this work as a transitory concept mediating African traditional institutional practices and those of modern Europe. In this sense, African modernity is a hybrid new construct which can neither be fully understood in terms of only African traditions or customs nor be reductively qualified in terms of only modern European institutions. African modernity is a hybrid, new construct that is being continuously forged out of both old and new institutional practices within the continent. This interconnectedness is what stands out in the work of Mahmood Mamdani when he argues in his book, *Citizen and Subject: Contemporary Africa and the Legacy of Late Colonialism*, that modern African subjectivities are caught between the demands and loyalties to the modern state as "citizens" and traditional institutions as "subjects." These demands and attachments are also ethnically based; hence there is a continual creative process of negotiating both traditional and modern institutional practices as well as inter-ethnic relations.

This ambivalent relationship of being caught between loyalty to either the "old state," built on internal colonialism and power structure around a dominant ethnic group which is represented by a pre-colonial African kingdom, and "modern African states," patched hurriedly together out of disparate ethnic groups at the Berlin Conference of 1884, is the source of friction and conflicts which seems to have acquired an independent force of their own in the emergent ethnic conflicts symbolized in the Old Biafran secession project in Nigeria, Tutsi-Hutu ethnic conflicts in the Great Lake region, and other classic cases in Senegal, Liberia, Sierra Leone and Côte d'Ivore. This incidentally also brings me to the final concept, which is that of "subjectivity" or "agency" in modern Africa. Perhaps one should quickly state here that subjectivity and agency are being used here in a plural sense to refer to the creative negotiation implied in inter-subjective relations and adaptiveness by Africans as they try to construct new identities out of the competing institutional practices of traditional African society and their European or other [Arab, for instance] institutional practices. It is in this respect that Richard Werbner has defined subjectivities as follows:

In analytic terms, subjectivities may be defined as *political*, a matter of subjugation to state authority; *moral*, reflected in the conscience and agency of subjects who bear rights, duties and obligations; and *realized existentially*, in the subjects' consciousness of their personal or intimate relations. These terms are not exhaustive, of course. There may be consumer subjectivity, arising in subjection to a global market, and that may conflict with subjugation to state authority. There may be playful or aestheticized self-fashioning, and this may reflect adoption of the latest, most fashionable ways of being wholly Other and the actual appropriation of modern subjectivism, all of which may proceed through new, virtually global struggles to control identity and command highly explicit consciousness. (original emphasis) (Werbner, 2002: 2)

All of the above go to show the creative adaptiveness, which underlies modern African experience as a product of institutional and cultural hybridization. Equally important is Francis B. Nyamnjoh's injunction that African subjectivity and agency is best understood as a *collectivized* notion linked to that of social intersubjectivity. He argues *against* the individualization of the notion, which believes that "agency or subjectivity is an undifferentiated phenomenon in any society, open to some and not to others, and that those who have it must prove their independence through conflictual and antagonistic relationship with others and with society" (Nyamnjoh, 2002: 135). It is worth quoting his conclusion on this issue since both of us seem to share similar views on the nature of modern African subjectivity:

> The chapter also challenges the parallel impression that imputes agency to the West and celebrates the Westerner and his/her impact on the rest of the world where tradition and custom are portrayed as obstacles to individual progress and achievement. It argues against such reductionist views of agency, acknowledging the fact that agency may take different forms and, most particularly, that it is construed and constructed differently in different societies, informed by history, culture, and economic factors…The way forward lies in recognizing the creative and intersubjective ways in which Africans merge their traditions with exogenous influences to create modernities that are not reducible to either but superior to both. (Nyamnjoh: 135)

In essence, modernity has been conceptualized in this work as a mediating and transitory concept, which historically can be located within the ambit of the Euro-African contact, beginning from the 15th century, and which is helping to shape and reshape modern African identities. But as a developmental concept, attempts must be made to transverse the ahistorical, specific location of human development essentially within the ferment of the European colonial conquests and empire building projects of the 19th century. A more persuasive argument would be one, which sees European Enlightenment and its consequent Scientific Revolution as a cumulative build up of earlier human civilizations in the sense in which Martin Bernal conceives it (Bernal, 1987). Such a theoretical proposition neither diminishes or removes the essential globalizing character of the European Enlightenment nor devalues this character as the main force behind the current globalization of the world. What is challenged, however, is the essentialist Eurocentric conception of human development as a consequence of European colonization of much of the rest of the world.

Towards a Definition of African Cinema

The problem of definition of modern African expressive arts was first addressed in a controversial work by Chinweizu, Jamie Onwuchekwa and Ihechukwu Madubuike titled *Toward the Decolonization of African Literature*. This work emerged within the ferment of the radical Neo-Negritudian politics of the 1980s, which tried to distance itself from Marxist aesthetics, which was then quite fashionable within the Nigerian literary scene. Their project was essentially that of cultural authentication. In the main, they tried to theorize African literature by posing the following rhetorical questions and attempting to find answers to them: (i) what is African literature?; (ii) by what criteria should African literature be judged?; (iii) what is the proper relationship between this body of works and other national and regional literatures in the world?

In answering these questions, these writers argued that there are regional literatures which include many national literatures in different languages, e.g. the American regional literatures which include the literatures of the United States (in English), Canada (in English and French), the Caribbean and South America (in English, French, Spanish and Portuguese) - and language literatures, some of which include many national literatures, e.g., (i)

British national literature; (ii) the national literatures of those countries where an exported English population is in control, e.g., Canada, the United States, Australia and New Zealand; (iii) the national literatures of those countries where English, though neither indigenous nor the mother-tongue of the politically dominant population or group, has become, as a legacy of colonialism, the official language in countries such as Nigeria, Kenya, India, Malaysia, the Caribbean etc.

These writers further argued that attempts to incorporate African literature into European literature by critics such as Adrian Roscoe and John Povey, on account of the fact that they are written in European languages, was wrong because what determines a regional or national literature were shared values and assumptions, world-outlook and belief-systems, ethos and so on. Although they acknowledged the fact that language does embody, and is a vehicle for expressing cultural values, it is not the crucial generator of those values and cannot *alone* be relied upon to supply literary criteria for assessing those works based on the language. A useful example was that though the national literatures of Britain, the United States, Canada, Australia and New Zealand share English language as the medium of literary expression, this was far less than sufficient grounds to judge them as identical literatures.

These writers argued that literary works produced for African audiences, by Africans and in African languages, whether these works were oral or written, constitute the historically indisputable core of African literature. In addition, works written by Africans in non-African languages, and works written by non-Africans in African languages, would be among those for which some legitimate doubt might be raised about their inclusion or exclusion from the canon of works of African literature. To consider a work as African literature, they argued that such works needed to be appraised to determine: (i) the primary audience for whom the work is intended; (ii) the cultural and national consciousness expressed in the works, whether through the author's voice or through the characters and their consciousness, habits, comportment, and diction; (iii) the nationality of the writer, whether by birth or naturalization; (iv) the language in which the work was written.

According to Chinweizu *et al*, most African literature written in non-African languages, e.g., English, French, Portuguese,

Spanish, etc qualified as African literature for the first three reasons. Though the concept of Pan-Africanism upon which Chinweizu *et al* based their definition of African literature tends to be homogenizing in its suppression of the contending issues related to the national question in individual African countries and affiliated issues of class, gender, race, ethnicity, etc, this attempt for once tried to conceptualize the nature of African literature. The same however cannot be said for African cinema.

In a related development, Abiola Irele in the 1980s was also trying to conceptualize the basis for qualifying modern African literatures as "African literature" when he argued that

> there is an African sentiment, an African consciousness, an idea of Africa, and I believe, a common African vision unified not only by history but by a fundamental groundwork of values and cultural life. But there is no African nation; in other words, the felt idea and vision have not yet found an objective form. What we have is a plurality of African states, multinational, with a diversity of customs, folkways, and especially languages Irele. (1981:48)

This current work is being undertaken in the same spirit in which our literary counterparts tried to map and define their field of study in the 1980s. That such a work is late in coming should be understandable because the cinematic institutions of Africa are relatively young compared to their much older literary counterparts. My definition of African cinema is based on the tradition of an *imagined* African identity, in Benedict Anderson's sense, to which most people on the continent are committed. The term "African cinema" should be understood as a descriptive term in a plural sense to refer to the cinematic institutions of Africa as opposed to individual national cinemas. Under this descriptive rubric, individual national cinemas within the continent can be studied in all their complexities. For a film to qualify as an African film, its primary audience must be African, and this must be inscribed in the very conception and textual positioning of the broad range of African subjects, identities and social experiences, and its director must be an African. Such a conception and projection of African subject matters and personality are an adjunct of the imagined African nation, and their roots can be traced to the very structures of shared African belief-systems and world-outlook. The belief in the circle of existence: the world of the living, the unborn, and the ancestral world; the concepts of re-incarnation and predestination, and socio-cultural correlates such as respect for elders; rites of birth, adolescence, and passage; polygamy and the extended family; community and ethnic solidarity. These issues should, however, not be conceptualized in terms of traditional African cultural authentication because such a conceptualization would be ahistorical and would not fully account for the hybridized nature of modern African cultural practices. They should rather be conceptualized as transitory hybrid cultural practices, which are constantly being creatively reworked by Africans as they try to negotiate modern institutional practices in a globalized world.

Arguably, the historically indisputable core of African cinema is made up of films employing indigenous African languages as media of filmic expression. Even though the first set of African films that followed the release of Ousmane Sembène's *Borom Sarret* continued for a while the tradition of their much older literary counterparts by employing inherited colonial European languages as media of filmic expression, possibly as a result of the language debates initiated by African scholars of the Obi Wali school of thought in the early sixties, most African filmmakers are currently employing indigenous African languages as media of filmic expression, with subtitles in the inherited European languages (Wali, 1963, 1964; Wa Thiong'o, 1986).

The relevance of the issue of language to the definition of African cinema is important because James Potts' arguments with respect to the photographic qualities of the filmic medium and its discursive implications re-echo some of the initial problems of definition of African literature discussed earlier. A similar argument is implicit in Potts' essay titled: "Is there an International Film Language?" In the article in question, Potts equates the photographic qualities of the filmic medium with its significatory range and capacities — a literal equation of the medium with the message. Since he also argues that the medium is a Western invention, on the basis of technological determinism, he assumes that there is an international film language and style but that it is Western. The implication of such an argument is, of course, that Africans cannot fully utilize a modern representational medium for telling their own stories. The beginning of Potts' essay actually suggests that his arguments are geared towards implying that the technology of the medium may not necessarily equal the message but the discursive use to which it is put:

> it seems unlikely that the use of an Arriflex camera automatically imposes a Teutonic film style, that an Eclair gives Gallic flair, or that by toting a Japanese Super 8 mm. camera with a power zoom one starts perceiving the world through the eyes of an Oriental (however 'Westernised'). But it is becoming generally accepted that technology is not value-free: to some extent different technologies dictate the way in which we see the world, the way we record and interpret 'reality', and they influence the types of codes we use to communicate a message. *But technologies, whatever their source, seem to interact with the culture into which they are transferred; in some instances they are modified and new methods of using old technologies may be attributed to experimentation based on specific localized cultural needs not foreseen by the manufacturers of the equipment* (my emphasis). (Potts, 1979: 74)

However, a little further in the essay, he reverses his earlier argument by equating the medium and its narrative or significatory range and capacities with camera technology. He specifically states that: "I would argue that it is more to do with technology than anything else. Given a Box Brownie or an Instamatic camera with a pretty basic standard lens, the tendency is to take medium-shots (or medium long shot). Then one is sure of focus and depth of field" (Potts: 79). He uses this same argument to explain the emergence of new cinematic forms in Europe and North America. As he puts it: "The development of the Eclair camera resulted in a new French filmic dialect which quickly spread around the world. Independent but parallel developments in North America also contributed to the rapid 'internationalization' of *cinèma vèritè* and 'direct cinema' technique" (Potts: 80). By placing emphasis on technological determinism, Potts virtually overlooks both the historical and anthropological roots of these technological developments that preceded the discursive uses to which they were put. In other respects, he also overlooks the discursive aspect of the filmic medium which Annette Kuhn uses in her essay to argue against exclusive technological deterministic theories of the cinema. According to Kuhn,

> that 16mm. portable synch-sound equipment facilitates production is not in question; it becomes possible, for example, to undertake location shooting in natural light with fast film; to

follow the spontaneous movements of subjects in the film; to
film relatively unobtrusively with a two-person, or even one-
person, crew; to record unscripted sounds and speech. But to
suggest that technology is determining is a different argument
altogether: to pose the question this way is to suggest that
technology itself is outside of determination. It is, however, quite
possible to reserve the terms of assertion and to give good
grounds for doing so — in other words, to argue, in the
particular instance of documentary film, that certain types of
equipment were developed and marketed expressly to make a
specific type of film-making possible and that therefore the
technological developments were themselves not innocent of
historical/ ideological overdetermination. (Kuhn, 1978: 75)

In contradistinction to Kuhn who places emphasis on the
discursive aspect of film, Potts' arguments exclusively equate the
narrative range of film with camera technology. In the essay in
question, Potts also refuses to accept plurality of styles in cinematic
practices. He argues, for instance, that, "On the whole, I am
sceptical about 'schools' as I am about the structural or formal
elements in a film which are national or even ethnic (in the sense
that one is tempted to talk about them) as specifically African,
Japanese or Indian" (Potts: 79). In essence, all the productive
theoretical linkage which African film historians and critics such as
Mbye Cham and Manthia Diawara have built between African
cinematic narratives and traditional oratorical practices make no
sense because Africa did not produce the cinematic camera used by
Africans in film production.

Though Potts states that he does not recognize the existence
of regional styles, with regards to the question of queries which the
Chinese raised in respect of the aesthetic preferences of
Michelangelo Antonioni's documentary on China, he argues that
"quite apart from the question of the film's content, it is clear that
the Chinese are unfamiliar with the *conventions* and *cinematic language*
of 'Western,' neo-realistic, social documentary. Antonioni's 'tricks'
are standard practice by our norms" (my emphasis) (Potts: 79). By
this sheer double standard and Eurocentric definition of style,
Potts implicitly equates style with camera technology. In this
regard, Potts refuses to contemplate the idea of the existence of a
black or Pan-African (film) aesthetics. In other words, since
Africans did not invent the camera, they could not possibly tell

their own stories with it nor could there exist, by extension of such an act, an African film aesthetics. As he puts it,

> even Paulin Vieyra, film-maker and author of a number of books on African cinema (including a study of Sembène Ousmane), makes this misleading generalization: "The African sensitivity is entirely different from the European or American sensitivity. We have a view of things that is completely different from that of the West. Each person sees things according to his own background and culture. The world in which the African film-maker lives gives him a vision of Africa which is not exotic, not foreign, but uniquely 'African' in cultural content." (Potts: 81)

As earlier observed, Potts' general argument in this essay re-echoes that of Adrian Roscoe and John Povey, who sought to integrate African literature into European literature — albeit on a lower level — on account of the fact that African writers employ inherited European languages as medium of literary expression. Potts' own version of the argument is implicitly proposed in this format: camera technology equals the significatory range of the cinematic apparatus, cinematic narration and style. Since the camera is a Western invention, cinematic style is Western. By extension, since Africans did not invent the camera, there cannot exist an African film aesthetics, and by implication also African cinema. To define style in this manner would mean an equation of style exclusively with technology and medium. It will also suggest an exclusive separation of the formal structures of a text from its content, or narration from narrative.

Though African film style does not operate the type of rigid structures and strategies for narrative coherence and clarity which David Bordwell identifies with classical Hollywood style, a style derived from historical forms such as the well-made play, popular romance, and late nineteenth century short story, African film style is now generally acknowledged to derive its narrative forms and structures from traditional African oral narrative practices, especially that of professional griot genre (Cham, 1982; Diawara, 1988a). The structure of oral narrative has been studied in detail by African scholars such J.P. Clark-Bekederemo 1977; Okpewho, 1979; and Chinweizu *et al*, 1980. These studies have unearthed the wealth and complexities of traditional African oral narratives — the fact that transcribed oral narratives vary in length and contain various genres ranging from moralistic tales and fables, to epics, horror tales, fantasies, etc. These studies revealed further that

> African oral narratives contain both linear and episodic plots, with plot structures incorporating embellishments such as narrative digressions, parallelisms, flashbacks, and dream sequences, and that characterization is elaborate and well-developed in them, with both human types and anthropomorphic types, and that language is extremely figurative, with performances incorporating song, music, and dance. (Okpewho, 1979: 135-201; Chinweize *et al:* 22-146; Diawara, 1992: 11)

Regarding the cinema, both Diawara and Cham have revealed through their studies how oral narrative structures and performance elements such as songs, music, dance, etc., are employed by African filmmakers as authentic indices of African cultural practices and also as masks for revealing aspects of contemporary African politics and social practices. Diawara, for instance, has observed that in oral narratives, the principles of narrative action, causality, and narrative progression, are based on the subversion of a stable moral order by a negative element and/or vainglorious persona, who is contained or neutralized at the end of the narrative. In African cinema, on the other hand, some of these elements or traditional narrative principles are violated through inversion (Diawara: 12). Whereas in oral tradition, griots, being generally conservative and concerned with maintaining traditional values, always closed their narratives through restoration of social order, in African cinema, the end of most narratives are much more ambiguous and open to several interpretations. Though griots often manipulated narrative point-of-view in their stories to coincide with the point-of-view of the central character with whom we are compelled to empathize, point-of-view in African cinema is much more diffused; character point-of-view, for instance, may not necessarily coincide with narrative point-of-view, and central characters such as El Hadji Abdou Kader Beye, in Ousmane Sembène's *Xala*, are not necessarily set up to invoke our empathy, but as objects of moral lessons.

Diawara also observes that while Western directors often achieve recognition by letting their stories tell themselves through various delegated narrative devices, the African director, like the griot, masters his craft by impressing the spectator with his or her narrative performance. Though the basic narrative format in instances of dialogue between characters is shot/reverse-shot, spatial representation is strongly marked according to gender lines. As he puts it: "The external space in Africa is less characterized by the display of emotion and closeness between man and woman, and more by a designation of man's space and woman's space in society" (Diawara: 12-13).

African film style is a transitory construct that is continuously being reworked and is creatively adaptive, in keeping with the dynamics underlying the construction of modern African subjectivities and social history. However, in the midst of this transition, there is the need to define the status of shot composition, camera movement, placement, and duration, and the general spatio-temporal order of representation for films of the folkloric or return to the source genre, set mostly in rural areas, as opposed to films set within urban milieu where the pace of life is relatively faster. There is no doubt, however, that African oral narrative tradition is one of the major sources of influence upon the emergent African film style. This is not to say that African cinema is isolated and not influenced at all by Hollywood (and other) cinematic styles, but to question the basis of Potts' assertion that there is no African film style but a universal film style which is Western.

With respect to the question of definition of African cinema, the argument has been made for the necessity of such an exercise. For a film to be qualified as African film the filmmaker must be an African by birth or naturalization and the film must be based on African social experience. This qualification does not, however, imply that there is a unified perspective to African social experience or a unified approach to representing it. For instance, the concept of African personality, which is a sub-category within the pan-Africanist project, recognizes the multi-racial, multi-cultural, multi-ethnic, and multi-religious make-up of Africa, but it is also a recognition that carries with it, significant historical implications for black Africans. As Abiola Irele puts it,

> ideological development in Africa, either in the form of Négritude or under its English designation, 'African personality,' has been largely a strategy with which to confront the contingencies of history. It had the primary objective of awakening the African consciousness so as to render us apt for

action. ...But if African thought has been largely a transposition to the intellectual plane of the responses to the colonial situation, it is also inscribed within a broader perspective which brings out the implications of the encounter with Europe in the very fact that we, as Africans, have become conscious of ourselves as a distinct category of men, with a responsibility to other men, it is true, but with a commitment to our particular destiny as a people. (Irele, 1981: 112-113)

The definition of African personality, together with its underlying structures of belief-systems, world-outlook, ethos, and social practices, has always been restricted to black Africans. However, the Pan-Africanist project, of which African personality is just a sub-category, has always, above all else, been a secular social vision of African unity. In this regard, it incorporates both North Africans who subscribe more to Arab culture than black Africa's, and European-Africans who subscribe more to European culture than black Africa's. Therefore, when one insists that for a film to qualify as an African film, the filmmaker must be an African either by birth or naturalization, and that it should be based on African social experience, it should be taken for granted that the term, African cinema, acknowledges the multiplicity of social experiences implicated in it.

Even within black Africa itself, there is no unified social experience as such, at the level of the *content* of every day's life. There are, however, African scholars like Wole Soyinka, Abiola Irele, Ousmane Sembène, Ngugi wa Thiong'o, Chinweizu *et al* — scholars who are Afrocentric in the sense of arguing from a cultural center while admitting the hybridized nature of modern African identities and social experience. In essence, modern African subjectivity is always being mediated by traditional African cultural values such as a collectivized social mentality, defined in terms of kindred responsibility that is not limited solely to blood relations but covers a broad range of experiences driven by the underlying impulse to make some sacrifice on behalf of one's extended family, one's community, and one's ethnic group, in order to better fit into the amorphous colonialist state created by Europeans. In other words, this collectivized social mentality owes its origin to the ambivalence of being caught between the demands and loyalty to the modern state as "citizens" and to traditional African institutions as "subjects." The belief that apart from the accident of belonging to a geographical region known as Africa, and of having had an identical historical experience of slavery and colonialism, *most* black Africans share a unified *structure* of belief-systems and world-outlook whose form is discernable in black Africa's social practices.

It is also instructive to note that there are other African scholars such as Valentine Mudimbe, Pauline Hountondji and Anthony Appiah, who, while being generally sympathetic to the social vision of the Pan-Africanist project, argue that there is no collective metaphysical outlook or social practices within black Africa to recommend it. They argue that, if anything, it might be anchored on the accident of geography, i.e., as a designation of ethnicities within the geographic enclave known as Africa and the historical experience of slavery and colonialism (Mudimbe, 1988: 153-186; Appiah, 1992: 74-171). Finally, in arguing that an African film should be based on African social experience, one does not intend it to be a legislation on approach or appropriate manner of representation but only as a commonsensical logic that an African film can only lay claim to such a designation by virtue of being produced by an African, for a primary African audience, and in representing African social experience.

In keeping with the conceptualization of modern African subjectivity as a hybrid social construct, one does not see any reason why borrowed critical frameworks cannot be applied in the criticism of African cinema. After all, modern African cinematic narratives have been borrowing freely from Western or other cinematic narrative techniques. Artistic freedom of expression is highly recommended because it can only help in further enriching African cinema. Arguably, narrative structures are basically the same all over the world. What differs from culture to culture and region to region is narrative or story-content. Theories of narration formulated in any part of the world are applicable beyond the borders of their formulators, but since the story-content or narrative differs because of the intertextuality of narratives and their implication in culture specific codes and social discourses, criticism should be responsive to these specificities by adopting a comparative approach in the analysis of texts.

The Two Major Schools in African Cinema

Traditionally, historians of African cinema have noted the existence of two radically different aesthetic schools in African cinema: "the Med Hondo school," and the "Ousmane Sembène school," "that differ in opinion with respect to the formulation of an African film style. The Med Hondo school is said to argue that propaganda does not reside only in the content but also in the form of Hollywood cinema. Scholars of this school of thought argue that African cinema should adopt an anti-imperialist approach to counter Hollywood's images and representations of Africans by devising an appropriate film style different from Hollywood's. On the other hand, the Ousmane Sembène school argues that African cinema should be conceived in terms of its destination: the post-colonial African public. Since the taste of this public has been conditioned by what he refers to as a "cinema of distraction," African filmmakers should take account of this conditioning in the production of their films if they want to cultivate and retain public patronage of their works. In the current historical phase in the development of African cinema, it is necessary to retain a form of "classic" — that is to say, comprehensible — narrative without, however, taking up all the clichés of Hollywood cinema (Bouhgedir, 1982c: 83-84; Ekwuazi, 1987: 88-93).

While there is some sense in acknowledging the existence of different aesthetic views by African filmmakers with respect to the question of an African film style, such views should not be overemphasized because African film style is continuously being creatively molded in keeping with the changing nature of modern African subjectivities, social history and politics, and because of individual filmmaker's social background. Besides, works such as Med Hondo's *Soleil O* (1969), *West Indies* (1979), *Sarraounia* (1986), and Ousmane Sembène's *Emitai* (1971), *Ceddo* (1976), *Gwelwaar* (1991) and Sembène and Thierno Faty Sow's *Camp de Thiaroye* (1988), all carry strong anti-imperialist tones. However, there is certainly a preoccupation, at least in Hondo's current fictional films, to emphasize the historical ambience of the colonial era, while those of Sembène tend to bestride both the colonial and post-colonial periods. Equally important is the need not to overlook the revolutionary post-colonial atmosphere within which the debate ranged. These were times when the more radicalized and anti-imperialist the views one held, the more popular one was considered in public reckoning, especially among the youths who were disenchanted with post-colonial African leaders.

The Historicity of Modern African Knowledge, Negritude, and the Rise of African Cultural Nationalism

Officially, the Negritude Movement began in 1934 in Paris, when African and Caribbean students such as Aimé Cesaire, Léopold Sédar Senghor, Léon Demas, Allioune Diop, and others, gathered to reaffirm their humanity in the face of racism in Europe. However, to fully understand the roots of the cultural reawakening experienced by these students, there is the need to link up with the American black intellectual and literary ferment of the post-First World War period generally referred to as the New Negro Movement, which blossomed in the Harlem Renaissance in the works of Claude Mckay, Langston Hughes, Counteé Cullen, Jean Toomer, Rudolph Fisher, Wallace Thurman, Zora Neale Hurston, and James Weldon Johnson. (Taylor, 2001: 126-127) But as Carl Pedersen notes, the Harlem Renaissance was part of a larger black diaspora intellectual and literary ferment, which also covers Caribbean cultural reawakening of the same era. To buttress this point, Pedersen cites the poem, "The Tropics in New York," from Mckay's collection *Harlem Shadows*, which is often cited as marking the beginning of the burst of artistic creativity known as Harlem Renaissance, and Jean Toomer's collection, *Cane*, as works of Caribbean immigrants in exile in New York. (Pedersen, 2001: 259-269)

The Negritude Movement, which essentially manifested itself in cultural/racial self-revalidation, was the result of the experience of racism and of racist discourse and of the encounter between the torchbearers of the Movement and the intellectual and literary works of the African diaspora as encapsulated in the Harlem Renaissance.

Writing on the framework within which the Harlem Renaissance emerged, Geneviève Fabre and Michel Feith have noted the essentiality of racial consciousness, pride and empowerment that underlay the project:

> The Harlem Renaissance was a moment of hope and confidence,
> a proclamation of independence, and the celebration of a new

spirit exemplified in the New Negro. Against the grain of
enduring stereotypes, in defiance of disparagement or
subservience, this rebirth and awakening seemed to herald a new
age, calling for heightened race consciousness and creativity.
Such confidence came from an awareness of changing times, of
better opportunities created by the Great War and the Great
Migration that set African-Americans flowing through the
United States and between continents. (Fabre and Feith, 2001: 2)

Drawing inspirations from the black diaspora cultural/racial
awakening of an earlier age, the Negritude philosophers and literary
writers were to create a body of work which not only bore a
critique of rationality/aesthetic theory, racial biological theories and
their hierarchies of subjecthoods, but also had to reflect on the
need for self-revalidation as Africans and as human beings, through
archaeological excavation of African history, traditional thoughts
on philosophical rationality/aesthetics, ethics and morality, and the
broad spectrum of African artistic engagements, all of which, in
their various disciplinary practices, articulated Africans' experience
of modernity in manners that can at best be qualified as hybrid in
relation to their European equivalents. These hybridized modern
African philosophic and artistic expressions are often reflected in
the ambivalent relationship, which is continually constructed out of
the colonial experience, between the desire for African authenticity
and traditions and the demands of European modernity.

African Political Nationalism and the Struggle for Independence and Modern African Identities

A major factor, which helped to speed up the process of African
modernity, is the demystification of the European myth of
invincibility, which Africans had imagined prior to the Second
World War. As a result of the peculiarity of the uneven levels of
development between Europe and Africa prior to the 15th century
contact, and the fact that traditional African society identifies the
color white with transcendentalism, Africans related to Europeans
with some awe when they first came in contact. After all, ghosts
and other categories of transcendental beings were often
represented in traditional African horror tales as white. The color
also figures prominently in African rituals in which it is supposed
to aid the priest/priestess who ties white cloths during such rituals

to facilitate contact with communal deities or the ancestral world. Europeans looked like ghosts and their warfare tools happened to have been so potent that Africans imagined them to possess the invincibility and potency of ghosts. Also, during wars of colonial conquests, Europeans did all within their powers to recover their wounded and the dead from battlefields, thereby further re-enforcing the myth of invincibility.

This myth was shattered when Africans fighting alongside their white counterparts during the Second World War saw, them being felled like fellow Africans by bullets, the wounded had cry out for rescue, medical attention, and help, like other mortals. This experience shattered once and for all the perceived invincibility of Europeans. Having shed their precious blood to save the mother country, represented by either Britain or France, the war-hardened African veterans no longer feared the white man but most importantly, they felt they deserved to take their destiny in their own hands. In other words, they deserved self-governance. The post-war agitation culminated in the convening of the pan-African Congress in Manchester in 1945, where Africans and African diaspora intellectuals, war veterans, students, and the British radical community called for the independence of African and Caribbean countries.

One of the key players at the Manchester Congress was Kwame Nkrumah, who left for home in 1947 to help change the course of the struggle for independence of the then Gold Coast. After gaining independence for Ghana in 1957, Nkrumah rallied around himself fellow continental and black diaspora pan-Africanists and helped to champion the cause of Africa's liberation from colonialism. Nkrumah's pan-Africanist spirit found a soulmate in Gamal Abdel Nasser's pan-Arabism, thereby creating a united platform across Africa for the decolonization of the continent.

Nkrumah always matched rhetoric with action, and the proof of this was the series of pan-African congresses that he convened in 1958 to unite the continent. They included a congress of heads of governments of independent African states called in April 15, 1958 and an All African Peoples Conference called on December 8, 1958. At the December conference, Nkrumah also laid the groundwork for the kind of modernity he would want to see across

Africa after liberation from colonialism. He laid down his vision of African modernity as follows:

> And here we must stress that the ethical and humanistic side of our people must not be ignored. We do not want a simple materialistic civilization which disregards the spiritual side of the human personality and a man's need of something beyond the filling of his stomach and the satisfaction of his outward needs. We want a society in which human beings will have the opportunity of flowering and where the humanistic and creative side of our people can be fostered and their genius allowed to its full expression. Much has been said about the inability of the African to rise above his low material wants. Frequent reference is made to his non-contribution to civilization. That this is an imperialist fiction, we all know. There have been great Empires on this African continent, and when we are all free again, our African Personality will once again add its full quota to the sum of man's knowledge and culture. (Nkrumah, 2001: 366)

The series of pan-African congresses called in the 1940s and 1950s were a great source of inspiration for the emergent liberation movements then struggling for independence across the African continent.

After the first wave of independence of several African colonies in the 1960s, the ideals of pan-Africanism, the whole idea that Africans should not consider themselves free until every vestige of colonialism on the continent had been uprooted, served to guide the relationship between independent African states and the liberation movements in the settler colonies which required armed struggles to secure independence. The settler colonies began to gain independence in the 1970s, with all the Portuguese colonies of Angola, Mozambique, and Guinea-Bissau and the Cape Verde Islands in 1975, the French Comoros and Djibouti in 1975 and 1977 respectively, Zimbabwe in 1980, Namibia in 1990, and finally the achievement of multi-racial democracy in South Africa in 1994.

The path leading to the construction of an African identity and modernity is strewn with the complexities and contradictions of the colonial enterprise. In the first place, colonialism was not a unified project. There was an implicit duality of purpose underlying the entire project, which in turn manifested itself either in terms of partial residency and exploitation (non-settler colony) or of full-fledged residency and exploitation (settler colony). However, whether the talk is of settler-colony or non-settler colony, in terms of the rationalization of the colonial project, colonialist discourse produced a unified schema of racial hierarchization in which the European was positioned in terms of the so-called evolutionary paradigm of humanity, and of the production of both ancient and modern civilizations, as next to God, with Africans placed at the bottom next to primates, and with supposedly little contribution to human civilization.

This discourse of racial superiority versus inferiority or of civilization versus barbarism led to the inauguration of counter-discourses of racial validation and to cultural nationalism in Africa thereby helping to inaugurate the concept of an African identity. Cultural nationalism produced the Negritude Movement and a broad range of ambivalent artistic responses, with very little to show by way of social or political restitution and admission of Africans into the institutional privileges and gains of the modern experience: freedom of association and expression, multi-party democracy, the rule of law, equality and social justice, free market participation and industrialization.

The restrictions created by the colonialist state to hinder Africans from participating fully in the affairs of state and of the emergent modern economy led to political agitation for self-governance at the end of the Second World War. The reasoning then was that once independence was achieved, Africans would be free to fully exploit the broad range of institutional gains of modernity. This reasoning underlined the crux of Nkrumah's injunction to fellow Africans still struggling for independence:

> My advice to you who are struggling to be free is to aim for the attainment of the Political Kingdom - that is to say, the complete independence and self-determination of your territories. When you have achieved the Political Kingdom all else will follow. (Nkrumah: 366)

What the founding fathers of modern African nation-states didn't reckon with were the post-war contradictions of Cold War rivalries and politics. Henceforth, the world would be divided into the Socialist Bloc led by Russia and Eastern Europe and the Capitalist Bloc led by the United States of America and Western Europe. This ideological division of the world left Africans and their newly independent states little room to maneuver. Every political or development policy direction was assessed by the West in terms of East-West ideological rivalries. To compound matters for most post-colonial African leaders, their anti-imperialist rhetoric classified them as budding communists who must be routed out by all means before they contaminated others. In this respect, these leaders' every move was monitored by the Western intelligence community which wasted no time in creating crisis situations resulting in the overthrow of blacklisted regimes such as that of Kwame Nkrumah in Ghana or outright elimination of the leader as happened in the case of Patrice Lumumba in the Congo. Liberation movements were equally classified as breeding grounds for communists which must be contained either through proxy allied regimes or outright military intervention. In this way, the apartheid regime in South Africa was used for many years to suppress the liberation movements in Mozambique, Zimbabwe, Angola, and Namibia. Caught in this web of international East-West ideological rivalries, more than four decades of post-colonial years have been wasted in Africa. If today the continent looks poor, underdeveloped and crisis ridden, the Cold War factor must be considered alongside the corruption of most post-colonial African leaders, as reasons why the continent is considerably backward compared to the rest of the world.

To compound issues further, decolonization preserved colonialist state apparatuses/institutions that needed reforms. Reforms would be misinterpreted as signs of political disloyalty on the part of the imperial powers. As earlier noted, once political reforms were conceived, strategies for containment of perceived disloyalty were put in place by Western powers and often took several forms: sponsorship of military coups (after all the armed forces were mentally and psychologically dependent upon the imperialist powers for military supplies and training), withdrawal of development aid or loans, and sometimes outright economic embargo as was the case in Guinea-Conakry at the times of President Sékou Touré. All of this created distractions from the set-goal of nation building and the pursuit of modernity by post-colonial African leaders. As the populace became alienated, gradually, the post-colonial state came to assume the image and likeness of the colonialist state it replaced.

A feeling of betrayal of trust and of angst towards the post-colonial state began to replace the grand optimism that preceded the struggles for liberation and independence. This feeling of betrayal of trust on the part of the masses also produced its own broad range of ambivalent artistic practices in relation to the concept of African modernity. On the part of the leaders themselves, there was also a general feeling of insecurity and alienation from the populace and a dilemma of helplessness arising from an inability to embark on proper reformation of inherited colonialist state apparatuses for fear of misinterpretation of their intentions by the imperialist powers and of consequently being overthrown.

Caught between these two devils, post-colonial African leaders decided to sacrifice their local constituencies by keeping the colonialist state intact thereby subverting the modernization projects in their countries. The casualty of this development was multi-party democracy and its institutional checks and balances that were replaced by dictatorships of one-party system. This subversion led to the polarization of the post-colonial state and of its social institutions and social relations. What was essentially a dictatorship of an individual soon began to be interpreted as a dictatorship of an ethnic group, with the ethnic group of the dictatorial leader being read as the privileged one. Those ethnic groups which felt alienated from power first protested and either resorted to armed struggles for self-determination or bid for power through the musical chairs of coups-counter-coups and the experience of ethnic cleansing and massacres in Nigeria, Rwanda, Burundi, Liberia, Sierra Leone, Côte d'Ivoire, Central African Republic, and the Democratic Republic of the Congo. The end-product of this general atmosphere of insecurity is, of course, the perennial postponement of the full realization of the set-goal of an African modernity. In the midst of the failures of the post-colonial state in Africa, how have African artists and writers represented the desire for and experience of modernity on the continent?

The Significance of the Modernity Thesis to the Criticism of African Cinema

As an institution, African cinema can be grouped alongside other modern media of mass communication such as the radio, the telegraph, the telephone, the television, and the print media as modern communication media introduced into Africa through colonialism. Another contemporary medium already making a strong impact is the Internet.

The introduction of these modern communication media also came hand in hand with other institutions such as modern state institutions of governance, educational systems, modern transportation, policing and legal institutions, modern bureaucracy, systems of accounting and record keeping, modern armed forces, the printing press, and modern manufacturing processes and labor relations. The introduction of the foregoing factors of modernization marked the entrance of Africa into modernity. As is common knowledge, the contact between Europe and Africa is not without its downside in the generation of social experiences such as the trans-Atlantic slave trade, colonial conquests, forced labor, and the attendant social mentality of racial superiority/inferiority complex. However, as is to be expected, the peculiar process of Africa's entrance into modernity has produced a feeling of ambivalence towards the whole project of modernity in Africans.

The root cause of this ambivalence can be traced to educated Africans' contact with a body of European racist and colonialist discourse that tended to negate the humanity of Africans. Reactions to this body of discourse have produced a complex body of discursive responses in both literature, the arts, letters and the cinema, works which show that while Africans eagerly embraced the process of modernization and its institutions as introduced by the European colonial powers, Africans also rejected racist and colonialist discourse, an uncanny process which often manifest in ambivalent simultaneous acceptance/rejection of modernity. Modernity has, therefore, been embraced with a lot of suspicion and ambiguity.

The range of reaction has sometimes swung between cultural nationalism (as in Negritude), political nationalism (in the pre-independence years), antipathy towards the post-colonial state and its institutions, and towards the whole project of modernity. The current moment has been marked by the discourse of Afro-pessimism. The context within which this ambivalence emerged towards modernity is to be examined shortly. For now, there is need to consider the issue of the peculiarity of the African experience in modernity because as people literally thrust into modernity, their experience of it is not exactly the same as that of Europeans whose peculiar socio-history helped produce the historical moment referred to as modernity.

Africa's experience of modernity is, to a certain degree, like that of Europe, marked by the phenomena of the modern nation-state and state institutions; the introduction of new technologies and modern transportation systems; rapid urbanization and population growth; modern armed forces and crime-control institutions; extensive rural/urban migration and international immigration; the explosion of modern forms of mass communication; the introduction of modern forms of mass amusements, merchandizing and consumerism; the introduction of modern accounting/bookkeeping systems; the expansion of heterosocial public circulation and interaction of the sexes; the emergence of distance/space between home and workplace, and the emergence of capitalist production processes, and their attendant peculiar labor relations.

From my tabulation, one can see that the experience may not be too different from that which Ben Singer has tabulated for the European or North American experience of modernity in his book, *Melodrama and Modernity: Early Sensational Cinema and Its Contents*. (Singer, 2001:21) However, when it comes to the question of the social mentality which modernity has produced among Africans, one finds that not every aspect of the phenomenon of modernity has been wholeheartedly assimilated. This is to be expected because Africans had their own traditional institutions prior to European colonialism and the subsequent emergence of the continent into modernity. The tendency is, therefore, to be selective in terms of assimilation of culture-specific institutions. For instance, the full range of scepticism and rationality, which marked the idea of modernity in Europe, has not been the case in Africa, at least, not yet. The African psyche is still very much submerged in metaphysics and a worldview that is grounded in traditional African religion and belief-systems. There is a very strong belief in a triangular and interrelated cosmology: the world of the living, that of the ancestors, and that of the unborn. Traditional African religion derives from this belief-system. This belief-system is also manifesting itself in the African diaspora, in terms of the manifestation and proliferation of spirit medium-ship, possession in religious worship which manifests in terms of temporary disabling of the human agency, the worship of various types of water spirits, exercises in spiritual exorcism, divination and propitiation, and a strong respect for institutional sacred mediators such as priest/priestesses.

Orthodox religious practices such as Islam and Christianity have attempted, albeit unsuccessfully, to demonize traditional African religious practices as pagan worship. Such process of demonization marked the early part of Christian proselytization across Africa but in West Africa, the rebuff of indigenous cultural and performance practices in church worship, coupled with the rise of cultural nationalism, led to the birth of indigenous church movements such as the Alladura and Celestial Churches, which were syncretic and hybridized in their marriage of traditional African mode of worship and those of Christianity. Beginning in the first quarter of the twentieth century, this movement had by the beginning of the new millennium given rise to a rash of religious revivalism of the Pentecostal brand of churches which are still very much marked by the syncretic nature of early indigenous churches. Today the foundation of indigenous churches in Nigeria and elsewhere in West Africa is laid on traditional African religious practices.

This strong pull of love for the sacred does not invariably have a uniform manifestation within the populace, but its social impact has circumscribed the secularization of ideas and social thought. One can, therefore, surmise that even among the educated African elite the scepticism and rationality which is the hallmark of European Enlightenment have not been embraced with as much enthusiasm by Africans. In this respect, most educated Africans perceive science as purely the application of natural laws to finding solutions to the problems of modern life. The inquisitiveness, scepticism, irreverence, and rationality which marked European quest for knowledge, and the application of scientific principles to the development of modern technologies, has been very tenuous in Africa. There seems to be a separation between scientific inquiry and scientific outlook.

Though progress has been made with respect to harnessing scientific principles to solving developmental problems, lack of good governance and transparency in public institutions, corruption, nepotism, lack of strong civil and democratic institutions, and the preponderance for ethnicity and ethnic loyalty over nationalism have combined to subvert laying a strong foundation for industrialization across Africa. Scientific breakthroughs in academia have not been matched by their transformation into usable new technologies because priority is not given to the establishment of engineering infrastructures. National priority across Africa has been that of how to share the proceeds from the exploitation of natural resources such as crude oil, gas, gold, diamond, iron ore, and from the sale of cash crops such as cocoa, rubber, groundnut, palm oil, and tea. Most African countries have been mired in the production of unrefined natural produce.

Another aspect of the social mentality of modernity cited by Singer and which Africans have experienced unlike Europeans is the issue of cultural discontinuity. Perhaps this is a result of the fact that modernity was imposed from the outside. Rather than cultural discontinuity, we find attempts at refinement of traditional African cultural practices [as is the case with modern fashion designs and sewing machines helping to refine the designs and production of traditional garments] and cultural hybridization, as seen in the mode of worship in indigenous churches and occasional cultural discontinuity in extreme cases of forceful ejection as was the case in the settler colonies of East and Southern Africa. Even in cases such as indigenous ethnic groups of the Kalahari Desert, which covers parts of Botswana and Namibia, there are now movements towards cultural restitution of some sort.

While modernity has arguably fostered social mobility in Africa, it has failed to induce the phenomenon of individualism, as it exists in Europe or North America. The African practice of the extended family system and its sense of communality have been reinvented even in cities. The experience has been such that affluent members of an extended family who have migrated to the cities often feel morally obliged to help favorite cousins within the extended family by taking some of them to the city and helping to sponsor them through either trade schools or even through the regular school system. This offer of help is, however, not without its conflicts, especially among house wives who think their husbands are financially spreading themselves thin in the name of helping relations. Since most men are also aware that when such help is extended to the relations of the woman in the house such criticisms do not surface, the onus has often rested with the man to be pragmatic in this aid program. Surprising, as this may seem, there are many Africans in Europe and North America who are sponsoring chains of cousins either through school or in business enterprise. Even within the same country, when one is staying very far away from one's ethnic geographical location, one automatically adopts and refers to a fellow member of one's ethnic group living within the same vicinity as one's "brother" or "sister" even though there is no blood link. Another aspect is the proliferation of "ethnic unions" or "societies" in cities across Africa whose role is to offer some form of ethnic rallying point in situations of celebration or bereavement. All of the foregoing factors have served in one way or another to reinforce and reinvent the tradition of the extended family system in modern African communities.

An aspect of modernity which Africans share with their European colonizers is that of the sensory-perceptual dynamics of a modernity which is peculiar to the urban environment and which Singer observes is "markedly quicker, more chaotic, fragmented, and disorienting than previous phases of human culture." According to Singer, this phenomenon of modernity is marked by "unprecedented turbulence of the big city's traffic, noise, billboards, street signs, jostling crowds, window displays, and advertisement," all of which subject "the individual to a barrage of powerful impressions, shocks, and jolts" (Singer: 35). It is on this experience that the modernity thesis of the cinema is anchored. But while Africans share the peculiarity of the sensory-perceptual dynamics with Europeans by virtue of the growth and development of cities in Africa, Africans' cinematic representation of this modernity has also been mediated by their concept of space and time in African culture.

In African culture, the tendency is to conceive space and time in communal terms. There is always a network of the social dynamics that privileges the communal perspective above that of the individual both in society and in narrative. Cinematic narrative may begin with the exploitation of an individual's desires, fears, anxieties or aspirations and even occasionally adopt narrative markers of an individual's flashbacks, dream sequences, thought distortions and projections, but the overall narrative perspective which frames that of the individual is the social communality of the African experience. In essence, the revelation of narrative space/time is not pre-eminently anchored on the movements and actions of the leading protagonist of the narrative as in classic Hollywood narrative. The basis of the African cinematic representational practice is borne out of the dictum that in Africa the individual is defined through the community, whereas in the European experience the community is defined through the individual. This practice is what is extended to the ways in which space and time are handled in African cinematic narratives.

Of course, one could argue that there are exceptional cases, but such cases are treated as exceptional, unorthodox, erratic or avant-garde; in other words, as deliberate cases of experimentation. Another way of looking at the practice of communal spatial/time representation in the cinema would be that of considering it a peculiar practice noticeable in most "Third World" cinematic practices (as opposed to the notion of "Third Cinema" which could be "First World" or "Third World," and essentially political in orientation). But again, the peculiar social history of European modernity *vis-à-vis* the external imposition of modernity in most Third World countries could be the root cause of the differences in spatial/time orientation in cinematic representation. Again, whether the experience is peculiarly Third World in orientation in no way invalidates the Africanness of the practice of African filmmakers because the concept of time/space is tied up with other issues of metaphysics and worldviews.

Another aspect of the modernity thesis, which has greatly impacted on African societies, is that relating to social mobility and its attendant rural-urban migration and the cultural and linguistic ambience of this reality. No doubt, rural poverty and lack of infrastructures have led to mass rural-urban migrations. This has in turn led to the growth and development of urban shanties or ghettoes. These shanties are helping to shape and reshape modern African identities, urban space and linguistic affiliations. Culture in urban shanties in Africa is highly hybrid. In this cultural melting pot, children are exposed to the languages and cultures of other ethnic groups. Often, the cultural mix has also led to the evolvement of hybrid languages such as Pidgin English in Nigeria. Pidgin English is the most widely spoken language in Nigeria even though the official language and language of instruction in the schooling system is Standard English. In addition to transnational social mobility, there is also the issue of international immigration arising from unfavorable political and economic realities in Africa. International social mobility has been facilitated by the advent of modern transportation in Africa. Both international social mobility and modern mass media have helped to bring about hybridization in African fashion, culinary practices, popular music, dance, and inter-ethnic marriages, all of which tend to undermine the social coherency of traditional African life.

Since there is a preponderance of illiteracy across Africa and a restricted access to modernity by those residing in the countryside, modern communication institutions and modes such as telephone, telegraph, radio, television and modern monetary transactions such as money orders and monetary transfers appear strange to the illiterate segment of the African populace. This often creates a lot of suspicion about the advances of modernity at the same time as it engenders marvel. This ambivalent relation to modernity sometimes manifests in terms of selective appropriation of aspects of modernity. In broad terms, however, African scholarly and artistic representations of the notion of modernity can be divided into three phases: Negritude and cultural nationalism, political nationalism and the struggle for independence, and the phase of the failed post-colonial state. All three phases articulate the notion of African modernity differently.

Writing on how the concept of Negritude and cultural nationalism has affected Africa's scholarly and artistic notions of modernity, Chinweizu has suggested that despite any contrary opinion about Negritude, this movement which he defines as "a generic term for the various impulses of black consciousness, and the various movements for rehabilitating black African culture..." had Francophone, Lusophone, and Anglophone strands (Chinweizu, 2001: 321). In this sense, the works of Lépold Sédar Senghor, Aimé Césaire, Frantz Fanon, Léon Damas, Nnamdi Azikiwe, Jomo Kenyatta, Agostinho Neto, Amilcar Cabral, Mbonu Ojike, Chinua Achebe, Ngugi wa Thiong'o, Camara Laye, Okot p'Bitek, Ayi Kwei Armah, Ola Rotimi, Wole Soyinka and many other scholars and first generation African writers can be considered cultural nationalists in their discursive responses to colonialist discourse or European notions of modernity. It couldn't be otherwise because colonialist discourse adopted a unified derogatory racist rhetoric in its qualification of black people and their culture. Africans were left with no choice but to revalidate their humanity and their culture. Chinweizu puts the whole experience in the following perspective:

> The invaders' caricatures were disseminated not only in Europe and America but also within Africa. Colonial settlers, traders,

and administrators held up that image daily. But this scorn on African soil inevitably challenged the youth of the era. While some sought to wrest political control from Europeans, others sought to rehabilitate the image of black Africa. Through essays, scholarship, and the stories they told, they set out ... to show "that African people did not hear of culture for the first time from Europeans; that their societies were not mindless but frequently had a philosophy of great depth and beauty; that they had poetry and above all, they had dignity." (Chinweizu: 321)

Chinweizu adds that regardless of the specific aspects or locale of the colonial encounter, colonialist discourse helped to foster a consciousness of pan-African identity.

While most scholars, writers, and artistic articulations of modernity in Africa between the 1940s and the late 1960s either revalidated African identity by representing opposing notions of tradition versus modernity or through production of grand narratives of struggles for liberation and independence, as from the 1970s, the loss of faith in the post-colonial state began to engender a feeling of angst and pessimism in African scholarship and literary creation as shown by titles such as Ngugi wa Thiong'o's *Devil on the Cross*, Achebe's *The Trouble with Nigeria* and *Anthills of the Savannah*, Soyinka's *The Man Died*, *A Play of Giants*, *Beatification of an Area Boy*, *Opera Woyonsi*, Ola Rotimi's *If...*, Femi Osofisan's *Kolera Kolej*, Ayi Kwei Armah's *The Beautiful Ones Are Not Yet Born*, Kwame Anthony Appiah's *In My Father's House*, Manthia Diawara's *In Search of Africa*, etc. These works have in their unique ways addressed the issue of the failed post-colonial state and the betrayal of the dream of an African modernity.

Writing on how African fine artists have articulated the notion of modernity, Chika Okeke has noted that the "signs of modern consciousness in the work of African artists have invariably been tethered to the civilizing mission and disciplinary procedures of European colonial project" (Okeke, 2001: 29). According to Okeke, the view that colonial education acted as agent of African modern art cannot hold ground because the colonial education system was interested only in producing low-level manpower such as clerks for the civil service of the colonial state. Whenever the curriculum included art, it was restricted to the notion of craft. He also submits that the final inclusion of art in the syllabus began in sub-Saharan African in the first decade of the twentieth century when the region's first modern artist, Aina Onabolu (1882-1963), began his lone crusade to convince the colonial administration in Lagos to establish art courses in secondary schools (Okeke: 29). According to Okeke, in North Africa, it also took the intervention of Prince Yusef Kamal - a member of the Egyptian National Party, which advocated independence from Britain - for the first art school, The School of Fine Arts, Cairo, to be established in Egypt in 1908. Lack of advanced training facilities also drove Egypt's first modern artist, Mahmoud Mukhtar (1891-1934), to enroll at the Paris École des Beaux-Arts after graduating from the Cairo School of Fine Arts. Lack of training facilities equally drove pioneer South African artists such as Ernest Mancoba (born. 1904) and Gerard Sekoto (1919-1993) to immigrate to Europe (Okeke: 31-32).

With respect to artistic production, Okeke has noted that during the colonial period, a large body of sculptural and performance practices flourished, engaging the colonial project with trenchant critique, humor, and empathy, and exploring above all what the modern condition implied for Africans in terms of alienation (Okeke: 29). He notes that the alienation took two forms in terms of artistic significations. First, at the level of subject matter, the figure of the colonialist was parodied in its presumed control over African artistic productions. Second, alienation also emerged through the alteration of the traditional artistic canons in the process of their signification in modern media and forms. The end-product of such experimentation was that new artistic products were able, according to Okeke, to construct "a field in which a dialectical discourse on power relations was played out, with the audience immediately recognizing what the colonial caricature meant within a classical African corpus" (Okeke: 29). The result left the colonial officer lost and unable to decipher the mockery that underlay what was interpreted as mimicry of European artistic forms.

In the post-colonial era, modern African art has adopted a pragmatic practice that fused European forms and inherited traditional African arts in their creative endeavors. However, while the new art combined the media and techniques studied in art schools, they encouraged less reliance on European subject matter and styles and instead preferred an aggressive recuperation of traditional art forms in all their historical variants. Emphasis was also placed on the role of the artist in a society and culture in transition. The techniques of the new art were invariably acquired in art schools established prior to independence. The oldest of these art schools were in Egypt, South Africa, and Sudan. However, with growing agitation for the inclusion of art in the school curricula, a new awareness of the importance of art developed. Art school were therefore established in Kumasi, Ghana (1936), Khartoum, Sudan (1946), Makerere, Uganda (1953), and Ibadan and Zaria, Nigeria (1955).

The curricula of most of the art schools were fashioned after those in Europe. But at the Zaria Art School, a group of students came together and formed the Zaria Art Society, which signaled a movement towards indigenization of artistic practices in Nigeria. Some of the leading voices in the Society such as Uche Okeke (born 1933), Demas Nwoko (born 1935), Bruce Onobrakpeya, and Irene Nwangboje started drawing inspiration from either traditional artistic practices or from myths and folklore. This returning to the source inspired Nigerian artists to draw their inspiration from the mural arts of the Igbo women known as *uli*, from Yoruba mythologies or from other ethnic grand narratives of origination. Those in North Africa such as the Egyptian, Ibrahim Salahi (born 1930), the Moroccan painter, Ahmed Cherkaoui (1934-1967), and his co-patriot, Farid Belkahia (born 1934) derived their inspiration from Islamic calligraphy and traditional Berber artistic practices. In South Africa, Cecil Skotness (born. 1926) and Sydney Kumalo (1935-1988), helped to steer black South African artists towards seeking inspiration from traditional artistic forms (Okeke: 33-34). As Africans began to witness the crumbling of the post-colonial state, African artists started to question the meaning of nationhood and notions of collective and individual identities in a post-modern world of hybridized cultural, social and political practices.

With respect to cinematic practices, the peculiarity of mostly non-industrialized societies venturing into film production, an industry that is built, supported and sustained by structures of industrialization, has often thrown up its own contradictions, most of them having to do with seeking financial aid from the very sources to which African filmmakers direct their critiques in their cinematic narratives. Manthia Diawara, while noting the emergence of three generic narrative impulses in African cinema: the historical colonial confrontation film, the social realist film, and the return to the sources film, has lamented the fact that African filmmakers have tended in their cinematic narratives to shy away from the crucial historical moment of social and political struggles for independence. Diawara writes,

> I realize, however, that for political reasons, the former colonizers do not want to see the retelling of African independence stories on film. Insofar as such a story is told from the perspective of the post-colonial filmmakers and depicts the former colonizers and oppressors and violators of human right, it is unacceptable to the West, which would rather deny that past. The former colonizers still consider their occupation of Africa to have been a civilizing mission... The paradox, therefore, in which the filmmaker finds him-or herself is the following: European institutions provide funding to produce films... But these institutions will not allow the production of stories that call into question the West's commitment to human rights in Africa.... (Diawara, 2001: 347-348)

This ironic dilemma faced by African filmmakers can specifically be read as unique to filmmakers in Francophone Africa where the French, through the institution of the Ministry of Foreign Cooperation, had provided funding for African cinema. The British, unlike their French counterpart, remained stuck, even in the post-colonial era, with their colonial policy of association or pragmatic engagement and never extended funding to post-colonial filmmakers in its ex-colonies. To compound matters, post-colonial governments in Anglophone Africa, nurtured under the Griersonian documentary tradition, were not interested in providing funds for the production of feature films, preferring instead to engage in propaganda and information related documentaries. The situation of filmmakers in Anglophone Africa required them to raise either the funds necessary for their film projects through private channels or to forget their dreams of capturing the important impulses of African modernity on film.

Faced with this unenviable situation, many Anglophone African filmmakers often braved the challenge by either mortgaging individual or family properties or by borrowing money from commercial loan sharks such as the banks. The end-result was that in the event of the film becoming a commercial failure, due in part to lack of distribution channels or discrimination by multi-national film distributors or lack of modern exhibition venues, the filmmaker invariably was worse off for it. A case in point is Nigeria's Ola Balogun, a highly prolific and innovative filmmaker

who became a music producer/club owner due to lack of readily
available sources of funding for his film projects. His co-patriot,
Eddy Ugbomah, joined the bandwagon of video filmmakers, not
because he likes working in the medium but just so that he could
remain relevant professionally while also earning his living in his
chosen career. Recently, the post-apartheid South African cable
network, Multichoice, assumed the mantle of sponsorship of post-
colonial Anglophone African filmmakers. How long this marriage
will last, only time will tell.

From Diawara's account of the contradictions faced by
Francophone African filmmakers, producers of the bulk of African
films, Anglophone African filmmakers' envy of their Francophone
cousins may be misplaced. Besides the contradictions of seeking
funding for film projects intent on critiquing the colonial enterprise
from the colonialists themselves, the realities of the post-Cold War
European Union politics is further making it impossible for
France's Ministry of Foreign Cooperation to continue providing
funds for Francophone African filmmakers. Indeed, faced with the
onslaught of globalization, the only option left to Africans is
embrace regional unity as advocated by Diawara in his
autobiography, *In Search of Africa*, pp. 134-162. Such is also the
position being canvassed by African statesmen such as Presidents
Olusegun Obasanjo of Nigeria, Thambo Mbeki of South Africa,
Abdelaziz Bouteflika of Algeria, and Abdoulaye Wade of Senegal,
whose advocacy of continental unity through their pet
development project tagged New Partnership for African
Development (NEPAD) has received the blessing of the Group 8
industrialized countries and is now being used as a building block
towards not only continental unity but also for facilitating an
African Renaissance which, it is hoped, would launch the continent
on the path of full industrialization. In a recent workshop on Pan-
African Business Forum in NEPAD, organized by the
Commonwealth African Investment Forum in Abuja, Nigeria's
Federal Capital, President Obasanjo said with respect to the aims
and objectives of NEPAD:

> Africans have the responsibility for creating the necessary
> enabling environment for intra-African trade and investment.
> While some African resources may be legally invested outside
> the continent, a lot of illegal transfers derive from endemic and
> pervasive corruption in the system. Africa ... needs to reverse

this trend… through rigorous anti-corruption campaigns, transparency and accountability at all levels. (Onuora, 2002: np)

The new thinking calls for self-examination on the part of every African, with a view to dropping old negative habits which negate the realization of the benefits of modernity on the continent. There is a clarion call to Africans to take their destiny in their own hands by spearheading the movement for an African Renaissance.

A Critical Reading of Ousmane Sembène's Representation of Modernity in Mandabi and Borom Sârret

Ousmane Sembène is one of the pioneering fathers of African cinema. Most of his earliest works have dwelt on either the theme of European and Arab colonialism or of Africans' relation to the emergent reality of modernity. In films such as *La noire de/Black Girl* (1966), *Borom Sârret* (1963), *Mandabi/The Money Order* (1968), *Emitai* (1971), *Xala* (1974), *Ceddo* (1976), *Camp de Thiaroye* (1988) (co-directed with Thierno Faty Sow), *Gwelwaar* (1991), *Faat Kine* (2000), Sembène has continually exploited both themes with a view to shedding light on the complex issues of slavery, colonialism and post-coloniality in Africa. The current study analyzes his representation of Africans' relation to the emergent reality of modernity in two of his films, *Borom Sârret* and *Mandabi/The Money Order* will be analyzed.

In *Borom Sârret*, Sembène reflects upon the living standards of poor urban dwellers in the wake of the euphoria of post-colonial self-rule across Africa, a theme which had engaged his attention in his first film, *La noire de*. In this film, he uses the typical daily experience of a cart driver's life to examine the impact of modernity and of post-colonial government on the masses in Senegal and other newly independent African countries. Even in these early days of post-colonial government, one could already see that right from the outset, post-colonial African politicians did very little to breakdown the inherited colonial boundaries erected by erstwhile colonial masters. Cities across Africa remain divided in accordance with the principles of colonizer/colonized binary dichotomy. In Dakar, as in Lagos (the former capital of Nigeria) and other cities across Africa, the uptown/downtown dichotomy reigned, with Africa's new post-colonial rulers fully entrenched in the downtown area formerly occupied by the European colonizers, and totally cut off from their co-patriots whom they claim to be governing.

The film begins in the morning as the cart driver says his daily morning prayers before setting out for work and ends in the evening when he is deserted by his wife. The events, which take place between both narrative poles, include the details of the daily work. After his daily prayer, he sets out for work armed with a piece of kola nut, given him by his wife as lunch pack, since there is no food in the house. As he drives out of his neighborhood, in his village on the outskirts of Dakar, he picks up one of his regular passengers, a poor market woman, who goes to sell her wares daily in a market within the native quarter of uptown Dakar. Business seems to have been bad for the woman, so the cart driver has been taking her to market daily, hoping that one day, the woman will pay him. Another regular passenger who joins the cart along the way is Monmadou, a retrenched worker who has been on the job market for six months, and who daily follows the cart driver to Dakar in search of a job. This picking and dropping of poverty ridden ghetto-dwellers living on the fringe of modern Dakar continues until the cart driver is apprehended and dispossessed of his cart by a corrupt policeman in downtown Dakar which used to be the exclusive European quarter in the days of French colonialism but has now become the exclusive abode of the emergent African elite. Dispossessed of his only means of livelihood and robbed of his money, the cart driver walks home dejected, lamenting what independence meant for downtrodden people like him. As if to add insult to injury, his wife equally deserts him as the film ends.

Within this simple narrative framework, Sembène examines issues such as the dividends of independence for the post-colonial working class urban poor who made a lot of sacrifices during the dark hours of the struggle for self-rule across Africa. Going by the experiences of the poor black girl in *La noire de*, and that of the cart driver in *Mandabi*, it seems like his characters, Sembène sees very little to cheer about in the euphoria which followed the attainment of independence across Africa. The reason for his pessimism can be traced to the selfish interest of most pioneer African politicians as exemplified in the behavior of the parliamentarians whom we encounter in his first film, *La noire de*. In that work, Sembène showed the parliamentarians to be more concerned with their personal welfare than that of the electorate who voted them in power. In retrospect, when one takes cognizance of the current failure of the post-colonial state in Africa, one can only say that Sembène has been a prophet in his assessment of the role which greed, corruption, and self-centeredness of post-colonial African leaders will play in aborting the dream of a prosperous future for the continent.

In *Borom Sârret*, Sembène also examines the ambivalent relationship between Africans and imposed foreign religious practices such as Islam, and concludes that despite being converts to their new religious faiths, Africans consider them as complementing their indigenous African religious practices. In other words, African converts to foreign religions appear caught between loyalty to traditional African religion and the imposed foreign ones. This perhaps explains why they quickly turn to indigenous African religious beliefs in times of unexplainable personal misfortune. Sembène examines the issue through the early morning chores of the cart driver prior to his departure for work. After his morning prayer as a Muslim, we see him arranging and rearranging his protective charms and amulets as if to say he trusts his forefather's religion than the imposed foreign one. Again, before he ventures into the forbidden territory of downtown Dakar, he also calls upon the *marabous* or traditional medicine men for protection. Even though he is not a polygamist like Ibrahim Dieng in *Mandabi*, his lack of education in the modern sense of the word or lack of competence in a modern trade has left him vulnerable within modern Senegalese society. This is the point that Sembène is making. Those who refuse to prepare themselves for the challenges of the modern African society will continue to remain vulnerable even in the midst of opportunities for self-advancement. Hence, in film after film, we see Sembène projecting images of youths embracing modern education as a means of self-development.

Borom Sarret, like *La Noire de*, is narrated mostly through internal monologues of the central protagonist of the film, the cart driver. Both films deal with the destiny of the downtrodden urban poor masses in post-colonial African countries. In *La noire de*, a desperate search for a housemaid job by Diouana, a young woman in Dakar, takes her to Antibes in the French Riviera, where she is supposed to take care of her mistress's children. Once there however, she's turned into an all-purpose housekeeper — a cook, laundry woman, house cleaner and child-minder. To make matters worse, she is hardly allowed out of the house. House-bound and treated by her mistress like a slave, her dreams of seeing the glittering lifestyle of France fades, and she is left with no option but revolt and suicide rather than continue to be enslaved by a white woman. In both films, as well as in *Mandabi*, symbols of traditional belief-systems and social experience continue to haunt orthodox religious practices and the project of modernity.

In *Borom Sârret*, as in the other two films being referred to here, there is a marked division of city space into two residential spaces, with each reflecting the inherited colonial political divide of European quarter/Native quarter, colonizer/colonized, ruler/ ruled, rich/poor, opulence/poverty. As earlier noted, the irony of the post-colonial experience in Africa is that post-colonial governments have refused to reform the inherited institutions and political structures of the old colonial state. The instruments of social containment put in place by the colonial masters were left intact. The armed forces and police which were created and used by colonial masters to enforce compliance to colonial laws were left intact and turned against fellow co-patriots who dared to express any contrary opinion to that of the new rulers. The European quarter, which used to be a dangerous space for natives to venture into in the colonial era, has now become a dangerous space for the urban poor and marginalized to venture into, as the experience of the cart driver in *Borom Sârret* shows. In this film, as in the others, Sembène uses the element of narrative contrast, to show the differences in architecture and city space-layout between the inherited European quarter, which is marked by well-laid out, tree-lined streets and boulevards, with side-walk spaces provided for pedestrians, modern high-rise flats and bungalows, and the ever protective watchful presence of the police force, to the disorderly rundown architecture of the Native quarter, marked by unpaved and over-crowded streets, street trading, beggars, petty crooks and thieves, and all shades of poor urban dwellers scrambling to earn a living. Just as the urban poor live in poverty at the periphery of the inherited modern colonial state, living almost impassively and anonymously compared with the ebb and tide of officialdom, so too are the rural dwellers whose experience of modernity is marginal, and who continue to live more by the precepts of traditional culture and social practices than by the dictates of modernity.

In *Borom Sârret*, as in *Mandabi*, Sembène offers a critique of aspects of traditional African cultural practices, which he thinks ought to be discarded in the light of modernity. In *Mandabi*, he focuses on the patriarchal traditional marriage practice of polygamy which treats women like personal household objects of the men. For holding on to such a moribund practice without visible means of sustaining a large family, he punishes his protagonist, Ibrahim Dieng. But as earlier noted, several factors are working in favor of the continued existence of polygamy. These include an emergent wealthy middle class, which can financially afford it; and for others, Islamic faith, which permits believers to marry up to four wives, as long they can be treated equally and can be financially sustained. In *Borom Sârret*, Sembène also examines the exploitative capacity of the *griot* caste in traditional African praise singing performance practice. Though the cart driver in *Borom Sârret* belongs to the caste of warriors whose exploits are recounted and preserved by the *griots* in traditional African societies, modernity has in most cases upturned the fortunes of griots and their patrons, as the encounter between the cart driver and the griot shows in the film. As the better dressed and well-off griot sings the praise of the ancestors of the poor cart driver, one gets the feeling that he is engaging in an exercise of mockery. Actually, at the end of the exercise, the cart driver felt more mocked than praised. It is as if the modern griot's praise singing is just another instrument for manipulating and exploiting a naïve and gullible public. But, to read the practice in such a simplistic terms is to overlook the emotional investment of the person so praised, and the influence of the charged atmosphere and overall ambience of the performance. Such is the power of the practice that Manthia Diawara, a self-professed modern man, with long years of residency and nationality in the United States, could not withstand the euphoria of the practice when he recently visited Mali, as he gallantly reports in his autobiography, *In Search of Africa* (Diawara, 1997: 112-115).

The film also focuses on the struggles of the urban poor to survive in the midst of the self-serving attitudes of post-colonial African rulers. Sembène's narrative strength in the foregoing films lie in his irreverent exposure of the poverty of vision and lack of political will on the part of post-colonial African governments to reform the inherited oppressive colonial state apparatuses. This lack of democratization of public institutions, coupled with corruption and lack of transparency in governance, nepotism, ethnicity and ethnic loyalties at the expense of nationality, have combined to slow down the pace of modernity in Africa. As things stand, for the continent to make any headway in modernity there must be a concerted effort at creating and sustaining democratic institutions. Africans must be able to elect and replace incompetent governments. In addition, they must subscribe to a private enterprise driven economy that has no room for governmental patronage of the sort that has come to characterize African state enterprises. They must also put in place the infrastructures necessary for translating scientific inventions in academia into usable technologies. Finally, governments across the continent must embark on the development of infrastructure to allow for easy mobility of people and goods within the continent, and between it and the rest of the world.

The next film earmarked for analysis is Mandabi. The film revolves around Ibrahim Dieng's attempt to cash a money order sent to him by his nephew, Abdou, a street sweeper in Paris. The amount sent is 25,000 Francs. Dieng was to give Abdou's mother 3,000 Francs, he was to get 2,000 Francs and to keep the remaining 20,000 Francs for Abdou, who is saving toward marriage and starting a family. The film basically uses the anxieties of illiterate and semi-literate segments of post-colonial Senegalese society to examine the relationship between traditional African institutional practices and those of modernity. Within this framework, issues such as problems of personal identity in urban societies, of patriarchal institutional oppression of women, of the relationship between traditional African belief-systems and imposed foreign religious practices such as Islam, of adaptation to a modern economy, of crass materialism and the urge to get rich quickly without hard work, of incompatibility between modern institutions and traditional African marital practices such as polygamy, and of the role of the extended family system in modern society are examined by Sembène. His verdict is that Africans need to adjust to the pace of change within their societies in order to avoid estrangement from modern institutions.

In this respect, his characterization of Ibrahim Dieng as a completely alienated entity in modern Dakar because of his tenacious attachment to moribund traditional African institutional practices is intended as a moral lesson to all those who are resistant to the forces of change in their society. Dieng's insistence on the practice of polygamy despite his lack of a tangible source of income makes him an object of ridicule. The climax of this symbolic public ridicule is represented in the piles of dishes from his wives that he is forced to consume in order to avoid charges of discrimination by them. His naïveté and pretentious lifestyle also make him a ready target to urban hustlers such as Mbaye Sarr and the phoney photographer out to make a quick buck in the survival game of city life. Sembène's representation of class conflicts in modern Dakar, as exemplified in the antagonistic relationship between Ibrahim Dieng and a representative of the capitalist class symbolized in the character of the neighborhood shop keeper, Mbarka, makes an interesting reading. Mbarka is characterized as a passionless capitalist blood-sucking leech located in the neighborhood for purposes of self-enrichment. But as a pioneer capitalist, he is also characterized as a master of the new economy, an adept at the manipulation of customers' psychology for purposes of entrapping them in debt-traps, not wholly unlike that which most African countries have found themselves in their relationship with Western monetary institutions like the IMF and the World Bank. Mbarka sells on credit to Ibrahim Dieng and grants him soft loans until he becomes entrapped in debt. Having cornered Dieng, his victim, he asks him to use his house as mortgage for his debts, a demand which in Dieng's reckoning amounts to an insult, and which results in a scuffle between Dieng and Mbarka.

With respect to the relationship between traditional African belief-systems and imposed foreign religious practices such as Islam, Sembène's characterization of Ibrahim Dieng, as a man caught between total conversion into Islam and tenacious attachment to African amulets and protective charms proves my earlier point that Africans cannot completely divest themselves of their traditional belief-systems. Everybody knows that despite strong protestations to the contrary, when things go unexplainably wrong in business transactions, in personal health, in marital relationship, in one's love life, in one's profession or place of work, in political aspirations/relationships, such personal misfortunes are said to have been caused by witches and wizards or other malevolent forces within society intent on frustrating the desires and personal aspirations of their victims. Such forces require neutralization either through special ritual sacrifices or wearing of protective charms and amulets as exemplified in the case of Ibrahim Dieng in the film, or require powerful Pentecostal prayers and anointing with specially blessed oil by indigenous church leaders and pastors adept at the ways of the African world. The question of how long this ambiguous behavior will continue in the face of modernity is open to speculation.

This film was set in the post-colonial era when the African elite has just assumed power across Africa. It was a period of hope when Africans were eagerly looking forward to the gains of independence. It was also a period marked by the mass exodus of Africans to Europe and North America in search of the proverbial golden fleece. The search was not restricted to formal education but also covered non-formal education. Many, like Abdou, went to Europe to learn a modern trade. Hence across Africa, in the years both before, and immediately after independence, many signboards in cities across Africa proclaimed messages of London or Paris trained tailors, barbers, barristers, photographers, etc. Of course, many who had never crossed the frontiers of their countries claimed they were London or Paris trained to gain respectability and clientele. It was also a period marked by an intensified growth and development of cities across Africa, in other words, of Africa's embrace of modernity. But that embrace as earlier noted is not without its ambivalence and contradictions.

Many, like Ibrahim Dieng, want to enjoy the fruits of modernity without dropping their traditional practices, and this is where they come to grief. The older generation, which also happens to be largely illiterate, were/are particularly guilty of this practice. Whereas in a traditional set-up, the notion of personal identity wasn't of great importance since everybody in a village could trace each other's genealogy and visitors can easily be identified, the mass population of cities and the anonymity of city dwellers require documented personal identity for business transactions to be verified. Again, the issue of documented personal identity is something which most African countries have not been able to solve up until now. In Nigeria, for instance, the issue of a national identity card has been politicized because of anxiety in certain regions of the country that has been fond of using population inflation for political gains. The idea of a national identity card is an indirect way of debunking their inflated population, especially when such drive is tied to the usage of the national identity card as a document for voting in national elections.

In circumstances such as this, it is only people engaged in the formal sectors of the national economy such as government bureaucrats; those engaged in industrial productions, the armed forces, the police, the teaching service and students, and those engaged in modern business transactions that have one form of documented personal identity card or the other. Residents of villages or the native quarters or sprawling ghettoes within cities, who have no link with these modern transactions, have no documented personal identity cards. Invariably, such people include the masses of urban dwellers in the various ghettoes in cities across Africa who are engaged in petty trading, masonry, daily paid laborers, market women, hawkers of various goods, domestic servants, petty crooks and thieves, etc., people such as those living in Ibrahim Dieng's neighborhood, lack such documented personal identity cards. Many of these people are also semi-literate and or illiterates. They particularly feel the pains of modernity since their nationality has been subtly circumscribed by their lack of personal identity cards. As the experience of Ibrahim Dieng shows in this film, possession of a voter's card is not a substitute for a personal identity card.

In a sense, *Mandabi* represents the anxieties and pains of those caught on the fringe of modern societies, those illiterate sectors of the populace barely scrounging a living on the fringe of numerous African cities and those whom Frantz Fanon referred to as "the wretched of the earth" in his book of that title. The film examines the pains and anxieties of these anonymous masses whose desires, dreams and aspirations do not figure in the developmental plans of the African elite living in the relative safety and opulence of the inherited European quarters vacated by the colonial masters. As the colonial masters were cut off from the natives whom they ruled by brute force of arms, so too are post-colonial African rulers cut off from their co-patriots whom they also rule by brute force of arms. Colonial societies were never democratic, nor have many post-colonial societies attempted to democratize. Just as the colonial rulers feared democracy, so too do many post-colonial African rulers fear democracy. The film continuously plays on this issue of personal identity and/or lack of it and the privileges that comes with its possession and/or disadvantages arising from the lack of it. In this process, the film also offers a critique of people like Ibrahim Dieng, who are caught up on the boundaries of traditional values and modernity. In fact, there is a sense in which one can argue that the film explores the lives of those anonymous masses caught on the boundaries of traditional values and modernity.

The opening sequence of the film examines the issue of traditional practices such as polygamy through the personal experiences of the central protagonist, Ibrahim Dieng. The film begins with a shot of the branches of a tree, a symbolic representation of the hybridization of modern African cultural practices and social identities, followed by a slow pan to a busy street in what looks like a ghetto or a native quarter of an urban center. This is followed by a cut to Ibrahim Dieng having a hair cut at a traditional barber's shop. In a carefully choreographed series of shots, we notice the care with which the traditional barber, using a sharpened penknife-like blade, carefully shaves his beard, his hair and nostril hairs. Feeling well spruced up, Ibrahim Dieng pays the barber and heads for home. Immediately he arrives, his senior wife, Maty, sets before him a sumptuous meal, which he voraciously devours amidst Maty's pampering. Although he is hardly through with the first meal, which he is unable to finish, his junior wife, Aram, abandons her crying baby to serve her husband another meal. Even though he is filled up, tradition demands that he has no right to reject his wife's meal, especially from his youngest and favorite wife, who is actually young enough to be his daughter. He manages to eat a few more morsels and barely rolls like a stuffed doll into bed, after which he summons Aram to massage him to sleep. In his lifestyle therefore, Dieng lives very much like a traditional chief in a traditional set-up, where he expects to be fed and supported by his subjects or his wives who are expected to toil on the land and feed him, having managed to pay their bride price. With two wives and eight children, and without a tangible source of income, Ibrahim Dieng is doubtless living beyond his means and, sooner or later, he may be forced to sell his only house. He also stands the chance of loosing his younger wife to an adventurous young man. The irony of Dieng's lifestyle is that he transfers the moral values of traditional societies to a modern city set-up.

In *Mandabi*, the city is represented as a dangerous place where traditional values stand little chance of withstanding the merciless onslaught of modern city life. Traditional societal values and his Islamic faith have taught him to give to the poor and less fortunate; it was a society built on good neighborliness and shared communal values. What Ibrahim Dieng doesn't know or is too naïve to realize is that in a modern city set-up, traditional values are bound to be manipulated and exploited by crooks and unscrupulous city dwellers driven by passion to amass wealth or survive by any means necessary. His naiveté opens him up for easy manipulation and exploitation by petty city crooks, professional city beggars and plain city spongers like the Imam and his other acquaintances, who are always trooping to his compound for one form of assistance or the other.

In other respects, even though the film does not condemn the retention of the extended family system, it seems to suggest that the peculiar circumstance of modern society is bound to circumscribe the practice. Such a reading can be inferred from the fact that Abdou's belief that his uncle would help him save the sum of 20,000 Francs toward his marriage and family plans is a misplaced trust. In fact, from the way Dieng and his family are already accumulating debts, even if he had succeeded in claiming the money order, there is little chance that Abdou would meet any money when he eventually returns home to marry. The African immigrant community in Europe and North America is full of tales of woes of those who, drawing their inspiration from traditional societal values, have sent large sums of money to close relations such as elder or younger brothers, sisters or aunts, uncles or other members of the extended family to use to buy plots of land and start a building for them, and many have returned home to find that such close relations have used such money to enrich themselves. Many have actually bought such lands, laid a foundation, abandoned the project, and then went ahead to use the money of their naïve relatives to build beautiful mansions for themselves.

Such naïve immigrants returned home to find a relation with little means of livelihood owning massive mansions, whereas they who slaved to send the money home have no tangible returns for their investments. This is why there is some sense in the way in which Sembène represents the dilemma of extended family members resident in Europe or North America. Sembène doesn't say that the extended family system is obsolete *per se*. After all, Amath, Dieng's nephew resident in the modern European quarter of Dakar, is represented in the film as uninhibitedly willing to assist his uncle in his time of need. What does seem obvious is that there is a certain ambivalence in the way the extended family system is represented in the film. We see that from the perspective of Amath's assistance to Dieng, that it is a noble traditional institution, but from the point of view of Abdou, it is open to manipulation and exploitation. Sembène's treatment of the extended family system is, therefore, much more open to ambivalent reading than the blistering critique which he offers of the polygamous system. In this regard, the film seems to suggest that worthy aspects of traditional societal values should be retained while those that are obnoxious like the polygamous system which treats women like personal objects within the patriarchal household should be discarded.

Sembène's treatment of the relation between Africans and their acquired foreign faiths, such as Islam, also makes an interesting reading. In the sequence following the first sequence of the film, symbols of religious authority are represented by a downward crane of the tall minaret of the neighborhood mosque, calls to prayer and an interior shot of the mosque packed with the Islamic faithful. But when we read this sequence against the grain of what is obvious from the example of Ibrahim Dieng's practice of this faith as shown in the opening sequence of the film, we come away with the impression that Islamic faith has not succeeded in undermining traditional African religious practices. In the scenes where Ibrahim Dieng is eating, we note that his arms are full of personal protective charms and amulets owing their roots to traditional African belief systems and religious practices and not to his Islamic faith. Indeed, as noted earlier, both Islam and Christianity have not succeeded in circumscribing traditional African religious practices. After his meal, Ibrahim Dieng tells his senior wife, Maty, to give the leftovers to the beggars, not as acts of Islamic charity, but so that they can take away the misfortunes of the family. Likewise, when he is on his way to the bank, he gives arms to the female beggar so that she can take away whatever misfortune there is on his way. All of this goes to show that even though he is a convert to the Islamic faith, he hasn't discarded his traditional religious belief systems.

In terms of the representation of city space, one finds architectural designs, street layout, and general iconography of the city strongly marked by the retention of the colonial division of urban space between the sector of the "colonizers," which was well-planned with modern architectural buildings, well-paved streets, with pedestrian sidewalks and street lights, and the sector of the "natives", marked by mud houses, make-shift buildings, dusty roads crammed with hawkers, street traders, petty crooks and thieves, and shop keepers such as Mbarka. In this set-up, the unofficial symbol of authority in the native quarter is the shop keeper whose wealth and position makes such persons highly esteemed members of such neighborhoods, but they can also for the same reason become victims of public hatred by virtue of their unscrupulous business practices as shown from the confrontation between Ibrahim Dieng and Mbarka. In other respects, the city is represented as a dangerous place packed full with strange fellows and look-alikes. A typical instance is the scene in which Ibrahim Dieng rests on a street-side rail while in deep thought over what line of action he is to take after he has been turned away from the city hall for not knowing the exact month of his birth. Someone looking exactly like his nephew, Amath, temporarily disturbs his sight line. When he succeeds however, in gaining the man's attention, he tell Ibrahim Dieng that he must be a lookalike of his nephew, adding that he is a poor fellow, just in case Dieng was thinking of begging him for money. The man is obviously a streetwise fellow from the way he subtly dismisses Dieng.

In terms of narrative time, the film's events take place within a period of nine days, between when Ibrahim Dieng receives the money order and when he realizes that, if he couldn't claim it in additional six day's time, the money order would be returned to Abdou in Paris. This realization of the impending deadline makes him appeal for more loans from Mbarka, even though Dieng is aware he already owes him some money. Of course, his desperation and naiveté lay open as easy prey to be exploited by the sophisticated crook, Mbaye Sarr. In his desperation, he is even prepared to pay Mbaye the sum of 3,000 Francs as commission,

having assessed him by his living standard that 1,000 Francs would
be too small a commission for a man of Mbaye's stature to charge.

With respect to the concept of modernity, one notices that the
film is crammed with symbols of modernity. They stretch from
long shots of the Eiffel Tower and City Gate in Paris, rendered
through montage shots showing Abdou's daily routine of activity as
a sweeper in Paris, to close-up shots of modern institutions such as
post and telegraph offices in both Paris and Dakar, and a police
station, banks, modern bureaucracy, represented by civil service
activities in city hall in Dakar, modern vehicular traffic and
crowded city streets, all of which Singer notes are products of
modernity. One also notices changes in dress codes, with Western
educated Senegalese wearing suits, and semi-literate and illiterate
Senegalese dressed in traditional clothing. It is instructive to note
that this tendency to wear suits in tropical African hot weather has
since given way to cultural resurgence which makes most people, at
least in West Africa, to dress in traditional African clothing which
is much more fitting for the hot weather.

In sum, Sembène Ousmane's film, *Mandabi*, addresses issues of
modernity the way they were experienced in the early days of post-
colonial self-governance in Africa when most Africans were full of
hope and expectations on the gains of independence. In the midst
of ongoing modernization process, desires, dreams and aspirations
for growth and development across Africa threw up a lot of
contradictions, many having to do with issues of documented
personal identity in modern business transactions, and anxieties
arising from what to do with traditional African cultural values in
the midst of modernity. In *Mandabi*, Sembène seems to argue that
there is need for universal personal documentation to avoid the
problem faced by Ibrahim Dieng in his attempt to cash his money
order, and that moribund traditional patriarchal African practices
like polygamy which oppresses women should be done away with.
But with the benefit of time, one can now observe that the
optimism that made filmmakers like Sembène think that modernity
would render polygamy moribund for reasons of the financial
implications of the practice in modern societies has been
misplaced. Polygamy is alive and kicking in both villages and cities
across Africa, and rather than becoming moribund, a combination
of factors such as cultural resurgence, and Islamic faith which

permits its believers to marry up to a maximum of four wives, have made this cultural phenomenon continue to thrive.

Summary

Thus far, one has been arguing that the cinematic medium, like other mass media institutions in Africa, is a product of modernity, and that it is one of the legacies of the historical encounter between Europe and Africa which started in the fifteenth century. The encounter highlighted the unequal power and knowledge relations between Europe and Africa. It also afforded the colonizing European powers the leverage to introduce European institutional practices in Africa. It equally created in Europeans a superiority complex that Africans have had to respond to in times of cultural awakening. These issues have often been played out, sometimes in binary terms, of tradition versus modernity. This is especially so because of the negative undercurrents which underlay the encounter in instances such as the trans-Atlantic slave trade, colonization and neo-colonial European domination of the continent. These instances have sometimes served to create in Africans ambivalent relation and responses to the project of modernity.

Within the cinematic institution, the crisis of identity, which is reflected in the hybridization of African cultural practices, is played out in urban centers across the continent. Initially, the cinematic institution was one of the colonial instruments used in the denigration of Africans, but in the post-colonial era, Africans have mastered the narrative techniques of the medium and have used it to interrogate the history of the colonial encounter.

This chapter has been rounded up with an analysis of Ousmane Sembène's *Borom Sârret* and *Mandabi*, to see how the master storyteller has handled the desires for, and anxieties of Africans, concerning the project of modernity.

ISSUES IN THE THEORY AND CRITICISM OF AFRICAN CINEMA

Introduction

This chapter conceptualizes African cinema by relating it to questions arising from concepts of national cinema, problems of "Third Cinema" theories in the Third World and classification of African cinema and rounds up with a proposed cinematic reading hypothesis anchored on the concept of subjectivity for the criticism of African cinema.

The Concept of National Cinema and its Implications to a Definition of African Cinema

As earlier observed, current African film scholarship is lopsided in favor of the history of the film industry at the expense of theory and textual analysis. Though these historical studies emphasize how patterns of colonial and post-colonial state sponsorship and the monopolistic influences of European and American film distribution conglomerates have affected the development of the film industry in Africa, by overlooking both the industrial and artistically specialized nature of cinema, they give one the impression that setting up a film industry is like setting up a factory to produce bricks or toiletries. If it were that easy, then Nigeria, Ghana and Burkina Faso, three West African countries with film laboratories, would have been self-sufficient in film production by now. The fact is that to build a viable film industry, a country requires, in addition to film laboratories, production companies and film studios, distribution companies and exhibition theatres, trained manpower comprising producers, directors, writers, actors and actresses, cinematographers, sound engineers and production recordists, light designers and technicians, editors, production and costume designers, stunts personnel, etc.; and the industry must be profitable enough to attract the unwavering patronage of both the financial and advertising sub-sectors of the national economy. Such viability in turn requires the patronage of a willing ticket-purchasing cinema audience. Finally, such a country should possess both the geo-political and economic muscle to ensure the international competitiveness of its national film industry (Bordwell and Thompson, 1976: 3-25; Bordwell, Staiger and Thompson, 1985: 243-337).

Thus instead of assessing the problems of the film industry in Africa in terms of the general gross underdevelopment of the continent due to lack of creative industrial policies, political and economic liberalization, and progressive educational policies, historians and critics of the film industry in Africa find a ready scapegoat in the erstwhile colonial authorities who, we are made to understand, conspired to let the industry remain underdeveloped (Diawara, 1986). To analyze the film industry in this manner is to fail to see it globally, in both its geo-political and economic terms, as an internationally competitive industry dominated by Hollywood film practice, with European and other national cinemas adopting creative policies for the survival of their national cinemas (Dickinson and Street, 1985; Elsaesser, 1989; Higson, 1989; Dyer and Vincendeau, 1992; Butler, 1992; and Crofts, 1993). Higson particularly foregrounds the political and economic imperatives at play in the construction of national identities through national cinemas when he argues that

> to identify a national cinema is first of all to specify a coherence and a unity; it is to proclaim a unique identity and a stable set of meanings. The process of identification is thus invariably a hegemonizing, mythologizing process, involving both the production and assignation of a particular set of meanings, and attempts to contain, or prevent the potential proliferation of other meanings. At the same time, the concept of a national cinema has almost invariably been mobilised as a strategy of cultural (and economic) resistance; a means of asserting national autonomy in the face of (usually) Hollywood's international domination. (Higson, 1987: 37)

According to Higson's theorization of the concept of national cinemas and identity construction, the concept is much more complex than most historians and critics of African cinema have conceived it. Stephen Crofts, in his reassessment of the notion of national cinema since the publication of Higson's essay, has tabulated seven categories that operate in terms of an agenda set by Hollywood. According to Crofts:

> the political, economic and cultural regimes of different nation-states license some seven varieties of "national cinemas" sequenced in rough order of decreasing familiarity...(1) cinemas which differ from Hollywood, but do not compete directly, by targeting a distinct, specialist market sector; (2) those which differ, do not compete directly *but* do directly *critique* Hollywood; (3) European and Third World entertainment cinemas which struggle with limited or no success; (4) cinemas which ignore Hollywood, an accomplishment managed by few; (5) anglophone cinemas which try to beat Hollywood at its own game; (6) cinemas which work within a wholly state-controlled and often substantially state-subsidized industry; and, (7) regional or national cinemas whose culture and/or language take their distance from the nation-state which enclose them. (Crofts, 1993: 50)

While conceding the overlapping nature of several of the categories with respect to the notion of national cinemas, Crofts highlights the geo-political, cultural and economic complexities that underlie the concept, and the strategies which individual nations or even ethnic groups or regions within the same nation, have adopted in response to the hegemonic domination of world cinema by Hollywood. What particularly stands out in his article is the fact that every nation, with the exception of the United States of America, is engaged in survival strategies aimed at preserving their national cinemas against the economic and cultural onslaught of Hollywood.

In a situation where both former colonial powers and their erstwhile colonies are engaged in the same fight for the survival or development of their national cinemas, it is naïve to expect that the former colonial powers in Africa would help to develop the film industry in Africa when the reality rather suggests that they need the African market, assuming they can wrestle it from the firm grip of Hollywood, to shore up their national cinemas. What most theoreticians and historians of African cinema fail to acknowledge is that pleas for the transfer of industrial technologies, either cinematic or otherwise, from Europe or elsewhere, to Africa, are futile exercises. It is like begging a neighborhood shop owner to assist you in setting up a competing shop on his street. To put an end to the embarrassment of such exercises, governments on the continent should follow the examples of other developing economies by setting up agencies for the funding of independent film producers, protecting and financing their national cinemas through control of film distribution and the building of movie theatres in both urban and rural areas as a matter of government policy, especially in those countries where indigenous businessmen and women have shown no interest in developing the cinema sub-sector of the national economy.

In countries where indigenous and/or foreign businessmen and women already own or manage movie theatres, they should be made to include all locally produced films in their programs, the films should be shown within a potential time schedule when they are most likely to attract audiences, and the price of tickets should not exceed those charged for foreign films. It is no use entering into contracts with owners of movie theatres only to have locally produced films scheduled solely for exhibition at the inauspicious hour of 11.00 PM. If movie theatres sustain losses from showing locally produced films, such losses should be deducted from their annual taxes to the state. African countries can only cultivate an audience for locally produced films if the audience has access to such films in the first instance. Finally, African countries should use import duties charged on foreign films to finance "independent" indigenous filmmakers until their economies are industrialized enough for them to enter into industrial film production for the competitive international film market.

The Concept and Problems of Third Cinema Theories

Traditionally, African cinema is categorized under the generalized rubric of "Third Cinema." The concept of Third Cinema was first theorized in the 1960s in Latin America though the general idea of revolutionary/Marxist aesthetics which underlies it was prevalent in most Third World countries both as a product of the ongoing liberation struggles for independence in parts of Africa and Asia or as a consequence of the guerrilla struggles for the overthrow of

Latin American dictators and fascist regimes. The notion of Third Cinema as expounded by the Latin American film theorists is also a product of the revolutionary cultural movement in Latin America of the 1950s, which climaxed with the Cuban revolution of 1959, and also inspired the pedagogical theories of Paulo Freire and the popular theatre theories of Augusto Boal (Freire, 1970; Boal, 1974).

Though the term, "Third Cinema," was coined by the Argentinean filmmakers, Fernando Solanas and Octavio Getino, in their key theoretical essay, "Towards a Third Cinema," the roots of Third Cinema practice can be traced to several factors: the pedagogical work of fellow Argentinean, Fernando Biri, and the documentary school of Santa Fe which he founded under the influence of Italian neo-realism and Griersonian social documentary practice; the artistic manifestoes of the Brazilian director and main proponent of *Cinema Novo*, Glauber Rocha, and the revolutionary culture thrown up by the guerrilla struggles earlier referred to.

According to Michael Chanan, the Third Cinema movement in Latin America was greatly influenced by Italian neo-realism and John Grierson's idea of the social documentary. Key proponents of the movement such as Biri and the Cubans, Tomas Gutierrez Alea and Julio Garcia Espinosa, studied film in Rome at the Centro Sperimentale, at the beginning of the 1950s and brought back with them to Latin America the ideals and inspirations of Italian neo-realism (Chanan, 1983: 2). Other major sources of influence include the social theories of Frantz Fanon and the literary theories of Bertolt Brecht and Walter Benjamin (Gabriel, 1979: 7-14; Willemen, 1989: 10-12).

In the area of film practice, the movement was launched with works such as Fernando Biri's *Tire die* (*Throw me a Dime*, 1958); Nelson Pereira dos Santos's *Vidas Secas* (*Barren Lives*, 1963); Glauber Rocha's *Antonio das Mortes* (*The Dragon of Evil Against the Warrior Saint*, 1968); and Solanas/Getino's revolutionary film, *La Hora de los Hornos* (*The Hour of the Furnaces*, 1968). In theory, the movement was launched with essays such as Biri's "Cinema and Underdevelopment," Rocha's "The Aesthetics of Hunger" and "The Aesthetics of Violence," Solanas and Getino's essay, "Towards a Third Cinema," Espinosa's "For an Imperfect Cinema" and Jorge Sanjines's "Problems of Form and Content in Revolutionary Cinema." As theorized in these essays, the concept of "Third Cinema" implies not only a break with "First Cinema" aesthetics identified with Hollywood practice and its imitators, but also "Second Cinema" practice identified with indigenous auteurist cinema.

In all the essays, "Third Cinema," is conceived as a tool for creating a revolutionary consciousness for the mass mobilization of society for social change. The emphasis is both on the decolonization of Third World societies, the institutions for anti-imperialist struggles both in the colonized and metropolitan countries in order to contain imperialist expansion, and the general decolonization of culture. Solanas and Getino for instance, argue that

> the anti-imperialist struggles of the peoples of the Third World and of their equivalents inside the imperialist countries constitute today the axis of the world revolution. *Third Cinema is, in our opinion, the cinema that recognises in that struggle the most gigantic cultural, scientific, and artistic manifestation of our time*, and the great possibility of constructing a liberated personality with each people as the starting point - in a word, the decolonization of culture...The culture, including the cinema, of a neocolonized country is just the expression of an overall dependence that generates models and values born from the needs of imperialist expansion (original emphasis). (Solanas/Getino, 1983: 18)

The Latin American film theorists and practitioners of Third Cinema considered their works as the artistic arm of the ongoing guerrilla struggles to overthrow the fascist and dictatorial regimes of the region. Solanas and Getino regard their cinematic practice as guerrilla cinema and their camera as "the inexhaustible *expropriator of image-weapons;* the projector, *a gun that can shoot 24 frames per second"* (original emphasis) (24). They also consider their works as part of the pedagogical crusade to create critical awareness and revolutionary fervour among the masses. In this sense, they saw themselves as members of the artistic vanguard of the revolutionary movement. They also consider revolutionary violence as a necessary appurtenance of the liberation struggle. Glauber Rocha, the key proponent of *Cinema Novo*, was even criticised by the more radical arm of Third Cinema practice, represented by filmmakers like Solanas and Getino, and Jorges Sanjines, for not being revolutionary enough. Yet, Rocha had argued that

> *Cinema Novo* teaches that the aesthetics of violence are
> revolutionary rather than primitive. The moment of violence is
> the moment when the coloniser becomes aware of the existence
> of the colonised. Only when he is confronted with violence can
> the coloniser understand, through horror, the strength of the
> culture he exploits. (Rocha, 1983: 13)

Finally, the Latin American theorists of Third Cinema also placed
emphasis on the cognitive rather than the emotive aspect of the
cinema. They did not necessarily emphasize a cognitive cinema at
the expense of pleasure. Julio Garcia Espinosa for instance,
compares the cognitive power of art to the power of a game for a
child. He argues that "aesthetic pleasure lies in sensing the
functionality (without a specific goal) of our intelligence and our
own sensitivity" (Espinosa, 1983: 29).

Willemen, in his assessment of Third Cinema theories, has
observed that filmmakers in Latin America, Asia and Africa, are
caught between the contradictions of technologized mass culture
and the need to develop a different kind of mass culture, while
being denied the financial, technological and institutional support
to do so. This dilemma, according to him, explains why the Latin
Americans have opted for a cognitive cinema. As he puts it,

> since the culture industry has become extremely adept at
> orchestrating emotionality while deliberately atrophying the
> desire for understanding and intellectuality, it makes sense for
> the Latin American avant-garde to emphasize lucidity and the
> cognitive aspects of cultural work, thus reversing the hierarchy
> between the cognitive and the emotive, while of course
> maintaining the need to involve both of them. (Willemen: 13)

Though Latin American filmmakers often expressed solidarity with
ongoing decolonization and anti-imperialist struggles in Asia and
Africa, they emphasized that their theories were borne out of their
search for an appropriate cinematic practice that would meet the
revolutionary needs of Latin America. They even expressed the
unique nature of each country's experience. In this regard, their
theories were regionally specifically tailored. Similar conditions of
underdevelopment, poverty, corruption, and mass illiteracy that
stimulated the guerrilla struggles in Latin America also exist in parts
of Asia and Africa. However, while the guerrilla struggles in Latin
America from the 1950s onwards were against independent
governments, those in Asia and Africa were in the main

decolonization struggles. What unites most Third World countries then, as now, are the structures of underdevelopment — institutionalized mass poverty, illiteracy, corruption, greed, nepotism, lack of democratic institutions — and the general technological backwardness of these countries.

The first attempt to systematically analyze Third Cinema as a tricontinental phenomenon, to paraphrase Julianne Burton (1985: 6), was carried out by Teshome Gabriel in his book, *Third Cinema in the Third World: The Aesthetics of Liberation.* Conscious of the range of cinematic forms and influences obtainable in most Third World countries, Gabriel, like the Latin American precursors of Third Cinema theories, emphasized that

> Third Cinema is moved by a concern for the fate of the Third man and woman threatened by colonial and neo-colonial wars. In selecting the themes and styles for his or her work, the filmmaker's choice is both ideologically determined and circumscribed...Their major concerns are twofold: (1) a rejection of the propositions and concepts of traditional cinema, namely, those of Hollywood; (2) the need to use film to serve an ideological and revolutionary end. (Gabriel, 1982: 1-2)

Gabriel was also fully conscious of the fact that Third Cinema is not unique to the Third World — that much at least is testified to by the title of his book, *Third Cinema in the Third World.* In fact, Solanas and Getino whose works Gabriel makes references to, cite the cinematic practices of *Newsreel,* a US New Left film group, the *cinegionali* of the Italian student movements, the films made by Joris Ivens and Chris Marker, those made by the *Etats Generaux du Cinéma Française,* and by the British and Japanese student movements, as belonging to the tradition of Third Cinema (Solanas/Getino, 1983: 17). In recognition of the fact that Third Cinema is not unique to the Third World, Gabriel has equally emphasized the fact that the "principal characteristic of Third Cinema is really not so much where it is made, or even who makes it, but rather, the ideology it espouses and the consciousness it displays" (Gabriel, 1982: 2). He additionally argues that "Third Cinema includes an infinitive variety of subjects and styles, as varied as the lives of the people it portrays" (ibid: 3).

According to Gabriel, point-of-view in Third Cinema does not function on a psychological or mythic level, but rather takes up an explicit position with respect to an ideological or social topic.

Furthermore, that point-of-view in Third Cinema is not a reflection of the consciousness or subjectivity of a single subject, i.e. a protagonist/hero; rather, the central figure in Third Cinema serves to develop an historical perspective on radical social change. Consequently, when the protagonist/hero casts a glance, in actuality, it is the masses or the people who give substance to the gaze. Gabriel therefore posits that the individual hero in Third Cinema is a trans-individual or a collective subject. Based on these arguments, he questions the suitability of applying psychoanalytic and cine-structuralist critical models, governed by the oedipal complex, to the analysis of spectatorial textual positioning and identification processes in Third Cinema. Finally, the aesthetics of Third Cinema moves between two poles: one which demands that the works engage the actual pressing social realities of the day, and the other that the film achieves its impression of reality, not simply by mirroring it but by transforming the given situation (Gabriel: 7-8).

In another essay published on the subject titled, "Towards a Critical Theory of Third World Films," Gabriel further refines his theory of "Third Cinema," this time by paying attention to "Third Cinema's" modes of narration. He argues that the patterns of viewing situations and spectatorial identification process are culturally determined. Furthermore, "Third World films are heterogeneous, employing narrative and oral discourse, folk music and songs, extended silences and gaps, moving from fictional representation to reality, to fiction — these constitute the creative part that can challenge the ideological carry-overs that technology imposes" (Gabriel, 1985: 361). He also restated his opposition to the application of psychoanalytic and cine-structuralist critical models in the criticism of Third Cinema of the Third World. He advances several reasons why he thinks it is inappropriate to apply Western critical models in the criticism of Third World films. He gives a comprehensive tabulation of Western and Third World (folk) conception of art and filmic conventions to back up this point.

Gabriel summarizes his arguments by stating that the conception and valuation of art and filmic conventions, which emanate from them reflect the world outlook and perceptions of a people and the position of the individual within the social set up. In his view, the major difference between the Third World and the

West, with regards to changing the community from a passive to a dynamic entity, is one of approach: while people in the Third World aim at changing the individual through the community, in the West, the community is changed through the individual. Both approaches, according to him, produce either a communal outlook or an individualist one, and they are in turn reflected through filmic conventions (Gabriel: 364). With regards to the conception of space and time in Third World and Western films, he states that where Western films manipulate time more than space, Third World films seem to emphasise space over time. The reason for such differences he traces to culture. Third World films grow from folk tradition where communication is a slow-paced phenomenon and time is not rushed but has its own pace. In Western culture on the other hand, a lot of value is placed on time — time is art, time is money and it has to be economized. If time drags in a film, the Western spectator grows bored and impatient, so a means has to be devised to cheat on time. Editing cuts off all that is considered cinematic excess (Gabriel: 365).

According to Gabriel, what is considered cinematic excess in Western cinematic practice is precisely where Third World cinema is located. He argues that some of the cinematic codes which are applied differently in both cinematic traditions include: (i) the long take, (ii) cross-cutting, (iii) the close-up shot, (iv) the panning shot, (v) the concept of silence, and (vi) the concept of hero. Gabriel argues that it is common in Third World films to see a concentration of long takes and repetition of images and scenes; and that in Third World films, the slow, leisurely pacing approximates the viewer's sense of time and rhythm of life. In addition, that the preponderance of wide-angle shots of longer duration deals with a viewer's sense of community and of how people fit in nature. He argues that when Michelangelo Antonioni and Jean-Luc Godard use these types of shots, it is to convey an existential separation and isolation from nature and self, rather than the unity of self and nature emphasised in Third World films.

On the use of cross-cutting in Third World films, he states that it shows simultaneity of action rather than the building up of suspense. Furthermore, that the power of images lies not in the expectation we develop about the mere juxtapositions or the collision itself, but rather in conveying the reasons for the imminent collision. Thus, whereas conventional cinema has often reduced this to the collision of antagonists, on a scale of positive and negative characters, in Third World films, this mechanism is used to imply ideological collision. Gabriel further argues that the close-up shot, a device used in Western cinematic practices to study individual psychology, is less used in Third World films, and that when it is used, it serves more of an informational purpose, than a study in psychological realism. Furthermore, the isolation of an individual, in tight close-up shots, seems unnatural to Third World filmmakers because (i) it calls attention to itself; (ii) it eliminates social considerations; and (iii) it diminishes spatial integrity (Gabriel: 365).

According to Gabriel, there is a preponderance of panning shots in Third World films because they help to maintain integrity of space and time, as well as help to minimize the frequent use of "the cut" or editing. The emphasis on space also conveys a different concept of "time," a time which is not strictly linear or chronological but co-exists with it. With regards to the use of sound and the concept of silence, Gabriel observes that the rich potential for the creative interpretation of sound as well as the effective use of its absence is enormous in Third World films. He cites the case of *Emitai* in which there are English subtitles for drum messages and cockcrows. He argues that silence is an important element of the audio-track of *Emitai*. He refers to the use of silence in this film as, "a cinema of silence that speaks" (367). However, he emphasizes the point that silences have meaning only in context. And that when they are employed in an extended manner, viewers wonder what will happen, accustomed as they are to the incessant sound and overload of music in conventional cinema. Finally, with regards to the concept of hero, he argues that even if a Western viewer cannot help but identify and sympathize with the black labor leader in *They Don't Wear Black Ties*, the lunatic in *Harvest: 3000 Years*, the crazy poet in *The Chronicle of the Years of Ember*, and the militant party member in *Sambizanga*, the films nevertheless kill those characters. He argues that the heroes are killed in these films because wish-fulfilment through identification is not the films' primary objective; rather, it is the importance of collective engagement and action that matters. The individual hero in the Third World context does not make history, he or she only serves historical necessities (Gabriel: 367).

Any critique of Third Cinema theories must take cognizance of the fact that they are historically and culturally products of the age, politics and rhetoric of both decolonization and anti-imperialist struggles in the Third World, and ultimately of the world socialist movement in general. Historically, the socialist countries were sympathetic to Third World decolonization struggles and gave military aid to liberation movements in these countries; but the West which was then engaged in Cold War politics of containing the spread and influence of Communism interpreted such aid in terms of the East's strategy for the spread of Communism.

As a result of the Soviet Union and Eastern Europe's aid to Third World liberation movements and of the general socialist rhetoric of equality of peoples, races, nations, and ethnicities, and solidarity among the oppressed peoples of the world, Marxist theories and aesthetics proliferated in Third World countries. In fact, Marxist theories and aesthetics offered some sort of liberatory utopia for an egalitarian society to which Third World people aspired to at a time when they felt Western political and economic structures, both in the Third World and in metropolitan countries, excluded them. As earlier noted, the historical circumstances within which Third World decolonization struggles emerged placed them in an awkward situation where the use of decolonization rhetoric was interpreted in terms of hostility to the West, Western liberal democracy and free enterprise. Third World countries were caught in a situation where they had few choices — to be moderate in such a historical circumstance as the period of decolonization era, to abstain from using anti-imperialist rhetoric, even if such rhetoric are empty self-consolatory ranting, amounted to being a sell-out to Western exploitation and imperialism; it was to be a collaborator with the West and a traitor to one's community. Caught in these circumstances, Third World decolonization struggles became casualties of the East-West Cold War politics. Third Cinema theories are therefore products of the historical circumstances which implicated them in the world socialist movement, together with its Marxist theories and aesthetics.

A lot of criticism has been made against Third Cinema theories. The foremost of these relate to the inadequacy of the very notion of Third World upon which Third Cinema theories are based. The notion is now perceived to be inadequate as a concept for assessing the level of development that exists in the so-called developing nations in contrast to the developed nations. Such contrasts between developed and developing nations are now perceived to gloss over a multiplicity of significant differences within and among both developed and developing nations. Every Third World nation is now conceived as including a First World component, just as every First World nation includes a Third World component. As Robert Stam puts it, the "notion of the 'three worlds' ...not only flattens heterogeneities, masks contradictions, and elides differences, but also obscures similarities. The first-world/third-world struggle takes place not only *between* nations but also *within* nations" (original emphasis) (Stam, 1991: 218).

Apart from the problematic involved in the homogenization of Third World experience, Third Cinema theories have also been found to neglect the national question. Willemen for instance, has noted that the effectiveness with which the national socio-cultural formations determine particular signifying practices is not addressed. Moreover, the split between a national dominant cinema competing with Hollywood, and a national authorial cinema, which also existed within Hollywood, is mirrored in the split between a politically oriented militant cinema opposing mainstream entertainment cinema, and a personal-experimental cinema opposing the literariness of authorial cinema, even if these categories tended to overlap at times (Willemen: 17). Such complexities are often overlooked in Third Cinema theories.

Stam also notes that the concept of the national carries an implicit nationalism which has always oscillated between its progressive and regressive poles, depending on the political character of the power bloc which mobilizes nationalism to constitute its own hegemony. He further argues that many early discussions of nationalism often took it as axiomatic that the issue at stake was simply one of expelling the foreign corrupting influence, in order to recover the national culture in all its plenitude and glory. This idea of the national is, according to him, simplistic:

> (1) it elides the realities of class, camouflaging possible contradictions between different sectors of the third world society, (2) fails to provide criteria for distinguishing exactly what is worth retaining in the national tradition (a sentimental nationalism was always liable to valorize patriarchal social institutions — Sembene mocks such valorizationa in *Xala* by

having his neo-colonized black elite defend polygamy in the name of "l' Africanite!". (3) Even apart from the question of class, every country is characterized by heteroglosia; nations are at once urban and rural, male and female, elite and non-elite. The nation as a unitary subject inevitably muffles the "polyphony" of social and ethnic voices characteristic of heteroglot culture. (4) The precise nature of the national "essence" to be recuperated, finally, is almost always elusive and chimerical. Some nationalist purists locate this essence in an organic past - e.g., prior to the colonizer's arrival — or in the rural interior of the country, or in a prior stage of development (the pre-industrial, or in a non-European ethnicity. But things are never so simple. (Stam: 227)

Such criticisms of Third Cinema theories have now broadened the grounds on which the question of representation as it affects issues of nationality, nationalism, ethnicity, class, gender, race, and belief-systems can be addressed. Coco Fusco has noted that the celebrated Latin American theorists and practitioners of Third Cinema were male, from the middle and upper class elites of their countries; and their sense of oppression was largely global and political, not microsocial or sexual. Their films became known through auteurist venues, particularly in Europe, in spite of their proclamations that their work was for the oppressed, the masses, or whoever else they designated as their ideal audience (Fusco, 1989: 10). Coming from such class background, their theories and cinematic projects, as Fusco has noted, often tended to homogenize, even at the regional level, the Latin American experience, thereby overlooking the equally important questions of race, ethnicity, gender, or nationality that are implicated in their theories and cinematic practices.

Most of the criticisms raised with regards to the Latin American theorists and practitioners of "Third Cinema," equally apply to Teshome Gabriel's theorization of the concept, especially, as it relates to Africa. Gabriel, and incidentally Julianne Burton (1985), in her critical review of Gabriel's book, often use the concept interchangeably to represent the totality of Third World film practice. Gabriel, in *Third Cinema in the Third World*, restricted the definition to the militant political cinema of revolutionary movements or filmmakers in Latin America, Asia, Africa, and its corresponding kindred practices in Western Europe, North America, and Japan, which drew their inspirations from Eastern European nations' concept of a revolutionary political cinema, as the Latin Americans originally conceived the concept of Third Cinema. Such a conception of Third Cinema seemed to be an acknowledgement of the existence of other cinematic practices in the so-called Third World countries: commercial entertainment cinema, often modeled after Hollywood practice, authorial cinema, of which most of Third Cinema practices could be considered revolutionary arm, despite their arguments to the contrary, and personal-experimental cinema. Besides, a generally accepted fact is that many of the so-called Third World countries such as India, Brazil, Mexico, or Argentina, are fairly industrialized nations that have now graduated into industrial film production. According to Stephen Crofts, in 1988, the Indian film industry produced 773 films, 262 films more than Hollywood produced that same year (Crofts, 1993: 56).

As Gabriel later theorized the concept in his essays, "Teaching Third World Cinema" and "Towards a Critical Theory of Third World Films," though he does not directly use the term, "Third Cinema," the definition and terms of reference applied to Third World cinema or Third World film practice seem to imply that he is using the terms interchangeably to represent the same concept (Gabriel, 1983; 1985). However, in another essay on the subject, "Colonialism and 'Law and Order' Criticism," Gabriel reverted to how he originally defined the term in his book, *Third Cinema in the Third World*, by making clear distinctions between Third Cinema, which is just one category of the cinematic practices in Third World countries, and Third World film practice in general. As he puts it:

> the discourse strategy of Third Cinema has a more political and ideological social focus. This Julianne Burton seems unable to understand — not all Third World film texts qualify as 'Third Cinema'. The territory is *not* the map. Third Cinema in the Third World is anti-imperialist, militant and confrontational cinema. (original emphasis) (Gabriel, 1986: 141)

In most of his writings on Third Cinema or Third World cinema to date, Gabriel has always objected specifically to the application of cine-structuralist and psychoanalytic critical models to the analysis of Third World films, and by implication, African films. The way he presents his objections, one could even discern a strain in his arguments that carries an objection to the application, generally, of Western critical criteria to Third World film practices; only that such an argument is in itself punctured by the very fact that his theorization of the concept of "Third Cinema," and his "political" or "ideological" criticism is propelled by Marxist critical theory, itself a major grid in Western critical theories (Gabriel, 1982: 5-14; 1985: 361-362). If perhaps his objection is restricted to infer reactionary and conservative Western critical theories, he ought to have been more specific. But even such an argument will be problematic, because the progressiveness or otherwise of Western critical theories, or any other critical theories for that matter, depend not entirely on the innate nature of such theories but on how, to what purpose, and who mobilizes them as critical canons for textual analysis. As a result, it will be difficult to subscribe to arguments that object to the application of Western critical theories or other critical theories not derived from Third World countries, to the analysis of Third World films. It is not which theories, where they are derived or even by whom, that ensures the suitability of critical theories as frameworks for textual analysis; it is how and for what purpose, these critical theories are mobilized, that ensure the progressiveness or regressiveness of them as the case may be. Critical theories are relative terms with relative meanings and applications. Ultimately, all critical theories become theories in translation the moment they are mobilized as critical canons for textual, social, and artistic analyses. They become implicated in the personal projects of whoever mobilizes them as frameworks for analyses. In other words, their progressiveness or regressiveness depends on the manner of their application.

In the case of Gabriel, the only reasons he gives for his objection to the use of the two critical models, cine-structuralist and psychoanalytic models, which he singles out for mention are:

(i) the conception and analysis of film which emerges from cine-structuralist criticism is uniform and static. He does not however state what is uniform and static about it. He also states that cine-structuralism strives to find immanent meaning in works whose deeper meaning is concealed. Therefore, he argues that since the films he earmarked for study do not try to hide their true meaning, the burden of search implicated in the project of cine-structuralism is irrelevant. But the question is, is there any work that has such an outlook, and if there is, is it impossible to read complex meaning into it. Gabriel is in this instance underestimating the labor of criticism and of the critical faculty. There is no work of art whose meaning is so virtually transparent as not to warrant the investment of the critical faculty. If there is such a work, it would not qualify as art. Without the labor of reading, of criticism, there would not be meaning in a work of art. Meaning is what we invest in a work of art in the process of reading. It is neither immanent nor innate; it is something that evolves, that we create in the process of reading.

(ii) Gabriel also argues that a psychoanalytic critical framework, with its mechanism of Oedipal Complex is also irrelevant to Third World film criticism because of its underlying nuclear familial model and its emphasis on individualism which he believes stands in contradistinction to the collective subjectivity and socio-political themes that are emphasized in most Third World films. (Gabriel, 1982: 5-14; 1985: 361-362)

Gabriel's objection to the application of cine-structuralist and psychoanalytic critical models to the criticism of Third World films, invokes the ghosts of criticisms that greeted the publication of Sunday Anozie's book, *Structural Models and African Poetics*, a pioneering structuralist study of African literature, art, and culinary art. In his critical review of the book, Anthony Appiah queried Anozie's approach to the whole project of structuralism. Appiah's general argument, part of which I subscribe to, is that though the book was intended as an introduction to a structuralist study of African literature, it does not define some of the key elements of structuralism, such as, the relation between *langue* and *parole*, *sign*, *signifier* and *signified*, and *synchrony* and *diachrony* and the role of linguistics in the promulgation of the structuralist project. As Appiah puts it,

> anyone who is even slightly unclear about the role that structuralism, whatever it is, has played in recent literary theory — anyone, that is, who wonders about the directness of the relevance of technical linguistics to literary theory, or about the distinction between *langue* and *parole*, or about the sense in which the nature of the 'signified' is as arbitrary as the nature of the 'signifier' — anyone who wonders about any of these things will find no help in Sunday Anozie's book. Despite the fact that he purports to offer us an introduction to the structure of structuralism, we enter its world *in media res*. (Appiah, 1984: 128)

Appiah further argues that the task of Anozie should have first started — since the work was intended to be an introduction to a structuralist study of African literature — with a definition of structuralism; second, he should have shown how it relates to certain features that he claims to exist in "African thought"; third, he should have made a case for why we should choose a structuralist approach in our efforts to account for the various semiotic systems of Africa (Appiah: 139). Due to these methodological problems, the book appears more like a mosaic selective application of structuralist models and key terms to the analysis of African literature than an analysis that proceeds from a systematic definition and application of structuralism to African literature. For all his criticisms of Anozie's book, Appiah is not against the application of structuralism or any other Western critical theory to the analysis of African literature. He specifically states that

> it is not that a structuralist poetics is inapplicable in Africa because structuralism is European; so far as it is successful in general, it seems to me as applicable to African literary material as any other. But we should not expect the transfer of a method to a new set of texts to lead to exactly the same results ...indeed, this would surely show that there was something wrong with the method. (Appiah: 145)

Though Appiah is not against the application of structuralism to African literature, he expresses philosophical and political reservations about the entire project of structuralism and post-structuralism. He observes that, though the fundamental idea of structuralism was to model our understanding of all meaning-bearing cultural systems on linguistics and, in particular, on the kind of linguistics pioneered by Ferdinand de Saussure, it is "by no means clear to many, among whom I happily include myself, what this project entails" (128). Despite his reservations about the general style of structuralist writers, Appiah moves quickly ahead to state in clear terms what he regards as the four basic theses of Saussure's linguistic theory: (i) the arbitrary nature of the *sign* and its constitutive parts, *signifier* and *signified*; (ii) the purely relational, or structural, character of linguistic systems; (iii) the importance of the distinctions between *langue* and *parole*; and (iv) the importance of the distinctions between *synchronic* and *diachronic* aspects of the linguistic systems.

To return to Teshome Gabriel, unlike Anthony Appiah who set about disagreeing with the project of structuralist poetics, and its application to African literature by Sunday Anozie, after he had systematically analyzed it and examined its implications for the criticism of African literature, Gabriel neither analyses cine-structuralism before dismissing it nor fully explains the implications of applying it to African cinema. The same goes for the psychoanalytic study of the cinema. To take the case of cine-structuralism as an instance, Gabriel merely observes that Christian Metz's widely read and analyzed book, *Film Language*, attempts to define film simply (Gabriel, 1982: 5). The fact is, Metz does not simply define film in the book. Rather, Metz's book is a systematic application of structuralism to the cinema.

Even though Metz does not claim to have exhausted all the semiotic potentials of the cinema, his systematic application of the linguistic model to the cinema does help to explicate its structural elements. Metz's structuralist analysis of the cinema is supposed to be a reading hypothesis, like the Marxist reading hypothesis which Gabriel favors in his analysis of Third World films, which anybody interested in textual analysis can apply to any set of films. Though Metz's book, *Film Language*, is a complex work, it cannot be critically reviewed by dismissing it the way Gabriel does by saying that it simply defines the cinema, for it was the first systematic application of the structuralist model to the cinema.

Regarding Gabriel's objection to the application of psychoanalytic critical model to African cinema on account of what he considers to be the centrality of the Oedipal Complex and its nuclear familial basis, I should like to state that though the Oedipal Complex is one of the central tropes of the psychoanalytic model, it is certainly not the most important. Current psychoanalytic criticism, derived from Jacques Lacan's re-reading of Freud, recognizes the Mirror Phase as the primal scene of identity formation.

Regarding film criticism, Edward Branigan states that the application of psychoanalysis to film criticism depends on an analogy that compares the processes of the unconscious, in a non-reducible manner, to the processes of language, and vice versa. An example of the former is the linking of condensation and displacement, respectively, to metaphor and metonymy. An example of the latter is the interpretation of the necessary distance between enunciation (narration) and enounced (narrative). The analysis of enunciation becomes an analysis of Freudian primary processes and the constitution of the subject. With condensation, a compression of two or more ideas occurs, so that a composite figure, image or name, drawing on and leaving out features of both is formed. In this way, a single image in a dream, for instance, is able to represent many different wishes or thoughts through compression of common features and elimination of (relevant) differences. In the case of displacement, the significant unconscious wish is able to transfer its intensity or meaning to an indifferent term, thereby allowing the latter to act as its delegate so as to disguise it. The insignificant idea is thus able to represent the more significant one without the repressed feature of the significant idea breaching the barriers of censorship. These two processes, which are the governing procedures of the psychical primary processes, function together to create the manifest dream and all other symptoms that so cleverly disguise and express the unconscious wish (Grosz, 1990: 87, Branigan, 1984: 11).

According to Branigan, psychoanalytic study of the film text, as derived from Lacan, begins with the fundamental distinction between narration and narrative. Both of these aspects of a text are conceived as organized along two axes: (i) a play of presence/absence between the author as subject and a narrator, i.e., any of the author's representatives in the text, e.g. a character who tells or acts out a story; and (ii) a play of identity or difference between the viewer as subject and a narratee, i.e, any of the viewer's representative in the text, e.g., a character who watches or listens. The narrator and narratee need not be personified as characters, but may sometimes be "effaced," i.e., be represented as implicit positions in the text. The purpose of these games, according to him, is not to move a message (information) betweeen a sender and a receiver (as in a communication model), but to replay the *mise-en-scène* of lack, i.e., castration, desire, or demand. Thus the self that the individual recognizes as his or hers depends, for psychoanalysis, upon what that individual rejects, fails to recognize, or *repressses*. The repressed text is therefore the true object of inquiry.

Character is no longer a stable unity (analogous to a human being) but a function in the text which is constantly being split, shifted and reformed elsewhere (just as the human subject is racked by contradictory drives from different conscious and unconscious levels). Character becomes a construction of the text, not *a priori* and autonomous. Character is, in this instance, not a "first fact" for criticism through which the remainder of the text is interpreted and made intelligible; rather, character exists to serve and mask unconscious forces as they are played out in a drama which implicates the viewer. Thus a character may at one moment be a narrator and at the next a narratee. And as the notion of character becomes more fluid, so too does the boundary between how the film presents a character and what that character presents within the film (Branigan: 11-12).

Like character, Branigan also states that the actions and events of a film are deconstructed by a psychoanalytic reading. For example, the desire to know often appears in the film as a set of enigmas posed, delayed and resolve. The classic text marshals desire and then moves to satisfy it; that is, to reassure the fears accompanying desire (which in turn constructs a replay of desire but only to conceal fear/desire anew). Desire is always a lack and so always lacking: the play of desire is a ceaseless lack of satisfaction of desire. The psychoanalytic search for the repressed text also upsets the notion of author. The circulation of desire, often repressed desire, in the text requires two points: self and other or I and you. Surface features of the text, such as character, voice-over narrators and voice-over narrates, are only transient masks for the desire to know and be known. The aim of psychoanalysis is not to expose an author who then "expresses" himself through a text but to analyze the network of desire which hold both text and author. Psychoanalysis does not also focus on the responses of real viewers (as they emerge from the movie theatre) nor accept a perfect viewer (perfectly objective and hence invincible), but rather postulates an intermediate, hypothetical viewer, like an intermediate hypothetical author, who is caught up by, and subject to, a system of desire. In psychoanalytic film theory, the viewer as a subject is positioned through its representative in the text (narratee) and through identification with other patterns of marks. Since both author and viewer are on exactly the same level as producers of the text, i.e., by being subjects of its systems, subjectivity is, strictly, neither in the one nor the other but in both and in a necessary simultaneity of self/other. The splitting of the subject is deemed the very ground of intelligibility of both discourse and the human. The split is that of self/other or various inflections of it such as Conscious/Unconscious, Id/Ego , and Ego/Id. In psychoanalytic studies, it is not the message which is fundamental but the constitution of the positions "I" and "you," which may not be separate "persons" and which may not be modeled through language. Starting with the text, psychoanalysis aims to reconstruct these various subject positions so as to ultimately reveal the "author as subject" and the "viewer as subject" (Branigan: 13-14).

Rather than the Oedipus Complex which Teshome Gabriel perceives to be the principal trope in psychoanalytic criticism, and therefore invoked to disqualify the application of psychoanalysis to African cinema, on account of what he considers to be its nuclear familial foundation, the Oedipus Complex, though a central trope in psychoanalytic studies, is just one of several. In addition, rather than the Oedipus Complex, the Imaginary Phase is the foundation of (mis)formation of subjectivity. The concept of the split subject that is emphasized in psychoanalysis and represented in the duplicity of discourses is a product of the Imaginary Phase. The Oedipus Complex, on the other hand, is a product of the mediation of the Symbolic Phase, a phase which institutes the subjection of the child to the laws, norms and values of society. But the individual, who is initiated into society through symbolic rituals of sanctions and prohibitions, is already an alienated individual on account of the (mis)formation of the individual that ties its subjectivity to the Other. Therefore, if there is an underlying tyranny in the whole project of psychoanalysis, it should be considered the tyranny of the Imaginary Phase and of the Unconscious with its triadic, intractable and insatiable structures of need, demand and desire.

In the manner in which it is currently theorized, human subjectivity seems to be held hostage to both Unconscious libidinal and social needs driven by insatiable desires. What worries me is that these desires or drives are attributed to primal sources and the Unconscious rather than the result of the social constitution, history, culture, and Conscious/Unconscious drives. The psychoanalytic theorization of the subject as an irretrievably split persona driven by both Unconscious/Conscious desires instead of Conscious/Unconscious ones, is what makes me sceptical of the model. It seems to explain away most human frailties and negative tendencies or symptoms, as products of repressed desires of the Unconscious. This makes the model a ready instrument for the architects of various social excesses or bigotry to rationalize their acts as products of malformed infancy and/or Unconscious desires. In addition, the Oedipus Myth/Complex is not a universal phenomenon because of its underlying nuclear familial structure. Such a structure cannot be said to underlie relations within the extended family system in Africa in which there is a constellation of authorities, with familial authority being centripetal rather than centrifugal and networks of authorities embracing the far reaches of the extended family system. The child in Africa is a child of the extended family and, ultimately, of the community, clan, ethnic group and society. Within such a structure with networks of surrogate fathers and mothers whose authorities sometimes supersedes those of the biological father and mother, the functionality of the Oedipus Myth/Complex is called into question.

Furthermore, while one subscribe to the notions of the sexed and split subject, both notions need to be considered as products of social constructs; and in particular, with regards to the sexed subject, one does not attribute the powers of patriarchy to the fear of castration. Rather, it is a product of the primal division of labor that tended to confine the mother to the home/domestic sphere, especially during the extended period of child birth/upbringing, and the father to the public sphere. Such a primal division of labor, especially the labor of child birth/upbringing, instituted the boundary between matriarchal and patriarchal power, and since the public sphere often moderate social intercourse and discourses, patriarchal power soon gained supremacy over matriarchy. This possibly explains the fact that though most African communities are matriarchal in structure, matriarchy continues to be subordinated to patriarchy as a result of the primal division of labor instituted by the labor of child birth/upbringing. Furthermore, though one subscribes to the psychoanalytic notion of the split subject, one considers that splitting to be product of the conflict between Conscious/Unconscious social needs and desires. Finally, one considers repressed desires as products of social sanctions and prohibitions rather than of primal miscognition of the Mirror Phase.

Despite some of the inadequacies of the psychoanalytic model which have been mentioned, to apply it to the criticism of African cinema is still possible after subjecting it to necessary modifications. Indeed, one of the most insightful critical studies of Ousmane Sembène's *Xala* is Laura Mulvey's psychoanalytic study. In her analysis of the film, she invokes Freudian/Marxist concepts of fetishism to explain commodity fetishism in post-colonial societies, and the historical structural imbalances and gaps which the disavowal value systems of capitalism, especially that of the neo-colonial state, impose on power structures and relations between men/women, elites/working class, and urban/rural areas of the post-colonial state. She refers to Sembène's cinematic discourse in this film, as a "kind of poetics of politics," and her analysis is undertaken within a framework of politics of poetics that appropriately translates through moderation, Freudian/Marxist critical concepts before applying them to an African text. Her submission in this regard is instructive:

> Sembène suggests that these fetished objects seal the repression of history and of class and colonial politics under the rhetoric of nationhood. His use of the concept of fetishism is not an exact theoretical working through of the Marxist or Freudian concepts of fetishism; however, his use is *Marxist* and *Freudian*. Furthermore, the interest of the film lies in its inextricable intermeshing of the two (original emphasis). (Mulvey, 1991: 36)

Mulvey's analysis of *Xala* demonstrates the fact that a psychoanalytic critical model can be applied to African cinema. As is the case with other European critical models, what is required of the analyst is a certain amount of sensitivity to the socio-historical world and cultural specificity of the film. In any case, African films, like films in general, contain the codes of their interpretation; and any critic who is sensitive to these should be able to give a fairly insightful reading even if he or she applies a European (or other non-African) critical model. Where the problem lies is when critics begin to use European (or other non-African) cultural norms and values as standards, not comparable cultural values but the standard against which its African counterparts are judged as pathological deviations or corruption of the ideal. When this happens, criticism has moved beyond the application of a critical model for discerning the narrational structures of narratives, a general textual reading hypothesis, to utilization of a different set of cultural values as judgemental models for appraising those of Africa. When this happens, African scholars have a right to denounce such criticisms for they are a product of colonialist mentality.

Gabriel's comparative study of European and Third World artistic valuation standards, performance styles, concepts of artist, and their filmic representations, tabulated in two tables in his essay, "Towards a Critical Theory of Third World Films," is only accurate, insofar as Africa is concerned, if one is dealing with the rural communities, and even there, only to a certain extent. In Africa, for instance, even in rural communities, master artists such as griots, song composers, choreographers, and master drummers are resorting to modern media of mass entertainment and information like radio, television, phonographic records and amplificatory equipment for popularizing their art. The drive to acquire modern amplificatory equipment and performance instruments, to acquire wealth, fame and star-status, have further led to the cultivation of individualist consciousness, thereby shattering the communal status of the master artist. The only unique aspect of this development is that during community ritual ceremonies and festivals which are still being celebrated even in major cities in Nigeria, for instance, the Eyo Masquerade festival in Lagos, master artists, in keeping with their sacred obligations to their communities, undertake free performances. However, such free performances, besides further popularizing the master artist and his company, also bring gratification in the form of spectators' spontaneous monetary gifts to show appreciation to the master artist during the course of performance.

Also during festival periods, wealthy members of the community invite such master artists for private performances during which special songs are dedicated to the ancestry and lineage of the patron, who in turn showers the performer with gifts and money. In the end, festival periods also become just another avenue for acquiring fame and wealth. What is still preserved in such performance is a style of presentation — performances are presented in arena-like or semi-arena spaces, with the performer and his company in the middle, and the patron(s) or elders occupying the innermost ring of the seating arrangement, next to the performer. Of course, there is also the spontaneous participation. This style of presentation is, however, unique to traditional performances. Modern African drama, even when it drew its inspirations from traditional festivals, history, myths and legends, was presented in proscenium stages. Only in the 1970s did directors like Ola Rotimi, Wole Soyinka, and Dapo Adelugba begin the movement towards restoring arena-like staging styles. Ngugi wa Thiong'O, Micere Mugo, and Ngugi wa Miiri began their innovations with plays such as *The Trials of Dedan Kimathi* and *I Will Marry When I Want* in the 1980s. In light of the march towards modernization on the continent, traditional artists are adapting and adopting modern media, especially the cinema, to popularize their art, and these are in turn transforming their personalities and their art.

With regards to cinematic conventions, as far as Africa is concerned, Gabriel's tabulation is useful also insofar as one is dealing with films set in the rural areas; the category of films which Manthia Diawara refers to as "the return to the source" genre in African cinema. According to Diawara, these films are characterized by the way the filmmakers look at tradition:

> it is a look that is intent on positing religion where anthro-
> pologists only see idolatry, history where they see primitivism,
> and humanism where they see savage acts. The films are
> characterized by *long takes and long shots with natural sounds most of*
> *the time. Unlike conventional film language, which uses close-ups to*
> *dramatize a narrative moment, the close-ups in these films, like most of the*
> *narrative devices serve to inscribe the beauty of the character and their*
> *tradition.* Pointing to their aesthetic appeal, some film-makers and
> critics have acclaimed the return to the source movement as the
> end of "miserabilism" in African cinema, and the beginning of a
> cinema with perfect images, perfect sound, and perfect editing.
> Others, on the contrary, have criticized the films for being
> nostalgic and exotic in their representation of Africa. They argue
> that the return to source films are influenced by the vision of the
> European anthropologists that they seem to put into question.
> (Diawara, 1989: 123)

Some of the films, which according to Diawara belong to the return to the source genre include, *Wend Kuuni* (Gaston Kabore, 1982), *Yeleen* (Soulaymane Cisse, 1987), and *Yaaba* (Idrissa Ouedraogo, 1989) (Diawara: 122-126). Though Diawara does not say so, the films of the folklore genre, or what Hyginus Ekwuazi and Onookome Okome, respectively, refer to as folklore cinema in Nigeria, derived largely from Yoruba Travelling Theatre tradition in Nigeria, also use these cinematic conventions. In this regard, films such as Ola Balogun's *Ajani-Ogun* (1976), *Iya Ominira* (1977), and *Oru Mooru* (1982) belong to this category. Gabriel's tabulation, with regards to cinematic conventions, therefore fits only the return to the source or folklore genre in African cinema. Finally, though he does not state so, Gabriel's theorization is greatly influenced by the

Negritudian ideas and the craving for a pure state in African culture and personality, free of European influences and the corrupt advances of modernity. These cravings are usually marked by a certain tendency to theorize African art in general, and African cinema in particular, by situating it in the imagined recesses of rural Africa, supposedly the area with its preserved traditional performances untainted by the corrupt influences of modernity.

On the contrary, one has stated that such a pure state of traditional performances and master artists do not exist in Africa. The rush for modernization is transforming the structure, practice, and status of traditional African performances and artists. Though performances are still inspired by oral history, myths and legends, these are presented through modern mass media, of which the cinema is just one example. If the pace of most African films is slow, in comparison to those of Europe and Hollywood, it is because filmmakers choose to subject editing to the dictates and rhythms of African social ceremonies and speech rhetoric, which demand that elders be heard out. Besides, cinematic conventions or codes of narration belong to the realm of paradigmatic choices that individual filmmakers face in the process of film directing. They are part of the director's prerogative and critics cannot legislate to directors on the best approach to preserve African cultural values through filmic representation. To imagine that African film critics are necessarily more patriotic than African filmmakers, is wrong.

To round up this section, most of the criticisms which have been made or cited with regards to the theorization of Third Cinema or Third World Cinema also apply to Roy Armes's, *Third World Film Making and the West*. Even though this study is quite ambitious in the scope of its analysis, it is greatly constrained by the fact that Armes generally treats the culture and narrative forms of Third World countries as pathological deviations from or imitations of European or Hollywood film practices. Some of the book's inadequacies which Stam has noted include:

(i)   A self-acknowledged ethnocentric approach to the study of Third World cinema.

(ii)   The repeated characterization of technology as Western, an idea which Stam considers flattering to First World narcissism. Stam states that quite "apart from the historical existence of non-European science and technologies (the Egyptian origins of Western science, African agriculture, Chinese gunpowder, and Aztec architecture, irrigation, plumbing, and even brain surgery), Armes underestimates the interdependence of First and Third Worlds."

(iii)   In the area of formal structures, Armes argues that Third World filmmakers depend not only on Western originated technology but also formal structures of narrative derived from the West. A view not too different from that which Potts (1979) puts forward in his essay, "Is There an International Film Language?" Stam notes that this formulation ignores the extent to which some Third World films draw on formal structures not derived from the West; for instance, African films and the influence of oral narrative structures and traditions, Indian films deriving from Hindu legends and Brazilian films building on Amazonian folktales.

(iv)   Though Armes pays some attention to the question of national cultures, he continues to employ colonialist and Eurocentric terminologies in his description of these cultures. For instance, he describes Brazil's African derived religions as "primitive" and "semi-pagan," terms which according to Stam, have long been abandoned by even Euro-Brazilians.

(v)   Finally, Stam has also noted that Roy Armes's standards for judging a Third World film as international are based on European criteria. Armes, according to Stam, contrasts "local" films with those "achieving" a "truly international standards," and merely "regional filmmakers" with "filmmakers of international stature," a dichotomy premised ultimately, on Eurocentric assumption of the "universality of its own values." (Stam: 221-224)

Most of the inadequacies notable in Armes's book are avoidable mistakes of the types that dogged early European criticism of African literature, but which most European critics of African cinema such as Angela Martin, Françoise Pfaff, Laura Mulvey and Philip Rosen have happily avoided. As earlier stated, it is not a question of whether it is appropriate or inappropriate to apply European critical models to African cinema, nor is it even one of whether European, or even other non-African critics, can give a fairly insightful reading of African cinema. It is a question of whether the critic, African or non-African, who applies European and other non-African critical models, is prepared to be sensitive to the socio-historical world and cultural specificities of the film.

The Categorization of African Cinema

Boughedir has proposed a classification of African films that proceeds not from the politics of subjectivization in film texts, themes or generic types but according to the principal motivations of their auteurs and the ultimate function and effects of their works. He argues that there are three principal motivations for making films, and in this respect, three types of African filmmakers. They are: (i) those who make films in order to be of service to their peoples; (ii) those who make their films for themselves; and (iii) those who make their films for money, glory and career. While agreeing that these positions or tendencies sometimes overlap, he stresses that there is always a dominating function in their films. On the basis of this auteurist functionalist theory, he argues that there are six auteurist functional tendencies in African cinema, which can be taken to represent emergent generic categories. These are: (i) the political tendency; (ii) the moralist tendency; (iii) the commercial tendency; (iv) the cultural tendency; (v) the "self-expression" tendency; and (6) the "narcissistic intellectual" tendency (Boughedir, 1982b: 79-81).

Films of the "political tendency," Boughedir argues, proceed from a preliminary political analysis of the reality they describe. In constituting this reality, however, they assemble the elements in such a way as to provoke reflection by spectators, to raise their consciousness and mobilize them against the injustices of their reality. Films which he includes in this category are Sembène's *Borom Saret* (1963), *Black Girl* (1966), *Emitai* (God of Thunder, 1971), *Ceddo* (1976), and Hondo's *Soleil O* (1969). Filmmakers of the "moralist tendency" tend to criticize the negative aspects of their society without attempting to examine the roots of the social malaise. Often, they depend on the goodwill of the individual to reform society. They tend to think that only individuals ought to change and not the social structures responsible for breakdown in morality. These films, according to Boughedir, concentrate in general, on scapegoats: fake marabous and Westernized young women with wigs and mini-skirts who, having taken the wrong path, drag all those who emulate them into moral and social degeneration. He argues that the spectator in these films is positioned as a morally superior person, and from such an elevated moral pedestal, he or she is made to laugh at the misfortunes of the stereotyped morally degenerate characters. Films which he includes in this category are Moma Thiam's *Karim* (1971), and *Baks* (*Cannabis*, 1974); Mahama Johnson Traore's *Diegue-bi* (*The Young Woman*, 1970), and *Lambaaye* (Graft, 1972); and Moustapha Alassane's *F.V.V.A. - Femme, villa, voiture, argent* (*Wives, Villa, Car, Money*, 1972).

The primary objective of films of the "commercial tendency" is the desire to please the largest number of spectators possible, by selling them emotions, e.g., of laughter, fear and violence. He argues that auteurs of these films never admit that their works are intended as commercial films, and often hide behind the screen of nationalism, moralism or even social satire in their narratives, but their structures, copying the proven box-office successes of the Western cinema of "evasion," always end up contradicting these principled declarations. In this category he groups films such as Tidiane Aw's *Le bracelet de bronze* (1974) and Daniel Kamwa's *Pousse Pousse* (1975), to which one could also add Eddy Ugbomah's *The Mask* (1970), structured after the popular James Bond series.

Films of the "cultural tendency," claim to have as primary function, the re-evaluation of African culture in the aftermath of colonialism. Filmmakers of this category attempt to restore, with the greatest possible authenticity, the way of life and thought of the African popular masses. They often combine a critique of ill-fated traditions with a truly accurate gauging of the aspirations of the popular masses. Examples include Soulaymane Cissé's *Cinq jours d'une vie* (*Five Days in a Life*, 1972), and Dikongue-Pipa's *Muna Moto* (*The Other's Child*, 1974). Regarding films of the "self-expression tendency," Boughedir states that their critical acclaim depends more on their form than their content, whether the latter is political, cultural, or moralistic. The principal function of these films is to allow an auteur to express his or her personal vision of the world, to "create," taking a given subject matter as pretext. Though these films please Western film critics, they hardly attract the patronage of African spectators. Films which he groups in this category include Timite Bassori's *La Femme au couteau* (*The Woman with a Knife*, 1968), Désiré Ecaré's *Concerto pour un exil* (*Concerto for an Exile*, 1968), *A nous deux, France* (*For us both, France*, 1970); and Djibril Diop Mamberty's *Touki Bouki* (*The Hyenas's Journey*, 1973).Finally, films of the "narcissistic intellectual tendency" belong to a sub-category of the self-expression tendency. He argues that auteurs of this category of films belong to that group of intellectuals who have been alienated by their contact with the West and have taken their personal problem to be that of the whole nation. Filmmakers in this category dwell upon the conflict between tradition and modernity; between the so-called soulless West, and a nostalgically conceived idyllic Africa. He states that on the ideological level, these films perpetuate the myth of the "noble savage" so prevalent in ethnographic films of the colonial era. Examples include Phillippe Maury's *Les Tams Tams se Sont Tus* (*Drums Stopped Playing*, 1972); and Daniel Kamwa's *Boubou-Cravate* (*Cross-Breed*, 1972) (Boughedir, 1982b: 79-81).

Though Boughedir's classification of African cinema is instructive in that it helped to initiate the process of categorization of emergent generic types of African films, his method is greatly undermined by his introduction of auteurist functional intentionality as the main plank of critical analysis. Boughedir's placement of emphasis on auteurist intentionality bears all the too recognizable trademarks of his French training and the influence of "la politique des auteurs" proclaimed by the writers of *Cahier du Cinéma* in the 1950s and 1960s. In retrospect, auteurism is now generally identified as a product of the romantic phase in film criticism, which is itself an outgrowth of romantic literary criticism that sought to apotheosize a certain category of writers, authors or filmmakers/directors whose works were said to display a high level of originality, finesse, and personal style, attributes which romantic critics ascribed to genius. Boughedir's schema for the classification of African cinema would have been adequate for the task he set himself if he had not anchored it on an auteurist theory of functional intentionality.

In the light of current theories of the author, text, subjectivity, and spectator, there is a need to reconceptualize these terms in relation to the African cinema. Such a reconception will entail a moderation of Boughedir's classification of African cinema by relating it to authorial desires for the ideological subjectivization and thematization of African social discourses, mythopoetics, politics, and culture, and the generic types which these desires have produced. Finally, such a reconceptualization must conceive the author and spectator as personas implicated in the text through the identification processes produced by psychic regimes of desires implicated in the social discourses of the day. In this regard, the author cannot be identified with some God-like pre-textual authority standing outside of discourse with rigid preconceived functional intentionalities, a point to be more fully explained below.

Another scholar who has attempted a classification of African cinema is Manthia Diawara. He bases his categorization on thematic preoccupations which he argues has produced three types of films: "the social realist film," "the historical colonial confrontation film," and "the return to the source film." According to Diawara, films of the social realist genre,

> draw on contemporary experiences and oppose tradition to modernity, oral to written, agrarian and customary communities to urban and industrialized systems, subsistence economies to highly productive economies. The film-makers often use a traditional position to criticize and link certain forms of modernity to neo-colonialism and cultural imperialism. From a modernist point of view, they also debunk the attempt to romanticize traditional values as pure and original. The heroes are women, children and other marginalized groups that are pushed in the shadow by the elites of tradition and modernity. (Diawara, 1989: 111)

He argues that the social realist genre uses narrative forms such as melodrama, satire and comedy in its narrative thrust and that it is the most popular of the three genres because it uses popular traditional African performance elements such as song, music, and dance, popular theatre and music stars. He states that to capture the spectator's desire on film — a spectator who is constructed as ordinary urban working class, unemployed, or rural peasantry — the filmmakers transform polemics against the elites into jokes made at the expense of the elites. Such films also include popular musicians and songs, the latest fashion and jargons of the cities, and deal with the themes of polygamy, witchcraft, women's liberation, and contemporary politics in their narratives. Films which he includes in this category are Ousmane Sembène's *Le Mandat* (1968) and *Xala* (1974), Moustapha Alassane's *F.V.V.A. — Femmes, Villa, Voiture, Argent* (1972), Mahama Johnson Traore's

Njangan (1974), Daniel Kamwa's *Pousse Pousse* (1975), Soulaymane Cissé's *Baara* (1978) and *Finye* (1982), Ben Diogaye Beye's *Sey Seyti* (1980); Kramo-Lacine Fadika's *Djeli* (1981), Ngangura Mweze and Benoit Lamy's *La vie est belle* (1986).

In Diawara's second category are films of "the historical colonial confrontation genre." These films deal with confrontations between Africans and their European colonizers during the colonial era. He argues that, on the one hand, the majority of African spectators view them with a sense of pride and satisfaction that at last a history of the period from an African perspective is being rendered, and on the other hand, some European spectators characterize them as polemical, poorly constructed, and belonging to the 1960s rhetoric of violence. He equally states that between 1987 and 1989, both French and British critics used such adjectives about *Sarraounia* (1987), *Heritage Africa* (1988), and *Camp de Thiaroye* (1988), even though these films have been among the most popular during public shows at FESPACO '87 and '89. According to Diawara, these films position their spectators to identify with African people's resistance against European colonialism and imperialist drives:

> these stories are about colonial encounters and they often pit African heroes and heroines against European villains. They are conditioned by the desire to show African heroism where European history only mentioned the actions of the conquerors; resistance where the colonial version of history silenced oppositional voices; and the role of women in the armed struggle. For the film-makers, such historical narratives are justified by the need to bring out of the shadow the role played by the African people in the shaping of their own history. It is also the case that they want to film a liberation struggle to keep it forever in people's mind. (Diawara: 116)

Some of the films which he places in this category include Ousmane Sembène's *Emitai* (1971) and *Ceddo* (1976), Ahmed Rachadi's *L'opium et le Bâton* (1970), Sarah Maldoror's *Sambizanga* (1972), Mohamed Lakhdar-Hamina's *Chroniques des Annèes de Braise* (1988), and Flora Gomes's *Mortu Nega* (1988). Boughedir overlooks this extremely important category of films in his classification of African cinema, preferring instead the general generic type of the "political tendency." But while many African films can be said to carry underlying political messages, they cannot all be claimed to be dealing with this, in addition to the important exclusive theme of historical confrontations between Africans and Europeans during the colonial era.

The last category in Diawara's classification, are films of "the return to the source genre." I will refer to them in this study as films of the folkloric genre because of their nostalgic treatment of folkways and folkloric themes, and by virtue of their narrative being set mostly in the rural areas. Films which Boughedir classifies under "cultural tendency" also belong here. According to Diawara, there are three main reasons why African filmmakers resort to "the return to the source genre." They are, (i) to be less overt with the political message in the film in order to avoid censorship; (ii) to search for pre-colonial African traditions which can contribute to the solution of contemporary problems; and (iii) to search for a new film language. The underlining desire behind making these films is to prove the existence of a dynamic African history before the advent of Europeans in Africa and European colonization of the continent. As he puts it,

> unlike the films about historical confrontation which are conventional on the level of form, these films are characterized by the way the director looks at tradition. It is a look that is intent on positing religion where anthropologists only see idolatry, history where they see primitivism, and humanism where they see savage acts. The films are characterized by long takes and long shots with natural sounds most of the time. Unlike conventional film language which uses close-ups to dramatize a narrative moment, the close-ups in these films, like most of the narrative devices, serve to inscribe the beauty of the characters and their tradition. (Diawara: 123)

Films which he places in this category include Idrissa Ouedraogo's *Poko* (1978), *Issa le Tisserand* (1985) and *Yaaba* (1989), Oumarou Ganda's *L'Exilè* (1980) and Gaston Kabore's *Wend Kunni* (1982). In addition to these, most of the films adapted from the Yoruba Travelling Theatre *oeuvre*, especially those dealing with folkloric themes, belong here.

Though there is a need for the classification of African films, it needs to be relatively flexible, comprehensive and tidy enough to avoid generic duplication of the sort that would constrain rather than facilitate African film criticism. For instance, considering Boughedir's classification, besides overlooking films of "the historical colonial confrontation genre," he also overlooks the "the avant-gardist text," which is marked in general by a maverick narrative form and structure that is antithetical to general narrative coherency, He seems to classify avant-gardist films the category of the "self-expression genre." Moreover, most African filmmakers want to recoup the investments they have made in their film projects, in this respect, there is an underlying commercial tendency within most African film productions. This, in part, explains why most African filmmakers construct their spectators as urban working class/unemployed, and rural peasantry. These people have traditionally formed the bulk of cinema-going audience in Africa.

Though it is true that many of the filmmakers that Boughedir groups under the "commercial tendency" sometimes resort to Hollywood narrative genres as a strategy for ensuring the commercial success of their films, to argue that most African films that have enjoyed commercial success are films that have adopted proven Hollywood formulae would be wrong. If anything, the reverse is the case. Most African filmmakers attracted to Hollywood genres have often met with commercial failures because they lacked the technological accompaniments of Hollywood. Since the majority of African spectators are used to Hollywood's renderings of genres, African filmmakers who attempt to imitate Hollywood's versions end up producing amateurish imitations. Such was the case, for instance, when Eddy Ugbomah tried to imitate the James Bond spy series in his production of *The Mask*. It was both a commercial and an artistic failure because Ugbomah lacked the technological and stunt expertise that create the thrill in this genre.

What ensures the commercial success of African films, among African spectators, apart from other narrative contingencies, is the adoption of traditional African performance elements such as song, music, and dance, not just as narrative embellishments, but as elements within the narrative structure. This is what has ensured the commercial success of New Nigerian Cinema, the fact that most productions are filmic adaptations of plays from Yoruba Travelling Theatre texts which were themselves popular dramatic renderings of myths, legends, and historical events, and which have traditionally enjoyed trans-ethnic patronage because the productions were based on the African concept of a total performance, that is, a narrative that uses traditional African performance elements like song, music, and dance, not just as embellishments or mood moderators, but as structural elements within the narrative itself. Rather than base the determination of a genre exclusively on the commercial tendency as Boughedir does, the commercial tendency should be considered as one of the underlying desires of the cinematic institution. Finally, at least for the time being, African versions of genres like gangster films, thrillers, and science fiction films, have not yet emerged in sufficient numbers, if they have even emerged at all, to warrant a genre theory of these forms that can be traced to commercial tendency.

The main problem with Diawara's categorization, on the other hand, lies in the rather generalized category of "the social realist films" into which he groups the majority of African films. His argument that films of this category draw on "contemporary experiences" and "oppose tradition to modernity," is quite problematic for three main reasons: (i) it seems to imply an underlying reference to the principle of verisimilitude with all its implications for equating representation with reality; (ii) if one considers alternatively that the narrative opposition he is referring to is one that is implicated in the politics of representation, one that considers "reality" as a product of the politics of representation, and as a critical construct, the restriction of his definition exclusively to "contemporary experiences" can be called into question because the opposition he is referring to actually began with the advent of Europeans in Africa; (iii) if his definition of social realism is identified exclusively with "contemporary experiences," one could question the rationale for excluding rural reality from contemporary experiences and if on the other hand, rural reality are included in contemporary experiences, Diawara has neglected to inform us what the root(s) of the cravings for alternative rural reality is implied by the generic category which he refers to as "the return to the source genre."

The kind of representation that Diawara describes as breaking with "the intellectualist tradition of African cinema," adopting "populist themes which are dear to the working class and the unemployed," and "transform[ing] the polemics against the elite into jokes made at the expense of the elite," can best be qualified as a "critical realist genre" (Diawara: 112). In fact, the whole category of films which he refers to as "the social realist films" ought to be referred to appropriately as "critical realist films." I am using the term "critical realism," in Brechtian terms to refer to the politics of representation, in terms of its goal, rather than its conventions (Lovell, 1983: 76-77). These are films that basically condemn bribery and corruption, nepotism, ethnicism, political and administrative incompetence, traditional practices like caste discrimination, ritual murders and human sacrifices, etc. On the other hand, films of the folkloric genre, or what Diawara and Boughedir, respectively, refer to as the "return to the source" or the "cultural tendency genres," are films driven principally by nostalgia and the desire to protect, what filmmakers of this category perceive to be the erosion of traditional African norms and values. But beneath this manifest nostalgia, there is also a latent desire to invoke tradition, in response to racist and colonialist discourses. Often because of the proliferation of racist and colonialist discursive representations of Africans or people of African descent, most filmmakers who resort to this genre have come to believe rather erroneously that the problems of modernity and urbanization are not the problems of modernization as such but the symptoms of the advance of European civilization. This mentality, as Robert Stam (1991) has argued, is essentially a product of racist and colonialist qualification of science and technology as an exclusive European invention and legacy to the rest of humanity, an argument that equates science and technology with culture and civilization — hence the equation of science and technology with Europeanness and, *ipso facto*, world culture and civilization with Europeanness.

Faced with the racist argument that Africans have made no contributions whatsoever to human civilization, the apostates and defenders of Africa's contributions to human civilization either lay claim to ancient Egypt or march off into the nearest underdeveloped rural African village and begin to postulate on how self-contented and self-sufficient it was before European intrusion. By invoking the ghost of the "noble savage," they inadvertently play right into the hands of the perpetrators of these racist arguments. For the sake of argument, let me state that even if Africa made the greatest contributions to human civilization, even if Ancient Egyptian civilization was built by blacks or grew out of older civilizations within the lower Nile river region, even if there were other equally valuable civilizations elsewhere in Africa, even if humanity itself originated in Africa, these facts cannot in themselves erase the legacies of our history — we were enslaved and colonized by Europeans and, to a large extent, they still dictate the state of affairs on the continent. To acknowledge European hegemony in modern world affairs is different from qualifying science and technology as an exclusive European invention.

African scholars, writers, artists, or filmmakers who, because of Eurocentric discourses, qualify and equate science and technology with Europeanness, also equate modernization with Europeanness, a position that seems to imply that if one uses ball pens, televisions and satellite dishes, drives a car, travels by jet plane, or even sets up a factory to produce these or other items of modern life style, one is becoming European. To equate science and technology with Europeanness is to imply that the entire on-going process of social development in Africa is a Europeanization of the continent — hence the often hysterical drive for the return to the source. While one does not intend to downplay the proliferation of European culture in Africa as a result of colonialism, there is a need to reconceptualize the experience as an interactive two-way phenomenon. Furthermore, the craving for the source or for folk traditional values is an essential human craving, one that is first and foremost a product of dissatisfaction with one's present state, and nostalgia for the past, a past that is romanticized in terms of a golden age that in actual fact never existed. What further complicates the African experience of such a craving is that the very existence of a canon of discursive practice that devalues the humanity of Africans means that such cravings, more often than not, carry far larger implications than a mere desire for closeness to nature. While it is true, as Diawara argues, that there are instances when filmmakers resort to mythopoetics in order to avoid censorship, equally the case is that the context of such productions often implicates such films within the realm of "critical realism."

From all indications, therefore, there are presently three distinguishable genres in African cinema. They are: "the critical realist film," "the colonial encounter film," and "the folkloric film." However, the majority of films currently produced on the continent, fall within "the critical realist" category. While many of the films criticize the excesses of the elites, the problem of ethnicism, and corruption, they also enjoin the masses to cultivate the spirit of self-help and self-reliance as a strategy in community development. Finally, many of the films are also concerned with the question of the most appropriate strategy for negotiating one's way through modernity without losing valuable traditional African norms and values. The remaining part of this chapter proposes a general cinematic reading hypothesis based on the concept of subjectivity as a theoretical framework for the criticism of African cinema.

Toward a General Cinematic Reading Hypothesis of African Cinema

Some of the major problems currently plaguing the criticism of African cinema are: lack of attention to the specificity of the cinematic medium, especially with regards to the nature of narration in film; the question of subjectivity and its attendant aspects like the representation of the relation of subjectivity to race, ethnicity, gender, and class; and the questions of authorship and spectatorship. In proposing a general cinematic reading hypothesis of African cinema, I am responding to these key issues with a view to making the criticism of African cinema much more responsive to the specificity of narration in film. My main argument is that comprehending the nature of film narration is a prelude to understanding film and of rendering a critical analysis that is responsive to the specificity of the medium. The proposed reading hypothesis is anchored on the concept of subjectivity and its relation to the nature of narration in film, to concepts of narrator, authorship, narrative authority, race, ethnicity, gender, class, and spectatorship, and the general spatio-temporal articulations within a text. The term "subjectivity" is used throughout this study to refer to a general theory of characterization and character representation in African cinema.

To understand the nature of filmic narration a major distinction needs to be established from the outset between the activity of narration and what is narrated, between the act of telling (narration) and what is told (narrated). It is a distinction which Emile Benveniste renders in establishing the role of pronouns in the location of the subject in utterance, distinguishing between subject and predicate, and ultimately between "histoire" and "discours," in which the former (history) involves an utterance from which all markers of enunciation have been effaced, and the latter (discourse) involves an utterance in which such markers are present (Stam *et al*, 1992: 210-211, Nowell-Smith, 1981: 232-241).

Film is a form of discourse, a textual system which implicates the subject in the activity of telling, viewing, and listening. The result of that activity is an object: what is told, viewed, and listened to; e.g. character, events and themes. Subjectivity therefore can be used to distinguish between levels of narration in film. For instance, character narration, e.g., the point-of-view (POV) shot, is an indication of a shift in the level of narration as well as reception. In the POV shot, we see what a character sees from his or her point in space. It is the transference of the authority of narration to an agent within narrative. Though what the character sees, talks about or listens to, is an object of narration, both "subject" and "object" are not fixed terms but indicative of a relationship between two elements in narration. For instance, a riot scene may be the object of vision of a character that may be the object of a voice-over narrator who may be the object of attention for a viewer. Thus the boundary lines between subject and object, narration and narrative, are never absolute; rather, they shift according to the scope of narration. To comprehend a film text, therefore, one needs to understand the successive shifts in the relation of subject to object in narration.

Subjectivity can also be used to measure the level of temporality in film narration. For instance, in a POV shot, diegetic time is usually continuous, whereas in a subjective/character flashback, discontinuity is established between diegetic time and the time range of the events related in the flashback. In *Chocolat* (Claire Denis, 1988) for instance, the subjective flashback which relates events in the life of young France (Cécile Ducas) in colonial Cameroon, events which form the main body of the film, is established through adult France's (Mireille Machinard) contemplation of her father's diary. Memory recall is effected through a look directed at the diary. The events related in the flashback cover several years, whereas adult France's visit to Cameroon is more of a tourist engagement of a few weeks.

Subjectivity or character narration can be classified into four broad categories: subjective flashback (cited above), mental process narration, character reflection, and character projection. Mental process narration involves the representation of a character's dream or projected thoughts in space. Such projected thoughts could be day-dreaming or fantasizing one's desires. In both dream sequences or projected thoughts, the character's mental condition serves as the unity or coherence of the representation. In mental process narration, discontinuity is established in temporal relations; time is no longer continuous or simultaneous. Time becomes a property of the dreamer or the character whose thought is projected. In character reflection, on the other hand, a character projects his or her body into space, not just the mental state. Character reflection is often achieved through a mirror surface placed in the *mise-en-scène*. Hence when a character looks into a mirror, he or she sees himself or herself as both subject and object. In character reflection, there is both simultaneity of action and temporality, except in cases where such process of self-reflection through looking into a mirror generates, additionally, past memories (Branigan, 1984: 73-100; Browne, 1981: 251-260).

Character projection, on the other hand, is realized through metaphorical identification of space with a character. It differs from character reflection because the subject's mental state is made explicit beyond the mere presence and normal awareness of a character. For instance, in *El Chacal de Nahueltoro (The Jackal of Nahueltoro,* Miguel Littin, 1969), after the psychopathic murderer (Nelson Villagra) has killed a widowed mother and her children who played host to him, to save them from suffering after they are ejected from their house by the land owner in whose farm estate the late husband of the woman worked, as he goes about giddily burying them one after the other, his mental state of drunkenness is reflected in the giddiness of the space, but since the space is not produced through a POV structure, dream state or thought projection, we attribute it to him nonetheless through metaphorical transference, especially since he was drunk before he carried out the crime. Through such processes of metaphorical transference, changes in color, scene, and lighting, may be attributed to a character once there is enough justification within levels of narration to warrant such a reading. In character projection, time is continuous with action. In addition to character narration through POV shot, character flashback, mental state, reflection, and projection, there is also aural POV in which we hear from a character's point in space. In an objective case, such hearing is of a direct nature that other characters within the narrative diegesis can share - e.g. telephone call, eavesdropping on gossip, etc. But there are also cases in aural POV in which we hear a character hearing imaginary noises and voices that diegetic characters do not hear.

Even though character narration is evidence of a second level of meaning in a text, evidence of delegated narration, underlining every such first person narration, is the authority of the third person omniscient narrator, which creates the fictional appearances of the other levels of narration within a text. Fundamentally therefore, there is a single activity of narration in a text or, personifying that activity, there can be only a single narrator in a text. In this regard, the delegation of the activity of narration to a character is an act of "framing." The new narrator must, therefore, be identified (referred to) before we recognize the initiation of a new level of narration, the incidence of a story within a story. In addition to cases of subjective framing in which a story is attributed to a character within the narrative diegesis, there are also cases of objective framing in which the new story is not a production of a single character. For instance, in a film, there may be a rehearsal of a play, dance piece, or opera, which may proceed into a production within the film; however, while such instances produce the structure of a story within a story, the framed story in this case is an act of objective production. Nevertheless, there always exists in a text an underlying omniscient narrator who authorizes the other levels of narration. The effect of a change in narration is that it signals a change in the relationship of the reader to the activity of narration. In other words, the introduction of a new narrator is a formal acknowledgement that the conditions have changed under which we acquire knowledge from the text. As a result of the superintending authority of the omniscient narrator, nominal narrators may indulge in lies, dreams, and fantasies, but the truth of the text is revealed in the end at the level of omniscient narration. Parallel to a first person nominal narrator, there may also be voice-over narrators as well as voice-over narratees who may fill in for the reader by voicing doubts, wondering, or laughing, as in the laughter track of television comedies (Branigan: 42-47).

Subjectivity can also be used in explicating the nature of filmic narration by examining the concepts of origin and destination of the sound/space within levels of narration in relation to differences produced in diegesis. Diegesis, as a concept of narration, is a subcategory of origin because it seeks to assign a source to the sound/space of a film with regards to specifying whether the production of sound/space is within or outside the story space. The diegesis in film comprises those elements within narration, which give rise to the fictional world of characters, landscape, and events in a text. The diegesis is thus the implied spatial, temporal, and causal system of the characters. It includes aspects of the fictional world, which are accessible to characters within the narrative. In this regard, a sound, for instance, is non-diegetic if it is not heard by a character within the narrative even if the sound later also functions diegetically by serving as a sound bridge between scenes. The problem addressed by the concept of diegesis is, therefore, one that deals with relating character to sound and space. As the relation between character and sound/space changes, so too does the viewer's relation to character and sound/space. The result of such changes is the production of different perspectives on the story.

By using the concept of origin, destination, and diegesis, we are able to give a proper breakdown of the classes of production with respect to narrators and readers. For instance, the third person or omniscient narrator is that level of narration which is assigned no origin by the text. Its authority lies in the fact that it presents the fictional world as if it is independently revealing itself. On the other hand, the subjective or first person narrator is that attributed to a particular origin within narrative diegesis (character) or outside the narrative diegesis (voice-over narrator). The obverse correspondence of the omniscient narrator is the voyeuristic reader or the unseen and unacknowledged spectator for whom an address is seemingly presented as if to no one — that is, the text does not acknowledge its viewer; it is as if the world is caught unawares. By contrast, the personal address is a direct second person address. In diegetic narration, the personal is a character who receives (listens, watches) the story, the bystander in a scene who exists only for his or her reaction shot. In most Third World films, a personal address are sometimes aimed outside the narrative diegesis — i.e., when a character stares direct into the camera and addresses a non-diegetic viewer. Though character is an important agent for determining the origin (or take-off point) of the story, or of determining the relation of sound/space to levels of narration, other sorts of entities like diaries, landscapes, and factories, can also serve a similar purpose. However, the unity and coherence derived from the application of such non-human entities as source or origin of narrative is a product of human agency or a mechanism of characterization. The reader's task therefore, is to determine those markers that divide the text into levels of narration (diegetic and non-diegetic) and the function of the narrator in the production of these levels (Branigan, 45).

The next element of narration, is the spatial properties of the text. The term required to specify the spatial properties of a film is the camera. I am considering the camera as the mechanism for reading the fluctuation of space. For instance, properties of the *mise-en-scène* such as acting, gestures, locale, lighting, costumes, and scenic decorations, are products of the structuring activity of the camera. This activity is realized through the properties of the camera such as lens, angle, positions, distance, focus, filters, and movement. The camera one is referring to is the reader's "camera," the spatial structuring principle of filmic narration, not the physical camera of film production. What the reader experiences are changes in the fluctuation of space. In specifying the classes of filmic narration, the place to begin is the spatial properties of the camera such as camera placement and movement. Camera placement may be characterized as either motivated or unmotivated. According to Branigan, a motivated camera is used to establish scenographic space, to follow or anticipate movement by a character or object, to select a narrative detail, e.g., an inserted dolly shot of an object or facial expression, and to reveal subjectivity. An unmotivated camera is evidence of an activity of framing which lags behind or searches out narrative details, i.e., when we seem to arrive at a scene of action a moment too late to witness significant events or when the camera seems to arrive long before the character (Branigan: 45).

To understand the narrational activity of a text, one must be able to make intelligible or comprehend the spaces of a film. Space can be defined as the placement and displacement of frame lines; the frame is stressed because it is the measure and logic of the simultaneity of textual elements — to frame is to bracket an array of elements. Frame is the perceptual boundary, which divides what is represented from what is not represented. Though the displacement of frame lines is the work of camera movement, other properties of the camera such as zoom shot, optical and special effects, rack focus, split screens, and animation, can also be used to effect frame displacement. In addition, properties of camera movement such as dolly, track, crane, pan, tilt and lateral tilt can also effect displacement in frame lines.

What has been examined thus far are codes of narration, narrational elements within the text which indicate levels of narration, the spatial and temporal signs of narration as they affect the concept of subjectivity. The next issue is that of codes of narrative and the effects they have on the concept of subjectivity. By codes of narrative, one is referring to the rules that couple or relate the elements of a syntactic type of a system to a semantic type. Different sorts of rules are involved with varying degree to correlate, shift, and replace elements in a narrative. Some of the codes of narration dealt with so far represent established social conventions, a cultural practice, within the cinematic institution that is acquired through training. In this regard, the structure generated by codes is a special sort of structure since it depends on skills or procedures, which are culturally acquired. Understanding the nature of the operation performed on codes in the production of a story is important in comprehending film narration and rendering critical analysis that is responsive to the specificity of the medium.

Roland Barthes, in his book, *S.Z.*, has classified the codes of narrative into five categories: the hermeneutic code, the proairetic code, the semic code, the cultural code, and the symbolic code. Though his formulations were conceived in relation to literature, Branigan has demonstrated their applicability to film. According to Branigan, the hermeneutic code is that code which at various times names a subject, states a condition, propose a question, delays its answer in multifarious ways, and finally discloses the answer (usually at the end), which is the truth of the narrative. The proairetic is a code of actions, consequence, gestures and behavior, which becomes sequences (e.g., stroll, murder or argument) when and because they are given a name in the process of reading. The proairetic is a cause-effect chain whose logic is that of the probable, of practical experience, of psychology, of culture, of history, of what is familiar: "the already done," "the already written," "the already seen." The semic code is that code which includes the connotations of persons, place, or object. The semic constructs the characters and ambience of narrative. The cultural or referential code refers to any generally accepted body of knowledge or wisdom generated by a culture — e.g., psychology, history, science, literature, aphorism. It is an inter-textual code because it strictly refers to other cultural texts. Finally, the symbolic is a code of meaning/relation based on the figures of rhetoric, the trait of the body, or economic (exchange) systems.

Branigan states that two basic operations may be performed on the codes: distribution and integration. He refers to distribution as the principle of articulation, segmentation, or form, a process along any one code, which disperses its elements, often inserting unpredictable expansions between the elements. In this sense, character development can be considered a distributional property of the semic code. On the other hand, he refers to integration as the principle of structuration and meaning, a relational aspect of two or more codes, a braiding and weaving of codes. The operation or interaction of codes is necessary because no narrative code can stand alone and still form a narrative. In order for a narrative to exist, the codes — both those pertaining to the principles of narration in the medium, and those of narrative derived from the socio-cultural world of the text — must interact with each other at some minimal level. The function of integration is precisely to specify hierarchical relations among the codes. To speak of hierarchical relations or levels is therefore to examine the structuration of a work rather than to merely describe the structures within the work. Consequently, the process through which codes are structured into narrative is narration (Branigan: 35-36; Stam *et al*: 192-196).

The next issue to be examined is the question of the relation of the author and the spectator to the film text. This issue has its roots in auteurism, associated especially with *Cahiers du Cinéma*, *Movie* and Andrew Sarris. In retrospect, auteurism is now identified as a product of the romantic phase in film criticism, which is itself an out growth of romantic literary criticism that sought to apotheosize a certain category of writers, authors or filmmakers/directors whose works are said to display a high level of originality, finesse, and personal style. The hallmark of the elevation of this critical policy to a theoretical construct, itself a product of the mistranslation of "la politique des auteurs" to auteur theory in the early sixties by Andrew Sarris, is predicated upon the application of technical competence of the director, his or her distinguishable personal style, and the interior meaning of a film, as critical criteria for filmic analysis. This critical practice depended on the recognition of a "pantheon of directors" and the cultivation of the cult of directors (Buscombe, 1981: 22-34; Sarris, 1981: 62-67). By elevating the director to a God-like pedestal of individual personal expression, auteurist critical practice places him or her above the flux of social discourses in which he or she is implicated and from which he or she creates. This critical practice is also built on the communication model in which the director/filmmaker is conceived as an active communicator of a message, which is then taken up by a passive spectator/viewer — a model that does not account for the labor and activity of viewing.

In its extreme negative instances, auteurism sometimes takes a path of critical inquiry that involves using a director's biographical data as material for discovering the director's functional intentionality — a kind of inquisition into the social background, psychological make-up or disposition of the director as made manifest through choices of codes and forms of narration, and thematic emphasis. On the other hand, in extreme creative instances, auteurism involves the analysis of *mise-en-scène* as the site of directorial creativity; but the elevation of *mise-en-scène* to the exclusive site of creativity also undermines, as John Caughie points out, the effectivity of visual discourse: "In auteurist criticism *mise en scène* begins to be conceived as effectivity, producing meanings and relating spectators to meanings, rather than as a transparency allowing them to be seen" (Caughie, 1981: 13). As he further observes, the intervention of semiotics or psychoanalysis into the field of film theory "has tended to shatter the unity of the author, scattering fragments over the whole terrain, calling into question the possibility of a theory of the author which is not also a theory of ideologies, of discourses, of commodities and, crucially, of the subject" (Caughie: 200).

It is also interesting to note that as a result of the attempt to correct romantic notions of the author, certain theorists, especially those influenced by the work of Roland Barthes, have attempted to define the author as an effect of the text. This is the position taken by Edward Branigan in his influential work, *Point of View in the Cinema*. Rather than conceiving the author as someone standing outside of language, discourse, and ideology, as the source of the text or at the other extreme end as an exclusive effect of the text, the author is conceived as a subject-author, driven by both conscious and unconscious desires. He/she is implicated in the text through language, codes and forms of discourses — both filmic and extra-filmic or cultural referential discourses — as a unifying term for the organization of language, cultural and filmic codes, into forms of filmic narration and discourse, with implications for character-subjectivity and spectatorial textual positioning. This is the sense in which Stephen Heath conceived of the relation of the author to the text when he argued that

> the function of the author (the effect of the idea of authorship) is a function of unity; the use of the notion of the author involves the organization of the film (as 'work') and, in so doing, it avoids — this is indeed its function — the thinking of the articulation of film text in relation to ideology. *A theory of the subject represents precisely an attempt, at one level, to grasp the constructions of the subject in ideology (the modes of subjectivity)*; it thus allows at once the articulation of contradictions in the film text other than in relation to an englobing consciousness, in relation, that is, to a specific historico-social process, and the recognition of a heterogeneity of structures, codes, languages at work in the film and of the particular positions of the subject they impose (my emphasis). (Heath, 1981: 217)

As the author is a subject implicated in discourse, so is the spectator. Unlike models of mass audience offered by empirical or sociological approaches to the study of film — i.e., conceptions of the spectator as a mass audience who go to the movies — and unlike the notion of a consciously aware viewer hypothesized by formalist approaches, i.e., as people who have conscious artistic ideas and interpretations about what they see, the spectator is conceived, in psychoanalytic terms, as someone liable to manipulation because of the psychic implication of the spectator in the machinery of filmic production, through projections or withholding of one's desires and fantasies upon character-subjectivities in texts. This is the sense in which Stam *et al* conceive the relation of the spectator to the text when they argue that

> psychoanalytic film theory sees the viewer not as a person, a flesh-and-blood individual, but as an artificial construct produced and activated by the cinematic apparatus. This spectator is conceived as a "space" that is both "productive" (as in the production of the dream-work or other unconscious fantasy structures) and "empty" (anyone can occupy it); to achieve this ambiguous duality, the cinema in some sense

"constructs" its spectator along a number of psychoanalytic modalities that link the dreamer to the film viewer. But a film is not exactly the same thing as a dream; in order for the film spectator to become the subject of a fantasy that is not self-generated, a situation must be produced in which the viewer is more immediately vulnerable and more likely to let his own fantasies work themselves into those offered by the fiction machine. (Stam *et al* 147)

Psychoanalytic theorization of the spectator therefore hinges on the distinction between the real person (as an individual) and the spectator (as a construct), and it draws on the operations of the unconscious to explain it. Five intersecting factors go into the psychoanalytic construction of the viewer: (i) the production of a state of regression; (ii) the construction of a situation of belief; (iii) the activation of mechanisms of primary identification (onto which secondary identifications are then grafted); (iv) the putting into play of fantasy structures, such as family romance, by the cinematic fiction; and (v) the concealment of the "marks of enunciation" that stamp the film with authorship. The success achieved in the manipulation of the spectator depends very much upon the psychic nature of human desires and their roots in fantasy. Christian Metz, in his essay, "The Imaginary Signifier," also acknowledges the "dual kinship" between the psychic life of the spectator and the financial or industrial mechanisms of the cinema in order to show how the reciprocal relations between the psychological components of the cinematic institution work to create in viewers not only a belief in the impression of reality offered by its fictions, but deep psychic gratification and a desire to continually return. He further states that the cinematic apparatus is made up of four interlocking processes that make up the cinematic viewing situation: (i) the technical base (specific effects produced by the various components of the film equipment, including camera, lights, film and projector); (ii) the conditions of film projection (the darkened theatre, the immobility implied by the seating, the illuminated screen in front, and the light beam projected from behind the spectator's head; (iii) the film itself, as a "text" (involving various devices to represent visual space, the creation of believable impression of reality); and (iv) that "mental machinery" of the spectator (including conscious perceptual as well as unconscious and preconscious processes) that constitute the spectator as subject (Stam *et al*. 147).

Although the cinematic apparatus is defined as a complex of four interlocking processes, the most salient feature of this apparatus is its construction of a "dream state." Certain conditions make film viewing similar to dreaming: we are in a darkened room, our motor activity is reduced, and our visual perception is heightened to compensate for our lack of physical mobility. As a result of this viewing situation, the film spectator enters into a "regime of belief" where everything is accepted as real. Stam *et al* state, for instance, that the cinema can achieve its greatest power of fascination over the viewer not simply because of this impression of reality, but because this impression of reality is intensified by the conditions of the dream state which produces an affect known as "fiction effect" (Stam *et al*. 142-144).

It is this fiction effect, which allows the spectator to have the feeling that he or she is actually participating in the production of the cinematic fiction, dreaming the images and the situations that appear on the screen. With the spectator locked in a dream state, there is an inducement of artificial regression, which makes it difficult for the spectator to distinguish between self and other. This trans-sexual, racial, ethnic, and class dream state of artificial regression that makes it possible for the spectator to get locked into a state of identification with character subjectivity. For instance, when as a child I identified John Wayne as my hero, it was an identification that entails the projection of my sense of heroism upon the actor, John Wayne; it was a purely apolitical self-narcissistic act which we all engage in as uncritical spectators. Incidentally, structural mechanisms of film narration such as the setting up of struggles between villains and morally upright persons, the activation of mechanisms of suspense, and delayed revelation of narrative enigmas make the spectator much more vulnerable to identifying with the textually constructed spectatorial subject positions. Yet, the position of the "critical spectator" needs distinguishing from the "hypothetical spectator" constructed in the text. The term, "critical spectator" is used to distinguish the level of critical interpretation, an instance of critical reading by an informed viewer who, because of his or her knowledge of the processes and strategies set in motion through filmic narration, is able to adopt alternative critical position antithetical to that constructed by text.

Thus far, one has been arguing that understanding the activity of filmic narration is a necessary prelude to giving critical analyses that are responsive to the specificity of film as a narrative medium. In addition, character-subjectivity is pivotal to understanding the nature of filmic narration because it is helpful in distinguishing between various levels of narration within a text and the agent(s) responsible for their production. For instance, through character-subjectivity, the various types of character narration and their modes of production can be mastered. Mastering these codes of narration is an important step to mastering the spatial and temporal orders of a film text.   Furthermore, an understanding of the manner in which character-subjectivity is constructed textually in relation to race, ethnicity, gender, and class, is necessary for determining the nature of spectatorial textual positions constructed in a text, and the power relations implicated in such constructions. Reading a film involves making a lot of inferences and hypotheses about the nature of the spatial and temporal orders produced in a text and the agent(s) responsible for their production. A cinematic reading hypothesis is therefore not just anything a reader may conceive in a text but what is internally justified in it and, ultimately, the ideas justified in a text reflect shared assumptions or expectations of a community with respect to a set text. The way we read is inter-subjective and inter-textual, and depends on cultural conventions just as a language belongs not to an individual but to a group.

Summary

This chapter has attempted a definition of African cinema and examined its nature with respect to emergent generic types. Equally analysed is the issue of how African filmmakers have dealt with the problems of modernity, African identity and subjecthood, belief-systems and culture. Finally, a general cinematic reading hypothesis, anchored on the concept of subjectivity, has been proposed as a theoretical framework for the criticism of African cinema.

4 COLONIALIST AFRICAN DISCOURSE

Introduction

In this chapter, the origin of colonialist African cinema is traced to both colonialist African literature and an existing canon of colonialist African discourse in European archives. The view canvassed is that, to understand the resilience of this mode of representation, the uneven power and knowledge relations that underlay the contact between Europe and Africa, and the subsequent slave trade and colonialism, which followed, should be taken into account. Though Brian Street and some scholars seem to overlook both the canonical authority and the contextual and intertextual influence of colonialist discourse in their studies of the novels of the British Empire, as will be evident in this study, there is sufficient justification for acknowledging the fact that the value judgments made in novels of the empire have canonical authority that dates back to the classical era.

Critical Perspectives on Colonialist African Discourse

In analyzing colonialist African discourse, the role played by power and knowledge relations in the constitution of African subjectivity and culture during and after colonial rule in Africa has been investigated. Also examined, is the question of how certifying institutions and instruments of power and authority that underlay colonialist discourse are masked, thereby making the represented and representation seem unconstrained and natural. The essence of the study is to establish the root of not only colonialist African discourse but also of colonialist African cinema.

One fact, often neglected in the analysis of colonialist African discourse, is that the so-called primitivism and barbarism of the African was a colonialist invention. In other words, the concept of cultural primitivity presupposes the superiority of the colonial culture and its practices. It also entails that the superior individual is in a position to impress such notions of superiority, hence primitivity entails the underlying factors of power and authority. Implicit in conceptions of colonialist discourse, therefore, is the Europeans' awareness of the authority, which they wielded, or still wield over those whom they conquered and colonized.

Colonialist discourse is a complex term, which covers the broad spectrum of colonialist portrayal of those who have been colonized. The areas of intellectual activity covered by colonialist discourse include anthropology, fine art, literature, autobiography, cinema, theology, government commissioned reports, philosophy, biological sciences, and memoirs and travel accounts. In fact, colonialist discourse covers the whole spectrum of human knowledge. The negative tenor of views expressed in these works seems to suggest that the inability of the colonized races to defend their territories and integrity is a manifestation of their mental and material inferiority. The speciousness that underlies such reasoning seems to disregard the fact that there are historical evidences of intra-racial conquests of people whom one may consider to be relatively of the same level of development. For instance, Napoleon's France once overran large portions of Europe; England overran the Irish, the Welsh and the Scottish, and Hitler's Germany once threatened the rest of the world. In the case of the European experience, would one be correct to argue that the countries, which France, England and Germany once overran, fell victims of aggression because they were primitive and inferior? Indeed, would it not be justified to argue that those who reason along this line subscribe to the triumph of militarism? Arguably, it would seem that colonialist discourse is more a practice of rationalization of the exploitation of conquered peoples rather than primitivity and inferiority.

Dorothy Hammond and Alta Jablow argue in their work, *The Myth of Africa*, that they find little reason to distinguish between fictional and non-fictional colonialist works about Africa because, as they put it, they are all governed by one tradition:

> there was no need to treat fiction and nonfiction separately since both are governed by the same tradition...fictional and nonfictional treatments of African material differ only in respect to greater or lesser consistency and integration. The fiction is by no means more fanciful than the nonfiction. (Hammond and Jablow, 1970: 44)

In broad terms, the foregoing assertion confirms and underlines the image of African barbarism as projected in, for instance, both literature and anthropology. But one cannot ignore the ironic qualities of imaginative works, which, no matter how much they are constrained by colonialist thought, manage, through self-negation, to create openings for native counter-discourse. The main argument presented by Hammond and Jablow is that colonialist representation of Africa, especially that of the British tradition, is a product of ethnocentrism; they are projections upon the African continent and

> the literature of this popular tradition yields relatively little empirical knowledge about either Africa or the history of the British in Africa. Reality is nearly irrelevant to the tradition. What is relevant, and indeed, integral to it, is ethno-centrism. This means that all perceptions are made through the lenses of one's own system of values and beliefs. (Hammond and Jablow: 5)

Hammond and Jablow argue that an ethnocentric point of view admits only one valid way of life, and that cultures which differ from one's own are perceived as negations of that single set of values rather than expressions that take cognizance of other different sets of systems (Hammond and Jablow: 15). Though this argument is valid, it is inadequate, because it neglects the question of the role played by the supervening, uneven power and knowledge relations in the construction of otherness. In the light of this, the most obvious shortcoming of this work lies in the authors' lack of acknowledgement of the distinction between fiction and non-fiction in their articulation of colonialist thought.

The same may be said of Edward Saïd's *Orientalism*. Even though the work makes only passing references to Africa, some of the arguments which he makes in regard to Orientalism as a mode of discourse can be applied to colonialist African discourse. *Orientalism* is a deconstructive study of Euro-American representation of the Orient from classical to modern times. What Saïd calls "Orientalism" is a rather complex mode and methodology of discursive practice that had its roots in Classical Studies, Philology, and Anthropology, but which later branched out to incorporate, as part of its analytical tools, theorization in Sociology, Political Science, Biological Sciences, Philosophy, and Cultural Studies, on the construction of the Orient. Using the classical era as his starting point, Saïd undertakes a deconstructive study of authors, nationalities, texts, text-projects, and contexts of discourses. He then analyses them within the overall ambit of the Orientalist fixation of the Orient and of the Orientalist practitioner.

Saïd's *Orientalism* is based the theorizations of Michel Foucault and Antonio Gramsci and, thus can be considered as an archaeological study of the representation of otherness and difference as a discourse of power and authority. Most of the arguments he makes are directed at explaining why it was possible for European and American writers and scholars to write about the Orient the way they did. The most important reason, which recommends the book as very useful for the analysis of the African situation, is the awareness and constraining authority of the colonial heritage. The area, he argues, fell prey to the colonial and imperialist adventures of ancient Greece, Rome, modern France, Britain and the United States of America.

Saïd distinguishes between two types of Orientalist discourse: "latent Orientalism" and "manifest Orientalism." What he calls "latent Orientalism" is essentially the hegemonized and institutionalized form of colonialist discourse. He argues that it is the discipline, which this institutionalized mode of representation imposes on writers and scholars who work in this field, that ensures the fixed construction of the Orient. In this regard, he asserts that whatever the disagreements that arise among Orientalists, these are matters of individual style and national priorities. This individual or nationally prioritized coloration within Orientalism is what Saïd refers to as "manifest Orientalism." At best then, "manifest Orientalism" would translate into different approaches and methodologies in colonial administration and discursive practices.

As noted earlier, one of the shortcomings of Saïd's *Orientalism* results from his failure to make a clear distinction between fictional and non-fictional works. It was from this angle that Dennis Porter and other scholars criticized the work. Porter's disagreement with Saïd stems from the fact that, not only does Saïd neglect to make a distinction between fictional and non-fictional works, but he also does not account for the counter-discursive tradition in Orientalism. In addition, Porter suggests that the work "presupposes the impossibility of stepping outside of a given discursive formation, by an act of will or consciousness" (Porter, 1985: 180-181).

My own disagreement with the work stems, not only from Saïd's lack of distinction between fictional and non-fictional works but equally from his neglect of the economic factor. In my view, if colonialism entails the hegemonization of "negative" representation, apart from the rationalization arising from the institutionalization of field studies of the colonialist category, and the geo-political implications of such studies, there must have been a motivating factor, what one would like to call the "initiating" factor, in the case of colonialist field studies. That initiating factor was, and still is, economic. Saïd's neglect of this factor is most unfortunate because, in doing so, his work sinks into the category of the over-theorized works that tend to undermine the contextual issues that underlie colonialist discourses.

While Saïd's *Orientalism* can be said to have rigorously criticized Orientalist discourse, the same cannot be said for the Orientalist colonialist project. If he had addressed the issue of Orientalism as a colonialist project with economic imperatives, he would have found out that Orientalist discourse, in addition to other projects, were meant to rationalize the Orientalist enterprise. Having argued appropriately in the beginning of the work that to "say simply that Orientalism was a rationalization of colonial rule is to ignore the extent to which colonial rule was justified in advance by Orientalism, rather than after the fact," (Saïd, 1978: 39) one assumes that he will at least return to this point later as the work progresses, since its avoidance does not preclude the fact that Orientalism rationalized colonial rule in the Orient. As it turns out, he never returns to this argument. In addition, he also fails to link his work up with those of other Third World scholars like Frantz Fanon and Walter Rodney. For these reasons, the work can be characterized as a formalist study of Orientalist discourse. Its importance therefore, lies in its textual and inter-textual deconstruction of the Orientalist canon. Saïd's *Culture and Imperialism* has made up for the lapses in *Orientalism*, by explicitly acknowledging the distinction between fictional and non-fictional representations in colonialist discourse, as well as linking his work with the tradition of colonialist counter-discourse.

The first major work to address the issue of the African experience in colonialist discourse by an African scholar is V.Y. Mudimbe's *The Invention of Africa*. Mudimbe's project is not different from that of Saïd, except that his work is dedicated to the African experience in colonialist discourse. Also, in contradistinction to Saïd's literary critical approach, Mudimbe's study proceeds from a philosophical perspective. First, he establishes the epistemological roots of colonialist discourse as the intellectual and spiritual arm of the colonial enterprise. Second, he examines the historical contexts of the emergence of concepts such as "Oral Philosophy", "Ethnophilosophy", and "African Philosophy." Finally, he examines the historical context within which African scholars attempted a philosophical reclamation of their history and cultural identity.

Mudimbe's critical analysis of colonialist discourse is based on the theoretical assumption that it is essentially a product of the intellectual rupture of the nineteenth century. He argues that during this period, a major shift in the order of knowledge occurred; and that the *episteme* that allowed General Grammar, Natural History, and the Theory of Wealth, was radically altered, and in its place emerged, Economics, Biology, and Philology. The philosophical and scientific works of men like Linnaeus, Blumenbach, Darwin, and Gobineau, helped to erect a theoretical framework and classificatory systems, which anthropologists inherited and utilised in the representation of Africa and Africans. This is the basic argument that Mudimbe pursues with respect to locating the epistemological roots of what he calls Africanist discourse (Mudimbe, 1988: 24-25).

Mudimbe's theoretical approach does not, however, account for the roots of works with underlying colonialist thought, such as Shakespeare's *The Tempest* and *Othello,* and of classical texts such as those of Herodotus, Diodorus of Sicily and Pliny. Mudimbe does acknowledge the existence of colonialist rhetoric in the classical texts, though what he fails to mention is the initiating authorities of the discourse, the fact that they were also products of an imperialist era. At the time classical scholars wrote their works, much of the African continent, especially North Africa, was under the colonial authority of the ancient Roman Empire. Apart from the colonial presence in North Africa, Roman imperialist influence was also felt at the northern tip of the Sahelian region — in places like Mauritania, Chad and much of the Lower Nile region. It can be argued that the imperialist framework that allowed scholars like Herodotus, Diodorus of Sicily and Pliny, to travel through parts of Africa as itinerant scholars, also permitted their counterparts from the fifteenth century onwards to do the same.

The writings of classical scholars, as they pertain to alterity, were essentially "anthropological" discourses, like those of their latter day counterparts. The epistemological order, which informs the practice of colonialist discourse, is essentially that of power and authority, nourished within the context of domination. The end product of such a discursive order, especially in situations where rational reasoning has been sacrificed to racial jingoism, is a sense of superiority complex or ethnic bigotry. What has made the Afro-European experience unique is the order of colonialism. The first political structure, which produced what Mudimbe, refers to, as an African *gnosis*, for European consumption, was the product of a European power, ancient Rome. That of the nineteenth century was, coincidentally, that of European powers again. In addition to these strings of coincidences, one must also add the influence of the concept of blackness in the European imagination. Much of European experience is subtended by Judeo-Christian thought, in which black is regarded as the symbolic color of evil. Satan, the archenemy of the Judeo-Christian God, is generally portrayed as black. On the ethical plane, when one is dirty, one is considered black, whether the thought is one of physical dirtiness or moral dirtiness. Of course, blackness does have its positive value when it is imagined to be the color of strength as well as athletic ability. Consequently, in locating the sources of colonialist discourse of the African experience, one must not lose sight of these factors, which Mudimbe's study overlooked. The thrust, here, is that superiority complexes always manifest whenever one group of people, even within the same race, militarily overwhelms another. Mudimbe's main contribution to the debate on colonialist discourse lies in placing the growth of Africanist knowledge in a genealogical order, and the response of scholars of African descent to it. Also, the lapses, which Dennis Porter noted in Saïd's Orientalism, have been accounted for. Colonialist discourse and counter-discourse were and is still very much a collaborative work between African and European scholars.

One of the most important debates in the current study of colonialist discourse is that opened by Homi K. Bhabha's re-reading of Frantz Fanon's *Black Skin, White Masks*. Fanon's work was written in an act of self-liberation, and it is intended essentially to help people of African descent to drop what he calls "the white man's artefact," inferiority complex, through self-pride and self-consciousness (Fanon, 1967: 16). It should be recalled that Fanon diagnoses the double-binding nature of racism and racist discourse — what he refers to as the "dual narcissism and the motivations that inspire it," the fact that some whites consider themselves superior to blacks, and some blacks want to prove to whites at all costs "the richness of their thought, the equal value of their intellect" (Fanon: 12). For the black dilemma, Fanon diagnoses both masculine and feminine categories: the Jean Veneuse and Mayotte Capecia syndromes. He equally diagnoses the Prospero and Miranda complexes as its corresponding white categories.

Although he undertook a psychoanalytic study of the phenomena of superiority and inferiority complexes, he insists that the roots of racism and racist discourse are economic as well as historical. He specifically mentions slavery and colonialism, part of the argument being pursued in this study, and queries the arguments of Mannoni in *Prospero and Caliban*, which, Fanon opines, gives the impression that "inferiority complex was something that antedates colonization" (Fanon: 85, 202). Having placed colonialist discourse in its historical context and having explained its double-binding nature, the fact that it fixes both the colonizer and the colonized; Fanon makes an impassioned plea for the recognition of the humanity of all races and, specifically, of the black race. He bases his plea on the recognition of the equality and sameness of human races, in terms of their humanity. He also affirms the right of peoples of African descent to fight for recognition should their humanity be called into question by racial bigots. As he puts it, "if the white man challenges my humanity, I will impose my whole weight as a man on his life and show him I am not that 'sho' good eatin' that he persists in imagining" (Fanon: 229).

As earlier observed, most of the debates which once raged around Fanon's classic work have to do with Bhabha's re-reading of *Black Skin, White Masks*. That reading was intended both as a critical analysis as well as a theoretical elaboration on colonialist discourse. The tenor of Bhabha's arguments is expressed in three leading essays: "The Other Question," "Forward: Remembering Fanon — Self, Psyche and the Colonial Condition," and "Of Mimicry and Man: The Ambivalence of Colonial Discourse." These essays are analyzed in order to place in perspective Bhabha's main arguments, and their implications for studies in colonialist discourse.

The tenor of Bhabha's arguments as expressed in "The Other Question" is that colonialist discourse is dependent on the concept of fixity in the ideological construction of otherness, and also that stereotypification, one of its main discursive strategies, rests on vacillation and consequently ambivalence. As he puts it,

> it is the force of ambivalence that gives the colonial stereotype its currency: ensures its repeatability in changing historical and discursive conjunctures; informs its strategies of individuation and marginalization; produces that effect of probabilistic truth and predictability which, for the stereotype, must always be in *excess* of what can be empirically proved or logically construed. (Bhabha, 1983: 18)

He recommends that the study of colonial discourse should shift "from the *identification* of images as positive or negative, to an understanding of the process of *subjectification* made possible [and plausible] through stereotypical discourse" (original emphasis) (Bhabha: 18). Bhabha is not questioning the regime of stereotype as such. His concern is only with the process of stereotypification and the ambivalent subjecthood that emerges through this agency. Suffice to say for the mean time, that this theoretical approach has deep political implications for Africa's drive for modernization.

Bhabha questions Saïd's work, *Orientalism*, because he feels Saïd does not elaborate on Foucault's concepts of power and discourse. He argues that Foucault's concepts of power reject an "epistemology, which opposes essence/appearance, ideology/ science" (Bhabha: 24). Saïd, according to Bhabha, has used this concept by identifying "the *content* of Orientalism as the unconscious repository of fantasy, imaginative writings and essential ideas, and the form of manifest *Orientalism* as the historically and discursively determined, diachronic aspect" (24). By introducing this concept of binarism, Bhabha believes that the effectiveness of Saïd's argument is sabotaged by what he refers to as the polarities of intentionality. According to Bhabha, subjects are disproportionately placed in opposition or domination through the "symbolic decentering of multiple power-relations which play the role of support as well as target or adversary" (24).

Bhabha equally argues that Saïd's theorization fails to see representation as a concept that articulates the historical as well as the fantastic in the production of the political effects of discourse. The function of the stereotype as phobia and fetish, he argues, renders the racial schema incomprehensible to the colonial subject while opening more scenes of desire to the colonialist. As a result of the theoretical inadequacies, which he notes in Saïd's work, Bhabha proposes a theoretical approach, which argues for the reading of the stereotype in terms of fetishism. He argues that the "myth of historical origination — racial purity, cultural priority — produced in relation to the colonial stereotype, functions to 'normalize' the multiple beliefs and split subjects that constitute colonial discourse as a consequence of its process of disavowal" (Bhabha: 26). He sums up his theorization by arguing that

> the stereotype is not a simplification because it is a false
> representation of a given reality. It is a simplification because it is
> an arrested, fixated form of representation that, in denying the
> play of difference (that the negation through the Other permits),
> constitutes a problem for *representation* of subject in significations
> of psychic and social relations [Original emphasis]. (Bhabha: 27)

Even though Bhabha's theorization may be correct with respect to his analysis of the discursive agency of stereotype, he does not account for the authority of the regime of discourse. Bhabha's refusal to account for the epistemological roots of colonialist discourse and its regimes of authority renders his theorization inadequate as a critical tool for the study of colonialist discourse.

Bhabha's reading of Fanon is predicated upon Fanon's deep insight into the contradictory nature of identity construction as it relates to racist discourse. While conceding that Fanon yearned for the total transformation of men and society, Bhabha insisted that Fanon speaks most effectively from the uncertain interstices of historical change: from the area of ambivalence between race and sexuality: out of an unresolved contradiction between culture and class; from deep within the struggle of psychic representation and social reality. (Bhabha, 1986: ix)

In addition, Bhabha argues that Fanon "is not principally posing the question of political oppression as the violation of a human 'essence'" (Bhabha: xii), although he concedes that Fanon occasionally lapses into such a lament in his more existential moments. He argues further that in, posing the question, "What does the black man wants?," Fanon provides an answer which, through "privileging the psychic dimension of what we understand by a political demand, transforms the very means by which we recognize and identify its human agency." Furthermore, it is "one of the original and disturbing qualities of *Black Skin, White Masks* that it rarely historicizes the colonial experience" (Bhabha: xiii) and that there is no master narrative or realist perspective that provides a background of social and historical facts against which emerges the problems of the collective psyche.

These arguments are quite disturbing because not only do they misrepresent the views of Fanon, they do so flagrantly through a de-historicization of the main pillars of Fanon's arguments. As earlier noted, one of the reasons why Fanon took issues with Mannoni's book, *Prospero and Caliban*, was to put the facts of black inferiority complex in their proper historical perspective. But as we can observe from Bhabha's reading of this aspect of the work, he has had to de-historicize Fanon's arguments in order to make him fit into his post-Marxist discourse.

Bhabha continues that in

articulating the problem of colonial cultural alienation in the psychoanalytic language of demand and desire, Fanon radically questions the formation of both individual and society and social authority as they come to be developed in discourse of social sovereignty. (Bhabha: xiii)

He further adds that the representative figure of such a perversion is the image of post-Enlightenment man, tethered to but not confronted by his dark reflection: the shadow of colonized man, that splits his presence, distorts his outline, and breaches his boundaries by repeating his actions at a distance, thereby disturbing and dividing the very time of his being.

Bhabha proposes his theory of identity construction by arguing that the process entails that of "metaphoric substitution, an illusion of presence and by that same token a metonym, a sign of its absence and loss" (Bhabha: xviii). He further adds that as

> a principle of identification, the Other bestows a degree of objectivity but its representation — be it the social process of the Law or the psychic process of the Oedipus — is always ambivalent, disclosing a lack. (Bhabha: xviii-xix)

And he indicates three instances, which recall the ambivalent nature of identity construction. These are: (i) to exist is to be called into being in relation to an Otherness, its look or locus; (ii) the very place of identification, caught in the tension of demand and desire, is a space of splitting. It is not the Colonialist Self or the Colonized Other, but the disturbing distance in-between that constitutes the figure of colonial otherness; (iii) the question of identification is never the affirmation of a pre-given identity, never a self-fulfilling prophecy — it is always the production of an "image" of identity and the transformation of, the subject in assuming that image.

It is instructive to note that, even though Bhabha claims to be using Lacanian theories in his identity schema, in order to avoid the intrusion of historical and therefore political imperatives, he has limited his schema to the Mirror Phase of identity construction, thereby proposing a construct that is not only devoid of historical intrusion, but also involves interminable re-runs between agent and agency, without the moderation of the stabilizing force of the Symbolic Order. In contradistinction to Bhabha, JanMohamed, who also uses Lacanian theories to explain colonialist discourse, places the process of its identity construct in clear historical terms thus:

> if every desire is at base a desire to impose oneself on another and to be recognized by the Other, then the colonial situation provides an ideal context for the fulfilment of that fundamental drive. The colonialist's military superiority ensures a complete projection of his self on the Other: exercising his assumed superiority, he destroys without any significant qualms the effectiveness of indigenous economic, social, political, legal, and moral systems and imposes his own versions of these structures on the Other. (JanMohamed, 1985: 66)

In addition, he argues that by subjugating the native, the European settler is able to compel the Other's recognition of him, and, in the process, allow the latter's identity to become deeply dependent on his position as a master. Thus, this enforced recognition from the Other amounts to the European's narcissistic self-recognition. Furthermore, JanMohamed adds that the gratification that this situation affords is impaired by the European's alienation from his own unconscious desire. In the "imaginary" text, the subject is eclipsed by his fixation on, and fetishization of, the Other: the Self becomes a prisoner of the projected image. Even though the native is negated by the projection of the inverted image, his presence as, an absence, can never be cancelled. For this reason, the colonialist's desire only entraps him in the dualism of the "imaginary", and foments a violent hatred of the native (JanMohamed: 67). The educational facilities of the colonialist liberate the native, but in the colonialist's imagination, the native remains just that — a native. Thus, like Fanon, JanMohamed also places colonialist discourse in historical perspective.

Bhabha's main point of disagreement with Fanon stems from Fanon's attempts to draw "too close a correspondence between the *mise-en-scène* of unconscious fantasy and the phantoms of racist fear and hate that stalk the colonial scene" (Bhabha: xix). He argues that Fanon turns

> too hastily from the ambivalences of identification to the antagonistic identities of political alienation and cultural discrimination; he is too quick to name the Other, to personalize its presence in the language of colonial racism. (Bhabha: xix)

On his own part, Bhabha suggests that the non-dialectical moment of Manicheanism is the answer, and that by following the trajectory of colonial desire, in the company of that bizarre colonial figure, the tethered shadow, it becomes possible to transverse alienation, even to shift the Manichean boundaries; for, as he puts it, where there is no human nature, hope can hardly spring eternal.

In my opinion, Bhabha has misread Fanon. In his haste to use him as a theoretical framework, he strips Fanon of those relevant portions that have made his theorization stand the test of history. To return to my original point, Fanon believes that Africans, both continental and diasporic, must cure their inferiority complex through the apprehension of the phenomenon on two levels, psychological and historical levels, since historically they influence each other. He equally recognizes the fact that the interdependence of both levels of cognition is not automatic. Therefore, he recommends that reality be studied both at the objective level and on the subjective level (Fanon, 1986: 13).

The problem with Bhabha's theoretical approach lies in the fact that, unlike Fanon, he pursues psychoanalytic study entirely on a *textual* level, as if the psyche is a self-constitutory organ. Fanon diagnosed the double-binding nature of racism and racist discourse, what he refers to as "dual narcissism"; but he equally wrote of "the motivations that inspire it" (Fanon: 12). Bhabha ends his theoretical construct at the level of dual narcissism, at the level of ambivalent concourse in colonialist discourse. In the place of the new man and woman who emerge through the crucible of liberation struggle, Bhabha elevates a historically backward Janus, the mimic subject that disrupts not only colonial texts but native ones as well.

Bhabha's theory of the mimic-subject is fully developed in his essay, "Of Mimicry and Man: The Ambivalence of Colonial Discourse," where he uses mimicry as a metaphor of sabotage within the authority signified by colonialist discourse. What he refers to, as a mimic-subject is an ambivalent personality construct with Anglicized features: never enough to warrant acceptance and incorporation by the English, yet with enough features to allow room for free movement. This mobility, because it transverses both the imaginary and physical boundaries of discourse, signifies the passage of colonialist authorized sabotage. Bhabha sees the mimic-subject, as an invention of colonial authority, as a product of necessity.

According to Bhabha, the subject emerged on the scene because the English felt the need to produce a class of interpreters between them and the millions whom they governed, subjects who would be "English in taste, in opinions, in morals and intellect — in other words a mimic man" (Bhabha, 1984: 128). Produced through an imported English public school system, the mimic-subject, according to Bhabha, is the effect of a flawed colonial mimesis, in which to be Anglicized is emphatically not to be English. The mimic-subject represents the problematic within the authority of colonialist discourse:

> a difference or recalcitrance which coheres the dominant
> strategic function of colonial power, intensifies surveillance, and

poses an immanent threat to both 'normalized' knowledges and disciplinary powers. (Bhabha: 126)

Rather than emerge from the construct as a subservient subject, the mimic subject soon becomes something of an authorized saboteur, who helps to fulfill the "civilizing" mission of colonialism, as well as help to sabotage it by representing it as a crossbreed between mimicry and mockery.

It is on this Janus personality construct that Bhabha hinges his theory. Furthermore, Bhabha's theory of the mimic-subject dwells only on one plank of the disruptive effects of the phenomenon, its effects on the "master" texts. Bhabha neglects the oppositional plank represented by this partial acculturation — the fact that the mimic subject is also partially acculturated in respect of native customary norms and values is totally neglected by him. Yet the partial presence and absence of the mimic-subject in colonialist discourse also represents a partial presence and absence in native discourse. Hence, unlike Bhabha who treats the boundary of discourse as a site for an eternal relay of ambivalence, in this work, it is considered a place of inter-cultural enrichment, and not one of perpetual fixation.

The boundary of discourse is a common ground for the mutual exchange of ideas, not one of eternal miscognition. In addition, discourse is conceived as the marketplace for the exchange of ideas, a trader-spot of some sort where ideas are exchanged in an inter-subjective engagement. Every man or woman goes there from a cultural center — be it family, ethnicity, nation, or even race. That certain opinions are presently dominant as a result of the uneven power and knowledge relations in the world does not mean that there is only one socio-cultural and historical center. To argue, as Bhabha does, by granting recognition to only one cultural center, in this instance, the European cultural center, from which the colonized can define his or her identity, is to engage in authoritarian discourse rather than the multiplicity of discursive traditions, which the media avails us daily.

Manthia Diawara has also criticized Bhabha's denial of subjecthood to blacks and other colonized groups in his essay, "The Nature of Mother in *Dreaming River*." In this essay, Diawara has demonstrated how difficult it would be to approach the analysis of the film, *Dreaming River*, by using Bhabha's theoretical perspective. The problem with Bhabha's theoretical proposition is not just that it takes only a single phase of Fanon's work, the early phase for that matter, as a standard for reading his entire corpus, but that he goes about it in a manner that seeks to foster self-doubt among colonized peoples, instead of the liberatory consciousness which Fanon's works propagate (Diawara, 1990). In his response to Bhabha's reading of Fanon, Neil Lazarus has observed that "Bhabha's Fanon would have been unrecognizable to Fanon himself" (Lazarus, 1993: 89).

Benita Parry has examined the dangers that lie in uncritically appropriating the theoretical propositions of scholars of the Spivak school of thought, to which Bhabha belongs. She has summarized the reasons why one disagrees with the theoretical propositions of the Spivak school:

> the significant differences in the critical practices of Spivak and Bhabha are submerged in a shared program marked by the exorbitation of discourse and a related incuriosity about the enabling socio-economic political institutions and other forms of social praxis. Furthermore, because their theses admit of no point outside of discourse from which opposition can be engendered, their project is concerned to place incendiary devices within the dominant structures of representation and not to confront these with another knowledge. (Parry, 1987: 43)

In order to avoid the kind of textual essentialism which Parry has noted, it is necessary to analyze colonialist [African] discourse by situating it within the context of the discipline of the colonialist canon as it exists since classical times; and in modern times, within the context of the slave trade and colonialism. The remaining part of this chapter examines the genealogical origins of colonialist African discourse with a view to establishing the roots of colonialist African cinema.

The Genealogy of Colonialist African Discourse

Although scholars, like Snowden (1970:169-195), would want us to believe that, prior to colonialism, European scholarly and artistic works on Africa were devoid of racist discourse, similar studies carried out by Kathrine George on classical texts suggest that, on the contrary, racist discourse is as old as contacts between Africa and Europe. George argues that, though European accounts of the inhabitants of Africa are in general scattered and brief, they tend, consistently, to emphasize the strange, the shocking, and the degrading qualities of African peoples and cultures. According to George,

> the classical consensus, then, is that these peoples in the hidden interior and on the farthest shores of Africa not only lack civilization but any worthy ethic of social organization or conducts as well. The most remote, in addition, are often denied the possession of a truly human form. The dominant attitude in these accounts conceived of civilization — Graeco-Roman civilization in particular — as an essential discipline imposed upon the irregularities of nature ... There was established thus early the pattern of thought which for many future centuries formed a basis for approach to Africa, and which defined them primarily not in terms of what they were and what they had, but in terms of what they presumably were not and had not — in terms, that is, of their inhumanity, their wildness, and their lack of proper law. (George, 1958: 64)

George traces the roots of Graeco-Roman racist prejudice to what she refers to as "the ego-flattering naiveté of the Aristotelian division of the world's population into Greeks and Barbarians, or freemen by nature and slaves by nature" (George: 62). She further argues that, though accounts of the representation of Africans in classical texts are scanty and scattered, they are nevertheless characterized by an attitude of superiority and disapproval, and the substitution of antagonistic fantasy for fact. She cites both Herodotus and Diodorus to buttress her argument. For instance, she quotes Diodorus as saying the following about Africans:

> the majority of them ... are black in color and have flat noses and woolly hair. As for their spirit, they are entirely savage and display the nature of a wild beast ... and are as far removed as possible from human kindness to one another and speaking as they do with a shrill voice and cultivating none of the practices of civilized life as these are found among the rest of mankind, they present a striking contrast when considered in the light of our own customs. (Cited in George: 63)

One only needs to compare the statements of Diodorus and those of sixteenth-century voyagers, such as John Lok, to apprehend fully the extent to which the classical texts were reproduced through the centuries. Writing in the sixteenth-century, Lok refers to Africans as a people of beastly living, without a God, lawe, religion, or common wealth ... people whose women are common: for they contract no matrimonie, neither have respect to chastitie. The region called Troglodytica, whose inhabitants dwell in caves and dennes: for these are their houses, and the flesh of serpents their meat, as writhed Plinie, and Diodorus Siculus. They have no speech, but rather a grinning and chattering. There are also people without heads ... having their eyes and mouths in their breasts. (Cited in Hammond and Jablow: 20)

This account largely reproduces the classical texts. In reference to the foregoing views, Kabbani has aptly argued that European anthropological discourses are driven by the desire to cater to the "needs of sedentary audiences desiring depictions of the extraordinary" (Kabban, 1988: 3). An analysis of the discursive terminologies applied by Diodorus in describing Africans affirms George's observations that, as early as the classical period, a pattern of thought was already firmly established with regard the representation of Africans. Not only were the external features of Africans well defined, a classification of the assumed psychosocial qualities of Africans was also included in Diodorus' description. Nor was the practice restricted to Diodorus. According to Mudimbe, the geographic and historical texts of both Herodotus and Pliny reflect the descriptive pattern of Diodorus, a patterns which was similar to that applied by European scholars from the sixteenth-century onwards (Mudimbe, 1988: 70-71).

Though both George and Mudimbe do not fully explore the contexts within which the classical colonialist discourse emerged, Bernal's study formally foregrounds the role of colonial conquests and counter-conquests to the evolvement of classical civilization within the Mediterranean region (Bernal, 1987: 189-223). Bernal's study also demonstrates how changes in Afro-European power structures affected the tenor of emergent discourses. He notes that the revision and replacement of the ancient model of history with the Aryan model is a demonstration of the role of power structures in the promulgation of discourses. Bernal also acknowledges the role of Aristotelian theories in the promulgation of racist discourse. According to him, Aristotle linked "racial superiority" to the right to enslave other peoples, especially those of a "slavish disposition" (Bernal: 202). European philosophers, beginning from the late seventeenth-century onwards, to legitimate the enslavement of Africans, later used similar arguments.

Apart from the existence of a classical canon in colonialist African discourse, one must add the influence of the widespread Biblical assumptions among Europeans that Africans were the descendants of the cursed Ham of the Genesis story (George: 66-67). According to Cowhig, hostility towards blacks in Renaissance England was the product of this Biblical assumption:

> the hostility would be encouraged by the widespread belief in the legend that blacks were descendants of Ham in the Genesis story punished for sexual excess by their blackness. Sexual potency was therefore one of the attributes of the prototype black. Other qualities associated with black people were courage, pride, guilelessness, credulity and easily aroused passions. (Cowhig 1985: 1)

The works of English Renaissance writers such as Shakespeare in *Titus Andronicus, Othello,* and *The Tempest,* Ben Johnson in *Masque of Blackness,* Thomas Peele in *The Battle of Alcazar* and Thomas Dekker et al, in *Lust's Dominion,* drew upon both canonical authorities and Biblical assumptions. Cowhig's study of the Renaissance theatre shows, for instance, that the representation of blacks did not depart very much from the classical texts:

> In these ... plays, black people are represented as satanic, sexual creatures, a threat to order and decency, and a danger to white womanhood. They are a loud presence, they rant and they curse their way through the plays with obscene antics and treacherous behaviour. (Cowhig: 4)

Even though canonical authorities and Biblical assumptions helped to sustain the growth of the colonialist African discourse, the single most important factor in modern history that helped to proliferate it is the Portuguese expedition to the West Coast of Africa, and the resultant slave trade in the fifteenth-century. Before the fifteenth-century contact, Arab middlemen handled black Africa's trade with Europe. After the Portuguese conquest of Ceuta in 1415, direct and consistent European contact with Africa, beyond the Mediterranean littoral, was fully established. According to François Latour da Veiga Pinto, the earliest navigators to round the coast of Africa were prompted by two economic motives: to discover the source of Sudanese gold, which had so far reached Europe via North Africa, and to find the sea route to India and her silk and spice markets (Pinto, 1979: 119). In addition to these economic motives, he also acknowledges that the ideals of the crusades equally played their part, and gave moral and religious backing to the expeditions. Furthermore, when the first sailor-knights rounded the coast of Africa, they hoped to find the kingdom of the legendary Prester John, with the hope of building a common alliance against the Muslim "infidels."

With specific reference to the foregoing, the first incidence of kidnapping and sale of Africans into slavery occurred in 1444. This initiated the mass enslavement of Africans in a proportion never before witnessed in the history of human slavery, the consequence of which was a proportionate mass devaluation of the life of Africans. According to Pinto,

> the first Negroes to be captured were taken by men convinced that they were doing a great feat — and also a virtuous deed, since everyone of the 'wretches' baptized meant a soul won for God. The technique initially used to acquire the first slaves, *filhamento* or kidnapping, was likewise inherited from the Middle Ages: surprise attacks were made on isolated nomad camps and the captives brought back to Portugal. (Pinto: 19)

The first sets of African slaves were made to provide both the domestic and agricultural labor of Spain, Italy and Portugal. The discovery of the Atlantic islands and, later, mainland America, was to bring about the rise of the sugar-cane industry and, consequently, pave the way for the beginning of the trans-Atlantic slave trade (Pinto: 119-120).

The question of the actual number of Africans lost through the slave trade is still unknown. Curtin gives a figure of around nine and a half million, which provoked heated disputations between him and Joseph Inikori in the 1970s (Curtin 1969, Inikori 1976, Curtin and Anstey 1976, Inikori 1976, 1979). In a UNESCO organized conference on the subject, the question of the actual figures of Africans lost through the trade ended unresolved between those whose calculations are based on estimated figures taken only from ships' manifests, as in the case of Curtin (1969), and those whose calculations cover the overall cost of the trade upon Africa (Inikori, 1979). The following summary of the UNESCO conference well illustrates these two opposing conjectures:

> according to some participants who wished to take into consideration factors such as losses during capture and land

journeys across Africa, and deaths during the sea crossing, Africa's losses during the four centuries of the Atlantic slave trade must be put at some 210 million human beings ... According to others the overall total of slaves transported between the tenth and nineteenth century from black Africa to the various receiving territories should be put at between 15 and 30 million persons. (UNESCO Report, 1979: 211)

Though the number of Africans lost through the slave trade is still unresolved, most scholars agree that the trans-Atlantic slave trade contributed a lot to the devaluation of African life (Hammond and Jablow, 1977: 23; Stepan, 1982: xii; Dabydeen, 1985; Brantlinger, 1986: 185). Stepan has argued, for instance, that as the slave trade grew in proportion,

> a black skin was taken as 'natural' outward sign of inward mental and moral inferiority. The association between blackness and inferiority produced by racial slavery was grafted onto an earlier, primarily literary tradition, in which blackness and whiteness comprised the terms of a binary opposition. (Stepan: xii)

Within this context of the devaluation of African life, racist theorists emerged in the eighteenth-century onward, with disputations over the question of the humanity of Africans. Curtin has argued, for instance, that though racism of some variety had existed before in Europe, it needs to be kept separate from "the full-blown pseudo-scientific racism which dominated so much of European thought between the 1840s and the 1940s" (Curtin, 1964: 19). The difference according to him lies within the period under consideration:

> science, the body of knowledge rationally derived from empirical observation, then supported the proposition that race was one of the principal determinants of attitudes, endowments, capabilities, and inherent tendencies among human beings. (Curtin: 29)

From such pseudo-scientific theorization, race became accepted as the sole determinant of the course of human history. Curtin, further, argues that as the slave trade progressed, so did Europeans progressively begin to believe that African skin color, hair texture and facial features were associated, in some way, with African way of life in Africa, and the status of slavery in the Americas:

> once this association was made, racial views became unconsciously linked with social views, and with the common

assessment of African culture. Culture prejudice thus slid off easily toward color prejudice, and the two were frequently blended in ways that were imprecise at the time — and even harder to separate after the passage of almost two centuries. (Curtin: 30)

Curtin, still further, maintains that though travelers' accounts of their visit to Africa contained culturally prejudicial statements, such accounts often condemned individual Africans as bad men. However, as the anti-slave trade movement began to gather strength in England in the 1780's, the African interest began to feel threatened, and a different kind of attitude emerged, when travelers began to ascribe qualities of individuals to the group — not individual men, but the collective term, African, began to be referred to as an inhuman savage. Furthermore, eighteenth-century biologists, who were trying to classify and arrange the whole order of nature in a rational manner, began, at this period, to use empirical data collected by travelers to systematize their classification of the order of nature. The major eighteenth-century classifications of nature began with Karl Linnaeus's *Systema Naturae*, first published in 1735, but later revised in 1758. According to Curtin, this work and its successors formed the basic framework of modern biological classification. It is structured on the hierarchic order of the "great chain of being", in accordance with the eighteenth-century belief that God had so organized the world that all creation could be classified and fitted into a hierarchy extending from human beings down to the smallest creature, whose existence could be discovered only by a microscope (Curtin: 37).

Since people were placed at the apex of the chain next to the Creator, eighteenth-century biologists believed that the varieties of humankind could also be arranged in a hierarchic order. In his classification, Linnaeus divided *homo sapiens* into six categories with physical and attitudinal qualities: *ferus* (four footed, mute, hairy); *americanus* (red, choleric, erect); *europeaus* (white, ruddy, muscular); *asiaticus* (yellow, melancholic, inflexible); *afar* (black, phlegmatic, indulgent); *monstrosus* (further subdivided into deviant forms from several regions) (Banton, 1987: 4).

Having thus classified mankind, eighteenth-century biologists then faced the second problem of the order of the quality of the races of mankind. According to Curtin, since there is no strictly scientific or biological justification for stating that one race is higher than another, the criteria for ranking had to come from non-scientific assumptions. Their assumptions invariably depended upon physical and racio-aesthetic chauvinism. Presumably, historical achievements in art and science were interconnected with physical form — in short, race and culture were closely interrelated (Curtin: 38-39). If whiteness of the skin was the mark of the highest race, darker races were presumed to be inferior in the increasing order of their darkness. Curtin submits that on this basis, Africans were put at the bottom of every classificatory order of the human race. Aesthetic judgments were introduced as well. Blumenbach, who later became a key figure of the monogenetist school of thought, and a champion of Africans, fell into this form of racio-aesthetic categorization. He described Caucasians as having "in general the kind of appearance which, according to our opinion of symmetry, we consider most handsome and becoming," and Africans he defined in the following manner:

> *Ethiopian variety.* Color black; hair black and curly, head narrow, compressed at the sides; forehead knotty, uneven, malar bones protruding outwards; eyes very prominent; nose thick, mixed up as it were with the wide jaws; alveolar edge narrow, elongated in front; upper primaries obliquely prominent; lips very puffy; chin retreating. Many are bandy-legged. To this variety belong all the Africans, except those of the North. (Cited in Curtin: 39)

Blumebach's description of Africans evidently uses Europeans as a standard for comparison. The major attempt to qualify racial distinction in the eighteenth-century was undertaken by Pieter Camper in Holland. Later, generally referred to as "Camper's Facial Angle," it was essentially a measurement of prognathism, derived by looking at a human head in profile. Measurement entailed drawing one line from the meeting point of the lips to the most prominent part of the forehead, and another from the opening of the ear to the base of the nose. The crucial angle was formed where these two lines met. Presumably, the wider the angle, the smaller the degree of prognathism, which suggested the headshape of animals. A wider angle was supposed to indicate a higher forehead, a greater skull capacity, a better aesthetic appearance, and greater intelligence. Camper, according to Curtin, claimed that if this angle were measured for men of various races (or even for animals), the measurements would fall into an ordered series, from Greek statuary as the ideal form, through European races, to negroes as the lowest human variety, and finally to the lower animals (Curtin: 39-40).

Towards the end of the eighteenth-century, a major bifurcation emerged among racial theorists. There were those, like Blumenbach, who held to the traditional and orthodox Christian view that God created man, a single pair, at some finite time in the past — the monogenists — and those who held that each race was a separate creation, distinct from the children of Adam, and permanently so; these were the polygenists, and included Edward Long and James Hunt. The polygenists were especially influenced by the works of eighteenth-century philosophers, who were concerned with finding a plausible and systematic explanation of the world outside Biblical orthodoxies. Philosophers like Voltaire and Rousseau suggested that negroes were naturally inferior to Europeans in their mental ability. Though the majority of European scholarly and scientific discourses in the eighteenth-century continued in the classical tradition by professing the inferiority of Africans, the influence of the anti-slave trade movement helped to polarize both scholarly and literary outputs (Curtin: 52).

Edward Long's *History of Jamaica* provided all the necessary "empirical" evidence of the inferiority of Africans, as he experienced it in Jamaica, to support the theorization of the polygenists. The Reverend James Ramsay, on the other hand, countered with a different set of "empirical" evidence in his major work, *Essays on the Treatment and Conversion of African Slaves in the British Sugar Colonies*. Ramsay's argument proceeds from Christian revelation, but he goes on to counter the biologists with biological arguments. He attacked the assumption that the negro could be considered a valid abstraction, by showing that even in their physical features, Africans were a diverse lot. Furthermore, biologists had not really established a definite relationship between the physical form and ability nor ability and climate. On the more detailed anatomical points, he showed that, even if negroes' skulls could be proven to stand between those of Europeans and those of apes, there was no evidence the that skull shape and size had any relation to intelligence, or any other human quality. He continued further that, even if it could be shown that the cranial capacity of negroes was smaller than that of other people, there was still no proof that this characteristic was permanent, and conclusive proof of mental incapability. He also contradicted Long's assertion that mulattos were relatively infertile, from his own observations in the West Indies. Finally he argued that, even if it could be proved that negroes were a distinct race, or even separate species, there was no proof that they were inferior. And if they could be proved to be both distinct and inferior as a group, there was no proof that individual Africans were inferior to individual Europeans. Even if all were inferior, he argued, there was still no moral case for their enslavement. Curtin has aptly and objectively observed that Reverend Ramsay employed critical rationalism, associated with science, in a way "scientists" had neglected to do (Curtin: 55-56).

The activities of Christian anti-slavery movements — like those of the Wesleyan Christian Sect and the Evangelical wing of the Church of England — and the secular rights-of-man philosophy of the eighteenth-century also supported the monogenist arguments. Individual reformers, according to Curtin, came into the movement with a variety of opinions about Africans. Granville Sharp, the principal leader of the fight against slavery in England, rested his initial case on purely legal arguments: the laws of England, he argued, have no bearing on slavery; therefore, any slave brought to England should automatically become a free man. This view already had some support in judicial decisions, and Lord Mansfield sustained it in 1772. Though John Wesley, like Sharp, was uncertain about the nature of Africans, on the specific issue of the slave trade, he too lent his support to the abolitionists (Curtin: 53).

From the foregoing circumstances, the literary convention of the "noble savage" emerged. The African of the cult of the noble savage had some of the characteristics of the biological African of the same period. He was just as much an abstraction, and begotten, just as much, from the needs of European thought as the biological African. The noble savage, as a literary hero, was essentially an abstraction, designed to depict moral lessons. His exceptional qualities of strength, intellect and virtue reflected or reinforced the ethical standards of the age. From seventeenth-century onwards, some heroes were drawn for the purpose of criticizing the artificiality of European civilization.

The first popular African hero of the noble savage convention appeared in English literature with Aphra Behn's novelette, *Oroonoko*. Hammond and Jablow suggest that Shakespeare's *Othello* may have provided the model for the characterization of Oroonoko. The storyline is woven around the tribulations of Oroonoko, an African prince and his princess, Imoida, who are captured and enslaved. Their tribulations at the hands of brutal white men, and their eventual heroic deaths, constitute the plot of the tale. It was later dramatized by Thomas Southerne, in 1696, and appeared in many other adaptations throughout the eighteenth-century (Hammond and Jablow: 25-26). The abolitionists later used Oroonoko and his like as vehicles for anti-slavery propaganda.

Though *Oroonoko* signified the initiation of this character-type, the fully conventionalized noble savage made its entrance only in the second half of the eighteenth-century, along with the cult of nature. Furthermore, though the use of the savage hero as a literary device helped to create a much more favorable emotional climate for Africans than they had hitherto enjoyed, the practitioners of this literary tradition had no intention of suggesting that Africans were equal to Europeans, or that their culture measured to that of Europe. In the same vein, the nobility of the savage hero was not a greater nobility than, or even equal to that achieved by a European. The literary theme of the noble savage climaxed during the last three decades of the eighteenth-century. Thereafter, its popularity began to witness a decline, with only occasional re-appearances throughout the first half of the nineteenth-century.

If the eighteenth-century signaled the emergence of racist biological thought, the nineteenth-century witnessed not only its climax but also its proliferating influence in all areas of human knowledge. In addition to tenacious stance of the biologist views, anthropological and philosophical discourses, geographical, religious, and socio-historical theses of scholars such as Robert Chambers, George Cuvier, James Hunt, William Lawrence, Josiah Nott, Charles White, Arthur de Gobineau, Charles Darwin, and James Prichard, continued to propagate the inferiority of Africans throughout the nineteenth-century and well into the twentieth-century.

For instance, Robert Chambers, in his study of the human embryo in 1844, drew the conclusion that before the Caucasian embryo is fully formed, its brain undergoes an embryonic transformation that includes transformations from the animal, through the Negroid, Malayan, American, to the Mongolian, before becoming a fully developed Caucasian:

our brain ... after completing the animal transformations, it passes through the characters in which it appears in the Negro, Malay, American, and Mongolian nations, and finally is Caucasian. (Cited in Banton: 25)

The face is also said to partake of these alterations. In short, the essence of his thesis is to prove that "the various races of mankind are simply representations of particular stages in the development of the highest or Caucasian type" (cited in Banton: 25). George Cuvier's study of *homo sapiens* in 1800 did not only place blacks at the bottom of the great human chain but also states that the lowly status of blacks accounted for their enslavement, while the racial superiority of Europeans accounted for their colonization of the world:

It is not for nothing that the Caucasian race has gained dominion over the world and made the most rapid progress in the sciences," he wrote, while the Negroes were "sunken in slavery and the pleasures of the senses. (Cited in Banton: 30)

Anthropological studies carried out by William Lawrence in the early part of the nineteenth-century also sought physical ethnographic evidence to prove an inborn racial difference of intellect and moral outlook between Africans and Europeans. According to Lawrence,

the distinction of color between the white and black races is not more striking than the pre-eminence of the former in moral feelings and in mental endowments. The latter, it is true, exhibit generally a great acuteness of the external senses, which in some instances is heightened by exercise to a degree nearly incredible. Yet they indulge, almost universally, in disgusting debauchery and sensuality, and display gross selfishness, indifference to the pains and pleasures of others, insensibility to beauty of form, order, and harmony, and an almost entire want of what we comprehend altogether under the expression of elevated sentiments, manly virtues, and moral feelings. (Cited in Curtin: 232)

In the United States of America, craniological studies carried out by Samuel Morton and Josiah Clark Nott, and George Robbins Gliddon, concluded that whites had the biggest brains, black the smallest, and brown people in between. Basing their arguments on craniological measurements, they argued that differences in brain sizes explained differences in the capacity for civilization (Banton:

34-46). In a similar vein, George Combe and William Lawrence employed the phrenological theories of the Austrian anatomist, Franz Joseph Gall, to prove the inferiority of Africans. According to Curtin,

> the essence of the phrenological system was the belief that the human mind could be divided into thirty-seven different "faculties", each of which was to be found in a different part of the cortex. For any individual, the strength or weakness of each of these faculties could be discovered by carefully measuring the shape of the skull. Thus character could be analyzed merely by external examination of the head. (Curtin: 234)

Though phrenology was untenable on almost every point, Lawrence used it in 1819 to prove that race and culture were interconnected as part of the permanent order of things. (Curtin: 234-235). George Combe, against the better judgement of Gall that the system should not be applied to analyze the character of an entire race, went ahead to apply phrenology in his characterization of what supposedly was the psychological make-up of Africans. According to Combe, the African's skull showed that

> the organs of Philoprogenitiveness and Concentrativeness are largely developed; the former of which produces love of children, and the latter that concentration of mind which is favorable to settled and sedentary employments. The organs of Veneration and Hope are also considerable in size. The greatest deficiencies lie in Conscientiousness, Cautiousness, Ideality, and Reflection. (cited in Curtin: 366-367)

Though the emergence of the Darwinian theory of the evolution of man, with the publication of Charles Darwin's *Origin of Species* in 1859, greatly refined biological thought, it allowed the errors of racist classification to stand. As Stepan puts it,

> for Darwin ... it appeared reasonable to think that, just as natural selection produced *Homo Sapiens* from animal forebears, so natural selection was the primary agent responsible for producing civilized races out of barbarity. As a result, Darwin's first general argument about man and evolution, for all its novelty concerning the descent of man from some ape-like ancestor, did not disturb the assumption in race biology of a great chain of races. (Stepan, 1982: 58-59)

Though the racist theories of scholars like Thomas Arnold, Thomas Carlyle, and Robert Knox, continued to proliferate and gain respectability during the nineteenth-century, the old divisions of monogenism/polygenism, ethnological society/anthropological society continued to produce scholarly discourses that reflected the liberal/conservative opposition in Euro-American scholarship.

Summary

Thus far, one has been arguing that colonialist African literature/films are governed by the existing canon of colonialist African discourse and the uneven power and knowledge relations resulting from modern contact between Europe and Africa, and the subsequent slave trade and colonialism. Though Brian Street, in his study of the novels of the British Empire, overlooks the question of both canonical authority and the contextual influence of colonialist discourse, he acknowledges that the value judgments made in the novels of empire are

> taken beyond the scope of "normal" ethnocentrism by their location in a supposedly scientific framework of race, evolution and hierarchy that lends respectability and authority to them. That framework underlies the trivial representations of the "other" that are found in popular novels and everyday representations alike and gives them significance and an ability to persist that makes them harder to overcome than simple "prejudice." (Street, 1985: 102)

Furthermore, it is necessary to sketch the genealogical order of colonialist African discourse because it is theoretically inadequate to situate its emergence exclusively within the intellectual ambit of the nineteenth-century. Only a conceptualization that takes into account the canonical roots of colonialist African discourse adequately renders a proper historiography of the subject, and locates the point at which its cinematic practice took off.

COLONIAL AFRICAN INSTRUCTIONAL CINEMA

Introduction

This chapter examines the historical context within which the practice of colonial African instructional cinema was instituted in Africa during the colonial era. It traces the origin of instructional film practice in Africa and examines how it was institutionalized through projects such as the Bantu Educational Cinema Experiment and those projects which later followed such as the instructional film practices of the Colonial Film Unit (CFU), the Film and Photo Bureau of the Belgian Congo and the Congolese Center for Catholic Action Cinema (C.C.C.A.C.) of the same territory. This background information is intended to establish the context within which the practices of instructional cinema emerged in Africa during the colonial period. My argument is that the practices of instructional cinema instituted a different regime of representation of Africa and Africans that stand in direct contrast to that of films of colonialist African cinema. In most writings on cinematic practices in colonial Africa, this distinction is never acknowledged (Malkmus and Armes, 1991: 3-35; Smyth, 1979, 1983; Richards, 1983; Diawara, 1992: 2-11). The impression one is left with is that all the films about Africa produced by Europeans during the colonial period were colonialist.

Though films of colonial African instructional cinema belong to the documentary form, which carries very strong suggestions of actuality, they are to be considered first and foremost as discursive texts with specific modes of representation and forms of subjectivities. No matter how close to reality representation in documentary form is imagined to be, it will always remain representation. As Bill Nichols aptly puts the argument,

> many documentarists would appear to believe what fiction film-makers only feign to believe, or openly question: that film-making creates an objective representation of the way things really are. Such documentaries use the magical template of verisimilitude without the storyteller's open resort to artifice. Very few seem prepared to admit through the very tissue and texture of their work that all film-making is a form of discourse fabricating its effects, impressions, and point of view. (Nichols, 1983: 18)

Nichols argues that documentary cinema is a discursive form and maintains that the discursive strategies deployed in the form, like narrative cinema, change and have history. They change because the arena of ideological contestation shifts and "new strategies must constantly be fabricated to represent 'things as they are' and still others to contest this very representation"(Nichols: 17).

Among the styles which have developed in response to shifts in conceptions of realism in documentary, Nichols cites the following: (i) the direct address style of the Griersonian tradition — or in its most excessive form, the March of Times' "Voice of God"; (ii) *cinéma vérité*; (iii) direct address, either by a narrator speaking directly to the viewer or character-narrators through interviews addressing viewers directly, or a combination of both; (iv) self-reflexive documentaries which mix observational passages with interviews, the voice-over of the filmmaker with intertitles, thereby making patently clear what has been implicit all along: documentaries always are forms of representation and never clear windows onto "reality"; (v) the modernist text which, through its application of a multiplicity of voices, direct and indirect forms of addresses and intertitles presents two levels of historical reference — evidence and argument — and two levels of textual structure — observation and exposition (Nichols: 17-18). Most instructional films belong to the first category of Nichols' classification, and they approach narration either through the "Voice of God" or voice-over narrator, as in the case of *Men of Africa* (Alexander Shaw, 1939), or are dramatized documentaries which use a combination of voice-over narrators and omniscient and character narrations as in the case of *Daybreak in Udi* (Terry Bishop, 1948). Though

Nichols does not include dramatized documentary in his categorization, his argument that documentary cinema is a form of discourse is enough for its inclusion.

To conclude this chapter, I consider a case study of two films belonging to the tradition of colonial African instructional cinema, *Men of Africa* and *Daybreak in Udi*. This is done to demonstrate how Africa and Africans are represented in instructional cinema and why the nature of African subjectivities that emerges of this practice is antithetical to that in colonialist African cinema of the same period.

The Historical Background of Colonial African Instructional Cinema

The introduction of instructional cinema into sub-Saharan Africa during the colonial era by the British colonial governments and other government and non-governmental agencies was informed by the desire to exploit the educational capacities of the medium as well as to counter the influence of Hollywood films in its colonies. Instructional film practice was introduced first in Nigeria in the late 1920s by the colonial government as a visual aid to an ongoing government campaign to eradicate an outbreak of a plague in Lagos in 1929. As a result of the success of this pioneering effort by William Sellers, the use of film as a medium of instruction and propagation of government developmental programs was extended to other British territories. The Central Office of Information (COI) bulletin gave the following account of how the cinema was adopted as a medium of instruction and propagation of government policies in British colonies:

> in the late 1920s lantern slides were being used to illustrate lectures on health in Nigeria, and it was in this territory, to combat an outbreak of plague in Lagos in 1929, that the film was employed for the first time in any colonial territory as medium of information and education. In the campaign, the film was used to illustrate to Africans the way in which rats carry the disease and to enlist the co-operation of Africans in killing the plague-bearing rats. The success of the campaign was such that from that time the film was increasingly used in West Africa. (Central Office of Information (COI) Bulletin No. R. 3161, October, 1955)

Despite the success of this pioneering effort, no immediate serious effort was made to institutionalize the practice of instructional cinema until 1939, when the Colonial Film Unit (CFU) was established. By the second half of the 1920s, however, the Colonial Office began to explore the implications of the cinema for the colonies and for colonial power. The initial impulse to regulate the influence of the cinema in British territories resulted from a perceived threat to British interests of the commercial cinema, especially Hollywood. Rosaleen Smyth has noted that

> in the African colonies the concern of the Colonial Office was how the cinema affected British economic and political interests, and how Britain might use the cinema to promote what it determined to be the economic, social, and moral welfare of the colonial peoples. Britain felt that both her economic and political interests in Africa were threatened by the stranglehold which the American film had gained on the commercial cinema circuit in the 1920s. (Smyth, 1983: 129)

Attempts made to break the influence of Hollywood failed because many colonies, especially those in Southern and Eastern Africa, had already entered contractual agreements with South Africa based film distributors for supplies of commercial films. As a result, the Colonial Office was forced to limit itself to the negative sanction of censorship and urged colonial governments to be aware of films that might discredit the armed forces or arouse undesirable racial feeling. Also during this period, the Colonial Office began to give serious thought to an alternative form of cinema to the dominant Hollywood practice, one that would combine instruction with entertainment. Since most Africans were at this time illiterate, the cinema was thought to offer bright possibilities as a medium of instruction.

In 1927, Hans Vischer, Secretary to the Advisory Committee on Education in the Colonies (ACEC), recommended to the Colonial Office Conference on Education in the Colonies, that the cinema should be used to spread general knowledge about health and economic development in the colonies. In 1929, Julian Huxley went to East Africa for ACEC to test African reactions to instructional films. He concluded after observing reactions to the pilot program for the education of adults that the cinema could be used for both educational and propaganda means. At the time Huxley carried out his pilot program, however, local experiments were already being made on the use of film as an instrument for the dissemination of government health policies by two colonial government health officials, William Sellers in Nigeria, and A. Paterson in Kenya (Smyth: 130).

After the pilot program by Julian Huxley in 1929, the Colonial Office had agreed in principle that the cinematic medium was an invaluable tool for adult education and social development. Still, it would not commit itself financially to the implementation of its findings. Indeed, this lack of financial commitment by the Colonial Office towards the development of the colonies was the subject of several reports that were critical of British colonial administration, which appeared just before the outbreak of the war. The consensus was that the British government needed to spend more money on colonial development; hence the enactment of the Colonial Development and Welfare Act of 1940 (Smyth: 131-132). As a result of the Colonial Office's lack of financial commitment to instructional cinema, the ultimate credit for the actual institution of the practice of instructional cinema goes to the pioneer of the program, the International Missionary Council (IMC).

In 1932, the Department of Social and Industrial Research of the IMC sent a commission under the leadership of J. Merle Davis to Northern Rhodesia and the Belgian Congo to study the effects of the heavy industries of the Copper Belt upon African customs and life-style. Among the findings of the commission was that the rapid pace of industrialization in the region was undermining the social fabric of African society. One noted feature of this process was the widening gap between the outlooks and ways of life of urbanized Africans in contrast to those of the rural areas. Another finding was the lack of recreational facilities for urbanized Africans who were being cut off from their traditional forms of entertainment. As a result of their urbanized outlook, after their training in missionary or government schools, youths tended to live in a world that was quite bewildering to their elders in the villages. The commission recommended that the cinema should be used as a means of explaining to the elders the new world, which was rapidly advancing upon them as well as a means of providing entertainment to urban dwellers. Towards this end, in 1933, the Department of Social and Industrial Research of the IMC attempted to organize a research project dedicated to the production and exchange of cultural films on an international scale.

According to Merle Davis, on the advice of F.P. Keppel, President of the Carnegie Corporation of New York, the scope of the project was limited to the East African region with emphasis on motion pictures as a means of adult education. It was at this stage in the conception of the project that became known as Bantu Educational Cinema Experiment, that Major L.A. Notcutt (rtd) and G.C. Latham entered it (Davis, 1937: 9-13).

Before he was contacted, Major Notcutt, like some colonial government officials, e.g. William Sellers and A. Paterson, had, under the inspiration of the documentary film movement spearheaded by John Grierson at the Film Units of both the Empire Marketing Board (EMB), and the General Post Office (GPO), been experimenting with instructional films. In 1926, he was managing a group of sisal plantations in East Africa and, like many other planters, thought that an estate cinema might be an effective method of maintaining a contented labor force. Towards this end, he made a few films with Africans as actors and was surprised that they were well received. It then occurred to him that there might be commercial possibilities in the development of a native cinema. In 1930, he returned to England and spent some time studying film production. The idea of using the cinema as a means of instruction rather than commerce was inspired after reading Julian Huxley's *African View* — a report of his pilot program. In addition, a letter to *The Times* by Frank Melland, a former provincial commissioner in Northern Rhodesia, further encouraged Notcutt to look towards the direction of instructional cinema rather than commercial cinema. He worked out a scheme in rough details and discussed it with Melland, who encouraged him and linked him up with Merle Davis (Notcutt and Latham, 1937: 24).

In 1933, Notcutt received a letter from Davis asking for an estimate of the cost of a two-year experiment in the production of educational films for Africans. Subsequently, generous grants were made by the Carnegie Corporation of New York towards a project for experimenting in the production and exhibition of cultural, recreational, and educational films for Bantu people. This was how the Bantu Educational Cinema Experiment — precursor to the instructional cinematic practices of the CFU, the Film and Photo Bureau, and the C.C.C.A.C. — came into being. Other financial contributors to the project included the Roan Antelope Copper

Mines Ltd Rhokana Corporation Ltd, and Mufulira Copper Mines Ltd. The experiment was originally planned to last for two years but, when a professional cameraman was added to the staff in accordance with the expressed wish of the Colonial Office, it had to be scaled down. The project was conducted under the auspices of the Department of Social and Industrial Research of the International Missionary Council in conjunction with the Colonial Office and the British Film Institute. Frederick Luggard was appointed chairman of the Advisory Council of the project, which also included representatives of the principal British groups concerned with the welfare of the people of East Africa. Merle Davis was appointed director-general of the project and L.A. Notcutt as the field director, while G.C. Latham, a former director of Native Education in Northern Rhodesia, was appointed educational director. The aims and objectives of the project, as set out in the printed pamphlet issued on its launching, were to find out how best the cinema could be used for the following purposes:

(1) To help the adult African to understand and adapt himself to the new conditions which are invading and threatening to overwhelm him.

(2) To reinforce the ordinary methods of classroom and lecture hall.

(3) To conserve what is best in African traditions and culture by representing these in their proper setting as stages in racial development and as inheritance to be cherished with pride.

(4) To provide recreation and entertainment (Notcutt and Latham: 27-28).

Some of the films produced included Post Office Savings Bank, Tanga Travels, Tax, The Chief, The Hare and the Leopard, Food and Health, Hookworm, Ugandan Boys Scouts, and Infant Malaria. The most popular of these films, Post Office Savings Bank, treats the issue of home-kept savings and theft. The story tells of two plantation workers who return to their villages after receiving their pay. One buries his money in the floor of his hut and is seen doing so by a thief who watches through a crack in the wall. In the evening, the man and his wife go to a dance and the thief, noting their arrival there; sneaks back to the hut and steal the money. The next morning the man looks at the place where he buried his money and, on discovering that it has been stolen, raises an alarm and informs his neighbors of the theft. One of them informs him that a stranger was seen early in the morning on his way to a nearby township. The man sets off to the township with one of his neighbors who say he can identify the stranger. On arrival at the town, they meet his co-worker and the man tells him of the theft of his salary. His co-worker tells the man's neighbors how he guards his money from thieves and takes them to the Post Office where the workings of the Savings Bank are explained to them. On returning through the town, they see the thief outside an Indian shop buying a shirt; as soon as he sees them, he takes to his heels, thereby giving himself away. A Hollywood style chase scene then follows, after which he is apprehended and brought to justice. The film propagates the importance and safety of the Post Office Savings Bank. According to Notcutt and Latham, this film was shown more than seventy times, and was always one of the most popular films of the project (Notcutt and Latham: 31-34).

The Bantu Educational Cinema Experiment lasted from March 1935 to May 1937. Within this period, the team produced thirty-five films, which included nineteen on agriculture and six on health. A singular feature of the project was that the people who made the films also showed them throughout East and Central Africa. According to Rosaleen Smyth,

> they were taken by Latham on lorry tours throughout East and Central Africa to test audience reactions. In five months he traveled nine thousand miles and gave ninety screenings to more than eighty thousand people, most of whom had never seen a film before. (Smyth, 1983: 131)

The instructional cinema project faced a lot of criticisms because of the poor technical quality of the films. Latham had conceived an ambitious plan for a central organization in London with local production units in the colonies, a structure later adopted by the CFU in 1939, but the East African governments were opposed to the institutionalization of the Bantu Educational Cinema Experiment for financial reasons and also because they felt the technical quality of the films were poor. There were complaints of imperfect synchronization in the sound-on-disc technique adopted for the project. Latham, however, argued that given the limited finance available and the fact that instructional cinema was still at an experimental stage, one could not be too much of a technical purist. Northern Rhodesia (Zambia) was the only colony that favored the continuation of the project. It was more cinema conscious than other parts of black Africa because, as a result of the mine cinemas on the comparatively urbanized Copper Belt, it probably had the largest concentration of African cinemagoers outside of South Africa.

Part of the explanation given for the termination of the Bantu Educational Cinema Experiment was lack of financial commitment by the Colonial Office. Until the outbreak of the Second World War, the policy of the British government was that colonial governments should pay their own way. Colonial governments did not, however, particularly rate experimental instructional cinema as a top priority in the midst of more fundamental areas such as health, education and agriculture. As a result of the criticism of the financial policy of the British government to its colonies, the Colonial Development Welfare Act of 1940 was passed in Parliament. One of the positive results of the criticism of the British government's colonial stewardship was that the Colonial Marketing Board (CMB) managed to find £4,175 to pay the Strand Film Company to produce a propaganda film, *Men of Africa* (Alexander Shaw, 1939). This film adopted the instructional format of the Bantu Educational Cinema Experiment in its depiction of the role of colonial governments in the development of the colonies. Smyth has noted that "the case of *Men of Africa* demonstrates that it is easier to find money for films in defense of the empire, to counter criticism of British neglect of the colonies, than it was to find money for films as an aid in imperial development" (Smyth: 132).

This argument is further reinforced by the fact that, when money was found for the establishment of a Colonial Film Unit (CFU), it was in furtherance of British defense and war strategies rather than for educational purposes. As I noted earlier, when the Ministry of Information (MOI) established the CFU in 1939, to make and distribute war propaganda films in the colonies in aid of the British war efforts, there was already a fairly thriving tradition of government officials using films to propagate government policies. Beside earlier efforts such as those of Sellers and Paterson, the Bantu Educational Cinema Experiment had also further demonstrated the instructional and propaganda potentials of the medium. When the government decided to recruit staff for the take-off of the CFU, some veterans of instructional cinema such as

William Sellers — who was appointed producer of the CFU — were drafted into war propaganda efforts (Jones, 1948: 4-8; Pearson, 1948: 23-27). The war propaganda films, which the CFU was charged to produce, were meant to counter the German war propaganda machine which represented Britain as a decadent and rapidly dwindling world power with a slave empire ruthlessly exploited and cruelly repressed (Richards, 1983: 247; Mackenzie, 1984: 74-75). The CFU films were, therefore, meant to correct these views as well as inform Africans why the war was being prosecuted, and why they should support British war efforts.

To achieve its set objectives, William Sellers and George Pearson, respectively producer and artistic director of the CFU, developed a specialized type of filmmaking which they considered suitable for illiterate people: the films should be slow in pace, avoid trick photography, leave nothing to be inferred, and pay special attention to continuity, the basic assumption being that the comprehension of films is a gradually acquired skill rather than a natural talent. Stating the fundamental stylistic principles of the CFU productions, Pearson in a paper titled "The Making of Films for Illiterates in Africa," presented at the 1948 British Film Institute conference on "The Film in Colonial Development," argues as follows:

> we hold fast to two fundamental rules in our screencraft. First, to keep rigidly to those principles of education based on the laws of all human mental progress. In essence, that all acquired knowledge derives from experienced sensations, of which those of the eye are ever the strongest; that these myriad sensations are held in the memory, to form our thought material — our perceptions; that with these stored perceptions stimulated by imagination we can move to new mental comparisons and associations — our conceptions. From the known to the unknown. That is our constant touchstone in shaping pictorial choice and pictorial flow; realizing always that all *present* thinking depends on *past* experience; knowing always that our vital task is the arousing of the imagination that functions between past apprehension and present comprehension. (Pearson: 24)

Working from these fundamental stylistic assumptions, Pearson argues that the narrative style of modern cinema, with its brief scenes carrying the story forward, with all the time and space gaps covered by narrative conventions of mixes, wipes, montages, and fades, varying its scene form with dolly shots, pans, and more, confuse illiterate spectators. He recommends fades as the most appropriate narrative convention for indicating the passage of time, because the approach of darkness and dawn helps the illiterate spectator to understand the fade-out and fade-in as an indication of passage of time, of an ending or a new beginning. He also recommends the maintenance of visual continuity from scene to scene, and the avoidance of parallel montages, so that the attention of the spectator is not distracted. As he puts it, "It is all a matter of using the very simplest ways of explaining something with our pictures, in the same manner that a good teacher speaks with the simplest words to his pupil eager for understanding" (Pearson: 25). Ordinarily, it would seem the fundamental stylistic principles of instructional cinema are very well suited to the set objective of using the film as a pedagogical instrument for social development, but a close scrutiny of the views of contributors at the conference, many of whom cite these production stylistics as keys to their arguments, reveals that they often use them as an approving stamp for the need to develop an alternative film aesthetics for Africans because they are inferior beings incapable of distinguishing between facts and fictions. Most of the arguments are often anchored on the imagined negative impact of commercial cinema on Africans. Instructional cinema was, therefore, seen as a way of redressing the negative images of Europeans projected in commercial cinema and the negative impact they were imagined to be having on Africans. The idea was to use British and selected American instructional films to counter Hollywood images of Europeans (Jones, 1948: 4-8; Beale, 1948: 16-21).

The question is if Africans understand the narrative conventions of Hollywood productions, which after all established and canonized the narrative conventions of the cinema, why was it imagined that they would be confused when these same conventions are used in instructional films? In general, I do not see anything wrong with the production stylistics that Pearson has enumerated because I consider them suitable for the nature of film practice they were aimed at. However when considered in conjunction with the views of earlier practitioner of instructional cinema such as those of Notcutt and Latham, and new interpretations attached to them outside their original framework by people like Jones and Beale, one is much more inclined to believe, in common with other African scholars, that the production stylistics of instructional cinema were not inspired by the altruistic set objectives of humanistic instruction.

By 1944, the total number of films carrying the CFU's label was 115, although not all were actually produced by the CFU. The Colonial Office, which played only an advisory role in the activity of the CFU, objected to the narrow concentration on war propaganda films and lobbied successfully to have the CFU's work extended to include the production of instructional films. To this end, in 1942, as the CFU widened its scope, funds and staff were increased, although the Treasury insisted that the main activity of the CFU should continue to be the production of war propaganda films. During the war period however, the Colonial Office continued to plan ahead for the post-war era when it expected that the CFU would concentrate on the production of instructional films. In anticipation of a drive for mass education to be launched after the war, with funds to be provided under the Colonial Development and Welfare Act, ACEC produced the report, *Mass Education in African Society* (1944), which acknowledged the cinema as the most popular and powerful of all visual aids in mass education. The report further advised that documentary films should be used to broaden the outlook of rural dwellers and help them to adjust to changes in the political, economic and social conditions of their societies. The content of the report had much in common with the aims and objectives of the Bantu Education Cinema Experiment launched almost a decade earlier.

The war propaganda films can be classified into three categories: war information films, exhortation and goodwill films, and the projection-of-England films. Most of the war information films carried titles like, *This Is an Anti-Aircraft Gun* (Pearson, 1941) or *This Is a Barrage Balloon* (Pearson, 1941). Others were devoted to Africans fighting in the war, such as, *Pilot-Officer Peter Thomas, RAF* (Pearson, 1943), about a Nigerian who was the first African to qualify for a commission in the Royal Airforce. The majority of the war information films were geared towards explaining the mechanics of modern warfare. Others, such as, *Food from Oil Nuts* (Pearson, 1944) and *We Want Rubber* (Pearson, 1944), exhorted Africans to produce more rubber to help overcome the critical shortage of this commodity after the fall of Malaysia to the Japanese. On the other hand, films such as *Comfort from Uganda*

(Pearson, 1942) and *Katsina Tanks* (Pearson, 1943), were goodwill films made to show British appreciation for contributions made by the colonies towards the war efforts. The projection-of-England films, such as, *Mr English at Home* (Gordon Hales, 1940) and *A British Family in Peace and War* (Pearson, 1944), were films geared towards explaining English culture to Africans.

Towards the end of the war, as the clamor for independence grew louder in Africa, British colonial film policy was directed towards ensuring that the colonies stayed within the Commonwealth. The main objective was to persuade Africans that western democracy had more to offer them than communism. In this campaign, the weekly newsreel, *British News*, was considered invaluable, and news items were carefully selected for their informational, prestige and trade promotional values. Throughout the war years, the CFU produced only war propaganda films, and they were mostly all directed by the veteran filmmaker, George Pearson. After the war, the Central Office of Information (COI) replaced the MOI, and the CFU became a department of the COI under the controller of the Films Division. The COI had no policy making power; it was simply an agency whose function was to supply technical advice and facilities to ministerial departments. The Colonial Office formulated the film production policy of the CFU. Consequently, in keeping with its post-war plans of laying emphasis on instructional cinema, the Colonial Office instructed the CFU to develop infrastructures in the colonies for the production of instructional films. Lionel Snazelle directed most of the post-war instructional films. They included, *Toward True Democracy* (Snazelle, 1947), *Good Business* (Snazelle, 1947), which dealt with cocoa marketing co-operatives in Nigeria, *Village Development* (Snazelle, 1948), *Better Homes* (Snazelle, 1948), *Mixed Farming* (Snazelle, 1948), and *Animal Manure* (Rollo Gamble, 1950). As the titles indicate, most of the films were geared towards teaching Africans the importance of multi-party democracy, village planning and development, and modern methods of farming.

To facilitate easy exhibition of its films, the CFU established in each colony a Mobile Film Unit (MFU), which took these films on extensive exhibition tours of both rural and urban areas. The MFUs were first designed and operated in Nigeria before the system was extended to other British territories. The Central Office

of Information (COI) bulletin, in its accounts of the origin of
MFUs states that

> the first mobile cinemas — usually in improvised vans — were
> in use as long ago as 1929. It was in 1931 that the specially
> designed mobile cinema van was evolved in Nigeria, and since
> then the design has been steadily improved. Modern vehicles
> carry their own power-supply, are fitted for the projection of
> 16mm. films, silent or sound, and include film strip projectors,
> public address equipment and radio. The mobile cinema van is a
> many purpose vehicle, for according to the composition of its
> crew and program, it becomes a mobile health center, a
> veterinary center, or a school for a literacy or agricultural
> improvement campaign. (Central Office of Information (COI)
> Bulletin No. R. 3161, October, 1955)

Once the popularity of this form of free cinema was established,
itinerant salesmen began to exploit the system by setting up their
own MFUs to promote sales of their merchandise. The salesmen's
film exhibitions were often much more popular than those of the
government's MFUs because they showed mostly Hollywood
westerns while the MFUs showed mostly non-fictional
instructional films. However, through the combinatory efforts of
both groups, a thriving film culture was firmly established
throughout British colonial territories in Africa.

As the criticism of the British colonial government's
stewardship grew louder after the war, government propagandists
once more employed film — as they did earlier just before the
outbreak of the war, in the case of *Men of Africa* — to defend the
achievements of colonial rule. The product of this exercise was the
widely acclaimed £30,000 dramatized documentary, *Daybreak in Udi*
(Terry Bishop, 1948), which was produced by the Crown Film Unit
[a different government agency from the CFU] to demonstrate the
progress being made in the Udi division of Nigeria. *Daybreak in Udi*
is a classic example of an instructional film. It deals with the mass
mobilization undertaken by the people of the Udi division, under
the supervision of their District Commissioner, E.R. Chadwick,
who plays himself in the film, to develop the district. A detailed
analysis of this film is to be undertaken shortly. The film won the
1948 Academy Award for documentary film, and a British award
for documentary film in 1949 (Smyth: 141).

Beside this brief intervention by the Crown Film Unit, the main objectives of the CFU in the post-war years was the promotion of instructional film production in the colonies, whose governments, it hoped, would ultimately assume full financial and administrative responsibilities for the work in their respective territories. Toward this end, emphasis was placed on the decentralization and Africanization of the activities of the CFU. As part of this indigenization process, the CFU branch set up in Nigeria in 1945, was renamed the Federal Film Unit in 1946; the Central Film Unit was set up to serve Northern Rhodesia (Zambia), Southern Rhodesia (Zimbabwe) and Nyasaland (Malawi) in 1948; and the Gold Coast (Ghana) Film Unit was established in 1949. Altogether, between 1945 and 1950, the CFU established twelve film production units in eight countries in East and West Africa. The units were mandated to make films on subject matters suggested by local territorial governments and to train indigenous people in film production. To achieve this aim, a Film Training School was established in Accra, Ghana, in 1948. However, after the first six months, the Film Training School moved to Jamaica, and then back to London. By 1955, the CFU declared that it had fulfilled its goal of introducing instructional cinema to Africans. The CFU changed its name to the Overseas Film and Television Center, a place where Africans filmmakers, their counterparts from other former British colonies and other Third World filmmakers could buy film equipment and undertake post-production activities (COI Bulletin No. R. 3161, October 1955; Smyth: 138-140; Mgbejume, 1989: 38-39).

Instructional Cinema in the Belgian Congo

The activities of the Bantu Educational Cinema Experiment and the CFU inspired similar projects in the former Belgian Congo (Democratic Republic of the Congo), where the Belgian Ministry of Information established a Film and Photo Bureau in 1947, to produce films specifically for the Congolese. The Chief of the Film and Photo Bureau felt that just distributing films from Europe and the United States would not meet the need of providing Africans with their own cinema. The Bureau's project included the production of educational films for Africans as well as newsreels and documentaries about Africa for the Belgians. The films were shot with 16mm camera, and most of the post-production work, except for the laboratory processing of rushes, was done on the spot in the Belgian Congo. The Catholic Church in the territory, within this period, also became aware of the proselytization potentials of the cinema. Accordingly, it established a film production center called the Congolese Centre for Catholic Action Cinema (C.C.C.A.C.) and headed by Father Alexandre Van den Heuvel. Under the C.C.C.A.C., three major film production companies were established in the former Belgian Congo. Father Van den Heuvel was in charge of the Edisco-Films in Leopoldville (Kinshasa); Father Van Haelst managed Luluafilm Production Company in Luluabourg (Kanaga), in the western Kasai region; while Father De Vloo headed Africa Films in Bukavu and Kivu. The most popular instructional film produced by the C.C.C.A.C. was a series of animated colour cartoons called *Les Palabres de Mboloko*, directed by Father Van den Heuvel. In 1960, when Zaire became independent, both the C.C.C.A.C. and the Film and Photo Bureau stopped their African film production activities (Diawara, 1992: 2-11).

Critiques of Colonial African Instructional Cinema

Many African film scholars such as Kehinde Vaughan (1957: 218), Hyginus Ekwuazi (1987: 2-11), Onyero Mgbejume (1989: 1-16), and Manthia Diawara (1986, 1992: 2-11), have criticised the philosophy or general reasoning behind the institution of instructional cinema, especially as articulated by its practitioners. For instance, in their published report of the Bantu Educational Cinema Experiment, Notcutt and Latham gave the following reasons for the introduction of instructional cinema in Africa:

> yet surely reflection will convince any unprejudiced person that, with backward peoples unable to distinguish between truth and falsehood, it is surely our wisdom, if not our obvious duty, to prevent, so far as is possible, the dissemination of wrong ideas. Should we stand by and see a distorted presentation of the white races accepted by millions of Africans when we have it in our power to show them the truth? There is much that is silly and sordid in the life of the West, but white people have other interests than money-making, gambling, crime and the pursuit of other people's wives and husbands. (Notcutt and Latham: 22-23)

As earlier noted, most African scholars have criticized the general reasoning behind the institution of instructional cinema in Africa, either by citing the above views of Notcutt and Latham or similar views expressed by other practitioners, to argue that the whole project of instructional cinema was motivated more by paternalistic attitude than by genuine altruism. For instance, other practitioners of instructional cinema such as William Sellers and George Pearson, producer and director respectively of the CFU, reasoned that Africans needed a specialized, simplistic, kind of filmmaking that is slow in pace, and avoids trick photography. Van Bever, head of the Film and Photo Bureau in the Belgian Congo, also argued along similar lines when he stated: "for the great majority of Africans it would be necessary to film with a special technique. We must, therefore, make, ourselves, the largest share of films destined for Africans" (cited in Diawara, 1992: 13).

But while the practitioners reasoned that Africans were incapable of distinguishing between "truth and falsehood," and that they needed a special simplified cinema, Africans themselves, with their wealth of storytelling traditions, were giving their verdict on instructional cinema by showing preference for commercial entertainment films whose stock in trade is the peddling of what Biodun Jeyifo elsewhere refers to as "the truthful lie" (Jeyifo, 1985). Indeed, a cursory look at the few instructional films that were popular — such as *The Post Office Savings Bank*, *Les Palabres de Mboloko*, and *The Boy Kumasenu* — would reveal that they lean more towards feature films than to documentary. Furthermore, in 1958, Sellers himself, told a conference in Brussels on the cinema in sub-Saharan Africa that although the CFU's films were of technical and pictorial quality, many aroused little emotional interest among rural audiences. He recommended that more feature films with African subjects, directed by Africans themselves should be encouraged (Smyth: 138). A year earlier, in 1957, Kehinde Vaughan had similarly attested to the unpopularity of instructional cinema and its special simplified narrative techniques when he argued that

> Africans film audiences, daily growing larger, when faced with the choice of seeing the "simplified screen narratives" produced by the "Colonial Film Unit" and the foreign "commercial entertainment film" have overwhelming decided in favor of the latter products in spite of their "complicated technical conventions." In African towns like Freetown, Accra, Kumasi,

Lagos or Nairobi, Charles Chaplin and many popular stars of the screen are already household names. (Vaughan, 1957: 218)

Manthia Diawara, in a recent assessment of the instructional cinematic practices of the Bantu Educational Cinema Experiment and the CFU, also drew the conclusion that the whole enterprise was driven by paternalistic attitude rather than by altruistic aspirations. In his opinion,

> the Bantu Cinema Experiment and the Colonial Film Unit were in many ways paternalistic and racist. They wanted to turn back film history and develop a different type of cinema for Africans because they considered the African mind too primitive to follow the sophisticated narrative techniques of mainstream cinema. Thus they thought it necessary to return to the beginning of the film history — to use uncut scenes, slow down the story's pace, make the narrative simpler by using fewer actors and adhering to just one dominant theme. The ideology of these units denied that the colonized peoples had elementary human qualities. (Diawara: 4)

Though I agree with these African scholars with respect to qualifying the views of the practitioners of instructional cinema as paternalistic, I should like to argue that these views should be distinguished from both the stated aims and objectives of instructional cinema and from the films themselves. The stated aims and objectives were to teach Africans modern methods of social development, hence the emphasis on film as a teaching aid, on modern medicine, modern methods of farming, banking, village and urban planning for hygienic purposes, and co-operative societies. The films do not represent Africans as lacking knowledge of these things; they merely posit them as doing things in the old and traditional ways. As an analysis of *Men of Africa* and *Daybreak in Udi* can demonstrate, instructional cinema posits Africans textually as human beings capable of acquiring knowledge to improve themselves and as enthusiastic about acquiring any knowledge that will help them increase the pace of development in their various communities.

The representation of African subjectivities in instructional cinema as knowing and knowledgeable beings, as people with independent mind of their own capable of making decisions about what they want and, most importantly, as people capable of acquiring knowledge to improve themselves is antithetical to the practice of colonialist African cinema which represents Africans by drawing analogies between them and animals, either showing them as people who are bestial in behavior or as people incapable of social development. As a result of the progressive manner in which Africans are posited in instructional cinema, the practice needs to be distinguished from colonialist African cinema. However, the line between instruction and propaganda is, indeed, very thin with respect to these category of films. The reason for this can be traced more to the political atmosphere within which they were produced and how they were perceived by people both in the colonies and in the metropolis than in the nature of the representation. Most of the films were produced, as noted earlier, in the heat of post-war criticism of British colonial stewardship. In the colonies, the post-war period was marked by intense demand for independence. These demands, rather than being accepted as an indication of a growing wish for self-rule, were often interpreted as sign of dissatisfaction with the level of development within the colonies. The period therefore witnessed the initiation of various development projects, many having to do with the building of infrastructures, schools, hospitals and the development of the agricultural sector of the economy. In pursuing these development projects, cinema was perceived as a facilitator, a means of orienting and demonstrating to the people within the colonies, a new and modern way of doing things. The proceedings of the 1948 conference on the cinema and colonial development clearly demonstrate that colonial governments saw cinema as an aid to the propagation of developmental projects such as health and environmental sanitation programs, agricultural extension services and public information network. Even before this time, the production of colonialist African films such as *Sanders of the River*, *Song of Freedom*, *King Solomon's Mines* and *She*, was already going on in the colonies and, because of the images projected in these films, there was a growing hostility to the way the cinema was being used, in general, in the colonies. For instance, in his response to the release of *Sanders of the River*, Nnamdi Azikiwe, one of the nationalist politicians of the day, noted that

> whoever sees this picture will be shocked at the exaggeration of African mentality, so far as superstitious beliefs are concerned, not to speak of the knavery and chicanery of some African chiefs. I feel that what is being paraded in the world today as art

or literature is nothing short of propaganda. (Azikiwe, 1968: 153-154)

Similar views were often extended to instructional cinema for different reasons. Many of the critics earlier cited used the paternalistic views of the producers of instructional cinema to judge the films. To them, it is not so much a question of the very nature and purpose of the films themselves as of the views of their producers. Using these views, they condemn the narrative styles in these films as simplistic. But when one takes a closer looks at films like *Men of Africa* and *Daybreak in Udi*, as examples of colonial African instructional cinema, one finds that they are not more simplistic in narrative than most films of the period. Besides, the purpose for which they were made is often overlooked. Others considered them uninteresting because of the emphasis on documentary practice. They would have preferred striking a balance between fictional narratives and documentary films. To the emergent political elites, on the other hand, little distinction was made between these films and the commercial ones. While they were condemned for their negative representation of Africa, the instructional films were either treated as continuing the practice of colonialist African cinema or as colonial government propaganda.

The lack of distinction between colonial African instructional cinema and colonialist African cinema which one finds in the works of most historians and critics of African cinema, is a product of several factors: the politics of interpretation of both colonial governments' intentions and the views of the practitioners of instructional cinema, on the one hand, and of the vexatious practice of colonialist African cinema on the other. While colonial governments considered the CFU productions as instructional films, the emergent political elite of the time as well as most post-colonial African film historians considered them as propaganda pieces. Certainly, most of these films would have been packaged for the metropolis as informational/instructional works showing the role of the British colonial governments in the development of the colonies. But taking cognizance of the criticism preceding the enactment of the Colonial Development and Welfare Act of 1940 and the subsequent institution of the practice of instructional cinema, it is difficult to draw a strict line between propaganda and instruction in these films. If I am considering them here strictly as instructional films, it is because I am much more concerned with the nature and purpose of these films, with respect to the representation of African subjectivity and culture, than with the politics underlining their production. In the remaining part of this chapter, a critical reading of *Men of Africa* and *Daybreak in Udi*, is to be carried out. Though the two films were addressed specifically to British spectators, as evidence of the British colonial government's commitment to the development of its African colonies, *Daybreak in Udi* was widely shown in Nigeria as an instructional film in aid of community self-help development and a copy of the film is at the University of Ibadan Audio Visual Center.

A Critical Reading of Men of Africa and Daybreak in Udi

A Critical Reading of Men of Africa

Men of Africa (Alexander Shaw, 1939) is an instructional film produced by the Strand Film Company for the Empire Marketing Board (EMB), just before the outbreak of the Second World War, to demonstrate the role of British colonial rule in the development of the British East African territories of Kenya, Uganda and the mandated territory of Tanganyika. The film uses a lot of materials from archival holdings on various parts of the British Empire, as well as actual location shooting, to show the role of colonial rule in the development of the colonies, with special emphasis on colonial development in East Africa. There are eleven main sequences in the film, with scenes dealing with various phases and institutions of British colonial administration. Essentially, the film is structured around the theme of development and British agencies responsible for the development of the colonies. *Men of Africa* is a loosely structured film with its disparate sequences focusing on either a British colonial government agency responsible for development in the colonies or various phases of development, united by the theme of development. The film uses a combination of voice-over narration and illustrative spatial representation to reinforce what is being shown. As the narrator gives verbal descriptions or information about a government development agency or aspect of development projects, shots of scenes related to what is being said are shown to reinforce it. However, the film is not focused on individual subjects but on aspects and institutions of colonial development. In representing the scenarios of development, the contributions of Africans and British colonial administrators to the development of the region under focus are foregrounded. In this respect, one can make general judgements regarding the nature of African subjectivity projected in the film. In reading the film, I will pay particular attention to narrative details within each sequence with a view to analyzing the image of African subjectivity and culture that emerges in the sequence and the relevance of this to the overall theme of development in the film.

The first sequence is an introductory exposé on the range and magnitude of the British Empire. It begins with an animated map of the world with arrows indicating the locations of British colonies around the world. A voice-over narrator (Leslie Mitchell) informs us that the British Colonial Empire is made up of two million, five hundred thousand square miles, and that it stretches from the Antarctic to the Tropics, with dependencies in every continent and every ocean. We are further told that the people of Britain are directly responsible for the well being of the colonies, and that there are about sixteen million people in them, made up of men, women, and children of every race, color and creed, with a hundred different languages and hundreds of different cultures and ways of living. We are also told that to try and develop this large empire is not an easy task. At this point, scenes from various parts of the empire are used to illustrate the range of the empire, its peoples and cultures, physical geography, and state of development.

This exposé begins in the Far East with a long shot of a street scene in Hong Kong. Several other scenes, all dealing with the cosmopolitan nature of the colony, then follows. Next, there is a cut to several scenes from the Fiji Islands, Malaysia and Ceylon, all dealing with aspects of development, geographical outlook, culture, and occupation. From the Far Eastern colonies, the film shifts to Africa, which, the narrator tells us, is the home of more primitive people. To illustrate this primitivism, a scene of two brawny men paddling a canoe is shown. But since scenes from Ceylon and the Fiji Islands do not include any evidence of the sort of modern development associated with Hong Kong or Malaysia, and since they were not for this reason qualified as primitive people, the primitivism associated with Africa in this instance can only be read as product of the already existing historical practice in colonialist African discourse, in qualifying anything African as primitive and savage. From Africa, the film switches to the Mediterranean, and the narrator tells us that Jews and Arabs dispute tiny Palestine. This information is accompanied by a short pan of an open country scene to illustrate the aridity of the land in disputation. Next, the narrator takes us to Gibraltar and Malta, which, we are told, are homes to British Naval bases that guard the shortest route to the Far East. Three scenes are used to illustrate the importance of these territories. The first begins with a long shot of a cliff overlooking the sea, followed by a cut to the deck of a frigate with its mounted guns and lastly a long shot of a war ship on flag parade. From the Mediterranean, the narrator takes us to the Caribbean Islands of Bermuda and Bahamas. Women carrying bunches of bananas from the plantation illustrate this region. This is followed by a cut to mainland South America, where the focus is on the British territories of Honduras and Guyana. Images of Caribbean women selling bananas, oranges, and pineapples, in huge baskets, in a market scene, followed by typical street scenes with donkey-drawn carts, illustrate this region.

While the first sequence is a general introductory exposé on the range and magnitude of the empire, the second, third and fourth sequences, focus on the role of British institutions like the Colonial Office, the Imperial Institute, and the Imperial College of Tropical Agriculture in Trinidad, in the administration of the empire. In the second sequence, for instance, the narrator tells us that the Colonial Office controls the colonies. This information is accompanied by a downward crane shot of the massive Colonial Office building, resting on the wall plaque "Colonial Office." Next, the narrator tells us that it is here that major decisions affecting the empire are taken. A cut from the wall plaque is followed by an interior long shot of the office corridors, followed by a cut to individual offices and officers. Next, there is a cut to a close-up of a map of West Africa, followed by an establishing shot of the West African desk, and a close-up of file covers on the desk, the first of which deals with general medical matters. Scenes showing the nature of interior office arrangements within the Colonial Office are followed by an introduction to standard procedures in colonial administration: a member of Parliament phones to ask the Secretary of State for the Colonies whether he is satisfied with the standard of nutrition of the people of the British West African territories. In answer to this question, there is a cut to an establishing shot of a village scene in West Africa. This is followed by a cut to a long shot of a clustered rundown street filled with mud huts and children. Next, there is a cut to a close-up of two boys lying on a huge rock smiling, their plump faces indicating good nourishment. As the parliamentarian and the Secretary of State exchange views, the alternation of the scenes continues. The close-up of the two well-nourished boys is followed by a cut to a pan of a field with grazing cattle and an establishing shot of a women's adult literacy/cooking class held in the open air. Towards the end of the sequence, the narrator picks up the narration by informing us that a special committee advises on grants and money for development and research in all parts of the empire. This summarizing statement resting on research and development is used to introduce the role of the Imperial Institute in colonial development. But already, within what is shown in the scenes from West Africa, the developmental and instructional emphasis of the film can be noted, especially in the women adult literacy/cooking class. This developmental emphasis is to be fully exploited later in the film.

The next sequence focuses on the role of the Imperial Institute in colonial development. It begins with the narrator informing us that the Imperial Institute helps the colonies to improve the quality of their exports. This information is accompanied by a downward crane shot of the Imperial Institute building, followed by a cut to a scientist working in a laboratory and another cut to a harbor scene with a docking ship. We are told by the narrator that the man is working on the best sort of paper which can be produced from Malayan wood, and that the ship in the harbor is the *Discovery II*, a research vessel. Furthermore, that it is the world's best-equipped research vessel, and that it has just returned from a voyage around the Antarctic ice cap with information on how to help the whaling industry. The information on the research vessel is followed by a cut to the London School of Hygiene and Tropical Medicine, part of the Imperial Institute. The focus on the School of Hygiene and Tropical Medicine begins with a short pan of the building complex, followed by a cut to busy office scenes with research officials. This is accompanied by the narrator informing us that the Bureau of Tropical Hygiene collects reports from all over the world, attends to them and formulates policies related to the development of the colonies, and that the work of one scientist or doctor in one part of the tropics in the empire comes quickly to his fellow research-worker in other parts through the services of the Bureau of Tropical Hygiene. This information is illustrated by a cut from the scientists at the Bureau to an out-station in Entebbe, Uganda. We are told that research stations on the spot such as that at Entebbe regularly send samples of tsetse fly pupas by airmail from Africa to the Wellcome Institute so that long range experiments can be carried out on the control of tsetse fly and the disease it carries, sleeping sickness. This bit of information is illustrated by shots of research workers packaging pupas, stamping the packages, and loading them into mail vans. This is followed by a cut to the Wellcome Institute in London. The cut to the scientists at the Wellcome Institute ends the sequence on the role of the Imperial Institute in colonial development. What is of importance in this sequence is that we are shown young African scientists and research assistants working in cooperation with other scientists from other parts of the empire in scientific and development oriented projects. This image stands in contrast to that projected in the opening sequence where we are told that Africa is the continent of more primitive people. Far from sustaining the earlier image of primitivism, what we are being introduced to here is the discourse of progress and development which the earlier statement denies. For instance, the image that stands out in the scenes relating research activities at Entebbe is that which projects Africa as a developing continent and Africans, like people from other colonized continents, as people struggling to contribute to the development of their communities. It is this progress and development oriented discourse that colonialist African discourse also seeks to deny when it projects the image of Africa as a continent of primitive and savage people. Even though *Men of Africa* occasionally slips into colonialist discourse as the opening sequence shows, it is never sustained probably because of its development and progress oriented discourse.

The next sequence, which deals with the contributions to colonial development of the Imperial College of Tropical Agriculture in Trinidad, begins with a long aerial shot of tropical vegetation, followed by a cut to birds flying and another of two men wearing matted coconut leaf hats looking at a coconut tree. These opening shots are followed by the narrator informing us that Trinidad, with its tropical climate and typical conditions, made

Britain establish the Imperial College of Tropical Agriculture there to carry out research into problems of plant diseases and soil fertility. The cut from the medium shot of the two men looking at the coconut tree is followed by an establishing shot of the college compound. Next, there is a cut to a medium shot of a group of British students cutting and examining cocoa buds, and to a lone student using pins to note on a map of the world places where samples are taken. As these activities are going on, the narrator informs us that these workers are students from all over the empire, and that they are receiving practical training which will help them provide solutions to agricultural problems in their territories. This information is followed by a cut to a group of students in a tobacco farm, some examining the tobacco leaves, others resting. Next, there is a cut to an establishing shot of a classroom scene with a teacher writing on the blackboard, followed by a close-up of the teacher and the blackboard. The narrator intervenes by informing us that training is a vital factor in Britain's plan for the colonies, and that emphasis is placed on agriculture, hygiene, medicine, and teaching; furthermore, the success of Britain's colonial policies depends finally on the men and women administrators, doctors, agricultural officers and teachers executing the policies. Next, there is cut from the teacher, followed by a pan of the classroom, leading to a laboratory scene showing another group of students carrying out laboratory tests. The sequence ends with the transition of the pan to a dolly into the laboratory, accompanied by a flurry of uplifting atmospheric music.

After these three sequences dedicated to highlighting the activities of British institutions responsible for the administration of the empire, the narrative switches to a case study of colonial development in East Africa. At the level of narration, this switch is effected by a cut to the opening animated map of the world with arrows showing the location of British colonies, ending with a zoom into the East African countries of Kenya, Uganda and the mandated territory of Tanganyika. This focus is followed by the narrator informing us that British East Africa is made up of the Kenyan colony, the mandated territory of Tanganyika and the protectorate of Uganda, an area of 700,000 square miles with a population of 12 million Africans. This information is followed by an opening long pan of the Kenyan countryside, accompanied by traditional xylophone music, to indicate the Africanness of the environment. The long pan ends by revealing Masai cattle rearers tending their cattle in open country. Next, there is a cut to a medium shot of an elderly Masai man, followed by a long shot of the men and their cattle, and a medium shot of them. A cut from the Masai and their cattles is followed by a pan of open grassland. The narrator informs us amidst these camera movements that the Kenyans are a people who live by the soil, that some tribes such as the Macamba and the Masai herd their cattle on the plains, while others such as the Luo and the Kikuyu are farmers. This is accompanied by a cut from the open grassland to a medium shot of a woman and a young girl, possibly a mother and her daughter, weeding on a farm. Next, there is a cut from the farm to an establishing shot of a market scene, and a pan of men sitting in the shades of trees within the market and whiling away their time. The pan ends the scene with women selling fresh milk. The opening scenes of this sequence introduce spectator to the geographical outlook, ethnic configuration and the main occupations of people of this region.

Next, the narrator informs us that this simple life under the harsh African sky was once a life of fear and uncertainty and that hostile tribes ravaged their neighbor's villages and cattle. This is illustrated by a cut to a close-up of a night campfire, and an establishing shot of a group of Masai warriors gathered together around the campfire in preparation for an inter-tribal war. First, the spectator is introduced to the various ritual preparatory dances that precede such raids. In terms of narration, this historical retrospect begins with a cut to a close-up of the fire, another close-up of the stamping feet of the warriors in a war dance, a medium shot of their swaying torsos, and a close-up pan along their faces. From the pan, the camera switches to a long shot of several rows of dancing warriors, back to a close-up of their faces, and a close-up punctuation of an individual warrior's face. These elaborate camera movements climax with a medium shot of the side view of a single file of warriors dancing in a jumping formation, facing first the left-hand side of the screen, followed by the right-hand side. These dance movements, accompanied by humming and stamping of feet, with an occasional cut to the fire, metaphorically signify the stoking of the flame of inter-tribal warfare. The use of medium close-ups and close-ups in this sequence, and similar ones in other sequences, are not intended as aspects of character detailing and development or character accessibility. They are used here as forms of spatial illustration of narrative action, specifically the Masai ritual war dance.

The fade is followed by a long shot of a scene of a group of women carrying firewood on their backs with belts strapped to their heads and returning from farming. This is followed by a cut to a short pan of the women, and a long shot of cattle entering a compound with several mud huts. This is a typical Masai village. The long shot is followed by a brief pan of the roofs of the huts made of banana leaves, and a medium shot of a lone, desolate woman, sitting on the bare ground in front of a hut with a hen clucking behind her. The narrator informs us that British rule has brought peace but that there is still a long battle to be fought against poverty, ignorance and disease. Furthermore, that the squalor of the villages and the lack of proper food still make their communities easy victims to the diseases of the tropics. These, we are told, are the problems Britain is trying to solve in East Africa. The squalor of the Masai village, signified by the rotting banana leaf roofed huts and the lone desolate woman sitting on the bare ground in front of a hut, is followed by a brief pan of a model village in construction. The roofs of the new village are constructed first, with tightly matted branches of trees, and then plastered with mud. This scene also ends the fifth sequence, which deals with British colonial development efforts at the village level. The historical retrospective nature of this sequence can be considered a form of narrative flashback aimed at propagating the necessity for the present British colonial rule — which is represented through the current construction of the model village — as the main force behind peace among the hitherto warring ethnic groups and the new methods of village planning and development.

From village development efforts, the narrative switches focus to urban planning and development, with the narrator informing us that in these lands, there are so many changes to be made, that much can be achieved by money and the initiative of the white man. Rivers are already being harvested to bring electricity to urban areas, and harbors and docks are already being built in Mombasa to open up the town. We are also told that elsewhere in the country, bridges, new roads and railways are being built to open up districts long cut off from the rest of the country. The sequence on urban development begins with a pan of a building site with several rows of partially completed modern flats. This is followed by a cut to a long shot of a power station, a medium shot of a sub-transmitting station, an establishing shot of a harbor scene with several ocean liners, a medium shot of a car entering a bridge and a long shot of the bridge. All these scenes illustrate ongoing phases of development. From urban development, the narrative switches to health care services with the narrator observing that a good medical service is essential for development, that medical services at urban hospitals and village dispensaries have been steadily expanding and that minor injuries are treated in out-patient departments by native dressers, while serious ones are handled by well equipped hospitals. We are further told that as a result of the success in health care, the fear and suspicion of the modern European health services is rapidly breaking down.

The sequence on health care services begins with a focus on a village dispensary. The opening scene begins with a medium shot of a male village dispenser coming out of a dispensary. This is followed by a cut to a pan of a group of patients, mostly men, sitting on benches in front of the dispensary. The dispenser calls a boy who is at the front of the queue into the consulting/treatment room. As they move in, there is a cut to a hospital scene. This opens with shots of a consulting room, a ward full of patients in bed, and several other patients outside in beds, in the shade of tree. This is followed by a shot of the exterior of a maternity ward, with several mothers, their babies, and expectant mothers sitting on the lawn in front of it, waiting for treatment. The voice-over narration informs us that the testimonies of mothers who use medical services like those offered by hospitals have been helpful in dispelling suspicion about modern health care; that in Kenya, one in every twenty-four women have their babies in hospitals; and in the Kiambu district where the hospital in focus is, the figure is as high as one in every five women. This information is followed by a cut from the women sitting in front of the hospital to a nurse carrying a newly born baby, a group of little children playing within the hospital ground and a close-up of a child excreting into a potty. What is interesting in both sequences is that, as in the earlier ones, we find educated Africans, including engineers, doctors, nurses, and pharmacists, at work, contributing to the development of their communities, and the image that comes out of such scenarios is that of a dynamic society with a progressive outlook.

From the health sector, the film switches to environmental sanitation programs with emphasis on insect borne diseases. This begins with the narrator informing us that the anopheles, the malaria mosquito, enemy of health and progress in Africa, is at last meeting defeat at the hands of modern science because health departments collect the larvae of mosquitoes from their breeding spaces for laboratory study and breeding lands are sprayed with paraffin and heavy oil which destroys the mosquito larvae before they hatch. This information is illustrated with shots of mosquito specimens in cages, a man collecting larvae from a pool and a laboratory attendant labeling the specimens for post. This is followed by a cut to two men, with spraying equipment strapped to their backs, and spraying stagnant pools of water. We are further told that mosquitoes have made large areas of rich lands uninhabitable, and that at Kisumu, the Papara swamps are being reclaimed. This is followed by an establishing shot of the Papara swamps, and a series of medium shots of half-naked workmen cutting into the roots of the swamp shoots, upturning them and dragging them to high ground. Others then fill the muddy waters with rocks. From the mosquito menace, the focus switches to the tsetse fly and sleeping sickness, with the narrator informing us that the tsetse fly, the insect responsible for the spread of sleeping sickness, infects nearly the whole of tropical Africa, and that it kills the cattle upon which many tribes depend for their living, besides spreading the deadly disease among the population. We are told that two-third of Tanganyika cannot be inhabited because of the tsetse fly but that scientists are already studying its habits and movements in order to find ways of controlling its spread. This information is followed by a pan of a tsetse fly infested forest, followed by a close-up of a tsetse fly perching on a white man's arm. There is a cut to a group of white scientists and their African assistants collecting specimens with hand-held loop nets. As these activities are going on, the narrator informs us that there are twenty-one varieties of tsetse fly in East Africa and that each is given a detail study. Furthermore, in twenty-six years, sleeping sickness has almost been wiped out in British East Africa. This is followed by a cut to an inoculation scene, a long shot of a group of people arriving in canoes for medical inspection and inoculation, and a group of women and children sitting in a field waiting to be inoculated. The narrator informs us that these people are the

Bagandas of Uganda who have been summoned by their chief to one of the frequent medical inspections, that most Africans suffer from malnutrition, and that, sometimes, they either do not have enough food, lack the right type of food, or do not properly eat the food they have. As a result, we are told that many Africans are not strong enough to resist diseases and that malnutrition is a basic problem to all doctors in Africa. The sequence on health and medical care ends with a group of children being registered, inspected, and inoculated.

The eighth sequence focuses on modern methods of farming and marketing of farm produce. The government officials whose activities are highlighted in this sequence include veterinary officers and agricultural extension workers/officers. The sequence begins with a brief pan of a demonstration farm with several farmers and agricultural officers. This is accompanied by the narrator informing us that the farmers are being taught how to manure their crops, engage in mixed cropping, live stock and cash crop farms. In addition, that they are also encouraged to form farmer's cooperatives through which they can market their farm produce at better bargains. This information is followed by a medium shot of weighing tables for graded coffee, and an establishing shot of a market scene with cuts into medium close-ups to show various grades and types of potatoes on display. Next, the narrator informs the spectator that Masai cattle owners are taught modern ways of drying their hides and skins, and that they are also encouraged to inoculate their herds of cattle as well as taught to shift their cattle from one grazing ground to another more often, to combat the problem of over-grazed lands. To illustrate this point, scenes of cattle inoculation are intercut with those of cattle dipping and an over-grazed land. The problem of soil erosion and how it is being tackled is also highlighted. The sequence ends with a long shot of cattle grazing in a field, followed by a cut to a medium shot of the same scene.

The ninth sequence focuses on the contributions of colonial educational institutions to the development of the British East African territories. The sequence, which begins with a shot of school children learning in the shade of a tree, is accompanied by traditional African xylophone music. A slow pan of the scene reveals several sets of classes being taught by black female teachers under the supervision of a white missionary headmistress. This is followed by cuts to other scenes with children reading and writing or singing happily to express the joy of learning, and children being taught how to bathe themselves properly. At this point, the narrator intervenes by observing that education must be related to the practical needs of Africa, that at Makerere College — then a college of the University of London — doctors, engineers, teachers, and nurses are undergoing training, and that they will be leaders of the new Africa, combining the best in their tradition with that of the West. This information is illustrated with a campus scene at Makerere College, intercut with a broadcast by the Secretary of State for the Colonies, in which he proclaims that a new world is coming into being in Africa. This proclamation is followed by scenes of construction sites, followed by Africans working in a railway workshop. At this point, the narrator intervenes to inform us that the railway workshop technicians in Nairobi are as skilled as their counterparts anywhere in the world. A cut from the technicians is followed by a long shot of a railway locomotive engine traveling by pulleys to the repair workshop, and a medium shot of a technician welding part of an engine. The sequence ends with a cut to an establishing shot of a football match between two secondary schools, and cuts to boy scouts keeping order at the match ground.

The tenth sequence focuses attention on the development of democratic institutions in colonial East Africa. It begins with the narrator informing us that the role of democracy in social development is being emphasized, and that, to this end, there has been delegation of authority to the heads of local tribes. This information is accompanied by a cut to a shot of a traditional council in session, with a district officer in attendance. Scenes of tax collectors performing their duties, and of a native court in session, then follow. The narrator informs us that the Lukikos of Uganda have even formed their own local Parliament with an elected Speaker. As illustration, scenes of Lukiko parliamentarians wearing jackets over traditional outfits of wrapper, with top hats and walking sticks to match, on their way to parliament, are intercut with scenes of the local Parliament in session, and the British parliament in session in London upon which it is structured. Also highlighted in this sequence is the role of the modern communication system in the transmission of information.

The film climaxes in the eleventh sequence with a focus on an Empire Day celebration with a huge fair where various departments of government exhibit and demonstrate models of their services. The celebration, which is attended by the resident governor of the territory, begins with parades by a detachment of the local constabulary, traditional dances by colorfully dressed women, and parades by school children with the governor taking the salute. On display at the fair are model huts and houses, demonstrations of how to build them, a model bed with fitted mosquito nets, soil erosion and control methods, and a demonstration of the importance of vegetables to a balanced diet, nutrition problems and their solutions. Each of the departments has assistants soliciting the attention of spectators and demonstrating their services. This climactic sequence therefore summarizes in microcosm the various services rendered by the British colonial government in East Africa. The film ends with a cut from the Empire Day fair to a pan of a tropical forest, followed by open fields and farms. The narrator summarizes the events by stating that the drive for change and modern development should be matched by a preservation of the good ways of old Africa.

Of great interest to me in this film is the balanced and objective way in which African subjectivity is constructed textually. At the time the film was made, a lot of developmental programs had already been initiated in various parts of the continent. These include the establishment of primary, secondary, vocational and tertiary institutions. The building of modern infrastructures such as roads, railway, airports, and harbors, were also in progress in various parts of the continent. The film acknowledges all these ongoing developmental programs in the region on which it focuses. The foregrounding of this sort of progress or development oriented discourse is one of the elements which distinguishes colonial African instructional cinema from colonialist African cinema. The other is the constitution of African subjectivity as knowing and knowledgeable beings capable of self-initiative and self-development. In *Men of Africa*, Africans are not merely positioned as objects of ethnographic and visual interest; they are positioned as conscious agents and subjects in action, contributing to the development of their communities. This kind of development and progress-oriented discourse is suppressed in films of colonialist African cinema. When one watches films like *Sanders of the River*, *King Solomon's Mines*, *Song of Freedeom*, and *She*, the impression one gets is that there were no ongoing develop projects at the time they were made, save the business of exploration and colonial conquest. But as a matter of fact, the business of colonial conquest had been concluded more than three decades earlier. The denial of development which one notices in colonialist African cinema is therefore both an exercise in the legitimization of colonial authority as well as the legacy of an already existing canon of colonialist discourse. It is as if to say that to represent a progressive outlook of Africans is to acknowledge their humanity. This is where films of colonial African instructional cinema are different. Though in the opening sequence of *Men of Africa* we are informed by the voice-over narrator that Africa is a continent of more primitive people, the overall picture of Africa and Africans that comes across in the film itself is one of a developing continent and of a progressive people contributing to the development of their society. In the third sequence of the film, for instance, this progressive outlook is highlighted during the focus on the activities of the Imperial Institute. In one of the scenes, a cut from British scientists working at the Bureau of Tropical Hygiene in London is followed by that of African research assistants working in a research out-station in Entebbe. In addition, from the fifth sequence onwards, when the film shifts its focus to East Africa, there is a gradual build up of a picture of a society in transition from traditionality to modernity, with Africans effectively positioned as agents of development. Though the point is made that African agricultural extension workers, veterinary officers, teachers, medical doctors, nurses and engineers, were trained by British educators and institutions, in the performance of their duties, British colonial officers are sparingly referred to in the execution of their duties.

The model Masai village is built by African workers, the spraying of the mosquito breeding stagnant pools is carried out by them, and the railway workshop technicians of Nairobi whom we are told are as skilled as their counterparts anywhere in the world are all Africans working alone without a British supervisor. There are African doctors, nurses, and teachers, either working alone or under the supervision of their superior British officers. Most importantly, the role of education in colonial development is greatly emphasized in the film. We encounter scenes of primary, secondary, and tertiary institutions in session, with Makerere College given special mention. The overall picture which one gets in this film of Africa and Africans is one, which positions African as knowing and knowledgeable agents of development. Africans are also positioned as people capable of handling their own affairs in the absence of colonial authority. In fact, the sequence, which focuses on the development of democratic institutions in Africa stresses the point, that Africans are being prepared for self-governance. This is something that one hardly encounters in colonialist African cinema where the preoccupation is with the perpetual degeneration of Africans into a state of barbarism at the slightest absence of colonial authority, as in the case of *Sanders of the River*.

In sum, *Men of Africa* is an instructional film released just before the outbreak of the Second World War to demonstrate the role of British colonial rule in the development of East Africa. The film neither romanticizes Africans under colonial rule nor represents them as degenerate primitive people incapable of self-development. It represents them as progressive people struggling under colonial rule to develop their society. Furthermore, the society represented in *Men of Africa* is a dynamic one in a state of transition from traditionality to modernity. In this regard, the experience of Africans was not too different from that of colonized peoples elsewhere in the world in the period under review. Finally, even though the title, *Men of Africa*, seems to suggest erroneously that it is the activities of only men of Africa that is highlighted in the film; the actual text itself does not foreground gender politics by giving preferential spatial treatment to any of the sexes. The "men" in the title is therefore a neuter subject term arising from the authority of patriarchy in British colonial government. However, where gender politics does occasionally figure in the text, as in cases of separate sitting positions of men and women in seating arrangements within scenes, its roots can be traced to the patriarchal separation of male/female space in traditional African society. Genderization of spaces figures prominently in *Daybreak in Udi*, to be analysed below.

A Critical Reading of Daybreak in Udi

Daybreak in Udi (Terry Bishop, 1949) is another example of an instructional film produced to demonstrate the role of the British colonial government in the development of the colonies, with specific reference to Nigeria. The Crown Film Unit produced it after the Second World War, in response to the growing criticism of the British government's stewardship in the colonies. The film is a dramatized documentary of the self-help development programs embarked upon by the people of Umana village in the Udi District of Nigeria with the support and encouragement of the District Officer, E.R. Chadwick. It sets out to propagate the concept of community self-help development, supported by government. The implicit argument underlying the film is that the British colonial government alone cannot serve as agent of development and that development must be a joint community/government effort. As a propaganda piece, the film seems to respond to the critics of the British colonial government's stewardship in Africa by arguing that development should be a joint community/government effort, while as an instructional film, it offers itself as a model of how people can spearhead development efforts in their communities.

The film tells the story of how two schoolteachers, Dominic (Harford Anerobi) and Iruka (Fanny Elumeze), spearhead the development of the village of Umana in Udi district of Nigeria by mobilizing the people into building a community maternity clinic. In pursuit of this goal, they seek the advice and help of the District Officer, E.R. Chadwick (who plays himself in the film), who supports the project by offering government aid as well as helping to mobilize the elders of the village to support the project. The project runs into conflict when a prominent elder of the village and head of the ancestral cult, Egwugwu, Eze (Joseph Amalu), attempts to mobilize public opinion against the project, for fear that it will bring about changes within the community that might undermine the authority of the cult. When he fails to win public support for the abandonment of the project, he makes a last desperate attempt after its completion by embarking on a scare campaign that any woman who delivers in the maternity clinic will lose her child during childbirth. In addition to this, he mobilizes members of the cult and invades the maternity clinic at night in an attempt to scare away its city bred midwife and her first patient. On the night of the invasion, Iruka, who has gone to keep the midwife company, throws hot water, which she has heated for a warm bath of the woman in labor, at the leader of the cult. This climactic act of courage finally defeats Eze and his cult members. The woman delivers safely and others soon follow suit. The film ends with an official opening ceremony of the maternity clinic, presided over by District Officer Chadwick.

In terms of narrative structure, the story is told in a simple straightforward manner without many narrative complications. It begins with a prologue bearing an intertitle message relating to the geographical location of the ethnic group whose self-help development projects it sets out to highlight, and ends in an epilogue with a work song expressing the spirit of self-help development and the dignity of labor. The central conflict arises from Eze's attempt to undermine the building of the maternity clinic. Once this conflict is resolved, narrative action moves quickly towards conclusion. The film is narrated mostly through an omniscient form of narration with occasional interventions by delegated narrators in the form of voice-over commentary by Chadwick and point-of-view shots of Iruka and the midwife. There are nine main sequences in the film, with each sequence dealing with a major event within the narrative. They are: the opening sequence which deals with the mass literacy campaign; the child paternity right case, and the proposition by the school teachers, Iruka and Dominic, for a community maternity clinic; a village council meeting called to discuss the teachers' proposition and Eze's opposition to the project; clearing of the maternity clinic site, molding of blocks and laying the foundation of the building; completing the project; arrival of the city bred midwife and Eze's scare campaign to boycott the maternity clinic; the invasion of the maternity clinic by members of the ancestral masquerade cult, the Egwugwus, led by Eze, and the delivery of the first baby in the clinic; the official opening ceremony of the clinic; and the road construction sequence.

The main theme of the film is self-help development, and it is introduced right from the opening intertitle message, which serves as a prologue to the main narrative as well as highlighting the geographical space and ethnic configuration of the area in focus. The prologue begins as follows:

> in a distant region beyond the River Niger, an ancient African tribe, the Abaja Ibos, have undertaken an ambitious program of community development which has seldom been equaled. Together they are teaching themselves to read and write, and are building schools, maternity homes, cooperative shops, and many

miles of roads. With few resources but their own strength and spirit, they are starting to bridge the centuries dividing their way of life and ours.

In the opening sequence, the theme of self-help development highlighted in the prologue is immediately taken up in the first narrative action of the film. It begins with an establishing shot of an adult mass literacy campaign gathering of the people of Umana in the village square. This is followed by a cut to a medium shot of rows of men, with the front row occupied by men sitting on the bare ground and others standing behind them as in a family portrait. A gradual pan to screen left reveals a male teacher, Dominic, standing in front of a blackboard. The camera dollies into a medium close-up of Dominic and cuts to a medium shot of a female teacher, Iruka, and her blackboard facing her women pupils. The first four shots of the film effectively establish the division of public space along gender lines in which we see first, the male teacher and his male pupils, and then, the female teacher and her female pupils. Both sets of pupils occupy a different arch of the circular space created around the village square. As I noted earlier, this gender division of public space owes its authority to the patriarchal division of public space in traditional African society. What the film has done is respect this tradition in the representation of public space. There are many other scenes within the film that are marked by this gender division of public space. I will be referring to some of them shortly.

To return to the adult literacy class, a continuation of the leftward pan of the arch reveals a profile of the rows of women, some with babies on their laps, others breast-feeding their babies while concentrating on the ongoing lesson. This is followed by a cut to a medium close-up of a boy in the male section of the arch, pointing a stick to the letter "a" and pronouncing the sound for the elders, and another cut to a close-up of an old man and a small boy pronouncing the alphabet after the boy. Next, there is a cut back to the medium close-up of the boy continuing to teach them the alphabet, followed by another cut to a medium shot of three chiefs sitting on chairs in a front row, equally concentrating on the lesson. Thus apart from gender division of public space, class division is also established in the opening sequence. Usually, in traditional African societies with reigning monarchs, the king and his council of chiefs, made up of mostly elderly men who have distinguished themselves either in their trades or through services to the community, constitute the apex of the power structure. Below them are the council of elders, made up of both elderly men and women of the community, and then the age grades, in order of seniority. There is no king in this adult literacy class, but there are titled chiefs in attendance, an indication that the community takes the mass literacy program seriously. Though the power/class hierarchy of traditional African society is marked through representation of the spatial division of public space, it is not given special treatment in the order of representation.

The scene with the boy teaching the elders the alphabet is soon followed by a cut to a medium shot of Dominic and a cut to a close-up of a section of his male pupils, which shows a man with a child on his lap, sitting among several children, all of whom are concentrating on the lesson. As he continues with his teaching, we see the dispersal of children in the background, indicating the end of their lesson. As soon as he notices this, Dominic ends his lesson. The sequence ends with a fade as Dominic cleans the blackboard. What is of special interest in the last scene is the close-up of the man with a child on his lap concentrating on the ongoing lesson. In one respect, this close-up is meant to signify paternal love in traditional African society, but it can also be considered as a signification of one of the customary ways of transmitting knowledge in traditional African society from one generation to the other. It is part of a long standing tradition whereby fathers take along their sons — ostensibly to help them carry their chairs, stools, and bags — to important elders' meetings where the sons are expected to sit inconspicuously among the elders and learn the art of public oratory and speech rhetoric. The womenfolk, through their sons, pick up most leaks from elders' council meetings. Of course, part of the game includes learning to keep one's mouth shut in the midst of prodding for information by the women. The use of close-ups and medium close-ups in this sequence is however not intended as a means of granting narrative authority to any of the characters in the sequence. It merely serves in this instance to locate the scene of narrative action as well as to highlight the genderization of public space in traditional Africa society. There are of course sequences containing conscious linkage of spatial articulations and narrative authority, to character development and spectatorial spatial accessibility. The issue of spectatorial textual positioning will be examined shortly.

Apart from the mass literacy campaign sequence, the next sequence, which directly addresses the theme of self-help development, is that dealing with the village council meeting called to discuss the proposed community maternity clinic. This meeting is significant for two reasons. First, it shows how local government functions in traditional African society as well as how public debates related to social welfare is conducted. Second, it serves to introduce the main conflict in the film: Eze's opposition to the project. I want to examine this sequence, to show how traditional African public discourse is conducted, who partakes in it, and how public opinion is mobilized for and against set common goals. The sequence begins with a pan of a group of village elders moving from screen right, through tree undergrowth, to a circular space in front of the chief's compound, on extreme screen left. The pan ends with a cut to an establishing shot of the village council in session, discussing the proposed community maternity clinic. This is followed by a cut to a long shot of rows of seated titled elders, and another cut to a pan from screen left to right that reveals Eze. In terms of spatial composition, there is a repetition of the earlier noted genderization of public space in the sitting arrangement. The men sit in the foreground, in an arch around the circular space, with the women standing in the background, behind them.

The meeting begins with an address by Eze. Though he speaks in Ibo and what he says is not immediately translated, Dominic will later reveal in his briefing of Chadwick when he later arrives, that Eze, a very prominent elder in the community, is opposed to the project. Even though Eze is opposed to the project, the chief of the village and other members of the council support it. For instance, while Eze is speaking, there is a cut to a reaction shot of one of the elders listening, with his chin resting on his right palm, and his left hand resting on his lap. This is followed by a cut back to Eze speaking in frenzy as he tries to mobilize public opinion against the project. Suddenly, the elder sitting in a provocative pose, who was highlighted while Eze is speaking, stands up and interrupts Eze by telling him that the community would go ahead with the project whether he likes it or not. As he says this, we hear background voices approving what he has said. In a cut back to Eze, other members of the council shout him down as he attempts to continue his interrupted speech. Seeing that the majority of the elders favor the project, he storms out of the meeting, promising that he will make sure the project does not succeed. As he walks away through the front of the women, they are brought into full focus through a cut to a medium shot, which displaces the men from the frame, and positions the group of women standing in the row immediate to the men in the foreground. Two brief reverse shots of Eze walking away, with the women booing him, conclude this scene.

This scene is typical of how traditional African public discourse is conducted. Debates are often conducted between two main public figures noted for their public oratory and opposition to each other's views. The speeches made by them often divide the house into two main camps, but the ethical and moral strength of each speaker's opinion as well as the general approving side-commentaries that it receives, often determine the argument that carries the day. If public opinion is equally divided, the chief or king presiding over such meetings must take a stand by supporting the argument which he considers most beneficial to the community's social well being. In this particular case, we find that public opinion is overwhelmingly in favor of the project. As the debate continues, there is a cut to Dominic and an Assistant District Officer dressed in Yoruba ceremonial outfits of *agbada* and cap, discussing in the foreground, with the elders in the background. Dominic asks his permission to try to persuade the elders to accept the project. Having received it, he addresses the elders in Ibo while standing in front of the chief of the village. The discussion scene between Dominic and the elders is in shot/reverse shot. While it is going on, Chadwick's voice-over commentary informing us that he has always been concerned with the progress of the village, intrudes into Dominic's speech. This voice-over intrusion is immediately followed by a cut to a long shot of Chadwick being led into the chief's compound by a youth of the village. As they walk through the tree undergrowth, into the compound, Dominic walks into the frame from screen left, to receive Chadwick. He asks Dominic if the village has come to a consensus over the project and he informs him that Eze, a prominent elder in the village, is opposing it. Chadwick then asks Dominic if the senior wife of Eze is in the meeting and he replies she is, adding that Eze has forbidden his wives to join the women's cooperative that is supposed to raise the money to pay the midwife's salary. Chadwick assures him that he will speak to Eze's wife as they move into the meeting ground, to the front of the chief of the village who stands up and shakes hand with Chadwick. As they greet, the three of them are brought into focus in a medium shot, with Chadwick and Dominic positioned in the foreground of screen right while the chief stands in the foreground of screen left. In the background, behind them are members of the elder's council sitting an in arch, towards screen right. Chadwick tells the village chief that he has heard that some villagers are opposing the project, but that if the majority of members of the community are determined to have one built, there is no reason why they should not succeed. He then walks over to the women and asks to be shown Eze's senior wife. After he is shown her, he asks the woman if she wants her children to benefit from civilization and she answers affirmatively in Ibo. Chadwick then cleverly sets her up by praising her as the bearer of many grown up and respected children in the village, and solicits her help to convince the women of the village to join the cooperative society. Having received her promise that she will work towards such an end, they return to the elders.

The conversation between Chadwick and Eze's senior wife is in shot/reverse shot that alternates between a full facial front view of Chadwick and the woman, and between him and Dominic, with the latter serving as interpreter to both of them. At the end of the scene, Chadwick asks for a song before he leaves. This request is followed by a cut to a medium close-up of Chadwick and the chief, as both of them greet each other in a traditional Ibo custom for titled elders — a process which entails hitting each other, back-palm to back-back, and front-palm to front-palm, gently three times in each movement. A short dance follows, interspersed with cuts to medium shots and medium close-ups of men raising songs and others chorusing, followed by a pull back to establishing shot as the meeting ends.

Besides highlighting the nature of traditional African public discourse, local government procedures, and introducing the element of conflict in the film, this sequence also deals with the nature of the relationship between the District Officer and the people of Udi District. From the way Chadwick conducts his discussions with the elders of Umana during the meeting, and the warmth and conviviality underlying their relationship, one can tell that the relationship between him and the people is built on mutual trust and respect. In fact, if you remove his color, the District Officer could well pass for a local government official in contemporary Nigeria. He does not for once adopt a bullying tone in the discussion between him and Eze's senior wife, even though, as an agent of British imperial authority, he could easily have his way with regards to how he wants to run the district. Instead of imposing his views on community development projects on the people, he canvasses their support by informing them of the benefits they stand to gain if they embrace such projects. He also does not show contempt for the culture of the people; rather, he partakes in it and in this way, he wins their confidence. For instance, when towards the end of the meeting he asks for a little song before his departure, it is a request born of desire to partake in the cultural practices of the area under his jurisdiction, not one by a person who wants to be entertained as an onlooker. He partakes in the dance he requests for. He knows the greeting rituals of titled elders in the community. Furthermore, throughout the film, he insists that the good cultural practices of the people should not be tampered with in the quest for development. Though there was a general British colonial policy in Africa to preserve aspects of good socio-cultural practice of the people, such a general guiding policy does not explain the good working relationship between Chadwick and the people of his district. It can only be explained as an individual trait of good leadership.

Chadwick also displays a high level of understanding of Ibo cultural practices in his handling of the child paternity case in the sequence preceding the village council meeting. I want to examine the scene dealing with the case because it shows that when the occasion calls for it, he knows how to strike a balance between moribund cultural practices that need discarding and modern cultural practices. The scene begins with an establishing shot of Chadwick's district office in which we find him sitting in the foreground, back to the camera, and in the background, the couple disputing the paternity right over their son with an elderly man who claims he paid a dowry on the woman when she was a young girl which was not refunded when she grew up and decided to marry a younger man instead of him. By Ibo tradition, the elderly man whose dowry was not refunded before the woman married has paternity right over children of such a marriage. Chadwick calls the child in dispute forward, and he moves into a mid-frame position between Chadwick and his parents. He asks the boy, who of the two men is his biological father, and the boy turns and points to the man in front of whom he had been standing. As he does this, there is a cut to a medium close-up of the full facial view of Chadwick, with the boy now occupying the foreground, with his back to the camera in extreme right of screen space, displacing Chadwick slightly into the background. When Chadwick asks him who buys his clothes, the shot is reversed with Chadwick in the foreground of the medium close-up, with his back to the camera while the boy occupies the middle of the frame, facing the camera as the main point of focus.

In answer to Chadwick's question, he points to his biological father. Next, Chadwick asks him if he goes to school, and he answers by nodding his head. He then asks him who pays his school fees and the boy points to his biological father while staring at the ground in front of him. Chadwick, who is probably unaware of the fact that in traditional African culture, it is a sign of rudeness to look one's elder directly in the eyes, especially in situations of close interrogation over culpable allegations, asks the boy to look him straight in the eyes while answering his questions. As the interrogation continues, the shot structure alternates with Chadwick and the little boy exchanging foreground/background compositional spatial positioning within screen space. Next, he asks the boy if he has seen before now the elderly man claiming paternity right over him, and as the boy turns to look at the man for the first time, there is a cut from the boy and Chadwick, to a medium close-up of the elderly man which positions him in the foreground of screen space, facing the camera, with a local constable in the background. This is followed by a cut back to a medium close-up of the boy and Chadwick, with the boy in the middle of the frame, facing the camera, as the main point of focus, and Chadwick positioned in foreground, back to the camera slightly to screen left. In answer to Chadwick's question, the boy shakes his head as an indication that he does not know the man. Next, the shot is reversed with Chadwick now occupying the middle of the frame, facing the camera as the main point of focus, while the boy occupies the foreground of screen right, backing the camera. Chadwick further asks him if he would like to live with the elderly man and the boy shakes his head to indicate he would not like to do so. He asks him whom he would like to live with and the boy points at his biological parents. Chadwick then tells him to go back to his biological parents. As the boy does that, there is a cut from Chadwick to the elderly man looking disconcertedly towards off screen right where the boy has just gone, with the local constable still standing in the background. This is followed by a cut from the man to a medium shot of the boy standing in front of his parents, with his father's hand on his shoulders. The interrogation then switches between Chadwick, the elderly man, and an office interpreter, shot mostly in medium shots.

Throughout the period of interrogation, both Chadwick and the man speak through the office interpreter. The elderly man does not state his side of the case, nor do the couple. Chadwick narrates the case in dispute through voice-over commentary. He asks the elderly man if he admits that the younger man is rightfully married to the woman and the man replies through the interpreter that he does. Chadwick then tells him that in paternity cases in modern times, the welfare of the child takes precedence over any paternity claims, which he may have over the boy because of customary laws. He tells the elderly man that he has examined the case thoroughly and that he is confident it would be in the child's interest to be under the custody of his biological parents. In addition, he warns him that he cannot hope to win the case in a modern law court should he contemplate taking legal action. He advises him instead to take his case to a customary court to seek recovery of his bride price. Chadwick's handling of this case shows that he not only has a firm grasp of the culture of his area of jurisdiction but also that he is fair and firm in dispensation of justice. In contemporary Nigeria, if such customs still exists, the elderly man would be given similar advice. Regarding the forms of narration, even though this scene displays a complex form of spatial articulation, especially in foreground and background composition, its use of medium shots and medium close-ups are non-discriminatory, and are not intended as means of exploiting aspects of character psychology or development. By this I mean that the spectator is granted equal spatial closeness to all the characters in the scene. For this reason, as in earlier noted similar forms of spatial articulation, medium shots and medium close-ups are used in this scene to locate the space of narrative action. The only time they are used, together with point-of-view shots, as forms of narrative authority, is in the sequence dealing with the Egwugwu's invasion of the maternity clinic. I should like to examine this sequence because besides consciously adopting this form of spatial articulation to grant narrative authority to Iruka and the midwife, it is also the film's climax.

The sequence begins with an establishing shot of the maternity clinic in pitch darkness except for two half-opened windows casting rays of light from the interior of the building. This is followed by a cut to a medium shot of the door. The midwife opens the door, comes out, and listens. There is a cut to the surrounding bush, followed by a slow pan of the bush towards screen right. At the end of the pan, we see nothing but hear noises. This is followed by a cut to a long shot of the midwife still standing at the door of the maternity clinic. She listens again. Hearing nothing more, she closes the door. Next, there is a cut to the interior of the building as she leaves the door and moves towards the rows of beds for expectant mothers. As she gets close to the camera, it pans away from her, towards screen left, to reveal the pregnant woman whom we saw Iruka taking to the clinic at the end of the last sequence. The midwife stands by her bedside, places her hand on the woman's forehead to feel her temperature and then, there is a cut to a medium shot of the midwife looking frightened in the direction of the door, back at the woman, and then, towards the door. This is followed by a cut to the bush outside. This time, we perceive movements in the bush but we do not see anything. Next, there is a cut to a medium shot of the pregnant woman in bed with a paraffin lamp by her bedside. This is followed by a cut back to the bush with the same noticeable movements, but once again we do not see anything. In a cut back to the midwife, we find her looking frightened towards screen right. She stands up from the woman's bedside and moves towards the opened window. This is followed by her point-of-view shot. But this time, there is a barely visible pair of horns jutting out of the bush.

In a cut back to the midwife, we notice that she has become notably frightened. As she moves away from the window, there is a cut to the pregnant woman in bed. Next, there is a cut to the midwife contemplatively opening the door and a cut back to the now equally frightened woman thinking possibly that the midwife is about to flee, leaving her alone in the building. In a cut back to the midwife, she closes the door and goes to sit by the woman's bedside. This is followed by the midwife's point-of-view shot as she looks outside through the opened window, and then we see the silhouette of a person entering the compound. The point-of-view shot is repeated as the midwife tries to look closely. She stands up and moves towards the window. Soon we begin to discern the figure to be that of a woman. Next, there is a cut to a medium shot of the midwife, framed by the window as she tries to decipher the figure that moves towards the door. As the figure gets to the door and knocks, there is a cut back to the extremely frightened face of the midwife. At the repeat of the knock, she moves towards the door, opens it, and discovers it is Iruka who has come to keep her company. Seeing that the midwife looks frightened, Iruka asks her whom she thought was knocking and the midwife replies she was not sure because a man came to see her earlier in the evening, to which Iruka replies that he must be Eze. The midwife then tells her that the man frightened her and warned her that their ancestors did not approve of these new developments. He had promised to bring out the dead (ancestral masquerades) that night to show her that the ancestors disapproved of her work in the maternity clinic. Iruka asks her if she believes in these things, and she replies that she does not but that she is frightened. Iruka then tells her that her patient too is frightened because there is no one to look after her. She then encourages her to go in with her to take care of the woman.

At the bedside, she asks the midwife if there is another lamp and she replies there is, Iruka tells her to look after her patient while she lights the other lamp. Next, there is a cut to Iruka heating water with a giant pot, and then back to both of them sitting beside the woman. As they sit there, Iruka tells her that she has not heard any noise since she arrived so it could be the midwife's own imagination, and the midwife agrees that it must have been. This conversation is soon followed by a cut to the bush. This time, we see a figure dressed in raffia leaves and moving in the bush. Next, there is a cut back to both of them sitting beside the pregnant woman. Iruka goes to bring the water we saw her heating earlier close to the bedside. As the woman begins her labor, the noises resume. In spite of her display of boldness, even Iruka is temporarily frightened by the sounds but she quickly recollects herself, puts on a bold face and moves towards the window. At the window, her point-of-view shot is given as she looks from screen right to extreme screen left and sees the face of a masked figure lodged in the bush. Next, there is a cut back to Iruka as she leaves the window thoughtfully and calmly. In a cut back to the bush, we see the earlier pair of horns jotting out of the bush. Gradually, the figure wearing the horns begins to move towards the compound. A shot pan to screen left where Iruka saw a masked figure a moment ago also reveals the masquerade she saw moving towards the compound.

In a cut back to the building, the now hysterical midwife tells Iruka that she is frightened. This is followed by a cut back to the bush, which reveals an additional monstrous-looking masquerade, bringing the total to three masquerades that are moving towards the maternity. Next, there is a cut to the frightened face of Iruka looking towards the window as the monstrous-looking masquerade, possibly the leader, positions its head by the window. As Iruka looks, the mask head is enlarged through a dollying in, followed by a cut to the frightened but thoughtful face of Iruka. Instantly, she grabs the pot and throws the steaming water at the masquerade. It screams and runs off. This action is intercut with the woman delivering her baby and a cut to a medium shot of the three masquerades, with the monstrous-looking one in the middle. This shot is punctuated by several others that reveal either an individual masquerade or groups of masquerade and a cut to an establishing shot of the compound, now full of masquerades. Seeing what has just happened to the one that stood by the window, they back off towards the bush, turn on their heels and flee. The shot lingers on a bit to signify the passage of time as the day starts to break. This is followed by a cut to Iruka sitting on the veranda of the maternity clinic in the morning. Shortly afterwards, the midwife moves into the frame from screen left and hands Iruka the baby. This is followed by a cut to a close up of the baby, and to a medium shot of Iruka smiling as she holds the baby and a fade.

In this sequence, point-of-view shots, medium shots and medium close-ups are used to grant narrative authority to the midwife and Iruka. In the case of point-of-view shots, we are made to see what both characters see from their point in space. There is therefore a transition from an omniscience form of narration, to character narration. Narrative authority in these instances lies with the characters. They anchor the story, and since one is granted access to their space, one is made to share their anxieties over the noises and movements in the bush. In the case of medium close-ups, they are used mostly as processes of character revelation and character psychology. In this sequence, this form of spatial articulation is used not just to locate the space of narrative action but also as means of granting the spectator access to the interior fears and anxieties of both characters. This is about the only time this form of spatial articulation is used in the film. Its usage in this sequence is recognition of the importance of events in this sequence to the resolution of the conflicts in the film. By allowing the spectator access to character psychology, through spatial proximity or point-of-view shots, the fears and anxieties of the characters can be shared by the spectator through empathy.

The final sequence deals with the opening ceremony of the maternity clinic. This sequence is significant because it contains Chadwick's speech, dwelling upon the film's central theme of community self-help development. This theme has implications for post-colonial development strategies. It begins with drumbeats and a long shot of a drummer sitting on a small hillside, followed by a cut to a long shot of the chief of the village in front of his compound with two of his wives. He moves towards the clinic as the drumbeats continue. This is followed by a cut to Eze moving towards his hut. He is soon joined by one of his wives handing him his hat. They exchange hot words and he moves towards the direction of the maternity clinic. Next, there is a cut to Chadwick moving towards his car. As he drives off, the scene ends. This brief scene registers people related to the project in one way or another preparing to go to the official opening ceremony of the maternity clinic. The next scene begins with a long shot of people and secular ceremonial masquerades dancing towards the compound. This is followed by a cut to Iruka standing by the window of the maternity clinic and a point-of-view shot of her as she looks at the group of young men dancing into the maternity compound. In a cut back to Iruka, we find her smiling happily as she leaves the window and moves towards the delivery room to meet the midwife and the newly delivered baby. This is followed by a cut to Iruka and the midwife excitedly congratulating themselves, seeing that many more women have now come to the maternity clinic for delivery after the successful delivery of the first woman. They chat a bit with sounds of drumbeats in the background and they move to join the pregnant women in their beds. Iruka lifts the baby from beside its mother, places it in a cot and stands a while admiring it. Then she moves outside to look at the youths dancing. As she looks, there is a shot pan from screen left to right to reveal the backs of seating elders, followed by a cut to a full frontal view of the elders, with Chadwick sitting among them. This is followed by a cut to the young men dancing outside the square space surrounded by the sitting elders and other standing spectators who have turned up for the official opening ceremony of the compound. Next, there is a cut to a long shot of the square space surrounded by the elders. An old man moves into the middle of the square space and begins to greet those who have turned up for the opening ceremony. He moves towards Chadwick and both of them greet each other in the traditional manner of Ibo titled elders. As the youths begin to dance into the open square space, we note that some of the spectators are holding little Union Jack flags, indicating that this is colonial Nigeria. They dance both in groups and individually before the gathered audience. This is followed by cuts to professional dancers performing in the middle of the square, and to a group of youngsters practicing their dance steps to the encouragement of the elders sitting closest to them. Next, there are brief cuts to display of finesse and mastery by both individual drummers and dancers.

The dancing scene ends with timed drumming and dancing by a single master dancer. At the end of these solo performances, there is spontaneous applause and then Chadwick addresses the gathering. He congratulates the elders and people of Umana village for building the community maternity clinic. He tells them that he realized it has not been built without opposition from some foolish people. As he says this, there is a cut to a reaction shot of Eze laughing and clapping like everybody else, but on noticing that they are looking at him, he casts a sneering glance towards Chadwick. On the mention of the word opposition, everybody begins to laugh again at Eze who, despite himself, soon joins in the laughter. Chadwick continues his address by telling them that the value of the work they have done cannot be measured by the number of bricks that they have made or even by the size of the building. He adds that the value lies in the power that they have demonstrated and the spirit they have put into it. He also tells them of an interesting experience which he had as District Officer when he first started working. According to him, he got to a village where the elders gathered £10,000 and came to him pleading that they

wanted to buy civilization. He informs the gathering that he told
people of the village that they cannot buy civilization like food in
the market, and that as far as civilization is concerned, people
matter more than money. He advises them that if they want to
catch up with modern people and improve their standard of living,
then they certainly have made a good start. He further informs
them that the village of Umana is just one of forty villages in the
clan that have embarked on self-help development projects. He
admonishes them not to stop with this single project but to move
ahead into others. He also tells them that they must build their own
future because nobody else can do it for them. He further informs
them that the people of his country will only be too grateful to help
them when they know that they are willing to help themselves. In
addition, he informs them that a neighboring village has embarked
upon the building of a road called Nkedimkpa — which means
"strength is important" — and invites the elders to the village to
see the work being done. Chadwick's address ends the sequence.
Chadwick's address virtually sums up the theme of the film: the
people need to take their destiny in their hands by embarking upon
community self-help development projects.

Ordinarily, the idea of community self-help development is a
lofty one, especially if it is made to complement government
projects. It is however wrong to base the progress and modern
development of a country — or countries since the film is
propagating this form of development in respect of all British
colonies in Africa — upon this form of development as the film's
thematic thrust seems to suggest. It is a rather ingenuous way of
absolving government of its responsibilities to the society it is
governing. Any government that collects taxes, custom and excise
duties and other forms of tariffs has a duty to develop that society.

While community self-help development needs to be
encouraged in every society, it should be considered the last resort
in the development strategy of a country. I say this because
watching this film has taught me a lot about the roots of the
contemporary Nigerian government's emphasis upon community
self-help development. Its roots lie in this colonial practice.
However, while British colonial governments may have adopted
this development strategy as a way of conserving funds and
ensuring that each territory pays for the cost of its government and
development, for that of most post-colonial governments in Africa,

certainly that of Nigeria, it is a strategy for absolving government of its development responsibilities to the people. Emphasis is often placed on community self-help development at the expense of a well planned development strategy, and funds saved from such a practice often end up in the private accounts of government officials in western capitals. In most parts of Nigeria today, development at the community level — the building of schools, maternity clinics, local dispensaries, postal agencies, and sometimes even roads – is based mostly on fund raising ceremonies and levies within the communities. This places financial burden on people since they have to pay these levies in addition to government taxes and other financial burdens. What annoys people most is the knowledge that though the government is not able to fulfil its obligation to society, individuals within such governments, with no known inherited wealth, have become millionaires over night by virtue of their public service. It is for these reasons that community self-help development has become a very unpopular development notion today in most African countries, and the knowledge that it is a colonial inheritance will certainly come as a shocker to many on the continent.

With respect to character-subjectivity and narrative authority, events in *Daybreak in Udi* are structured around the character of Chadwick. He is situated at the center of most events. Even when he is not physically present in a scene, he continues to control the flow of narrative actions by virtue of the omniscient powers invested in him, which allows him to float above and comment upon events. A good example of such narrative authority is displayed in the opening scene of the village council meeting where we hear his voice-over commentaries on events before his physical appearance. At other times, he is granted omniscient narrative authority in addition to his physical control of narrative action, as in the case of the opening scene of the child paternity case sequence. The overall omniscient control of narrative action which the Chadwick character displays is, however, not extended to the sphere of discriminating spectatorial spatial accessibility or inaccessibility in respect of his character and others in the film. By this I mean he does not enjoy any special close relationship with the spectator by way of exteriorization of his character psychological make up. The use of such forms of spatial articulations as medium shots and medium close-ups as studied approaches to character development or revelation are also not exclusively tied to the Chadwick character. Other characters such as Dominic, Iruka, the midwife and Eze all enjoy this form of spatial articulations. The only advantage Chadwick enjoys over other characters is his omniscient control over the flow of narrative action.

Apart from the Chadwick character, the other character, which enjoys a comparative level of narrative authority, is Iruka. The Iruka persona is constructed as a strong-willed modern African woman who has not only risen above the dogma of traditional African superstitious beliefs but is also aware that such superstitious beliefs are not unique to Africa. The defeat of Eze and members of the Egwugwu cult is due to her courage, imagination and swift reaction. It is Iruka who gives courage to the terrified midwife who is contemplating fleeing the maternity clinic before her arrival to keep her company. In scenes involving her, Dominic and Chadwick, she demands that she should be allowed to air her views on the proposed maternity clinic project when she notices that Dominic and Chadwick are monopolizing the discussions. Though the assertive nature of the Iruka character is not strange to African women, her interruptions of Dominic when he is speaking and her demands that she should be allowed to air her view are characteristically western. Though African women live in a male dominated society, they always put across their views on major issues — and those views are taken seriously — without adopting the confrontational attitude reminiscent of radical western feminists. Certainly, few educated African women of the late 1940s possess the assertive personality displayed in the film by the Iruka persona. Of course, there were powerful women activists during this period in Nigeria, like Fumilayo Ransom-Kuti, Margaret Ekpo, and Sawaba Gambo, who were notable political players and women leaders at the national level. But granted that these national activists possess the assertive personality of the Iruka persona, certainly a village schoolteacher of Iruka's caliber of the late 1940s would not possess such assertive personality qualities. It seems, therefore, that this character is drawn more with the behavioral characteristics of the western woman in mind than an African woman. Having said this, the Iruka character certainly enjoys a lot of narrative authority through spatial articulation, especially in the climactic confrontation between her and the leader of the Egwugwu cult, Eze.

In the scenes of confrontation, she is granted narrative authority through character narration by way of her point-of-view shots. In this respect, the relationship between the spectator and space of narrative action is articulated from her point in space. We are forced to see and feel the flow of narrative action from her point in space. In this way, we partake in her fears and anxieties of the mysterious noises that precede the physical appearance of the Egwugwus. Even though the midwife enjoys similar narrative authority through spatial articulation in this sequence, Iruka's display of courage and imagination, when it matters, is what is foregrounded in the sequence. She holds the key to the resolution of the film's conflict. For this reason and the strength of her verbal views, she is the most visible of all the African characters.

Beside Iruka, Dominic also plays a leading role in the realization of the project. Even though he is a young man, he has earned the respect of elders of Umana village through his humility and dedication to duty, both as schoolteacher and agent of social development. As representative of the elite class at the village level, Dominic and his colleagues serve as bridge between modernity and traditionalism, between the colonial state and the community. Due to their tenacious spirit and dedication to the processes of modernization, the adult mass literacy campaign and the maternity clinic project are realized. However, the Dominic character does not possess the sort of narrative authority imbued in the Iruka character. He is characterized in general terms as a dedicated schoolteacher interested in the development of his community.

Apart from Iruka and Dominic, the other visible African character in the film is Eze. Though the main conflict in the film arises from Eze's objections to the proposed community maternity clinic, his objections are represented as deriving from fear of the consequences of social change than anything else. Such individualist spoilers are not lacking in contemporary African society; nor are they lacking in other parts of the world. As represented in the film, the collective will of the people often neutralizes the individualist crusades of such people. It is possible also to take a sympathetic view of Eze's behavior from the perspective of his leadership of the ancestral cult, the Egwugwus, who are highly respected in Ibo society as custodians of tradition. The Egwugwus, by virtue of their calling, represent the most conservative arm of society. The cult members are recognized by the society as vehicles through which the ancestors maintain links, through their physical presence as masquerades, with the world of the living. Through the Egwugwus the ancestors are supposed to intervene in the activities of their lineage; hence the Egwugwus are recognized by traditional Ibo society as the highest arbiter in inter-family disputes. Looked at from this perspective, Eze's behavior becomes understandable. His objections to the project derive from fear of eroding the power of the Egwugwus to maintain adherence to traditional Ibo cultural practices. His objection also derives from fear of loosing of one's power — in this case, Eze's power as leader of the Egwugwu cult. But once he realizes that building the maternity clinic would not necessarily diminish the power of the cult, he begins to support the march towards development and modernity.

Daybreak in Udi was made after the Second World War when agitation for independence had already commenced in most African countries. If the producers so wished, they could have structured the narrative in accordance with the tradition of colonialist African cinema by dwelling on the fixed notion of African barbarism as in the case of *Sanders of the River, Mister Johnson, Man of Two World*, and *Simba*. This would have easily been realized, especially as the film chose the form of dramatized documentary in its treatment of colonial community self-help development. *Mister Johnson* and *Man of Two Worlds* also deal with the issue of colonial development but they do so from the perspective of colonialist discourse. Africans in these films do not take charge of their own affairs. They are represented as people who are incapable of independence of thought and action — as good laborers; full of energy and brawn but with little brains. Where one of them is credited with cognitive abilities as in *Man of Two Worlds,* he is represented as a victim of autosuggestion and superstition. This is where *Daybreak in Udi* is different. In general, the film neither romanticizes Africans nor romanticizes colonial community self-help development programs. Like every society in a state of transition to a new order, the people of Umana are not represented as exempt from the machinations of those who fear the consequences of change or the forces of change. Rather the film represents the pursuit of community self-help development as an endeavor full of stumbling blocks. The activities of Eze and his collaborators represent such stumbling blocks.

Another interesting aspect of *Daybreak in Udi* is that it is one of the very few films produced during the colonial period that has represented Africans as initiators of development projects. Though we know through Chadwick's voice-over commentary that the village of Umana is just one of forty villages in Udi District to embark upon self-help community development, the actual initiative to start the maternity clinic at Umana is credited in the film to the two school teachers, Iruka and Dominic. *Daybreak in Udi* also charts an alternative colonial realism by shedding the militaristic image of the District Officer of the sort that one confronts in *Sanders of the River* and *Mister Johnson*. E.R. Chadwick, the District Officer of Udi District in colonial Nigeria, is represented as a man of the people, a well trusted and much loved District Officer who partakes generously in the customary practices of the area of his jurisdiction. Even though he is a colonial agent whose power is superior to that of his subjects, he insists that the traditional practices of the people should not be undermined in the name of development and modernity. In upholding this cardinal policy of British colonial governments in Africa, he helps to preserve the good aspects of African tradition. Also noteworthy is that even though it is within his power to enforce the completion of the community maternity project by incarcerating Eze and his collaborators, he refuses to do this; instead, he subtly exploits the phenomenon of inter-village development rivalry and pride in colonial African society, to defeat Eze. As I noted earlier, he also displays a comparatively high level of understanding of Ibo customary practices in his handling of the child paternity dispute. His recommendations about the case are the sort that the elderly man will receive in contemporary Ibo society if such practices still exist.

In sum, *Daybreak in Udi* dramatizes efforts by the people of Umana village in Udi District of colonial Nigeria to develop their community. It also relates some of the conflicts, which the people have to overcome in their quest for development. In contradistinction to the discursive traditions of colonialist African cinema which represents Africans as degenerate barbaric people, the film represents Ibo society of the colonial era as a developing society — like any other of the colonized world — struggling against the forces of traditionalism in its efforts to develop and embark on the road to modernization. Regarding the film's central theme of community self-help development, I have argued that though the notion of community self-help development can be considered as an additional complementary strategy to a government's overall strategy for the development of its society, it is ethically wrong to suggest, as the film's underlying argument seems to imply, that the British colonial government should not be solely held responsible for the development of the colonies. If the film's theme is considered along this line of argument, as I believe it sets out to do — i.e., that it is produced in response to the growing post-war criticism of British colonial stewardship — to absolve the British colonial authorities of their responsibilities to the colonies, then it ought to be considered as a disingenuous attempt to pass the buck of development to indigenous communities even though they do not control the apparatuses of government and revenue collection. As earlier noted, this tradition of placing the burden of development in a country within the framework of community self-help development has been passed on to post-colonial governments in Africa where the system has become one of the abused loop-holes for siphoning public funds into the private accounts of government officials. For sure, community self-help development is worth encouraging, but only as a complementary strategy to government's overall plan for development. If the film had been structured to pursue such a line of argument, it would have been much more acceptable. The main line of argument pursued in the film is that if communities embark upon self-help development projects, British people will be only too willing to offer help and assistance. Though such a line of argument would be feasible in a post-colonial context, if it is considered as part of development aid to such communities, in a colonial context, such a line of argument would be a weak one, especially when it is considered as an argument in response to criticism of British colonial stewardship, because the onus of development lies with the British colonial government since it is the sole collector of taxes and other revenues in the colonies. It is ethically wrong to pass the buck of development to communities within the colonies and British philanthropists.

Summary

This chapter has examined the historical framework within which colonial African instructional cinema emerged. The point has been made that the practice(s) of colonial African instructional cinema should be considered as alternative cinematic practices, distinguishable from that of colonialist African cinema. Most film scholars who have written on African cinema have failed to make distinctions between the two cinematic practices that existed in colonial Africa. The result is that one is left with the impression that alternative voices or practices did not exist apart from the traditional discursive practices of colonialist texts. Another point canvassed, is the need to treat documentary films as discursive texts, and on the strength of this argument, *Men of Africa* and *Daybreak in Udi* have been analyzed as case studies of colonial African instructional cinema.

6 COLONIALIST AFRICAN CINEMA

Introduction

This chapter examines the historical context of colonialist African cinema. It also presents a classification of the various types of films, which constitutes the cinematic practice as a genre, and a tabulation of its general modes of representation. The main argument canvassed is that colonialist African cinema is an outgrowth of both the canon of colonialist African discourse and of colonialist African literature. In addition, some of the ideas, which inform these films, are nineteenth century racial theories that constitute Africans as subhuman beings in the evolutionary chain of human beings. This order of classification provides the framework within which the various metaphors of African savagery and bestiality are invented. My argument is that the association of Africans with bestiality in these films robs them of their legitimate rights as human beings. As a result, this set of films needs to be distinguished from colonial African instructional cinema which constitutes Africa as a developing society and Africans as knowing and knowledgeable human beings willing and able to learn and master modern forms of social development.

My textual analysis will be directed towards examining how African subjectivity is constructed in contrast to European or other subjective types in colonialist African films. To round up this chapter, *Tarzan the Ape Man* (W.S. Van Dyke, 1932), *Sanders of the River* (Zoltan Korda, 1935), *King Solomon's Mines* (Robert Stevenson, 1937), *The African Queen* (John Hurston, 1951), *Simba* (Brian

Desmond Hurst, 1955), *Chocolat* (Claire Denis, 1988), and *Mr Johnson* (Bruce Beresford, 1990) will be analyzed as case studies of colonialist African films.

The Historical Background of Colonialist African Cinema

The roots of colonialist African cinema can be traced to colonialist African discourse in general and colonialist African literature in particular. Most of the texts of colonialist African cinema are either adaptations from literary texts or personal memoirs. This pattern is, however, not peculiar to Africa. Robert Stam and Louise Spence note that

> colonialist representation did not begin with the cinema; it is rooted in a vast colonial intertext, a widely disseminated set of discursive practices. Long before the first racist images appeared on film screens of Europe and North America, the process of colonialist image-making, and resistance to that process, resonated through Western literature. Colonialist historians, speaking for the 'winners' of history, exalted the colonial enterprise, at bottom little more than a gigantic act of pillage whereby whole continents were bled of their human and material resources, as a philanthropic 'civilizing mission' motivated by a desire to push back the frontiers of ignorance, disease and tyranny. (Stam and Spence, 1983: 5)

An earlier collection of essays on colonialist African cinema, edited by Richard A. Maynard, *Africa on Film: Myth and Reality*, has equally traced the roots of the cinematic practice to colonialist African literature (Maynard, 1974), as has Jeffrey Richards, in his study of what he refers to as the "Cinema of Empire," which includes many of the films I have classified under colonialist African cinema. Richards also states that Hollywood's involvement in the practice was driven by two factors: "the desire for exotic and romantic escapism" and "the commercial factor" (Richards, 1973: 3). This perhaps explains the investments in the Tarzan series of films, the majority of which were set in Africa. Writing on the ideology of the "Cinema of Empire," Richards observes that

> what becomes immediately obvious when viewing these films is that, although they are made in the last decades of the Empire's existence, they do not reflect contemporary ideas about the

> Empire. The ideas they reflect are those of late nineteenth century... The constitutional developments in the Empire in the inter-war years find no place in the cinema of Empire. In films, the Empire is unchanged and unchanging. (Richards, 1973: 7)

The prevalent ideas propagated in the nineteenth century as they relate to Africa are racial theories aimed at proving the racial inferiority of Africans. As I have earlier noted, the fallacy of such theories has since been the subject of many scholarly works (Mudimbe, 1988; Stephan, 1990; Banton, 1987). But the fact that the cream of Euro-American scholarship propagated these racial theories for more than three centuries has left its mark. These same theories informed and continue to inform colonialist African films.

In colonialist African cinema, people who are different, not only in culture but also in skin color and physical outlook, are denied their difference and are measured by European concepts of social organization, cultural practices and notions of aesthetics. Categories of cultural experience and physical outlook which mark out Africans as different from Europeans are cinematically highlighted not so much to acknowledge them as such but specifically to disavow such differences or use them as representative paradigms of perversions of European ideals. In essence, colonialist African discourse or its cinematic practice is an arrested form of knowledge and perception.

It is a partial blindness that arises from the inability to see beyond oneself or one's cultural boundaries or the extension of one's cultural boundaries over others by means of physical force and discursive self-aggrandizement. Paul Bohannan has argued that "Africa was the 'Dark Continent,' but the darkness had much more to do with the European and American visitors to it, and workers in it, than it had to do with Africans" (Bohannan, 1974: 2). This fact is often overlooked in the representation of Africans in colonialist African films.

The discursive practice of colonialist of African cinema was instituted with documentaries such as *Tuaregs in Their Country* (1909), *Big Game Hunting in Africa* (1909), *Missionaries in Darkest Africa* (1912), *The Military Drill of the Kikuyu Tribes and Other Ceremonies* (1914), and films such as *How a British Bulldog Saved the Union Jack* (1906), which deals with the British-Zulu war of 1906-1907, and D.W. Griffith's *The Zulu Heart* (1908), in which a Zulu turns on his fellows in order to aid whites. However, most film historians now cite Griffith's The Birth of a Nation (1915), as the film that codified the stereotypical images of blacks in the cinematic medium (Pines, 1975: 7-32; Leab, 1975: 23-57; Cripps, 1977: 15; Nesteby, 1982: 27-57). Though The Birth of a Nation exploits white fears and anxieties about the black presence in America and, in this respect, can be considered as dealing specifically with the African-American experience in colonialist filmic representation, in the opening sequence, the film traces the problem of the black presence to Africa and the slave trade. Through this association, metaphors of African savagery and bestiality are transposed to African-Americans and vice versa. With respect to Africa itself, the works of Edgar Rice Burroughs and the Tarzan series of films based upon them helped to canonize these metaphors of African savagery and bestiality. Brian Street draws similar conclusions with respect to his analysis of the novels of empire when he states that

> Edgar Rice Burroughs, the inventor of Tarzan, for instance, helps to fix the notion for future generations of young readers that people like their ancestors may still be found in some forgotten jungles, dancing ape-like rituals in ways that European society has left behind. His florid jungle prose transforms the scientific theory of his day into vivid and memorable images. (Street: 98)

Not only do colonialist films deny Africans their individual identities and social values, as in almost every other aspect of the unequal Afro-European relationship, Africans are made victims of European psychic projections and fantasies. Africans are cinematically represented as sexual perverts, cannibals, sadists, despots, idlers, indolent, gutless, timid, superstitious and barbarous. Just about any social practice, which European and Hollywood film producers and directors consider uncivil, is projected upon Africans. When they are not being portrayed as childish and harmless, they are depicted at the other extreme as heartless despots and sadistic murderers; when they are not gutless, they are portrayed as irrational and bloodthirsty warriors. Broadly speaking, most colonialist African films can be categorized as melodramas. Theoreticians such as Rahill (1967), Smith (1973), Brooks (1976), and Gledhill (1987), have given varied definitions to melodrama. However, one thing that unites these definitions is the centrality of opposing complex moral orders and social values. Rahill defines melodrama as

> a form of dramatic composition in prose partaking of the nature of tragedy, comedy, pantomime, and spectacle, intended for a popular audience. Primarily concerned with situation and plot...more or less fixed complement of stock characters, the most important of which are a suffering heroine or hero, a persecuting villain, and a benevolent comic. It is conventionally moral and humanitarian in point of view and sentimental and optimistic in temper, concluding its fable happily with virtue rewarded after many trials and vice punished. Characteristically it offers elaborate scenic accessories and miscellaneous divertissements and introduces music freely, typically to underscore dramatic effects. (Rahill, 1967: xiv)

He also states that from its roots in late eighteenth century popular theatre, melodrama as a popular form was taken up by the popular novel and subsequently by film and television. As its audience grew in sophistication in the nineteenth century, especially with the rise of the bourgeoisie, it adopted a much more subtle approach to characterization. Furthermore, the use of music was curtailed and the extravagant embellishments in scenography were discarded. Heroes and heroines, who were not blameless, especially in love, began to emerge. So too were villains who were more to be pitied than censured. The unhappy ending also became common. He also states that melodrama with its structure of villain-heroine conflict, and a plot in which the heroine is persecuted, with events resulting in a happy ending; offer an almost perfect instrument for propaganda. He notes that during the nineteenth century, this instrument was pressed into the service of innumerable crusades, including national patriotism, anticlericalism, abolition of slavery, prohibition, and even tax and prison reforms (Rahill: xv-xvi).

With respect to film, Gledhill has offered one of the most comprehensive historical and theoretical studies of melodrama. In Gledhill's words, the "term denotes a fictional or theatrical kind, a specific cinematic genre or a pervasive mode across popular culture ...melodrama both overlaps and competes with realism and tragedy, maintaining complex historical relations with them" (Gledhill, 1987: 1). She further states that

> melodramatic desire crosses moral boundaries, producing villains who, even as the drama sides with the "good," articulate

opposing principles, with equal, if not greater, power. In so
doing it accesses the underside of official rationales for reigning
moral orders — that which social convention, psychic
repression, political dogma cannot articulate. Thus whether
melodrama takes its categories from Victorian morality or
modern psychology, its enactment of the continuing struggle of
good and evil forces running through social, political and psychic
life draws into a public arena desires, fears, values and identities
which lie beneath the surface of publicly acknowledged world.
(Gledhill: 33)

She argues that in film, the form has grown from its preoccupation
with the "realism" associated with the masculine sphere of actions
and violence to the woman film, with its emphasis on talk rather
than action. This generic shift has subsequently led to the
empowerment of women within this genre (Gledhill: 35). With
respect to colonialist African cinema, melodrama takes the form of
the opposition, through comparative schema, between European
and African subjects, culture and moral values, belief systems, and
other institutional practices. The genre does not empower Africans.

It represents them, like American Indians in the Western, as
degenerate and barbaric people. Villainy is identified with Africans
just as virtue and moral uprightness is identified with Europeans.
The only exceptions are the "good" African who collaborates with
the European colonial authority or the degenerate working class
European who fraternizes with Africans. African counter-
discourses emerge in these films, mostly through the
representations of violent confrontations between Europeans and
Africans. Though these violent confrontations are represented as
misguided and unwarranted savage attacks, since most of the films
do not explain the rationale for the attacks, this silence can be
interpreted as an admission of Africans' objection to European
colonial authority.

From the above definitions, one can deduce the fact that
melodrama is a complex generic form with various sub-genres and
categories. However, within this broad category, colonialist African
films constitute a genre by themselves since they employ
recognizably colonialist tropes of representation in their narrative
structure, characterization and spatio-temporal articulations. What
makes these films colonialist is that they are constrained by
colonialist thought. Thomas Sobchack has dwelt upon the various
manners in which genre films become constrained by the

conventions and thoughts underlying such forms. He observes that the genre film

> is a classical mode in which imitation not of life but of con-
> ventions is of paramount importance...Though there may be
> some charm in the particular arrangement of formula variables in
> the most current example of a genre, the audience seeks the solid
> and familiar referents of that genre, expecting and usually
> receiving a large measure of the known as opposed to the novel.
> Elevated and removed from everyday life, freed from the
> straight-jacket of mere representationalism, genre films are pure
> emotional articulation, fictional constructs of the imagination,
> growing essentially out of group interests and values. (Sobchack,
> 1977: 52)

Though most colonialist African films belong to one genre because they subscribe to colonialist thought, they do reflect additional sub-generic narrative and thematic contingencies that require distinction. While some like *Tarzan the Ape Man* (W.S.Van Dyke, 1932), *King Solomon's Mines* (Robert Stevenson, 1937), *The African Queen* (John Huston, 1951) or *Greystoke* (Hugh Hudson, 1984) can be grouped under colonialist adventure films, others like *Sanders of the River* (Zoltan Korda, 1935), *Men of Two Worlds* (Thorold Dickson, 1946), *Simba* (Brian Desmond Hurst, 1955), *The Kitchen Toto* (Harry Hook, 1987), *Chocolat* (Claire Denis, 1988) or *Mister Johnson* (Bruce Beresford, 1990) can be categorized as colonial burden films because of the predominance of the theme of burden of colonial administration in them. *Simba* and *Kitchen Toto* can additionally be qualified as decolonization conflict films or liberation struggle films, even though their British producers intended them to be some kind adventure thrillers exploiting the violent milieu of the "Mau Mau" for dramatic effects. Other sub-genres include colonialist safari films, of which a most typical example is *Mogambo* (John Ford, 1953), and colonialist autobiographical films.

General Modes of Representation in Colonialist African Cinema

The following are some of the general conventional manners in which Africans and African culture are represented in colonialist African cinema. Within the practice, the application of various metaphors of savagery and barbarity to Africans is carried out without discrimination, with respect to class, ethnicity or gender. As earlier noted, the only exception in this regard is the "good" African, and the good African is one who collaborates with British colonial authority:

(i) Prolonged emblematic panoramic shots of the African landscape. The preferred shot is that which I shall call the "safari shot." This is a shot that captures the landscape against the background of a broad spectrum of animals roaming the landscape. Its origin lies deep in European travel literature and explorers' memoirs, which described African as a hunter's haven. A classic example of these shots can be found in *Sanders of the River*, where there is prolonged gratuitous footage of animals being sadistically pursued by an aircraft in a games park possibly in Kenya. These types of safari footage are used in many of the films. The safari shots have both land and water varieties. The water variety displays the danger posed to explorers and adventurers by crocodiles and hippopotami. Such footage is extensively used in films like *Tarzan the Ape Man*, *Sanders of the River*, *The African Queen* and *Mogambo*. Even though they are supposed to provide visual pleasures for Western spectators, the application of such footage appears to be driven by geographic and ethnographic interests rather than the dictates of plot. The safari footage is therefore utilized purely for the sake of exploiting the geographic otherness and difference of the African landscape for the visual pleasure of sedentary spectators in Europe who do not have the financial wherewithal to engage in adventures and travels and have the benefit of physically beholding the scenes that are packaged for them in form of safari film footage. Through the safari footage, they are invited to partake in the wild pleasures of adventures.

(ii) The representation of Africans as cannibals. Examples of this kind of representation can be found in *Sanders of the River*, especially in the sequence dedicated to the killing of Fergusson by king Mofalaba. It is encapsulated in the Pidgin English exchange between Mofalaba and his subjects: "Who chop Fergusson?" meaning, "Who ate Fergusson?" to which they all answer in ironic defense, "the white man chop Fergusson."

(iii) The portrayal of Africa as a symbolic Garden of Eden — albeit one infested with dangerous diseases — through the use of surrealistic lighting. This type of cinematic framing of the African landscape is utilized in the opening sequence of *Men of*

Two Worlds, a film that deals with the theme of the clash of cultures. In this film, through the use of special lens filters, static camera pans, and expressionistic lighting, an atmosphere of ironic calm and serenity is created, even though the film has much to do with the deception of outward appearances. As the film unfolds, we begin to realize that the initial symbolic framing of the landscape as a "Garden of Eden" is intended as an ironic comment upon the fact that the area is infested with the deadly Lassa fever carrier, the tsetse fly. Much of the film has to do with the cultural and metaphysical confrontations that arise when a London based educated son of the village is imported to try and persuade his people of the need for resettlement elsewhere.

(iv) The organization of a cinematic scheme of binarisms that uses European criteria in judging traditional African institutional practices. The intention is to portray how radically inferior African cultural practices are in comparison to those of Europe. This is the organizational mentality behind colonialist film culture. The regime of this cinematic practice operates through comparative alternation of shots that displays the outward appearances of Europeans and Africans, the interior decors and furnishing of their dwellings, environments, social atmospheres and moods, or through narrative comments on African social practices. The whole reasoning proceeds from the use of European norms and values in the assessment of African cultural practices.

(v) The representation of Africans as a sexually perverse people eternally preoccupied with procreation because of their different marital practices. Typical examples of these tropes of representation abound in most of the films but they are much more explicitly portrayed in the sequences that follow the proposal and marriage between Lilongo and Bosambo in *Sanders of the River*, and also in the sequence that proceeds the departure for the "gorilla country" by the hunters in *Mogambo*, where the wives of one of the guides are paraded as an instance of the sexual perversion of Africans. I should like to add at this point that polygamy is an authentic ancient African cultural practice, one that is widely practised even today. The portrayal of this practice as an index of sexual permissiveness is another instance of Europeans projecting their values upon Africans.

(vi) The portrayal of African kings as despots and their subjects as oppressed people in need of European political redemption. While it is true that there is historical evidence of reigns of tyrannical kings in Africa — as there is in every other part of the world — the traditional mode of government had its own way of ridding itself of such bad elements. They were either given poison to drink publicly by the kingmakers as evidence of the society's dissatisfaction with their governance or compulsorily exiled from the kingdom (Crowder, 1962: 53-65). African kings or community leaders are portrayed as despots in *Tarzan the Ape Man*, *Sanders of the River*, *King Solomon's Mines*, *Men of Two Worlds*, and *Simba*.

(vii) The representation of the African environment, metaphorically, as a personal antagonist that must be overcome or defeated through symbolic heroic acts. Tropes of this representation are much more prevalent in adventure films like *Tarzan the Ape Man*, *King Solomon's Mines* and *The African Queen*, but they can also be seen in colonial burden films like *Sanders of the River* and *Men of Two Worlds*, where the struggle to conquer the environment is symbolically portrayed as the triumph of a dogged work ethic over debilitating sickness, Lassa fever or malaria fever, unleashed by the environment.

(viii) The cinematic constitution of two types of colonized African archetypes: the cooperative and therefore civilized African, and the rebellious and barbaric ones. Subjective camera positions are granted more to the former than the latter.

(ix) The organization of a cinematic narrative structure and subjective camera positioning around a European male protagonist whose "heroic" acts of physical and symbolic militarism are applauded as necessary appurtenances of the burden of "civilizing" the natives. All films with armed confrontations between Europeans and Africans are filmed this way.

(x) The representation of Africans and African cultural practices as objects of visual pleasures. This practice is most prevalent in those films that incorporate African dances into their narrative structures. Anybody well informed in traditional African performance practices will be amused by the incongruity of the transplantation. Often, they appear to have been grafted into the narrative for the purely visual pleasures of Western spectators since the dances do not further the progress of the narrative in any way.

(xi) The emblematic representation of pre-colonial African soldiers as spear and shield carrying or bow and arrow wielding warriors attired exotically with white-plumed headgears.

Invariably, all of the above do not occur in one single film. Historical periods and the thematic preoccupations in each sub-genre determine the choice of representation. Moreover, knowledge of the conventions of colonialist African cinema alone does not explain how colonialist thoughts are narrativized in a film. One needs to analyze the films, for only then can one demonstrate the manner in which such thoughts are articulated on film. In the remaining part of this chapter, seven randomly selected colonialist African films produced between 1930 and 1990, namely, *Tarzan the Ape Man*, *Sanders of the River*, *King Solomon's Mines*, *The African Queen*, *Simba*, and *Chocolat* will be analyzed.

My choice of films is based on sub-generic consideration and on easy accessibility. Though the selected films are mostly those based on Anglophone African experience, this does not mean that they are the only ones constrained by colonialist African discourse. The tradition extends to the whole corpus of Euro-American films of the colonialist African genre. In fact, until Hollywood and European cinemas cultivate alternative modes of representing Africa, its peoples, and its cultural practices; until Afro-European relationships move into the realm of equal recognition of each other's cultural norms and values, and until Europeans learn to recognize the humanity of Africans, their films set in Africa will continue to be constrained by colonialist thought.

A Critical Reading of Selected Colonialist African Films

Colonialist Adventure Films

Of the colonialist adventure films, the Tarzan jungle films need to be treated as a sub-genre if only in recognition of the sheer number of films based specifically on Tarzan's adventures. James R. Nesteby asserts that there are over forty American made Tarzan films alone, and that

> by 1918, film audiences clearly expected that Tarzan the white must lord it over the apes and the blacks and the beasts; the fact that Tarzan is indeed an English Lord by birth, Lord Greystoke, helps embed the contrast in black and white images. (Nesteby, 1982: 142)

By 1919, the year of the worst outbreak of racial rioting in American history prior to the mid-sixties, *Tarzan of the Apes*, the first in the series of Tarzan jungle films, had become one of the six biggest moneymaking films (Nesteby: 38). Edgar Rice Burroughs, the man who created the Tarzan series of stories which later inspired one of the most derogatory cinematic representation of Africa, had neither been to the continent nor was he ever genuinely interested in knowing it, its peoples and its cultural practices (Maynard: 27). To him, as well as to many others, the continent was a backcloth onto which one could project one's superiority complexes as well as avenue for commercial gains. In this study, I will be analyzing the first sound Tarzan jungle film, *Tarzan the Ape Man* (W.S. Van Dyke, 1932) that starred the Olympic gold medallist swimmer, Johnny Weissmuller.

A Critical Reading of Tarzan the Ape Man

The narrative of *Tarzan the Ape Man* revolves around a search for the legendary elephants' burial ground by Harry Holt (Neil Hamilton), James Parker (C. Aubrey Smith) and Jane Parker (Maureen O'Sullivan). The elephants' burial ground is thought to contain a million pounds worth of ivory. In the course of their search, they stumble upon a white ape-man, Tarzan (Johnny Weissmuller), deep in the forest. From there, the narrative takes on an additional twist by incorporating romance between Tarzan and Jane. The search, which after many perilous obstacles results in the discovery of the elephants' burial ground, consequently leads to the death of James Parker.

Tarzan the Ape Man is a product of the post-abolitionist era when European explorers and travelers crisscrossed Africa in an attempt to gain access to the hinterland and promote legitimate trade in European manufactured goods in place of the discredited slave trade. Those drawn to Africa during this period included explorers, anthropologists, missionaries, scientists, and seekers of wealth, attracted to the continent by tales of lost treasure lying buried somewhere in the hinterland. The James Parker expedition team can be grouped under the last category.

To gain a fair knowledge of the complex thoughts in operation in *Tarzan the Ape Man*, one needs to examine the predominating scientific thoughts in operation during the post-abolitionist era. As I earlier noted, the predominating thoughts of the period revolve around theories of racial evolution that placed Africans next to apes in the evolutionary chain. These theories served a dual purpose: first, they helped to legitimize the slave trade since Africans were considered sub-human; second, they helped to lighten the burden of guilty conscience that followed the abolition of the slave trade. I will explain the link between racial theories and the European fascination with apes and Africans in the Tarzan series. Suffice it to stress at this point that racial theories were later elaborated into philosophical and anthropological discourses (Banton, 1987). With respect to Africa, in the realm of political thought, there emerged in the post-abolitionist era a combination of paternalistic humanitarianism that saw the salvation of Africa as tied to some sort of European imperial presence on the continent. Such political thoughts were inspired by both Social Darwinist theories and changes in the industrial outlook of both Europe and America. Europe and America had by this time expanded beyond the needs of slave labor and was instead in dire need of foreign markets and industrial raw materials. In the artistic and literary sphere, there emerged a romantic sensibility that sought to portray pre-colonial Africa as a continent of noble savages living in pastoral freedom and innocence before the slave trade (Brantlinger, 1986:189). *Tarzan the Ape Man* is a product of this romantic sensibility. It is a film caught on the boundary between its own imaginative world of an Africa of noble savages and wild hunting grounds where Europeans can roam about in adventurous spirit and the real Africa populated by indigenous people proud of their independence. The adventure it promises its viewers is caught between its invented and romanticized world, and the real world it refuses to acknowledge. As a result, the adventures continue to suffer the intrusion of forces it refuses to acknowledge — indigenous people who are proud of their culture and independence. This is the quintessential conflict at the center of *Tarzan the Ape Man*.

Northrop Frye's essay on literary romance acknowledges the unattainable utopia that marks its nostalgic project, and his definition of the essential quality of the romantic genre is worth noting because it can be applied to the analysis of *Tarzan the Ape Man*. According to Frye, the romantic genre is plagued by a perennially child-like nostalgia or search for some kind of imaginative golden age in time and space, and its essential plot element is adventure. He also classifies the genre as possessing the quality of sequentiality or processional form which produces, at its

most naive form, an endless series of works in which a character
never develops or ages as he or she goes through one adventure
after another. This is a quality very much characteristic of all the
Tarzan series. Finally,

> the complete form of the romance is clearly the successful quest,
> and such a complete form has three main stages: the stage of the
> perilous journey and the preliminary minor adventures; the
> crucial struggle, usually some kind of battle in which either the
> hero or his foe, or both, must die; and the exaltation of the
> hero...the central form of romance is dialectical: everything is
> focussed on the conflict between the hero and his enemy, and
> the reader's values are bound up with the hero. Hence the hero
> of romance is analogous to the mythical Messiah or deliverer.
> (Frye, 1973: 187)

Most of the foregoing qualities elaborated by Frye can be found in
Tarzan the Ape Man. The film begins with a shot of black men
carrying ivory tusks. This is the symbol of the emergent legitimate
trade and the new source of wealth, which inspires the search for
the elephants' burial ground — the main subject matter of the
film's adventure. This is followed by the arrival of Jane and a group
of people at James Parker's General Store. Parker is shown
consulting an elderly man about the site of the burial ground:
throughout the scene, the old man merely points at the map in
front of him and mumbles "iyo" several times. When Jane arrives,
she sees her father, Parker, sitting with his back to the door,
looking at her picture. Feeling emotionally touched, she calls out
saying hello. Parker turns and looks, without recognizing her. At
her second hello, he comes to realize that she is Jane. They
embrace and after this emotional reunion, Jane says: "From now on
I'm sick of civilization. I will be a savage." In terms of the film's
narrative, to be a savage is to exist outside the orbit of European
civilization. Since Africans are represented in the film as "savages,"
Jane's' statement implies she wants to live like Africans.

Shortly after this statement, Beamish (Forrester Harvey),
Parker's cook, enters, excited to see Jane, who pats his cheeks as a
mother will pat that of a child. Next, Holt enters and Parker
introduces them. Jane tells Parker that they have already met. Holt
calls the boys (African men) to bring her load in. Beamish goes to
get her coffee. Holt teases Parker about the quantity of Jane's
luggage and leaves. Jane remarks that she likes Holt and Parker tells

her that he and Holt get on very well, that both of them are united by their hatred of Africa, and Jane replies that she does not believe that. She pulls off her gown and prepares to make up while Parker sits besides her, smelling the fragrance of her clothes. As she pulls off more dresses, he gets embarrassed and tries to get up and leave, she tells him that he will be embarrassing her if he leaves. She begins to clean her face. At this point, they hear the voices of people singing outside. She moves toward the window and through her point-of-view shot, we see several people, some leading cattle, moving from the background of screen left towards the foreground of screen right. Parker joins her by the window and she asks him who they are. He tells her that they are the Macamba who have come to sell their produce. In the next point-of-view shot of Jane and Parker, we find a group of warriors wearing white-plum headgear, carrying shields and spears, moving from the background of screen right towards the foreground of screen left. All the while, we note Jane dressing up and excited about the spectacle outside. She moves towards the dressing table, puts on a helmet and moves outside, followed by Parker.

Looking at the traders dancing, Jane asks if they always sing and dance when they come to sell. Parker replies that they always do and that they are praying to their gods to give them the best of the bargaining. In exclamation, she replies that he has done far better than she had imagined, as if in acknowledgement of his worthy discovery. She then moves closer to the dancers to get a better view of them. From the dancers, she moves towards screen right where she looks at a group of women and children standing in a single file like soldiers mounting a guard of honor. Holt joins them there and remarks that Jane is already breaking into society. Holt takes her to a group of Masai warriors, referring to them as boys, also standing in a single file. He tells her that the marks on the warriors' shields indicate the number of people killed by each warrior. At this information, Jane exclaims excitedly in surprise saying: "Really!" He also shows her a group of Macamba warriors and dancers performing a courting/fertility dance. Parker tells Jane that they should be going, and she asks him about a group of elders sitting in an arch formation and wearing exotic head-gears, their faces painted and smoking pipes. Holt recognizes the chief of the Luo, a man wearing a monstrous-looking headgear, and exclaims that the old chief, Ntala, is in town, that possibly he can tell them where the burial ground is. Parker replies that the chief will not, that he has been trying to get the information from the chief for years. They look at them for a while and, as they prepare to leave, Parker says he hopes when they (natives) are done with their dancing they will be in a good mood for some substantial trading. As they move away, Parker asks Jane if she remembers the story of the elephant burial ground and she replies she does and recounts it. Parker then tells her that the natives know where such a burial ground is but that they are forbidden to even look at it. Any native who breaks this taboo is put to death by the witch doctor of the tribe. He informs her that Holt and him are searching for that burial ground. She asks what she can do to assist him and he replies that she is not physically fit enough for such an adventure. She then pleads with Holt to allow her and he agrees. Holt, however, asks her if she can shoot and she replies she can. She is given a gun and a hat, which she throws and shoots before it falls to the ground. At the sound of the gun shot, the black servants scamper toward the house and Holt points at them laughing. The sequence ends after this incidence with a fade.

The opening sequence contains most of the conventions of colonialist African cinema. There is a parade of warriors with white-plum headgears, armed with shields and spears, and dance scenes containing both war and fertility dances. The whole of the dance scenes and the tone of conversation between Jane and Parker are structured to give the western spectator the false impression that Africans dance in procession to the market to sell their farm produce. In addition, men, women and children are lined up, as in a military guard of honor, for Jane to inspect. Throughout the dance scenes, the warriors, dancers, women, children and elders are made to look like mere objects of Jane's spectacle and pleasure. They are denied speech, and if the dance performance is taken outside context of pure entertainment for Jane, and by extension, western spectators, it would be difficult to justify its inclusion in the narrative. Towards the end of the sequence, the black servants are represented as people who have not heard gun shot before. This pattern of representation is adhered to throughout the rest of the film. In terms of spatial articulation, the spectator is not allowed spatial accessibility to the African characters since spatial articulation, especially in this sequence, is tied to the presence of Jane. It is only through her point-of-view shots or when she moves close to examine the dancers, warriors, women or elders that we gain access to them. As a result, African characters hover in the background and are anonymous when they not drawn into the spatial orbit of Jane.

Another fact that is also established in the opening sequence is the ambivalent nature of the romantic sensibility. Frye acknowledges the dialectical nature of the conflicting forces of romance as representative symbols of good and evil, but he neglects to add that these forces are played out in an ambivalent manner. In *Tarzan the Ape Man*, the ambivalent nature of the romantic drive is established right from the opening sequence when Jane arrives in Africa. In a conversation with her father, she says she is tired of civilized societies, that she wants to live a savage life, but the first thing she does immediately after her luggage arrives is to start making up — a humorous and ironic comment on her craving to escape western culture. The film is also fairly explicit on the question of who the good African is — he is the loyal and tame servant, Riano, the task master whose role invokes images of slave trade days when slave-traders and slave-foremen wielding whips ensured that the white man's orders are carried out.

The main source of conflicts in the film is the threat posed to the adventure team by the indigenous population. The first of these conflicts is played out at the first camp in the forest at night. The sequence begins with comparative shots of the African and European sections of the camp. Here, as well as in most other colonialist African films, Africans are portrayed in joyous singing mood in contrast to the European characters' meditation over how to locate the elephants' burial ground. Against the background of this singing, animal noises, and threatening persistent African drum sounds, the camera pans from one quarter of the camp to another only to rest momentarily on Jane's reaction to the whole atmosphere as she engages in conversation with Holt. As the drum-sound gets nearer the camp, the camera focuses on Jane, no longer pretending to enjoy the ominous sounds but scared stiff. This is followed by cuts from her to the pitch dark and threatening forest that surrounds them. A bloodied black man shouting "bwana" bolts out of the dark forest pursued by his assailants. To protect him, Holt covers him up with a white cloth and sits on top of him, smoking his pipe. Shortly after that, his assailants emerge from the dark forest, done up exotically in white chalk, the symbolic make up for African ritual executioners in colonialist African films. Their leader later identified by James Parker as the chief priest, challenges Holt to produce the man for execution. Holt denies that he is being sheltered at the camp. Frustrated and disappointed, they disappear into the dark forest from which they emerged. Shortly afterwards, Parker explains to his daughter that the man has broken an ethnic taboo and has been condemned to death. That taboo, from his explanation, has to do with his attempt to show Parker the elephants' burial ground. The point of interest for western spectators however, is the story of Africa's barbaric ritual murders. Unfortunately, by the time Parker is done with his tale of ritual murders in Africa, his treasured guide is found to be dead, having only vaguely pointed in a certain direction before collapsing.

In terms of imagery, Holts' use of a white cloth to cover the guide before sitting on top of him carries a lot of significant meaning. It can be considered a metaphor for colonialism. The white cloth signifies a framework of European protection, but the fact that the guide dies from it also signifies the danger that underlies such protective framework. With respect to the narrative itself from this point onwards, the expedition team stumbles from one obstacle to another, including climbing steep mountainous cliffs where they lose one servant who falls to his death. Jane also falls she is saved because a rope has been tied round her waist and secured to that of Holt as a precaution after the fatal fall of the servant. They also cross a crocodile infested river on rafts, whereupon excited hippopotami, made aggressive by being shot at, savagely attack one of the rafts thereby setting up a scene for prowling crocodiles to feast on human flesh. It turns out; however, these crocodiles are a discriminating species that specialize only in black men's flesh.

The highlight of *Tarzan the Ape Man* is the discovery of a white ape-man, Tarzan, living as king among apes deep in the tropical rain forest. This discovery shortly after the crossing of the crocodile and hippopotami-infested river gives a different twist to the adventure. First, Jane is abducted by Tarzan during an attack on the expedition team by pygmies and falls in love with him, thereby heightening suspense in the film since earlier on, at the night camp sequence, Holt had tentatively proposed to her. Second, and perhaps most important, the simultaneous appearance of Tarzan, the apes and the pygmies in this film, carries a lot of significance because it represents the enactment of both the social and hierarchical orders of evolutionary theories in vogue during the post-abolitionist and colonial eras. The enactment is organized through a cross-cut of shots between Tarzan, the pygmies, and the apes, which places in perspective the comparative bodily configuration and social mentality between the apes and the pygmies on the one hand, and between Tarzan and the apes on the other. In this filmic enactment of evolutionary theories, the pygmies are placed symbolically in succession to the apes by virtue of bodily configuration and bestial behavior in the film. In addition, they are also symbolically represented as the evolving line from which Africans can trace their roots since only height separates them from the pygmies. On the other hand, Tarzan with his animalistic gait provides speculative possibilities of the missing link in the Darwinian chain with respect to Europeans. Third, this scene sets the stage for the realization of the white supremacist ideas that underlie the film's narrative structure.

The idea of white supremacy is propagated through the character of Tarzan, Frye's archetypal mythical super hero, a white messiah who has perfected the act of survival in the savage world of the animal kingdom. The Tarzan character is invested with all the super-human qualities that only the purveyors of white supremacist ideas could subscribe to. Tarzan is characterized as a white ape-man who, though totally cut off from his white race, still possesses some of the qualities of super-human nature that white supremacists ascribe to themselves. Swinging from tree to tree like apes and walking upright like humans in fast skipping steps, his only possession that makes him lord of the forest is a hunting knife. How he came about possessing that knife, we are not told. What we do learn is that with the possession of that sole weapon, Tarzan is able to kill, without suffering much physical damage to himself, a leopard threatening his dwelling place and two lions in quick succession, when he is out searching for food. Even though he has lived all his life alone with apes in the forest, he seems to possess the noble qualities of the well bred which can only be explained as product of the biological notion of genes and hereditary. When he attempts forcibly to seduce Jane and she protests, he voluntarily goes out to sleep in the cold open space in front of his treetop dwelling place, another noble and gentlemanly quality. Furthermore, within the short period of their meeting, the narrative informs us that he is able to learn a few English phrases and also gain enough self-consciousness to know that his name is Tarzan. Surely, only a super-human person could have achieved such a feat within that short period. He is also portrayed as a protector of animal rights who saves elephants caught in traps set possibly by the pygmies. When in trouble, he knows how to summon his animal friends to his aid. But as a Darwinian creature, he also kills some of the animals in his kingdom for food.

The foregoing super-human qualities are fully realized within the overall context of the adventure story. I noted earlier that his discovery and consequent integration into the narrative serves to heighten the level of conflict and suspense in the film. To play out the conflict, Tarzan abducts Jane during an ambush by pygmies. This abduction introduces an element of rivalry into the narrative. For instance, we know that Holt has proposed to Jane and that he is armed with a gun in contrast to Tarzan who has only a hunting knife. We also know that Jane prefers Tarzan to Holt because of his display of chivalry and gallantry in the face of danger. This greatly increases the possibility of conflict between both men. This conflict is played out when one of the apes guarding Jane is shot. This violent act not only shatters the peace of Tarzan's kingdom but also symbolically represents the loss of innocence as far as the film's narrative is concerned. Where before Tarzan stood by ignorantly while a gun is being pointed at him without realizing its implied dangers, where before he reacted indifferently to the presence of the expedition team in his kingdom, the termination of the grand ape's life by the gun shot changes everything. From then onwards, he develops not only a self-preservative consciousness in presence of the team, but also a predatory and vengeful consciousness toward them.

As a result of the shooting of the ape, Tarzan in vengeance kills two of the black porters; a signification of the textual devaluation of African lives, thereby increasing Holt's determination to kill him. Jane intervenes and pleads that she should be allowed to appeal to Tarzan to halt the killing. Her voluntary return to Tarzan results in the blossoming of their relationship and also witnesses the symbolic re-enactment of the Judeo-Christian mythical Garden of Eden tale and the noble savage tradition. The film creates this Garden of Eden atmosphere by focusing exclusively on the evolving love story between Jane and Tarzan in the forest. This love story, represented with all the trappings of its patriarchal world-outlook, depicts Jane happily luxuriating in the "nest" built for her by Tarzan while he plays the role of hunter-gatherer searching for fruits and meat in the forest. The Edenic setting, reserved exclusively for them, comprises the whole forest with its wild fruits, various animal species, and a nearby pool where Olympic gold medallist swimmer Johnny Weissmuller exhibits his swimming prowess. The sequence ends with a cut to James Parker and his team searching for Jane. Her voluntary departure from Tarzan, this time with his consent, symbolizes the establishment of a bond between her and Tarzan. When they are later ambushed and captured by the pygmies, this bond enables Tarzan to intervene and effectively realize his role as a messianic savior of the team. I want to examine the sequence dealing with the capture of Jane and other members of the adventure team because it is the climax of the film and uses a lot of the metaphors associated with African bestiality.

The sequence begins with the capture of members of the adventure team, including Jane, by the pygmies who take them to their village. Their arrival at the village is greeted with singing and dancing amidst lowering the gate of the village. This is followed by a brief medium close up of a man, possibly the traditional ruler, casting an evil look at the captives as they are led into a prison. In the prison, there is a huge pit inside of which there is a giant ape. Opposite the pit, there is a grandstand packed with ropes wielding pygmies singing and dancing. They throw ropes across the pit to fetch the prisoners one by one into the pit for the giant ape to strangle. As it strangles the prisoner, there is a cut to the pygmies dancing happily and making gestures suggesting that the ape should squeeze harder. This whole macabre scene is represented as some sort of sport for the pygmies. The prisoners are fetched inside the pit, beginning with the black guides. The scene climaxes when Jane is trapped and lowered into the pit and Holt jumps in to save her. The ape throws Holt to the side of the pit and Parker jumps in with a burning stick and tries to use its flame to burn the ape. It disarms Parker and throws him out of the pit. This is followed by a cut to Tarzan, swinging from tree to tree and racing to Jane's rescue, having been informed by Cheeta, Tarzan's friend, that she is in danger. In a cut back to the pit, we find the ape carrying Jane in its arm. Just then, Tarzan arrives, looks into the pit, sees Jane in the ape's arm, removes his knife from his side and jumps into the pit. He attacks the ape with the knife but it throws him down. As it goes again for Tarzan, Cheeta (the young ape), his friend, jumps on the ape to distract its attention. It gets hold of Cheeta, swings Cheeta round its head, smashes it at the side of the pit and throws Cheeta out of the pit. As the ape makes for Tarzan a third time, he picks up his knife and throws it into the ape's forehead. Holt carries Jane out of the way. Tarzan then jumps at the ape from behind, pulls the knife from the ape's forehead and uses it to jab at the ape until it slumps to the ground. Having killed the ape, he calls the elephants in a triumphant wail. On seeing that the ape is dead, the pygmies begin to shoot at the captives with bows and arrows. However, they use the dead ape as shield. This is followed by a cut to a pygmy sentry blowing a horn made of ivory on sighting the elephants racing towards their village. On hearing the sound, the pygmies at the stand begin to flee. The elephants tear down the fence of the village and rescue Tarzan and the team. The sequence ends with the teams' departure for the elephants' burial ground.

The capture of the expedition team by the pygmies can be considered as part of the strategy of incorporating exotic elements into the narrative since their appearance, short rotund shiny bodies, represents departures from the norm even by the standards of colonialist African cinema. But apart from this physical deviation from the norm, they also symbolize the unconscious interjection of the counter-narrative currents represented by indigenous opposition to colonial presence. This climactic sequence is, however, devoted entirely to the exploration of stereotypical themes such as African sadism and childishness. In terms of representation, it involves the simultaneous denial and representation of the fundamental implicit native opposition to colonialism as some sort of trifle and sadistic child-sport. In line with this mode of representation, the narrative refuses to acknowledge why the team is captured and, when they arrive at the pygmies' kingdom, no formal case is held against them, only a momentary shot of an evil gaze meant to represent that of the ruler is offered. In this classic example of colonialist trivialization of native opposition to imperial presence, the film reduces this fundamental opposition to sadistic childish sport. To fully complement this picture, shots of pygmies wielding human-bones, an indication that they are cannibals, are incorporated into the frame. There is also an underlining fear of miscegenation in the sequence, especially in the image of the giant ape carrying Jane in its arm — an image that is fully exploited in *King Kong.*

Tarzan the Ape Man is a romantic film caught in the ambivalent desire to simultaneously denounce and acknowledge the qualities of industrial societies through racial affirmation. Despite its overt racist tone, the film occasionally incorporates elements of counter-discourse, though in most cases, it does so through inversion as for example, the presentation of native opposition to colonialism as some sort of sadistic childish sport. However, through this unconscious incorporation of implicit counter-discourse, the idea that Africa is one huge jungle and adventure ground, a symbolic "Garden of Eden," inhabited by wild animals where white adventurers can roam about unchallenged is questioned.

A Critical Reading of King Solomon's Mines

In her essay, "The Dark Continent: Africa as Female Body in Haggard's Adventure Fiction," Rebecca Stott states that almost "all of Haggard's romances involve the quest motif: usually a band of men must journey into the center of Africa in search of something or someone" (Stott, 1989: 71). One can even go even further to say that the quest motif is central to most adventure films set in Africa. It provides the main framework upon which *Tarzan the Ape Man,* *The African Queen,* and *Mogambo* are based. Stott, like Frye, also acknowledges the centrality of the perilous experience to the quest. According to Stott, the quest is usually full of danger and requires the physical and moral strengths of those involved to be tested at every stage of the journey. The quest motif becomes a quest for and initiation into manhood, a confirmation of virility (Stott: 71). Even though *King Solomon's Mines* (Robert Stevenson and Geoffrey Barkas, 1937) is not an all-male affair, since there is Kathy O'Brien (Anna Lee), its narrative structure is centered on the quest motif. The quest in this case, is for the legendary King Solomon's Mines that are supposed to contain secret chambers full of mined diamonds.

King Solomon's Mines is a melodramatic adventure freely adapted from Haggard's novel and it is the first of three versions so far inspired by the novel. The story revolves around the hunt for lost treasures of the sort we have already met in *Tarzan the Ape Man.*

And as in *Tarzan*, there is an underlying story of paternal desire to increase the inheritance of a loved daughter. In the case of *King Solomon's Mines*, the adventure story is driven by Patrick O'Brien's desire to accumulate wealth for his daughter, Kathy.

The storyline is straightforward: Kathy O'Brien (Anna Lee) and her father, Patrick (Arthur Sinclair), are stranded in Kimberly after they have tried unsuccessfully to sell a fake diamond. They beg and get a lift from Allan Quartermain (Cedric Hardwicke), a well-known hunter, who is on his way to meet two clients, Commander Good (Roland Young) and Sir Henry Curtis (John Loder). On their way, they come upon a dying man, Jose Sylvestra (Arthur Goullett), who informs them that he is on his way to the legendary King Solomon's Mines. Shortly after his death, they find among his possessions, a map showing the location of the mines. Patrick O'Brien leaves at night in search of the mines. From this point onward, the narrative becomes complex, having taken on the additional story of a daughter's search for her father. A search party comprising Sir Henry Curtis, Commander Good, and Allan Quartermain set out in search of Kathy. Having caught up with her, they offer to assist her in her search for her father with the assistance of the native guide Umbopa (Paul Robeson) who, it turns out, is the rightful heir to the throne of Kukuanaland. After overcoming the harsh conditions of the desert where they nearly die of thirst, they finally arrive at the mountain-pass that leads to the mines. There they are taken prisoners and brought before the throne-usurping king, Twala (Robert Adams), who rules Kukuanaland with the assistance of his spell-casting councilor, the aged witch, Gagool (Sydney Fairbrother). Gagool schemes for their death but Allan Quartermain neutralizes her plans by successfully countering her "black" magic with his "white" magic, offered by way of accurately predicting a scientifically forecast eclipse of the sun. A succession of warfare follows during which Twala is killed and the rightful heir to the throne, Umbopa, is installed as king. Finally, they go into the mines but are trapped by Gagool, who herself perishes in an eruption inside the mines. Umbopa saves Kathy and her search party after successfully rescuing her father. Patrick O'Brien, in show of appreciation, offers to share his diamonds with other members of the team since the mine is buried in the inferno that follows the volcanic eruption.

As in *Tarzan the Ape Man*, spatial representation in *King Solomon's Mines* is decidedly colonialist in nature and, like its narrative, aimed at geographic exploration of the unfamiliar and the exotic. The camera is used to map the landscape as the journey progresses through veldt, desert and mountainous regions into the thick rain forest. The whole process involves making the African landscape look familiar through filmic exploration. The fundamental drive for this mode of cinematography, as earlier stated, is the desire to exploit the geographic Otherness of the landscape for the visual pleasures of Western spectators. Thus once the adventure party moves into the open country, the short rapid cuts of the opening sequence give way to a combination of long takes and frequent slow pans as the company unwinds its way from the open country, through desert, and into the thick rain forest.

During the journey, the African landscape is symbolically represented as a personal adversary that must be conquered in the search for self-fulfilment. In this regard, the spiritual symbolization of the journey into the hinterland of Africa can be compared to an inward journey into oneself, a journey that involves exploring the unfamiliar regions of one's mind. Here spiritual vacuity is symbolized as desert while turbulent thoughts are represented by all manner of native threat. But in addition to such a metaphysical reading of the text, there are enough visual details that physically represent the threat to explorers of unfamiliar regions. These visual details represent part of the perilous experience of the romantic genre (Frye: 187). They include both visible and invincible forces at interplay in the film text. By visible forces, I mean the physical obstacles like desert, mountains and forest that are represented in the narrative; and by invincible forces, I mean the presence of indigenous people resentful of foreign intrusion which the text refuses to acknowledge directly as such but instead disguises as an intra-ethnic succession contest. For instance, the colonialist tone of the film is established right from the opening sequence when in response to Kathy's observation that she sighted somebody in the horizon, Allan Quartermain replies by saying that what she is looking at is open and uninhabited country. The remark, "uninhabited country," is a colonialist term used by Europeans to legitimize the forcible occupation or settling of lands. Of course, the film is silent on the geo-political significance of the intrusion into a foreign land; instead, it represents it in narrative terms, as the natural threat of invincible forces. In furtherance of this colonialist perception, when the hunting team arrives in the forest region, Sir Henry Curtis surveys the land and concludes that they are in uninhabited country, thus recalling Quartermain's observation of the opening sequence. This last observation is marked by ironic contradiction because shortly after his observation, the land becomes activated as it reveals its unacknowledged inhabitants.

Another visual detail established in the opening sequence is the feminization of the African landscape. This is visually captured through filmic exploration of maps and cartographic illustrations designed to make the landscape look feminine. For instance, in *King Solomon's Mines*, the actual act of penetration of the hinterland is preceded by a scrutiny of the map of the terrain. The camera is positioned like a searchlight as it probes the cartographic illustrations from the plains through Sheba's Breasts, down King Solomon's Road, to a triangle of mountains, with feminine sculptural adornments at the gate of the mines. In keeping with this mode of representation, the actual entering of the mines, guarded by the bat-like ageless witch, Gagool, which physically involves entering the womb of the earth, can be symbolically likened to nostalgia for one's original home in the female womb during conception. In addition, shots of the interior of the mines structured like a series of smoldering catacombs with craters and frothing lava can be considered as a symbolic representation of fear of the female body as well as of hell. As in every adventure story, the intention is simultaneously to scare the faint-hearted as well as grant them access to the experiences intrinsic to heroic acts and, as in most colonialist African films, *King Solomon's Mines* is organized around a cinematic scheme of comparison that portrays Africans as people with inferior behavioral attitudes such as preoccupation with singing and dancing and Europeans as endowed with rationality and reason. For instance, in the opening sequence of the film, contrasting shots of Allan Quartermain's camp at night show the African quarters of the camp alive with songs and merry-making while the Europeans in their quarter are shown deeply engrossed in the analysis of maps and calculations on how to locate King Solomon's Mines. These contrasting shots, also present in the forest camp scenes in *Tarzan the Ape Man*, help to portray Africans as emotionally expressive people bereft of rational reasoning.

In tandem with this inferior/superior comparative narrative structure, the battle sequence pitches European war strategies and weapons against those of Africa in an attempt to show the superiority of the former and inferiority of the latter. Thus while the European war camp is portrayed as building ramparts and positioning fighters for effective fighting, the African war camp is depicted as lacking any war strategy. While Europeans fight in formations, Africans are shown haphazardly pouring into the battle ground without formations, sustained only by unmitigated frenzy that usually ends in massacre. In this game of violence, the Europeans are shown as the good men backing the forces of justice by fighting on the side of their lackey, Umbopa, the rightful heir to the throne, while Twala's warriors are portrayed as the bad men fighting to sustain the evil rule of a fake king. The battle sequence climaxes in the fight between Sir Henry Curtis and Twala, in which Curtis, representing the forces of good, kills Twala, thereby making it possible for Umbopa, the rightful heir, to ascend to the throne. Here, as well as in *Sanders of the River*, which also features Paul Robeson in a similar role, we find his white masters assisting him to ascend to position of authority. In fairness to Robeson, much of the film's success can be attributed to his acting as well as singing prowess. His performance of the songs, "I'm not Afraid" and "Climbing Up" with its refrain of "Mighty Mountain!" is powerfully rendered. In keeping with his star status in the film, mostly low angle shots that frame a proportionally larger-than-life image of him against the skyline, especially in the scenes where he is singing, are utilized, thereby lending an air of vitality to the weariness and drudgery of the trek into Kukuanaland.

The film also adheres to colonialist African cinematic conventions in its utilization of traditional African costumes and dances. In the battle sequence for instance, the African soldiers are exotically dressed up in the emblematic battle gear of colonialist African films: these include a white plum-headgear, bows and arrows, spears and shields. Like the exotic battle gear, the dances included in this film are performed out of context and their inclusion is strictly borne out of the desire to cater for the visual pleasure of western spectators. Furthermore, while *mise-en-scène* in *King Solomon's Mines* can be qualified as effectively handled, especially in scenes like those involving dances and meetings, both in terms of exterior and interior decor positioning as well as in terms of the general set-up of the staging space, it is nonetheless constrained by the conventions of colonialist African films. For instance, the set of the dance sequence which has the stage situated in an arena-like space fenced in by several huts has the entrance to the king's hut adorned with human skulls, the iconographic representations of cannibalism.

In sum, *King Solomon's Mines* fully exploits the conventions of the colonialist romantic genre. It utilizes most of the characteristic traits of the romantic genre which Frye identifies as comprising the quest motif together with its perilous journeys and the romance; the nostalgia for setting in "unspoiled nature," the comparative opposition of a set of moral values, and the triumph of good over evil, with its element of messianism. In addition to its romantic vision, the film also adheres to the conventions of colonialist African films, which require the portrayal of Africans and African cultural practices as inferior in comparison to their European counterparts. Thus while the pattern of representation in *King Solomon's Mines* may be said to meet the entertainment requirements of those western spectators in search of exotica, the narrative is constrained by colonialist African discursive practices which require the setting up of Africans as objects of the westerner's gaze and visual pleasure, and whose subjecthood can only be defined as such or through special paternalist beneficence.

A Critical Reading of The African Queen

Of all the colonialist films set in Africa, none better reflects the intra-European conflicts and rivalries that attended the scramble for Africa than *The African Queen*. In this film, the continent is represented in gendered cinematic idioms within a romantic framework as was the case in *King Solomon's Mines*, but beside the feminization of the landscape, the romance has been nuanced in such a way that the intra-European conflicts and rivalries set up Africa as a treasured bride, symbolically represented in the film as "The African Queen," albeit one under the protection of British imperial authority. The other major suitor vying for the possession of Africa in the film is Germany, whose power is symbolized by her frigate, "The Louisa." The film is set within the context of the outbreak of the First World War in what was then German East Africa. The main theatre of war is, of course, Europe, but what the film attempts to do is to set up Germany as a villain both in the war as well as in her colonial enterprise in Africa.

Germany's villainy is established in the opening sequence of the film, which depicts the rampage of her colonial forces. But besides showing Germany as a villain, the film also propagates such themes like patriotism and loyalty to one's country in times of war as well as representing Africans as barbaric, indolent and unpatriotic. The whole romance between Charles Allnut (Humphrey Bogart) and Rose Sayer (Katharine Hepburn) is aimed at propagating the theme of patriotism and loyalty to Britain during the First World War. At the outset of the film, for instance, Charles is a plain mine-worker/mail-runner with little concern for nationalism and all its attendant jingoism, but after fate consigns him with Rose, after the destruction of their church by the rampaging German colonial forces, she convinces him of the necessity of helping the British cause in her war with Germany. The conflict, which is symbolically played out in The African Queen's sinking of The Louisa, shows how British ingenuity triumphed over German armament.

What is of interest to me in this film, however, is the manner in which the intra-European conflicts are extended to Africa and how the film represents the role of Africans in it. The film utilizes gendered cinematic idioms in which the continent is symbolically represented in feminine terms as a queen with contesting imperial suitors — Britain and Germany. The film proposes Britain as the worthy suitor by portraying Germany as a villainous colonial power whose forces destroy villages and send Africans to concentration camps. But in addition to portraying its rival as an unworthy suitor, the film also portrays Africans as simpletons helping the Germans to destroy their own people. This unpatriotic behavior is, therefore, subtly contrasted with the nationalist fervor of Charles and Rose.

Apart from portraying Africans as unpatriotic elements in the war, the film also adheres to the general conventions of colonialist African cinema in the representation of Africans. The whole of the opening sequence, which establishes the African atmosphere of the film, is dedicated to the recycling of stereotypical images of Africans. The church service scenes are full of such representations. For example, shots of the church congregation are structured in a contrasting pattern with the African members of the congregation deprived of any comprehensible speech. They are shown mumbling in an incomprehensible and disinterested manner in order to highlight the burden of missionary work. Amidst these rapid contrastive shots, which show Reverend Samuel Sayer (Robert Morley) and Rose Sayer trying desperately to retain the attention of the congregation, the sound of the African Queen's horn is heard and is shown to distract the congregation. Several shots of them looking childishly toward the direction of the sound of the horn are contrasted with that of Reverend Sayer and Rose singing frantically in an effort to retain their attention. The sound of the horn is shown to affect men, women, and children even though the narrative suggests that the steamboat is a regular caller at the village.

Before the boat is anchored, there are more shots of elderly African men running to catch its glimpse — a most unlikely thing for an African elder to do. Later, the elders receive gifts of cigar from Charles. After greeting them paternalistically, Charles moves to the front of the church where more interior shots reveal the helplessness of Sayer and Rose to contain the excited converts. Things come to a climax when Charles stylishly throws his cigar stub toward a group of adolescents seated indolently on the ground in front of the church. Even before the stub lands, expertly choreographed shots of both boys and men scrambling for the stub are shown. This is followed by a cut to shots of the arrival of the German colonial forces made up of Africans with German officers. The leading unpatriotic role which the African conscripts play in the burning of the village helps to reinforce the earlier image of childishness and indolence which the film had established in the preceding scenes.

In addition to the adoption of colonialist textual conventions in the representation of Africans, there is also a noticeable influence of Joseph Conrad's *Heart of Darkness* in the representation of the African landscape. Most of the colonialist regime of representation found in this novel is visually replicated in this film. The most common feature of this style of representation includes sailing in a steamboat through turbulent waterways bounded on both sides by thick tropical vegetation. In place of Africans that shoot arrows and throw spears at Marlow's steamboat from the shore, the film puts a German colonial force, made up principally of African recruits with German officers, who fire rifles at Charles and Rose, but the savagery this was meant to reflect cannot be lost on spectators familiar with Conrad's poetic description of a lonely steamboat sailing through an equally lonely but unpredictable river bounded by tropical forestation.

The sailing sequence with its perilous elements is shot mostly in long takes, slow pans and long shots. This gives the film a slow leisurely tempo. The long takes show the river as a very calm bluish body of water with thick greenish vegetation. Occasionally, there is a slow pan of the greenish riverbank almost from the water level as the steamboat glides along. This style of filming serves a dual purpose: on the one hand, it cinematically documents the flora and fauna of the landscape for the visual pleasure of western spectators; on the other hand, it represents an ironic comment upon the beauty of the water and the landscape. The subtlety of the style lies in the fact that this bluish body of calm water set within thick greenish vegetation with a clear blue skyline will be revealed to be a mask for its dangerous hidden cavernous rapids and gullies. Therefore, the long take depicting the calm river serve as a metaphor for representing the deceptiveness of the outward appearances of African landscapes. It is a style also effectively used in the opening sequence of *Men of Two Worlds*, where ironic inversion is adopted in the representation of the landscape. This ambivalent style of representation falls within the general conventions of colonialist African cinema. In *Men of Two Worlds*, the beautiful landscape is represented as being infested with the sleeping sickness carrier, tsetse fly, while in *The African Queen*; the beautiful calm river is shown to be a deceptive mask for hidden dangerous rapids. Furthermore, as in most colonialist African films, the landscape is symbolically represented as a personal adversary that must be defeated as part of the self-fulfilling aspect of the adventure. The romance between Charles and Rose is realized out of the circumstantial difficulties in which they find themselves. If the romance is captivating in the end, it is because we realize that it has withstood the test of the clash of two strong-willed personalities and of a treacherous environment.

The African Queen is a nationalistic romance set within the context of the colonial rivalries between Britain and Germany at the outbreak of the First World War. The nationalist romance has its captivating moments when circumstantial difficulties help to break down Rose's image of a sexless missionary spinster and transform Charles from a simple-minded hard-drinking mine worker into a war hero. But in the representation of Africa, its vision of patriotism is blurred by the constraints of colonialist African filmic conventions as it portrays Africans as simpletons and indolent children, and the African landscape as a treacherously deceptive landscape.

Colonial Burden Films

Colonial burden films are essentially films that propagate the necessity for colonial rule. For this reason, many of them tend to rationalize colonialism through a derogatory portrayal of institutions that obstruct the free flow of the colonial system. Historically speaking, the greatest opposition to colonial rule prior to the emergence of Western educated nationalists came from African traditional rulers. As a result of this, most of the films situated in this era tend to represent traditional African rulers as despotic and barbaric. Through this method of representation, the case for colonial presence is legitimated. However, in the process of legitimating colonial presence, the films also paradoxically expose the fragility of the whole system because of the potential for the slippage of Africans into barbarism in the absence of colonial authority. The strategy is to rationalize colonial presence, but it is a strategy that also inadvertently exposes the fragility of colonial rule. Evidence of this textual pattern can be glimpsed from *Sanders of the Rivers*, *Four Feathers*, *Old Bones of the River*, *Men of Two Worlds*, and *Mister Johnson*. This pattern will become clearer in our analysis of both *Sanders of the River* and *Mister Johnson*.

A *Critical Reading of* Sanders of the River

Among the films that I have categorized as colonial burden films, *Sanders of the River* (1935), Zoltan Korda's film version of Edgar Wallace's popular stories book of the same title, can today be considered as a classic in the sub-genre. Alexander Korda conceived *Sanders of the River* as part of an imperial trilogy that includes *The Drum* and *The Four Feathers*. Of the three films, one, *The Drum*, was set outside Africa in India.

Most of the reputed success of *Sanders of the River* can be traced to the fact that it was one of the very first set of films, in this sub-genre of colonialist African films, to deal with such a historically relevant subject matter as the potential problems of an archetypal colonial administrator at a time when the British had commenced colonial administration in Africa. Its success can also be traced to the elaborate use of Yoruba artistic carvings as objects of scenic decoration both in Commissioner Sander's office, in Mofalaba's court, and in Bosambo's private dwelling, its use of erotic African fertility dances in the sequence dealing with the marriage of Bosambo and Lilongo, and its elaborate use of songs and dances. All these combine to satisfy the entertainment needs of a broad spectrum of spectators. The film is reputed to have been so successful that, after its 1935 exhibition, it was re-issued in 1938, 1943 and 1947. The film inspired a stage version, *The Sun Never Sets*, which also starred Leslie Banks. Paul Robeson's recording of the "Canoe Song" also became a hit record (Richards and Aldgate, 1983: 25). Richards and Aldgate also state that the "box-office success of Sanders was such as to inspire Korda to produce *The Drum* (1938), set in India, and *The Four Feathers* (1939), set in the Sudan" (Richards and Aldgate: 25).

The film begins with Commissioner Sanders (Leslie Banks), who has been peacefully ruling a set of communities on the estuaries of a river in West Africa for several years without leave, preparing to go on an annual leave to enable him finalize his wedding plans. Commissioner Ferguson (Martin Walker) is sent to relieve him. But before he proceeds on leave, Bosambo (Paul Robeson), a Liberian ex-convict who has unofficially manipulated himself into position of chief of the Ochori, comes to seek official approval from Sanders. Sanders, playing the benevolent fatherly role, officially confers upon Bosambo the title of chief of the Ochori after chastising him for his naughty past behavior. Immediately Sanders goes on leave, the gin and gunrunners, Farini (Marquis de Portago) and Smith (Eric Maturin), spread the rumor that Sanders is dead. Ferguson, sensing that trouble is afoot, leaves for the Old King's country, on a peace mission, where he is murdered by King Mofalaba (Tony Wane). Not yet done, Mofalaba, who has been peeved by Bosambo's audacious obstruction of his slave raids into neighboring ethnic groups, plots his elimination now that his white master and protector, Sanders, is out of the way, by kidnapping Bosambo's wife Lilongo (Nina Mae McKinney) so as to lure Bosambo into his trap. Bosambo falls for the trap and is captured. On learning of all these developments, Sanders, who had been waiting for an auspicious moment to bring King Mofalaba to justice, sails up river in his steamboat, the Zaire, and arrives just on time to free the captives. The film ends with King Mofalaba being killed and Bosambo installed in his place.

As earlier stated, one of the reasons why *Sanders of the River* was successful was because of the choice of subject matter, the problems of an archetypal colonial administrator, especially one who served in Africa. This choice of theme and characterization helped to strengthen the narrative and I shall accordingly start my analysis through examination of its central character, Commissioner Sanders. Richards and Aldgate state that

> the characteristics that Sanders embodies are entirely in line with the criteria actually employed to select colonial administrators. The selection was virtually controlled from 1910 to 1947 (with the exception of World War 1 period) by one man — Sir Ralph Furse. Furse selected his men specifically on the basis of character and recruited them mainly from public schools. (Richards and Aldgate: 16)

Furse himself is famous for stating that without the caliber of men like Sanders, Britain would not have been able to run such a vast empire with a small band of men. In addition, he observed that "In England, universities train the mind; the public school train character and teach leadership" (cited by Richards and Aldgate: 16). On their part, Richards and Aldgate state that the "public school taught duty and responsibility; a sense of fair play, qualities of leadership, above all a benevolent paternalism" (16). To qualify for recruitment as a District Commissioner, one would supposedly have served one's apprenticeship years as a school prefect or have held leadership positions in voluntary organizations like the Boy Scouts or Boys' Brigade.

The character of Sanders is drawn to embody all the foregoing qualities. He is fair and firm toward his subordinates; he is mild mannered and good humored in the presence of his superiors; above all, he is benevolently paternalistic toward his subjects like Bosambo and the local chiefs appointed by him. Leslie Banks' interpretation of the role of Commissioner Sanders was deemed to be so realistically carried out that the Colonial Office came to project the Sanders character as a role model for newly recruited District Commissioners. One of them, Charles Allen, has explicitly recorded the central role played by this film in the lives of newly recruited District Commissioners: "Most of us had seen a film called *Sanders of the River* before we went out, and suddenly here was the thing, and it was real, one was walking behind a long line of porters — and it was just like the film." (Richards and Aldgate: 17)

Another talked of the "*Sanders of the River* touch" in the description of the conduct of his duties (Richards and Aldgate: 17). Therefore, the character of Sanders was set up as an ideal model to which all would-be District Commissioners could aspire. Since Sanders is the model character and protagonist, all other characters in the film tend to be defined in relation to him. Sanders is also the symbol of the uneven Afro-European power relations in this text. The contending levels of authority are represented Mofalaba on the African side, and Sanders on the British. The sequence, which most graphically represents this uneven Afro-European power relation, is that which deals with the meeting between Sanders and King Mofalaba after the first slave raid. This sequence will be examined to show how power is projected in the text.

The sequence begins with a medium long shot of soldiers standing on guard with their bayoneted rifles at the ready. This is followed by a cut to Sanders, Tibbet and Bosambo. Sanders orders the soldiers to stand at attention as Bosambo points with his spear towards King Mofalaba arriving in an entourage of armed warriors. Three of them then sit to await Mofalaba's arrival — Sanders and Tibbet sit on chairs, and Bosambo sit on the ground beside Sanders. As Mofalaba's entourage gets closer, the soldiers adjust themselves with their bayoneted rifles pointing aggressively towards them. This is followed by a cut back to King Mofalaba riding in a hammock. The entourage arrives at the meeting ground chanting a war song and a chair is placed down for the king. Sanders gets up to acknowledge his arrival, both of them bow to each other and they sit down, with King Mofalaba sitting opposite Sanders. A hot exchange then ensues between them, beginning with Sanders telling him that he called him for meeting but not with his warriors, and King Mofalaba replies that the guard of Sanders' little Chief (Bosambo) killed the captain of his guard. Sanders replies that Mofalaba's captain heard his orders but did not obey them. Mofalaba reminds Sanders that he promised that they (Sanders' subjects) should keep their customs. He informs Sanders that it is one of their old customs to buy women. Sanders agrees but adds that he permitted that only if the woman and the father consent. He warns Mofalaba that he will not tolerate slavery in his district. Mofalaba responds by reminding Sanders that his

(Mofalaba's) forefathers have ruled the area for three hundred years and that he is the greatest King in the country. Sanders replies that his King is the greatest King on earth and that if little Kings and chiefs disobey his King's order then he (Sanders) will remove them from their thrones.

At the end of this hot exchange, Mofalaba pauses and asks Sanders what he wants. Sanders tells him to take his spear and men back to his (Mofalaba's) country and he (Sanders) will release Mofalaba's men in his prison. Mofalaba replies that he will do what Sanders want because both of them are friends, but that he has nine war drums over which are stretched the skins of any chief who offends him. Casting an evil look at Bosambo, he adds that he knows the skin that will be stretched on the tenth. Sanders warns him that if he touches one servant of his King, be it as little as a pigeon, Mofalaba won't be King any longer. He adds, as a measure of finality, that the meeting is finished. Both of them get up and as Mofalaba prepares to leave, he casts an evil look at Bosambo. The entourage leaves amidst humming and Tibbet observes that he will be delighted to wring the king's neck, to which Sanders replies that the British tax payers won't be delighted. When Tibbet asks why, Sanders replies that it will cost about one million pound to do that, that war is an expensive thing.

Throughout this sequence, the authority of Sanders is visibly displayed. His soldiers are positioned at the meeting ground to respond to any eventuality should the meeting degenerate into confrontation. But even though Sanders has his troops standby for the meeting, to intimidate Mofalaba, he disapproves of Mofalaba's right to self-defense. Authority and power is what is on display in this sequence. But this authority and power is, in the context of this sequence, tied to military prowess. From the way Sanders exercises power in this sequence, we know that British authority and power is established in the district through military superiority. It is this military superiority that gives Sanders the sole authority to undermine indigenous power structures as well as appoint British Warrant Chiefs. With respect to the representation of African culture, the payment of bride price is deliberately linked in the narrative with the institution of slavery so that the condemnation of slavery is used to denigrate marital customs. This linkage is fully exercised in the Bosambo-Lilongo marriage sequence where Sanders uses his position as the sole authority in the district to impose a European concept of marriage, one man, and one wife, upon Bosambo. In keeping with the conventions of colonialist African cinema, King Mofalaba is represented as a barbaric despot who will go to any extent to impose his authority on his subjects, including killing and stretching the skins of disloyal chiefs over his drums. It terms of spatial articulation, the dialogue between Sanders and Mofalaba is shot in shot/reverse shots, with a brief cut to Bosambo's reaction shot when Mofalaba says he knows the skin which will be stretched on his tenth drum. Though Sanders does not enjoy more spatial authority than Mofalaba in this sequence, the strength and authority of his speech reflects the imbalance of power between him and Mofalaba.

The relationship between both contending levels of authority is based on suspicion, tension and violence. Sanders is always suspicious that the King is trying to undermine his authority while the King sees the appointment of Warrant Chiefs who owe allegiance to the British colonial authorities as undermining his right to appoint chiefs. Characterization also reflects the general conventions of colonialist African discourse in which collaborators like Bosambo become the good African and traditional rulers like Mofalaba, who oppose British imperial presence, however self-centered such opposition may be, become the bad African. But ironically too, the good African is the one who is treated with a lot of condescension, since the relationship between him and his British patrons is based on master-servant relationship not on equality. For instance, the Bosambo character is tolerated and patronized by Sanders. When he appears before Sanders in the opening sequence of the film, for the purpose of the conferment of the title of chief of Ochori, he remains standing while being addressed like a child summoned before his father or headmaster. To reduce him further in stature, Paul Robeson's huge frame notwithstanding, Sanders invokes his criminal past. This criminal past refers to his activities in Liberia. The fact that he is portrayed as a Liberian ex-convict symbolically links him up with Africans in diaspora, especially to African-Americans, since Liberia was created as a settlement colony for freed slaves of United States origin.

As a Warrant Chief, Bosambo is a servant of British imperial authority. During colonial era, Africans often perceived the chain of authority that dangles from the neck of the Bosambo character, as a symbol of collaboration. Thus, when confronted by Bosambo during a slave raid, the Captain of the Old King's warriors addresses Bosambo in terms used for pets by saying: "Whose dog are you?" However, as puppets of British imperialism, Warrant Chiefs enjoyed a lot of privileges. Besides wielding enormous authority on behalf of the British, their children enjoyed privileged education, thereby helping to perpetuate the tradition of a two-tier education system, with special elite schools forming the upper level, reserved for children of the emergent ruling class. This was how elite schools like Federal Government Colleges and Government Colleges were established in Nigeria. Therefore, Bosambo is reflecting this historical trend when he tells his wife, Lilongo, that if they persevere and remain in their present post, their children will have the opportunity to attend special schools for the children of chiefs.

In terms of characters' relationships, Sanders relates to Bosambo as well as other African characters in paternal terms. He supervises Bosambo's marriage to Lilongo and specifies the type of marriage by insisting upon one wife, one certificate. In line with this paternal relationship, when King Mofalaba kidnaps Lilongo and Bosambo is going to seek her release, he sends his children to Sanders to be brought up as wards of the government just in case Mofalaba kills him in the mission. Furthermore, in comparison with Sanders, who has kept his sexual and marital life under control, the Bosambo character, as well as other African characters, is portrayed as sexually promiscuous people. For instance, the scene that precedes the rescuing of the slave girls depicts Bosambo and the girls as sexually loose persons. In his inquiry before ordering the return of the girls to their families, with the exception of Lilongo whom he permits to marry Bosambo, the girls begin their confessions of sexual liaison with Bosambo amidst giggling, an indication that they did not mind going to bed with Bosambo. On his part, as the girls begin their confessions, Bosambo begins to fidget like a reprimanded child, in keeping with the film's representation of Africans as children.

The film also registers that underneath Bosambo's meekness, there is a valiant and dangerous underside. This is revealed in the battle scene where he confronts the captain of the Old King's warriors shortly after the slave raid and in the scene where he tries to teach his son the survival principles of his society. In this latter scene, a war song meant to portray him as a warmonger is introduced:

On, on into battle
Make the war drums rattle
Mow them down like cattle
On and on, on into battle, stamp them into dust...
Charge, kill, shoot, smash, slash...fight and slay!

The incorporation of this violence-laden war song seems to be the film's own way of explaining the root causes of violent activities like slave raids and inter-ethnic warfare in pre-colonial African societies. The film seems to suggest that the methods of instruction in pre-colonial Africa were responsible for inter-ethnic wars. Since one of the film's major themes is that of peace, peace in terms of total submission to British colonial authority, the film tends to blame this mode of instruction for lack of peace in colonial society. I have earlier stated that Mofalaba represents one of the contending levels of power and authority in this text by virtue of the fact that he symbolizes traditional African authority. However, while Sanders, his contending opposite symbol of authority is depicted as a fair and forthright ruler, the Mofalaba character is portrayed as a despot. However, this manner of representation is not unique to Mofalaba. It is consistent with the conventional pattern of representing traditional African rulers in colonialist African cinema. The King Mofalaba character is thus a reproduction of similar character types such as Twala in *King Solomon's Mines,* Magole in *Men of Two Worlds,* Simba in *Simba* etc. The traditional institution of authority is so derogatorily portrayed in *Sanders of the River* that no one is left in doubt of the necessity of British imperial presence.

The use of propaganda inter-titles in this film is also part of the overall strategy of discrediting the ruling capacities of traditional African rulers while celebrating British imperial presence. What is celebrated in this instance is the efficacy of indirect rule as the propaganda clip from *Sanders of the River* shows:

AFRICA
Tens of millions of natives under British rule, each tribe with its own chieftain, governed and protected by a handful of white men whose everyday work is an

unsung saga of courage and efficiency. One of them
was Commissioner Sanders.

With the penchant in colonialist films for spinning globes and
maps, the propaganda clip in the opening sequence of the film is
superimposed upon a fluttering British flag, the Union Jack, with
the spinning globe signifying the all embracing nature of British
colonial authority. But if indirect rule was efficient and cost
effective, as the film seems to imply, it also encouraged divide-and-
rule, and bred favoritism, suspicion, rivalry, violence and the breach
of peace, as the relationship between Mofalaba and Bosambo
indicates — the very things colonial authority wanted to avoid.

In addition to his subordination to Sanders, Mofalaba is also
portrayed to be childlike in nature. This is displayed most explicitly
in the sequence in which he kills Ferguson. An instance of this
childish attitude is shown during the brief verbal exchange between
him and Ferguson. When Ferguson tells him that Sanders is alive
and that Sanders will see to it that he, Mofalaba, is brought to
justice if he kills him, Mofalaba sways like a child and retorts that
Sanders is dead, as the gunrunner, Smith, had assured him. Indeed,
the relationship between Sanders and his subjects in this film, as
well as the relationship between European characters and their
African counterparts, is structured around European patronage and
paternal attitude towards Africans. For instance, when Sanders has
not been recalled from leave and Father O'Leary comes to report
to Ferguson the violent situation in the district, Ferguson remarks
that the arsonists who burnt O'Leary's church acted just like wild
beasts. Responding, Father O'Leary, in a paternalistic tone, says
they are not like wild beasts, rather, they are like misguided children
and, like a father, Ferguson must act quickly as Sanders would have
under similar circumstances. In another instance, Sanders while
introducing Ferguson to the chiefs of his district, addresses them
the way a headmaster would normally address his pupils or, better
still, the way a father would address his children. He specifically
tells them that they should obey Ferguson as if they were
Ferguson's own children.

Another colonialist trope exploited by the film is the
representation of Africans as sexually promiscuous people. This
mode of representation is foregrounded through the examination
of the traditional African marriage institution with specific

reference to polygamy. Polygamy is treated in the film as an index of sexual promiscuity. For instance, when the slave girls attempt to submit themselves voluntarily in marriage to Bosambo *en masse*, Sanders first applies all sorts of subterfuge to dissuade them. When that does not seem to work, he puts his foot down and insists that Bosambo must practise the doctrine of one man, and one wife. The girls' readiness to marry Bosambo despite the fact that he has sexually exploited them can be considered an indication of their sexual permissiveness. Furthermore, the choice of erotic African fertility dances featuring bare-breasted girls is also informed by this underlining colonialist convention. These dances, which are featured for a fairly lengthy time during the Bosambo/Lilongo marriage sequence, and also during the victory dance sequence when captured female slaves are displayed in the sequence following the departure of Sanders on leave, do not only represent Africans as sexually permissive people but also as primitive and barbaric.

In the Bosambo/Lilongo marriage sequence for instance, the shots switch from male dancers to bare-breasted dancing girls, to a set of women breast-feeding babies, to a group of children already perfecting the sexual rhythms of the dance. The shots appear ordered to represent the supposedly awesome procreation machinery of traditional African societies. The intention in this instance, as well as in similar ones already cited, is to portray the totality of African social experience as primitive and barbaric. More broadly, dances are utilized in the marriage sequence both to create an erotic atmosphere as well as to present African cultural practices to Western spectators as part of the film's package.

Although the film sets out to celebrate indirect rule in Anglophone Africa, it also paradoxically exposes the fragility of the whole practice. Indeed, as Richards and Aldgate observe:

> there is an implicit subtext in the apparent fragility of British rule, given that it collapses the moment Sanders leaves the scene. One of the great paradoxes of British imperial history was the simultaneous dominance of twin emotions, confidence and fear — confidence in the rightness of British presence in far-off lands and fear that British rule would be violently overthrown. (Richards and Aldgate: 18)

The news of the death of Sanders appropriately demonstrates the fragility that Richards and Aldgate refer to. The commotion which the news of his death brings to the carefully painted picture of a district that is as peaceful as an Edenic paradise also symbolizes the underlying fragility of British colonial rule as represented in *Sanders of the Rivers*. For instance, once the news of his death is relayed through the district in drum messages, there is a sequence of shots representing the rapid slippage of Africans into savagery. This social degeneration or slippage into barbarism is shown in the form of resumption and celebration of slave raids, a man rapidly climbing a tall coconut tree bare-handed like a bat, and of animals lumbering in and out of water as if in joyful celebration of the absence of the law from the river. Though the whole sequence is structured to signify a slippage into the old regime of jungle justice, it has inadvertently ended up portraying the fragility of British colonial rule through the exploitation of potentiality for such relapse.

Though *Sanders of the River* is not the first film to institute the conventions of colonialist African cinema, that tradition having been initiated by the Tarzan jungle series of films, there is no doubt that it stands out today as a classic example of the sub-genre of films which it did inaugurate, the colonial burden films. These films propagated the necessity for colonial rule. However, their attempts to reflect the contradictions of colonial societies often negate this message, thereby exposing the fragility of the whole project. This becomes both a lamentation and an acknowledgement of the burden of colonial rule. Evidence of this textual pattern can be glimpsed from *Sanders of the River, Men of Two Worlds*, and *Mister Johnson*. where attempts to portray the power play of colonial societies and the rationalization of colonialism result in the exposure of the fragility of the whole system.

A Critical Reading of Mister Johnson

Mister Johnson (Bruce Beresford, 1990) also bears the textual marks of a colonial burden film. It is based on Joyce Cary's novel of the same title and deals with the tragic consequences of a native clerk's attempts to live beyond his income. The clerk, Mr Johnson (Maynard Eziashi), in an attempt to imitate European life-styles indulges in all sorts of corrupt practices, including embezzlement of public funds and petty robbery in order to satisfy this lifestyle. His aspiration to live like a European makes him organise an expensive Christian wedding to a local village belle, Bamu (Bella

Enahoro), a wedding that leaves him much in debt. In his attempt to help his benefactor Judge Rudbeck (Pierce Brosnan) to complete his road project, he overreaches himself by falsifying public account records and aiding misappropriation of public funds. This earns him dismissal from the colonial civil service.

With the assistance of Rudbeck, he gets a sales clerk job in Sargy Gollup's store, where once again he earns a sack by holding a party in the store to the consternation of Gollup (Edward Woodward). After this second sack, Johnson goes into voluntary exile where he squanders his income. He returns like a prodigal son and is rehabilitated once again by Judge Rudbeck, who employs him as a pay clerk. Once again he gets the sack when he starts to collect illegal road dues at the successful completion of the road project. On this occasion, Johnson, without a job, and in desperation, takes to petty stealing. During one of his stealing sprees, he accidentally kills Sargy Gollup in his store while attempting to burgle his safe. His friend and benefactor, Judge Rudbeck, has to carry out the unenviable job of executing him after he has been condemned to death.

Joyce Cary, whose novel inspired the film, had colonial Northern Nigeria as the setting of his novel and in the process drew the ire of Chinua Achebe who felt that Cary's novel was a misrepresentation of the Nigerian character and society. Achebe reportedly started his writing career in an attempt to correct this misrepresentation (Pieterse and Duerden, 1972: 3-4). I have had to refer to these facts because unlike Cary who specified Nigeria as the setting of his novel, Beresford's opening inter-title de-emphasizes any specific country by locating the film's setting in West Africa of the 1920s. He has done this presumably to avoid the controversies that surround the novel in Nigeria where the film was shot on location.

The film begins with a shot of a blazing sun and cuts to a long shot of a dry riverbed, a signification of the ravages of drought in Africa. This is followed by an establishing shot of girls washing clothes in a muddy puddle of water along the riverbed and a cut to Johnson running and skipping elatedly toward the girls with an umbrella in hand. He is dressed in immaculate white trousers and shirtsleeve. This is followed by another establishing shot of the girls and a close up of Bamu, the village belle who has drawn the attention of Johnson. After teasing Bamu, Johnson runs and skips off toward Fada, the district headquarter, making sure he pulls off his shoes along the way so as not to damage them, and wears them again as he is about to enter the village so as to look respectable. This opening sequence establishes the pretentiousness of the Johnson character as well as making symbolic reference to the ravages of droughts in Africa.

Although _Mister Johnson_ exhibits the usual paraphernalia of British colonial power through parades and the ritual hoisting and lowering of the Union Jack amidst blowing of military trumpets, the film nonetheless makes implicit reference to the power play resulting from the challenges posed to British colonial authority by the Emir, the traditional ruler of the district. As a result of the existence of these contending levels of authority in the text, even though the British colonial authority is firmly in place, there is nevertheless a certain amount of discomfort arising from the looming authority of the Emir. The presence of this contending power structure imposes a certain amount of fragility upon British colonial authority in the text. But these contending power structures are represented in such a way as to legitimize British imperial presence. For instance, in keeping with rivalries between traditional African and British colonial authorities, the film portrays the Emir as a tyrannical ruler who, even though his presence is less visible, nevertheless has a despotic grip upon the people. Even his Prime Minister, the Wasiri, is flogged regularly in public if the Emir's policies and directives are not properly carried out. Besides, the Emir is also said to favor the policy of public flogging as a means of deterring women from prostitution. These barbaric practices recall Mofalaba's habit of stretching the skins of disloyal chiefs over his drums.

In fact, the first public meeting between Judge Rudbeck and the Wasiri, is devoted to the denunciation of this barbaric practice. In opposing the continuation of public flogging of men and women, the film demonstrates the superiority of British judicial process. In addition, it legitimates the necessity of British imperial presence as a means of bringing to an end such barbaric practices. As in _Sanders of the River_ and _Men of Two Worlds_, the old order that has been defeated militarily, but whose influence nevertheless still remains, is represented as decadent and reactionary in order to legitimate the new order symbolized by British colonial presence.

As is the practice in most colonialist African films, the African landscape, music and dance are fully exploited in *Mister Johnson* as a means of enriching its narrative structure. But in keeping with the colonialist manner of representation, we find that most of the dances are performed out of context and utilized more as exotic ornamentation. For instance, in the opening sequence of the film, a durbar is put on display with a group of traditional Hausa trumpeters, drummers and flutists in procession. Men leading hyenas and monkeys in accompaniment to the traditional orchestra help to establish a circus-like atmosphere in this opening sequence. The use of a combination of establishing shots and rapid close ups invoke a grotesque atmosphere since the rapid cuts and shot variations leave little room for leisurely contemplation. At the head of this procession is the Emir himself. The whole sequence is choreographed with no specific direction in mind — there is no clear specification of venue or ceremony that warrants the presentation of the durbar. It is only in the following scene that the whole purpose of the sequence becomes meaningful. Shortly after this noisy display, there is a cut to the European quarter in absolute quietude. This and other comparative schemas are used regularly in the film.

Apart from the above instance, this comparative schema is also used in the filming of the interior decors of European and African houses. In one such significant moment, after Johnson's return from exile, through parallel editing interior shots of the homes of the Rudbecks and the Johnsons are shown. While the Rudbecks' is represented as orderly in its simplicity, Johnson's is shown to be disorderly as well as scantily furnished. Significantly too, at the moment when Johnson makes exclamatory remarks of happiness over his rehabilitation by Judge Rudbeck, the music from Rudbeck's house is symbolically extended to the space of Johnson's house, thus affirming the authority of the former over the latter. Two things are emphasized through this comparative schema: first, the representation of Africans as disorderly people; second, the representation of European life-style in superior terms, in comparison to its African counterpart, thereby legitimating the necessity for colonial presence since the argument for that presence is said to be for humanitarian purposes of bringing development to primitive peoples.

In terms of characterization, the film is less firmly grounded in the propagation of British colonial authority through the projection of colonial administrators such as Sanders in *Sanders of the River*. The major European character, Judge Rudbeck, does not have the charismatic presence of Sanders; nor does he have his sense of quick judgement, independence of mind and action. The only quality Rudbeck shares with Sanders is paternalistic patronage of his African protégé, Mister Johnson. Rudbeck is enthusiastic about his road project but he lacks the vision of a purposeful set goal. Johnson has to complement his visionless enthusiasm with a sense of definite goal for the project to have a direction. Beside that, Johnson also has to devise an illegal means of financing the project before Rudbeck can realize his dream to build a road to link Fada with the outside world. This aspect of the film also shows how the British colonial system undermines itself by insisting upon strict application of civil service rules and regulations.

While the Judge Rudbeck character gains a lot of respectability by virtue of his official status, the same cannot be said of Sargy Gollup, a representative character of the British working class. He is portrayed in the film as a semi-literate ex-service British sergeant who has gone native by marrying a native woman and becoming a local trader. His tactless fraternizing with natives as well as his drunkenness and racist outbursts are represented as the result of his class upbringing. So too is his regular beating of his wife. Through this manner of representation, the film emphasizes the point that only Europeans of working class background degenerate to the point of marrying native women and that they are the ones who are racist in outlook. In addition, the film also emphasizes the point that the wages of fraternizing with natives are betrayal of trust and possibly death as is the case between Johnson and Gollup. This is the pattern of thought also expressed in the fraternization of the gunrunners, Farini and Smith, with the natives in *Sanders of the River*. The most significant point to note in these and other similar instances is projection of negative European attitudes onto those of working class background. In this regard, the character of Gollup is a reproduction of similar types like Farini and Smith in *Sanders of the River* and Delpich in *Chocolat*.

Regarding the representation of European women, the Mrs Rudbeck character occupies an ambivalent middle ground position in the colonial power structure similar to working class European males. Like them, she enjoys the privilege of being white and belonging to the ruling colonial authority. Furthermore, even though she is not directly involved in the exercise of colonial authority, by virtue of her marriage to Judge Rudbeck, she commands a lot of respect, in addition to being white, in colonial Africa. Her relationship with the natives of Fada is essentially that of an outsider, a sort of tourist. She goes about the village with a camera taking pictures of interesting backgrounds and people. The only person she relates to closely is Mr Johnson, her escort when she is newly arrived in the village. The film makes implicit reference to sexual relations between Mrs Rudbeck and Mr Johnson, especially during her first quarrels with her husband. On the whole, however, her character is less developed and is used as a foil to Judge Rudbeck. Beside this, she also functions as some sort of conscience with regards to arguments on the necessity of colonial domination.

Of the African characters, Mr Johnson stands out as the most developed as well as the most caricatured. As played by Maynard Eziashi, Mr Johnson is an exuberant semi-literate native colonial clerk caught on the boundary between African and European cultural values. Much of the humor in the film surrounds his attempts to transform himself into the ill-fitting role of a black English gentleman. Lacking in education, upbringing and financial wherewithal, his drive to become a black English gentleman leaves him in a grotesque and caricatured role, a mimic subject in Homi Bhabha's term. Bhabha defines the mimic subject as a personality construct which results from the "effects of a flawed colonial mimesis in which to be Anglicized is emphatically not to be English" (Bhabha, 1984: 128). Such is Johnson's status. What makes his character a comic caricature is that he is not even a thoroughly Anglicized character like most well educated African elites of the colonial era whose lifestyles were tailored to that of Victorian England.

Johnson's personality traits are revealed in detail through his relationship with his British patrons and benefactors, Judge Rudbeck and Sargy Gollup, most especially the former. Through this relation, he is portrayed as a compulsive liar, a spendthrift, an ungrateful and disloyal friend to Gollup, an embezzler of public funds and petty robber. The relationship between Rudbeck and Johnson is never allowed to go beyond the level of patronage, while that with Gollup, which does, ends in the tragic murder of Gollup by Johnson. There is also a noticeable European outlook in the conception of the Johnson character. For instance, the relationship between Johnson and his wife, Bamu, is a bit over-romanticized and is essentially built on the western model of one man, one wife.

Most of the other African characters are less developed in comparison to the Johnson character. The character of Johnson's wife and that of her father and brother are, for instance, thinly developed. His wife, Bamu (Bella Enahoro), seems to be eternally under the influence of her patriarchal father, Brimah (Hubert Ogunde). Besides the domineering influence of her father, the film also portrays Bamu as a disloyal wife, especially towards the end of the film, where she and her family frame up Johnson for arrest. Her father, on the other hand, is represented as a greedy and selfish patriarch who is ready to exploit his daughter as a means of personal enrichment. There are implicit references to the fact that he might have hatched the plans for Johnson's arrest for cash rewards. The significant point to note in the characterization of Brimah, however, is that his character offers the opportunity for the critique of African marital practice, especially with regards to the issue of bride price, as in the case of *Sanders of the River*.

Another interesting but equally less developed character in comparison to Johnson is the Emir's Prime Minister, the Wasiri (Tunde Fatoba). The Wasiri is represented as a cunning and wily character versed in the art of diplomacy and brinkmanship. In addition, he is portrayed as a spymaster who knows how to exploit the soft underbelly of officialdom in order to gain access into state secrets. We get an insight into the tyranny of the Emir through the Wasiri. Through him the Emir is revealed as favoring the policy of public flogging as a means of deterring women from prostitution. We also learn through his servant that the Emir publicly flogs the Wasiri occasionally for failure or poor execution of the Emir's policies. The Wasiri character is also represented as a homosexual, especially in his relation to young servant, Saleh (Jerry Linus).

The most hideous of all the African characters is the Emir. Even though he appears in the film briefly and only twice, in the opening sequence during the durbar procession and towards the end of the film after the murder of Gollup, his image and authority loom large throughout the film, thereby presenting a counter-weight to British colonial authority. This counter-weight is earned at a price of notoriety. He is portrayed as a tyrant who operates a barbaric judicial system as well as someone who resents progress. His conservative nature is revealed through his opposition to the road project, which he sees as a symbol of the erosion of his authority. The only time when a full-front view shot of him is revealed in the film is when he is giving an ultimatum to the Wasiri to find the killer of Gollup or capture any stranger who comes into town, through the new road, as a scapegoat.

One very significant element in this film is the road. It is significant both as a physical access for mobility and development and as a symbolic element for the infiltration of alien values and loss of authority. Most characters in the film recognize the changes the road might bring to the community and react for or against it, depending on how they imagine the changes might affect them. The Emir opposes it because he realizes it represents the beginning of total loss of his authority over the district. On the other hand, the villagers' refusal to work unless they are paid is portrayed as a sign of ignorance and primitiveness by the film. Tring opposes it on the grounds of keeping strictly to civil service rules and regulations that require that votes in other departments should not be expended in projects they are not earmarked for. Mrs Rudbeck feels the road will bring radical changes that the people are ill prepared for. Only Johnson of all the African characters supports the building of the road. Yet his support is hinged upon the fact that it is the pet project of his friend and master, Judge Rudbeck.

Mister Johnson is a typical colonial burden film and it employs most of its narrative strategy to legitimize colonial rule. The film begins on an individual note by building on the tragic consequences of Mr Johnson's spendthriftness and naive mimicry of English values and lifestyles and winds up examining the entire spectrum of the colonial enterprise through the symbolic element of the road. In tandem with the convention of colonialist African cinema, Africans are portrayed as lacking the initiative for self-development, thereby legitimating the necessity of colonial intervention. Furthermore, legitimate demands for remuneration are interpreted as a sign of primitiveness and lack of communal appreciation of the gains to be derived from the execution of the road project. In its overall narrative strategy and in keeping with the conventions of colonial burden films, the film tries to legitimize colonial rule by representing traditional African institutions of government as barbaric, and Africans in general as primitive and savage people incapable of self-government and initiation of development projects.

Colonialist Autobiographical Films

Colonialist African autobiographical films are based on the memoirs and autobiographies of Europeans who have lived, worked or traveled through the continent. Because of this attribute of personal first-hand knowledge of the continent, most of the films as well as the literature from which they are adapted seem to contain elements of nostalgia. These films are the most problematic of all colonialist films because of this underlining element of remembrance. Most of them genuinely admire many aspects of African society, such as respect for old age and elderly persons, the care and protections of the extended family systems, and African hospitality, but there is also the prevalence of ethnocentric and paternalistic views which make one wonder sometimes if the emotions expressed about certain aspects of African lifestyle are genuine. The films, which contain these textual qualities, include *Out of Africa* (Sydney Pollack, 1985) and *Chocolat* (Claire Denis, 1988). In this present work, I shall be focusing on *Chocolat*.

A Critical Reading of Chocolat

Chocolat is an autobiographical film which recalls Denis' childhood days in the French Cameroon of the 1950s. The film is unique in many ways. First, it is the first film set in Africa by a female European director. Second, it is Denis's debut as a film director. Before this, she had been assistant director to both Wim Wenders and Jim Jarmusch, and according to Margaret Walters, her work "avoids their stylized whimsy in favor of a transparent and very personal simplicity" (Walters, 1989: 47).

The film's narrative is a conjunction of two historical narratives: one dealing with the colonial era and the other with the post-colonial era in Cameroon. Though the narrative begins in present day Cameroon, this post-colonial narrative merely serves as a mirror for re-assessing events of the colonial period. For instance, many of the cinematic iconographies signaled in the colonial narrative in the form of the introduction of air transport and construction of air fields are recalled in the post-colonial narrative, especially in the departure sequence with all its modern airport paraphernalia. Though the film switches codes between the present and the past through memory recall, and though it uses the colonial narrative to comment on developmental progress in post-colonial Cameroon, there is a deliberate obliqueness and ambiguity as to whether the narrative strategy is meant to serve as some sort of sanction of the colonial project.

This ambiguity arises because even though the film uses most of the recognizable colonialist tropes of representation like emblematic postcard framing of the landscape and racist rhetoric, they are deliberately made oblique through the element of parody. For instance, when Delpich (Jacque Denis) gives food to his African mistress, Thérèse (Edwige Nto Ngon a Zock), he says: "Here's your grub sweetie," as if she were some sort of animal. Protée (Isaac de Bankole) later parodies this same phrase when he gives edible insects to the young France (Cecile Ducas) during the airfield construction sequence. Linda Hutcheon defines parody as follows:

> parody...in its ironic "trans-contextualization" and inversion, is repetition with difference. A critical distance is implied between the backgrounded text being parodied and the incorporating work, a distance usually signaled by irony. But this irony can be playful as well as destructive. The pleasure of parody's irony comes not from humor in particular but from the degree of engagement of the reader in the intertextual "bouncing" between complicity and distance. (Hutcheon, 1985: 34-36)

Most of the ambiguity in *Chocolat* comes from this continuous bouncing between complicity and distance in the textual construction of colonialist African discourse and in the representation of Africans. The resort to memory recall through France's subjective flashback is the main strategy used to avoid the complicity of colonialist rhetoric. Since memory recall, as a narrative strategy, is tied up with nostalgia, it tends to assume the quality of colonialist complicity because a European director made the film.

Chocolat is about the visit of France (Mireille Perrier) to post-colonial Cameroon in search of her father's colonial outpost where she spent her childhood. The film begins with a freeze-frame of a long shot of a beach which looks very much like a desert but for the accompanying wave-sound in the soundtrack. As the shot unfreezes, it becomes clear, with the rising and falling of the waves, that the scene is set at a beach. At first, the beach looks deserted as the opening credits appear. However, as the shot lingers awhile, two figures emerge from the waves, a man and a little boy. They play about for a while, splash water on each other and run off towards screen left. A gradual pan to screen right reveals a white woman sitting and contemplating on the beach.

From her sitting position and contemplative mood, it looks like she wants to go for a swim since she is wearing a swimming suit. However, instead of going for the swim, something in her seems to resist the water. A cut from her to a close up of the upper body of the black boy lying on the beach reveals the water to be of chocolate color, full of dirt. This is followed by a close up of an adult black hand and an establishing shot of the boy and the man. They later turn out to be the African-American, Mungo Park (Emmet Judson Williamson) and his son. A cut back to France shows her amused by Mungo Park and his son. Shortly afterwards, her countenance changes when through her point-of-view shot, we note that the water is full of dirt. She gets up from her sitting position, dresses, and leaves the beach because of the impurity of the water.

The association of the African natural surrounding with threatening impurities is not something unique to *Chocolat*. It is one of the conventions of colonialist African cinematic representation of the African environment. We encounter it in *The African Queen*, in the form of the deceptive leisurely flow of the river with its cavernous rapids, leech-infested waters and wasp-like insects; in *Men of Two Worlds*, the lush green vegetation, which is expressionistically lit to give it the uncontaminated purity of an Edenic garden, is later revealed to be infested by tsetse flies, bearer of lassa-fever and sleeping-sickness diseases; in *King Solomon's Mines*, the vegetation is represented as a cover for the threatening and perceivable presence of natives. In *Chocolat* too, rotting dead leaves of the tropical forest region of Cameroon, are said to possess a benumbing effect on Europeans.

Nikki Stiller, in her review of the film, has equally noted the film's parodic contrast of the attitudes of Africans and Europeans to nature and the surrounding. She observes that

the western attitude toward nature in this film appears as skewed, morbid, denatured. The American black and his chocolate son, in the opening scene, let the waves caress them. Never do the whites take pleasure in water this way. They contrive to shower indoors, thus depriving themselves of the best "sale de bain du monde", while the blacks are made to bathe in the open. The detained pilot fears the seasonal rain will ruin his runway. The film ends with a jubilant downpour. To the Africans it is part of life, perhaps a blessing. To the European intent on going elsewhere, the rain is merely an inconvenience. (Stiller, 1990: 52)

What Stiller says of European attitude to nature in *Chocolat* is true; what she fails to add, however, is that the representation of this western attitude is part of the strategy of parody in the text. The film complies with colonialist filmic practice in several respects. For instance, the representation of the African landscape follows the postcard-framing pattern noticeable in other films. Emphasis is placed on revealing the geographic otherness of the landscape. However, there is a highly contrastive element with respect to this film. Before and after the flashback, a combination of pans and fast tracks are employed to show the tropical vegetation and architecture of southern Cameroon. In the flashback sequences, similar shot compositions are employed, this time, to represent the sparse vegetation of the north, together with its round huts with thatch roofs, and rectangular mud houses with flat mud-roofed tops. The comparative schema is employed here to show western spectators the differences in geographic outlook and architecture between northern and southern Cameroon.

The sequences dealing with the journey, during, and after the flashback, are particularly significant for their contrastive qualities. Beside vehicular comparison of old-modeled cars and trucks for the colonial era and modern Peugeot cars and buses for the post-colonial era, the differences in road make up is also graphically registered. The post-colonial road is a modern asphalt tarred road while the colonial one is just an earth road. As noted earlier, the film is ambiguous about whether the narrative strategy of historical recollection through filmic parallelism and contrast is necessarily a manner of nostalgic sanction of the colonial project. Besides the noted colonialist influence in the representation of the landscape, the film also adheres to colonialist African cinematic conventions in the area of characterization. Most of the characters fall into the types already firmly established in colonialist African cinema: there is the liberal good natured, workaholic colonial administrator in the person of Marc Dalens (François Cluzet); the neglected colonial housewife in the person of Aimée (Giulia Boschi); the colonial white underdog in the persons of Delpich and Luc (Jean-Claude Adelin); and, of course, the black male servant in the person of Protée. All of these characters have correspondences in other colonialist African films.

Marc Dalens' type, for instance, can be found in Rudbeck in *Mister Johnson* and Sanders in *Sanders of the River*. These characters are often typed as workaholics whose single-mindedness and dedication to duty is contrasted as well as equated with dereliction of duty at the marital front. The call of duty delays the marriage of Sanders while the workaholic attitude of Rudbeck and Dalens leads to neglect of their wives. There are implied references to Johnson's sexual relations with Mrs Rudbeck. In *Chocolat*, Claire Denis' attempt to circumvent stereotypes of the black male servant somehow end up foregrounding them even though she does try to affirm the integrity of the character by making him refuse the advances of Aimée. This integrity is devalued through the incorporation of a sadistic underside to the character. Two of the most shocking moments in the film are devoted to the depiction of Protée's sadistic underside.

One of them takes place on the journey to Marc's station during the flashback. The event is recorded when the family stops for a lunch break. Protée's sadism is represented in this instance through comparison of parallel relations between him and Marc on the one hand, and between him and the young France on the other. When the truck stops, intimacy between Marc and Protée is represented through an establishing shot of both of them urinating side by side. What later transpires between Protée and the little girl seems to be a betrayal of trust. After Marc has gone back to the front of the vehicle, Protée collects France's bread and sticks ants with it taken from where they have just urinated, to make a sandwich for France. To underline the sadistic nature of the situation, Protée is made to go through the whole exercise in a mute manner. This pattern of behavior is re-established toward the end of the film when he takes vengeance on France by making her hold the hot exhaust of the generator.

The characterization of the white underdog is also typical of colonialist African cinema conventions. Two of the most perverse white characters in this film, Delpich and Luc, are white underdogs. Delpich is a coffee planter who has gone native by having a local woman as a mistress, while Luc, the ex-seminarian, in his relationship with the natives seems bound for such an end. These characters have correspondences with similar ones like Farini and Smith in *Sanders of the River* and Gollup in *Mister Johnson*. Colonialist African films often emphasize the point that it is Europeans of lower class backgrounds who are racist in outlook, a view that *Chocolat* seems to subscribe to. Luc, who is considered the most racist of all the European characters in the film, is a white underdog. According to Marie Craven, Luc is the most depraved as well as the most hypocritical of all the European characters:

> of all the European characters, the ugliest and most perverse is Luc Sagalen (Jean-Claude Adelin). At first he appears as a saintly ascetic one who has eschewed a culturally superior position, identifying himself with African worker. Yet his humility contains a sneer. He ostentatiously enacts the role of an outsider, a position that cannot exist, that can be adopted only with hypocrisy. In his misanthropy, political conviction becomes a weapon that maintains his sense of superiority against both Africans and Europeans alike. (Craven, 1990: 36)

The Luc character is, therefore, a typical white parasite that refuses to work but fully exploits the canopy provided by the colonial administrative structure. He is a social leech and a political pretender. His ascetic airs form a smokescreen for his failure to build up a career of his own. Though the film is critical of the Luc character, the criticism is offered within the colonialist convention of representing working class Europeans as degenerate whites.

Claire Denis's characterization of European women in *Chocolat* reveals most aptly the lot of European women in colonial societies. They were essentially appendages to their husbands. Their only social engagement involves playing host to visiting colonial bureaucrats just as Aimée does in the film. This role apart, most of the time, they were lonely as their busy husbands had little time for them. The only company they had was the black male servants who normally filled the husband's role in his absence; hence, the temptation for infidelity.

Characterization apart, the film can be read as an allegory on Franco-African relationship. This is borne out of the fact that the central character of the film is called France. The relationship between France and Protée is in many respects typical of Franco-African relationship. Though Protée is bigger and older than France, just as Africa is older and bigger than France, she bosses him around just as France today dominates parts of Africa formerly under her colonial authority. She also spoon-feeds Protée like a beggar from her bowl in a manner symbolic of the dependence of most Francophone African countries on French aid. Read along these lines, adult France's return to post-colonial Cameroon and her memory recalls can be considered as the allegorical return of France to the country to claim credit for whatever infrastructural development or modernization there is in her erstwhile colony, as product of France's colonial beneficence. In fact, through adult France's flashback, the representation of modern infrastructural development in post-colonial Cameroon such as roads and airports is linked to the road construction and the building of airfield, in French colonial Cameroon, as product of colonial heritage. The film seems to suggest that without French colonialism, Cameroon would not have developed its modern infrastructures. This is also the underlining argument in the whole genre.

Such an argument would be historically inaccurate because both before and after the slave trade, that is prior to colonialism, there was a flourishing trade and between Europe and Africa and documented evidence of autonomous efforts towards modernization on the continent. For instance, according to Chinweizu, as early as the 1490s, the reigning monarch of the Congo (Zaire), the Mani-Kongo of the Bakongo, Nzinga a Mvende, son of Nzinga a Nkuwu, decided voluntarily to embrace Christianity and Europeanize his kingdom, in his quest for modernization. Upon his baptism, he dropped his African names and titles and became Dom I, King of the Congo and Lord of the Ambundos. He learned to read and write Portuguese, Europeanized his court in both etiquette and dress, and sent some of his sons, relatives and noble youths to study in Portugal and Rome. One of them, Dom Henrique, served as Bishop of Utica, a city on the Mediterranean coast of what is today Tunisia. He returned in 1521, after an absence of thirteen years, to serve as Bishop of Bukongo. All through the long reign of Dom I (1506-1543), there were ambassadorial exchanges between the kingdom, Portugal and Rome. Dom I desperately wanted aid for autonomous development and set about building schools and cathedrals in his kingdom but his Portuguese trading partners wanted slaves. He wrote to the king of Portugal protesting this development to no avail. In the end, the Portuguese waged war against the kingdom and brought it under its authority, for resisting slave trade within its boundaries, and in their quest for slaves, gold, and copper (Chinweizu, 1978: 27-30).

The experience of Dom I and his successors is not unique in Africa. The Oba of Benin, Chief Nana of Itsekiri, and King Pepple of Bonny, all pre-colonial rulers in present day Nigeria, also sent their wards to study in Europe and exchanged ambassadors with European countries in a quest for autonomous development. The British later overthrew these traditional rulers for denying them access to inland trade. As a result of the existence of alternative paradigms of quests for autonomous development and modernization prior to colonialism, the rhetoric of colonial beneficence projected in the colonialist genre can, at best, be explained as part of the textual rationalization of colonial rule.

Chocolat is a very problematic film with respect to the representation of Africans. Though the film uses most of the acknowledged conventions of colonialist African cinema, the subjection of these conventions to parodic treatment makes it difficult to ascertain the extent to which nostalgia is informed by the sanction of the colonial project. The elaborate use of Abdullah Ibrahim's music further exacerbates the level of ambivalence in the film since most colonialist films use music as an element for marking the social segregation of colonial societies. The use of Abdullah Ibrahim's music seems genuinely borne out of love for African rhythms. One of the most memorable moments in the film has two small boys running after a public advertising bus playing indigenous music. The scene carries genuine memories of small towns' mode of advertising in Africa, one that is still widely practised. Unlike in *Mister Johnson* where European music is used as one of the elements for acknowledging the social segregation of colonial space, thereby reinforcing the colonialist structure of the film, the musical score of *Chocolat* is mostly African and is used both to open up spaces for native counter-discourse as well as create an African atmosphere for the film.

Decolonization Conflict Films

Most of the films that fall under the category of decolonization conflict films are films that deal with native revolts against colonial authority toward the end of British colonial rule in Africa. These films place emphasis on the barbarity of the coercive methods applied by leaders of the liberation struggle against colonial rule. The mass revolts are not represented as independence struggle movements; rather, they are portrayed as violent uprisings championed by a few misguided elements that recruit people by coercion and threats of violence. However, with the benefit of hindsight, these films can now be read as liberation struggles even though they were originally conceived as decolonization conflict films. As a result of the nature of the subject matter treated in these films, most of them seem to be set in regions where European settlement resulted in mass appropriation of lands and the dispossession of the natives. The two films that stand out in this regard, are *Simba* and *The Kitchen Toto*, both set in colonial Kenya. In this study, I will be focusing on *Simba*, the first film to deal with the issue of native revolt against colonialism in Africa.

A Critical Reading of Simba

Simba (Brian Desmond Hurst, 1955) was shot on location in Kenya toward the end of the Mau Mau uprising. The film is supposed to be about the Mau Mau revolt but its narrative is structured in such a way that issues which are central to the revolt, like the appropriation of native lands, are never referred to; instead, emphasis is placed on ritual practices like the process of oath taking which the film represents as barbaric. In addition, Africans are represented as simple-minded people who are coerced into the revolt through violent means. The reason for the revolt itself is relegated to the background, thereby making it look like a mindless uprising and discrediting the Mau Mau movement as a mass anti-colonial revolt. In my analysis of the film, I will be placing the Mau Mau revolt in historical context so that textual gaps created by the backgrounding of the central issue of the revolt, are brought into focus.

The origin of the Mau Mau can be traced to the British colonial settler policy in then East Africa Protectorate, later to be called Kenya, shortly after the annexation of the region in June

1895. The relatively temperate climate and good agricultural land around the Rift Valley region and the highlands attracted European settlements. But the impetus for this rapid settlement of the region by Europeans and Asians came with the opening up of the inland area by the East African Railway that was then being built from Mombasa to Uganda by the British colonial administration. This construction work brought in large numbers of Asians as construction workers as the war for the "pacification" of the region continued. With the successful suppression of the Nandis and the Kikuyus who led the opposition to British colonial settlement, large numbers of European settlers, mostly British, poured into the region. To realize the dream of a settler colony, the policy of land appropriation was vigorously pursued.

Vast agricultural lands around the Rift Valley region and the Highlands, the most fertile lands in Kenya, the rest of the country being mostly semi desert region, were appropriated, thereby creating a large population of landless Africans. Not that there was unanimity over the policy in Britain. There were noted disagreements between the Foreign Office, the Treasury and the Colonial Office. However, the relative powerlessness of the Colonial Office in the face of the Foreign Office's policy of encouraging European immigrants for the purpose of rapid development of the Protectorate, and the Treasury's decision to sell lands around railway lines in order to recoup expenditure for the rail project, led to the triumph of the policy of land appropriation. Africans who were ejected from these lands were either confined to area called Forest Native Reserves, very much like the American policy against native Americans, created by the colonial government, or they became squatters in their ancestral lands (Sorrenson, 1968: 31-43). Furendi has also noted the impact of this policy on the Kikuyu, who incidentally are the largest ethnic group in Kenya, and the ethnic group that spearheaded the Mau Mau revolt:

> of all the peoples of Kenya, it was the Kikuyu whose ways of life were most disrupted by colonial rule. Many of them were disposed of their land and were forced to work for European enterprises at a relatively early stage of the colonial era. But the impact of colonialism on the Kikuyu was more comprehensive than the simple loss of land. Central Province, the area where the Kikuyu lived, was swiftly drawn into the capitalist market and underwent major social transformation. (Furendi, 1989: 5)

In addition to this appropriation of land and forced labour, there was also the institution of apartheid and the restriction of the free movement of Africans. According to J.M. Karuiki, a key figure in the Mau Mau movement, detained alongside other leaders by the colonial government between 1953 and 1960, Africans during the colonial era, suffered all sorts of social degradation at the hands of European settlers:

> many Europeans refused to talk to educated Africans in any language but their deplorably bad Swahili; old men were addressed as boys and monkeys; Africans with land near Europeans were not allowed to plant coffee; there was a wholesale disregard for human dignity and little respect for anyone with a black skin. (Kariuki, 1963: 49)

As we shall later observe about *Simba*, the above derogatory language is what is used by Europeans to qualify Africans. In fact, there is a sense in which *Simba* legitimizes the revolt through adherence to this manner of address even though the film represents the mass revolt as a mindless uprising. The revolt itself was a product of the Squatter Movement, which evolved as a result of the land appropriation policy. The movement grew out of a loose association of squatters living on European farms as tenants, farmhands and house servants. Such associations as the Young Kikuyu Association (YKA) and the Kikuyu Central Association (KCA) started in the 1920s later grew into nationwide nationalist movement, the Kenya African Union (KAU). The Oath of Unity, which forms the central focus in *Simba*, was instituted by KAU to unite all the ethnic groups in Kenya into a strong nationalist movement. The movement itself was not called the Mau Mau. This was a derogatory term invented by the propaganda machine of the colonial government in order to discredit the movement. Kariuki explains its origins as follows:

> this is the real origin of the name 'Mau Mau'. Kikuyu children when playing and talking often make puns and anagrams with common words. When I was a child I would say to other children 'Ithi, Ithi', instead of 'Thii, Thii', (meaning 'Go, Go'); and 'Mau Mau', instead of 'Uma Uma'. One evening, people went to a house in Naivasha area where the oath was to be administered. That evening, the guard was given the instruction that, if he heard footsteps and suspected it was the police or an

enemy, he should shout the anagram 'Mau Mau' so that those in the house could escape. (Kariuki: 50-51)

According to him, that evening, the police did arrive on a tip off and the man on guard shouted the agreed anagram "Mau Mau." When the police arrived they found no one but the paraphernalia of oath taking. They reported back to police headquarters that they heard the words "Mau Mau" but found nobody in the scene. After this incident, a certain loyalist Church leader referred to as Parmenas is said to have popularized the term as part of the strategy of pouring scorn on the movement (Kariuki: 50-51). The nationalist movement was therefore tagged "Mau Mau" in order to qualify it as a childish movement. This manner of representation is also the pattern followed in the film *Simba*.

The film examines the Mau Mau revolt through the personal experiences of two European families, the Howards and the Crawfords. The central character, Alan (Dirk Bogarde), arrives in Kenya to find that his brother, David, has been murdered by Mau Mau fighters who have left their mark "SIMBA" (Swahili word for lion), scribbled in blood, on the doorpost. He is faced with two options, return to England immediately or stay on and defend the family property. He chooses the latter option even though he is by this time full of bitterness toward Africans. His suspicion that every African belongs to the Mau Mau movement puts a lot of strain on his relationship with Mary (Virginia McKenna), his white Kenyan girlfriend who feels it is possible for both blacks and whites to live together peacefully without racial hatred. Part of the film's project includes seeing the growth of the Bogarde character from the position of intolerance to one of understanding, but that growth is achieved only at the expense of black sacrifice in form of the death of Dr Karanja toward the end of the film.

The film begins with a long shot of a singing black man riding a bicycle along a lonely stretch of road. His song is soon interrupted by a cry for help from a white man fatally injured from an attack. The black man dismounts from his bicycle quietly, examines the scene to make sure that nobody is looking, brings out his machete and hacks the man to death. This opening sequence with its mindless killing is the film's way of representing the Mau Mau uprising. We are not told why the black man kills the white man. As the film progresses, this pattern are repeated without explanation, thereby giving the impression that the Mau Mau was a mindless murderous uprising. During the drive from the airport to the farm, this pattern of representation is further reinforced through portrayal of the landscape at the center of disputation as a semi desert region. The representation of the landscape as a wasteland where Europeans are managing to eke out a living makes them appear victims of unwarranted African violence. Through this manner of representation, the film solicits empathy to the cause of injustice. The African who was victim of British colonial land appropriation policy becomes the villain in a mindless murderous uprising. According to a reviewer in the *Monthly Film Bulletin* of March 1955, the film merely sets out to glamorize violence through exploitation of its dramatic potentials:

> simply to exploit the dramatic potentials of violence and mistrust in the present situation in Kenya is not enough; and *Simba*, though its intentions may be serious, achieves little more than this. Only in its admission of intolerance on the part of some British settlers does it ever get beyond the immediate obvious aspects of the situation. That is to say, it fails to acknowledge that Mau Mau represents something ... in the film ... one has the feeling that tension have grown up in a vacuum. The native people never express any cause of grievance against the whites, the implication being that through fear, ignorance and superstition, they have been influenced by a band of terrorists into believing they are bad. (*Monthly Film Bulletin* Vol. 22 No.254, March 1955)

In addition, many of the spectacular and emotional gratifications that *Simba* has to offer were initiated and realized at the expense of what were tragic moments for Africans. The film reduces the Mau Mau to a farcical ritual and employs some of the foulest colonialist form of verbal address. Its quasi-realistic project is built around principally derogatory form of address in which African men are referred to, as boys and monkeys and their behavior termed childish. The only exceptions in this practice are Mary (Virginia McKenna) and Dr Hughes (Joseph Tomelty) — and both are considerably minority opinions. As earlier stated, if this form of address served any purpose in the film besides reinforcing the colonialist structures of the text, it is to legitimize in an inadvertent manner, the Mau Mau uprising.

With respect to the representation of the African landscape, the film adopts the general conventions of colonialist African cinema. There are aerial photographs of the landscape with spectacular scenes of fleeing buffaloes, open beaches, forests and Savannah grassland. As in the earlier films, the photographic strategy is aimed at exploiting the geographic otherness of the landscape and its vast games reserves, for the visual pleasures of western spectators. The incorporation of market scenes, with their vast arrays of foodstuffs, animals and haggling market women, is also part of the ethnographic display of the racial and cultural otherness of the people. The setting of the interrogation scene next to the market serves to further the overall strategy of ethnographic display of peoples and cultures of Kenya.

The interior scenes of European bungalows with their teams of grinning but violence-prone house-servants further invokes images of grinning but cunningly scheming blacks popularized by early Hollywood's representation of African-Americans, reminding us, in accordance with the symbolic meaning in the tradition of its construction, that there is treachery lurking somewhere beneath the grinning face (Nesteby, 1988). The film seems to be saying that the Kenyan house servants might be grinning but they could also be spies or Mau Mau recruits.

Richard Dyer, in his analysis of the film, has observed that

> *Simba* is founded on the 'Manicheism delirium' identified by Frantz Fanon as characteristic of colonialist sensibility ... The film is organized around a rigid binarism, with white standing for modernity, reason, order, stability, and black standing for backwardness, irrationality, chaos and violence. (Dyer, 1988: 49)

This contrastive mode of representation reaches its climax in the parallel editing of the two meeting sequences — the African meeting called for the initiation of Mau Mau recruits and the European meeting called for vigilante plans in the settler community. Dyer's analysis of both sequences details how the underlying Manicheistic thought is realized cinematically:

> the white meeting takes place in early evening, in a fully lit room; characters that speak are shot with standard high key lighting so that they are fully visible; everyone sits in rows and although there is disagreement, some of it hot-tempered and emotional it is expressed in grammatical discourse in a language the British viewer can understand ... The black meeting, on the other hand, takes place at the dead of night, out of doors, with all characters in shadows; even the Mau Mau leader is lit with sub-

expressionist lighting that dramatizes and distorts his face; grouping is in form of broken, uneven circle; what speech there is ritualized, not reasoned and remains untranslated. (Dyer: 49-50)

Even though one could argue that the lighting of the African meeting is determined by the surreptitious and clandestine nature of the uprising, it is no reason for denial of speech and the reasoned persuasion of the Mau Mau recruits. Furthermore, by choosing to highlight the oath taking ritual ceremony instead of the central issue of land appropriation, the mass uprising is downgraded into a barbaric orgy of drunken stupor and ritual sacrifice. The overall impression one gets from the film is the official British colonialist view that the Mau Mau is a terrorist organization. In keeping with this line of thought, the film ends on a note of optimism as it looks into the future with the death of Simba (Orlando Martins) and a shot of an African child.

Simba is a colonialist film that deals with the problems of British decolonization in Africa. Based on the Mau Mau uprising, the film refuses to highlight what was responsible for the revolt, instead directing its focus on a ritual ceremony, which highlights the operational methods of Mau Mau. The methods are portrayed as coercive and barbaric in nature. By focusing only upon operational methods at the expense of land disputation and the practice of apartheid, the film solicits empathy for the white cause. It is only in displaying white intolerance through a derogatory form of address that the film touches on reasons of black discontent and revolt.

Summary

In this chapter, the historical roots of colonialist African cinema have been traced to colonialist African discourse, in general, and colonialist African literature in particular. In addition, the ideas that informed the films and the literary texts are nineteenth century racial theories, which constituted Africans as inferior beings. I have equally given a classification of the various types of films, which constitute the cinematic practice as a genre, and a tabulation of its general modes of representation, with respect to the construction of African subjectivity and culture, in comparison with the Europeans.

In my textual analysis, I have argued that, in general terms, most of the films structure their narratives by setting up a comparative schema which represent Africans as savages and bestial both in behavior and in cultural practices, and as people who are impulsive and emotional in their responses to situations. They are also represented as people lacking individual initiative, incapable of acquiring knowledge and by extension initiating development projects, and as people always on the verge of slippage into barbarism once white authority is not present. It is in this regard that they differ considerably from colonial African instructional cinema. On the other hand, Europeans are represented as civilized, calculating and rational in their responses to situations. With respect to spatial articulation, I have argued that in most of these films, space is defined by the presence of white lead characters. Africans remain in the background and are shot in mostly long shots, with spectatorial access to them tied in most cases to their movement into white space or when white characters move into theirs. Within this broad comparative schema, however, the colonialist structures of the films are undermined by the incorporation of counter-narratives linked with gender and class politics, especially with respect to the representation of European subjectivity, where negative character attributes are projected upon members of the working class as in the case of Farini and Smith in *Sanders of the River*, Delpich and Luc in *Chocolat*, and Sargy Gollup in *Mister Johnson*, but also with respect to Africans where such counter-narratives take the form of Africans' opposition to European imperial presence. These underlining counter-narratives within colonialist African cinema make its discursive structures ambivalent and the application of pure binarist schema simplistic.

FILM PRODUCTION STRUCTURES AND SPONSORSHIP PATTERNS IN ANGLOPHONE AND FRANCOPHONE AFRICAN COUNTRIES

Introduction

In this chapter, the nature of film production structures and sponsorship patterns in both English and French speaking African countries are examined. Emphasis is placed on how colonial and post-colonial production structures and sponsorship policies of countries within the two linguistic blocs have affected film production output and quality. The choice of countries in both linguistic blocs is informed by the fact that, together, they account for two-third of film production in Africa. This is followed by a comparison of the effects of British and French colonial and post-colonial cultural policies on the scope and quality of current film production in the countries under consideration. The quality of films are measured by the general artistic quality of production and their level of popularity and reception by African spectators, the people for whom they are meant, and the larger world spectators who may have the opportunity to see them and pass general critical judgments, including awards at both African and international film festivals. Of course, one is aware that a film may be of good artistic quality, may even win awards both locally and internationally, without being popular with African spectators. On the other hand, a production can be of poor quality and yet be popular among spectators; a case in point is some films of Yoruba folklore cinema productions. Such exceptional cases are acknowledged, but especially African film critics and scholars place special emphasis on those films, which were popular and yet were also critically acclaimed. The chapter begins with an examination of the nature of film production in colonial and post-colonial Anglophone African countries, followed by that of Francophone Africa.

Film Production Structures and Sponsorship Policies in Anglophone Africa

Colonial Film Production Structures and Sponsorship Policies in Anglophone Africa

Film production was introduced into most Anglophone African countries after the Second World War as part of the British colonial government's instructional cinema program. The British colonial government's perception of the cinema as a useful aid to development and modernization in what were then largely illiterate societies resulted in the establishment of the Colonial Film Unit (CFU) in 1939. Throughout the war years, the Unit concentrated its efforts on the production of propaganda films in aid of British war efforts. During this period, Britain also launched the "Raw Stock Scheme" under which it gave out 16 mm. cameras and raw film stock to British officials working in the colonies, especially information officers, to shoot newsworthy ongoing development projects and important ceremonies for the CFU. This scheme did not require the participants to have any specialized knowledge of the camera. They gained a working knowledge of the camera through experimentation. Later this scheme became a source of news materials for the CFU. Film footage shot under the scheme was sent to the CFU's studios in London for processing, editing and criticism by experts who forwarded their opinions through correspondence to participants. After the war, emphasis shifted to the production of instructional films in aid of the colonial governments' development efforts. The CFU, which hitherto had been concentrated in London, was also decentralized, with sub-Units set up in most African countries. The first CFU in Africa was set up in Ghana in 1945. Subsequent CFUs were set up in Nigeria in 1946, Kenya and Uganda in 1947, Gambia, Sierra Leone, Tanganyika, Zanzibar, and the Central African Federation, comprising Northern Rhodesia (Zambia), Southern Rhodesia (Zimbabwe) and Nyasaland (Malawi), in 1948. To facilitate the training of indigenous personnel in film production, a Mobile Film

Training School was set up by the CFU. The training school for Africans was organized in Accra, Gold Coast (Ghana) in 1948. Subsequent training schools were run in Jamaica for the West Indies in 1950 and in Cyprus in 1951, for the Middle East and Asia. The last training school was organized in London in 1955. The Accra Film Training School, which lasted for six months, was attended by three students each from Ghana and Nigeria. They were trained in both 16 mm and 35 mm equipment. Sam Aryetey and Adamu Halilu, who later became General Managers of Ghana Film Corporation and Nigerian Film Corporation respectively, were among the pioneer students at the Accra Film Training School. During the colonial era, most film productions undertaken by the Unit in each territory were government-t sponsored productions, and they formed part of their instructional cinema programs.

The Gold Coast (Ghana) Film Unit was organized on a professional basis in 1949, following the completion of the first Film Training School held in Accra in 1948. The Film Unit was under the overall control of the Director of Information Services in the Gold Coast, and its stated objective was the making of films in Africa for Africans by Africans. Despite this stated objective, Sean Graham, a former student of John Grierson, directed most of these films. Ghanaians trained at the Accra Film Training School had to wait until independence before they tried their hands at directing. They functioned during the colonial period mainly as actors and technical assistants to Graham. The Unit had facilities for recording, post-synchronization and editing. The laboratory work still had to be undertaken in London. The Unit had two sections, one of which produced scripted dialogue films, and the other, newsreel materials. The former section worked with amateur local casts and shot most of its films on location. It had sound track and other equipment. The films were mainly short story films meant to interest Africans in improving their standards of living such as *Kofi the Good Farmer*, about cocoa growing, and didactic features such as, *Amenu's Child* (1950), which deals with the consequences of neglecting modern health care in favor of traditional medicine; *Jaguar High Life*, which deals with the theme of acculturation; *The Boy Kumasenu* (1952), which deals with city life; *Freedom for Ghana*, a documentary on Ghana's independence struggles.

The Gold Coast Film Unit became independent in 1950, seven years before Ghana became independent. Two films of the Unit's productions, *Amenu's Child* and *The Boy Kumasenu*, attracted favorable attention at international film festivals and were publicly acclaimed. *Amenu's Child* was shown at the Edinburgh Film Festival and won an award at the Venice Film Festival in 1950. *The Boy Kumasenu*, the first full-length feature to be made in West Africa, was shown at the Edinburgh Film Festival in 1952 and was shortlisted for the British Film Academy. The film was widely distributed in Ghana and the United Kingdom. In 1957, Graham, the artistic director of the Unit left Ghana after its independence, and the President of Ghana, Kwame Nkrumah, nationalized both film distribution and production in the country. (Central Office of Information (COI) Bulletin No. R. 3161, October, 1955: 6; Diawara, 1992: 5-6).

The Federal Film Unit (FFU) of Nigeria, established in Lagos, also grew out of the Film Training School held in Accra. The Unit was set up in October 1946, although the government of Nigeria's legislation, which legalized it as a Division of the Federal Ministry of Information, was not enacted until 1947. Even before the Unit was set up in Nigeria, the Film Exhibition Section of the Federal Ministry of Information had already formed the nucleus of what was to become the FFU as far back as 1945. Originally, the Film Unit was a Public Relations Section of the Marketing and Publicity Department of the Federal Government of Nigeria. Its functions were to explore the country's resources and enhance the nation's economic growth. The FFU was established with N.F. Spurr as Film Officer, and it had a nucleus Nigerian staff made up of A.A. Fajemisin, J.A. Otigba and Malam Yakubu Auna, who were trained at the Film Training School in Accra, Ghana. In its early days, most of the films shown by the FFU were supplied by the CFU in London. Later, the FFU began to produce its own documentaries. Some of the films produced during the colonial period are *Empire Day Celebrations in Nigeria* (1948), *Small Pox* (1950), *Leprosy* (1950) *Port Harcourt Municipal Council Elections* (1950) and *Queen Elizabeth II's Visit to Nigeria* (1956).

In addition to locally produced films, newsreels were also provided by a commercial film distributor who imported two copies of *British Movietone* and one of *British Gaumont* every week. *Pathe (British) News* was also distributed in the country.

These films were shown in Lagos and in towns and villages across Nigeria by the Mobile Film Units. Shortly after the establishment of the FFU, the old three principal regions in Nigeria, Western Region, Eastern Region, and Northern Region, later set up their own regional Film Units. They received a supply of films and Mobile Cinema Vans from the parent body, the Federal Ministry of Information, through the FFU (Mgbejume, 1989: 43; Opubor and Nwuneli, 1979: 2-3). The political structure of Nigeria has since changed with the creation of the Midwestern Region in 1963. At present, Nigeria is made up of thirty-six states, most of which have their own Film Units.

In East Africa, Film Units were established in Kenya and Uganda in 1947, and Tanganyika and Zanzibar in 1948. The Kenya Film Unit was attached to the Kenya Information Department. Most of its early productions were documentaries released as part of the campaign against the Mau Mau Movement. Others were "Safari" documentaries aimed at promoting tourism in Kenya. The Kenya Film Unit produced 16 mm. films for showing to Africans, and 35 mm. news materials for world newsreel subscribers. Uganda started its productions in 1955. In 1951, the Tanganyika government set in motion an experiment to produce locally made entertainment films. A commercial company was commissioned to produce these films in the territory to a story line provided by the Tanganyika government. During a two-and-half year period, sufficient films were made to provide four complete entertainment programs. The stories of the full-length features include *Wageni Wema*, the adventure of a coastal family who left their overworked land and finally settled down among the Masai; *Mela Tuakwenda*, a village drama of love and hate; *Chalo Amerudi*, a story portraying the confusion that may arise in an educated African when the call of a job in town conflicts with his duties as head of a family living in the village. Film show programs were supplemented with documentaries and newsreels provided or produced by the Tanganyika Film Unit. The casts of these films were made up of Africans, and the experiment showed that local feature films could be made at a low cost.

In 1948, the Central African Council, an inter-territorial advisory body which linked the two Rhodesias and Nyasaland before federation, set up the Central African Film Unit to produce films to assist in the advancement of Africans in Southern and

Northern Rhodesia and Nyasaland, and also to make a limited number of tourism- promotion films. The Unit was later inherited by the government of the Central African Federation. From the beginning, the Central African Film Unit made most of its films in color, using 16 mm kodachrome films, which were sent to Johannesburg in South Africa for processing. As there are seven main language groups in the region, most of the films produced were silent films with local commentators serving as narrators. A few sound versions were produced with English commentary. Most of the Unit's productions were educational and informational films (Central Office of Information Bulletin, No. R. 3161, October, 1955: 7; Pearson, 1948: 22-27).

It can justifiably be opined that the CFU made a number of contributions to the introduction of instructional cinema into Anglophone Africa. After its war propaganda objective, the post-war phase of the CFU witnessed the establishment sub-Units in almost all British colonies in Africa. Most of the productions based in the colonies used indigenous personnel. The CFU also initiated a popular form of film exhibition, the Mobile Film Units (MFUs), which took films to the rural areas, thereby making it possible for rural dwellers in Africa to have an early exposure to the cinema. Unfortunately, since independence, most of the MFUs have either completely ceased operations or, where they still operate, they have become only occasional callers at the rural areas.

The CFU also laid the foundation upon which most of Anglophone African countries' state owned film corporations were established after independence. In West Africa the CFU Film Training School provided the basic training for the first batch of filmmakers and technicians in the region. The Accra Film Training School also helped to establish the Grierson tradition of documentary film making in countries like Nigeria and Ghana, which currently produce high quality documentary films geared towards mass instruction and social mobilization. However, most of these films are shown on television thereby making it impossible for poor rural dwellers without television sets to benefit. In the area of feature film production, the aesthetic influence of the Grierson documentary tradition has been noted in the works of Sam Aryetey and Adamu Halilu, both erstwhile students of the Accra Film Training School.

Post-colonial Film Production Structures and Sponsorship Policies in Anglophone Africa

The bulk of current Anglophone African films is produced within the West African sub-region, principally by Nigeria and Ghana. These two countries have set up their own film corporations, with modern production facilities for indigenous film production. In Ghana, for instance, the Nkrumah regime built a very sophisticated film production infrastructure between 1957 and 1966. The facilities included editing studios, and 16 mm and 35 mm processing laboratories. When the facilities were completed, most Ghanaian directors were still inexperienced, so foreign directors made use of them. Post-independence Ghana has also set up its own film school, the National Film and Television Institute (NAFTI), with the assistance of the Federal Republic of Germany. The Ghana Film Industry Corporation (GFIC) and NAFTI manage the training of personnel, production, censorship, and distribution of documentaries and information-related films in Ghana. In addition to the production facilities set up by the Nkrumah regime, the GFIC also inherited the facilities of the old Gold Coast Film Unit. In respect of the general quality of production facilities available in Ghana, Diawara has noted that, with GFIC alone, Ghana is better equipped than all of the other West African states, and it is capable of turning out more than 12 features a year. Ghanaian filmmakers trained at NAFTI and abroad find their first employment at GFIC and GBC [Ghana Broadcasting Corporation] (Diawara, 1992: 118). So far, the Ghanaian directors who have been able to direct their films by making use of the state-owned production facilities of GFIC include Sam Aryetey, who directed *No Tears for Ananse* (1968); Egbert Adjesu, *I Told You So* (1970); Kwate Nee-Owoo, *You Hide Me* (1971), *Struggle for Zimbabwe* (1974) and *Angela Davis* (1976); King Ampaw, *They Call it Love* (1972), *Kukurantumi* (1983) and *Juju* or *Nana Akoto* (1986). The most reputable Ghanaian director is Kwaw Ansah, and his film, *Love Brewed in the African Pot* (1980), was shown in Ghana and other African countries where it was well received (Diawara, 1992: 118; Bachy, 1987: 55-56; Pfaff, 1988: 11-18). Most of these productions were self-financed. However, the GFIC makes its facilities available free of charge to Ghanaian filmmakers.

In Nigeria, the complementary role of television broadcasting to the film industry needs to be acknowledged. Television broadcasting was introduced to sub-Saharan Africa by the Obafemi Awolowo regime of the old Western Region of Nigeria, when it set up Africa's first television station, Western Nigeria Television (WNTV), in Ibadan on October 31, 1959. Both the Eastern and Northern Regions soon followed suit with the Eastern Nigeria Television (ENTV), Enugu, on October 1960, and the Radio Kaduna Television (RKTV), Kaduna, in March 1962. In 1961, the Federal Government invited NBC International, New York, to help set up the federal television station in Lagos, and so the Nigerian Television Services (NTS), later changed to (NTV) Lagos, was established in April 1962 at Victoria Island, Lagos. The Midwest Television (MTV), later changed to (NTV), Benin, was set up in April 1973. In 1976, the federal military government of Nigeria decided to take over the ten television stations in the country. Decree number 24 of 1977 was promulgated to establish a government agency to coordinate the activities of television broadcasting in Nigeria. This agency was called the Nigerian Television Authority (NTA). The agency later took over the existing television stations, and began to establish new ones in new states or in states that had none. At present, almost all the thirty states in Nigeria have two television stations — one owned by the Federal Government of Nigeria, called (NTA) station, and the other by the state government. Most states decided to set up their own television and radio stations during the period of the civilian government of President Shehu Shagari because they felt the Federal Government was enjoying an undue advantage over them through a monopoly of information transmission. Currently, the television industry has been liberalized. Consequent to the liberalization in the 1990s, the Federal Government established the National Broadcasting Commission (NBC) to license both private and state-owned radio and television stations in the country. As a result of this policy shift, the country now has over 150 television stations, comprising of private and state-owned television stations.

Most of these television stations show films as part of their program schedules. Most importantly, through television broadcast, a lot of instructional and mass mobilization films are shown. Such television documentaries are designed to lead to a better and greater appreciation of government operations by the Nigerian populace. The objectives of such television documentaries include the followings,

> (i) Helping to educate the public on methods of improving its way and standard of living. This would be done through films on improved farming techniques, health schemes, factory methods and techniques, social organization, etc; (ii) Portraying the achievements of our culture both locally and internationally; (iii) Informing the public of news events in and outside of Nigeria. (Cited in Mgbejume: 45)

The FFU consists of eight departments, including Film Direction, Scripting, Camera and Sound, Editing, Laboratory, Exhibition, and Maintenance. The Camera section further includes sub-sections comprising Still Camera Section, Animation Section, and Live Action Section. Among the films produced by the FFU since independence, two films by Bayo Imeovbere are noteworthy. These are *Lagos* (1965) and *Nigeria* (1968). According to Françoise Balogun, *Nigeria* shows fine technical quality and great sensitivity. It takes us around Nigeria from the Arogungun Festival to the Museum in Ile-Ife, and from the palace of the Oba of Benin, to the mosque in Kano (Balogun, 1987: 22-23). In a report published by the FFU, which covers three years, October 1, 1979 to March 31, 1983, the Unit produced twenty-five documentaries, sixty-five news magazines, and three hundred and ninety news items (Balogun: 22).

One of the most important private documentary films about Nigeria is *Nigeria: Culture in Transition* (1963), a twenty-five minute dramatized documentary which reviews Nigeria's performing and fine arts, from antiquity up to 1963, showing the country's music, dance, drama, literature, painting and sculpture. The dramatized portion of the documentary was adapted from Wole Soyinka's play, *The Strong Breed*. The film was produced by Esso World Theatre, and it starred seasoned Nigerian actors and actresses of the 1960 Ibadan Mask, a theatre company formed by Wole Soyinka. Also included in the cast were veteran television actors, actresses, and producers. The cast included big names such as Yemi Lijadu, a prominent television personality in Lagos, and Betty Okotie, a very talented television and stage actress. Those in supporting roles included Segun Olusola and Ralph Okpara, both of whom were at this time prominent television producers. Other members of the cast included Rufus Bayo, a renowned painter, Tokunbo Odunjo, and Julie Olamijulo. When the film was premiered at the Federal

Palace Hotel in Victoria Island, Lagos, in April 1964, many important politicians, civil servants, professionals, business tycoons, and diplomats were present. Though privately financed, the film has since been incorporated into the corpus of FFU films.

Another important documentary in the category of *Culture in Transition* is *In Search of Myself* (1965), produced by the United Nations Television, in which Nigerian writers and artists discussed the link and conflicts between tradition and modernity. The film featured renowned Nigerian artistic figures such as Chinua Achebe, Onwura Nzekwu, Cyprian Ekwensi, Demas Nwoko, Simon Okeke, and Duro Ladipo. The main questions, which *In Search of · Myself* addressed, were the impact of modernity on cultural practices and the problems faced by literary and fine artists (Mgbejume: 68). Apart from these private productions, the FFU has, since the 1980s produced many documentaries of which the most significant are *Nigeria's First Executive President* (1980), a documentary on the swearing-in ceremony of Nigeria's first Executive President, Alhaji Shehu Shagari; *Framework for Survival* (1981), which shows the efforts of the Federal Government towards the "Green Revolution" project geared towards general improvement of agricultural production; *Progressive Years* (1981), a silver jubilee anniversary film; *22nd Independence Celebration at Abuja* (1982), a documentary on independence day celebration in Nigeria's new Federal Capital, Abuja (Balogun: 23).

The Federal Government manages the film industry through five government agencies. They include the Federal Film Unit (FFU), the Nigerian Film Corporation (NFC), the National Film Distribution Company (NFDC), the Federal Censor Board, and the National Film Archive. The NFC came into statutory existence with the promulgation of Decree No. 61 of 1979 by the federal military government headed by General Olusegun Obasanjo. However, the civilian government of President Shehu Shagari brought the NFC into actual existence through an enabling Act in 1982. Since the creation of the NFC, the profit-oriented ventures of the FFU have been inherited by the NFC. The FFU is now solely concerned with the production of documentaries. The NFC also inherited all the equipment, which the FFU had procured for the setting up of a film-processing laboratory. The NFDC has since become the Commercial Department of the NFC. The following are the stated objectives of the NFC:

the principal objective of the Nigerian Film Corporation is to act as the nucleus of a vital nation-wide motion picture industry. Rather than rival independent producers, the Corporation will use its resources to encourage and promote all film makers not only by financial assistance wherever possible, but by creating a larger market through the expansion of cinema distribution and encouragement of a movie-going culture. The NFC also hopes, through its programs and activities, to expand the range of creative expression by talented Nigerians, young and old, and to explore all aspects of creative, cultural, entertainment, health and social development through existing as well as new uses of cinema and its subsidiary forms. (Cited in Ekwuazi, 1987: 36-37)

The appointment of Bredan Shehu as the General Manager of the NFC in 1985 can be considered a turning point for progress in the history of the NFC. Since his appointment, the NFC has moved its headquarters from Lagos to Jos, Plateau State, its statutory location. The NFC is now the owner of an ultra-modern comprehensive color film-processing laboratory for both 16 mm. and 35 mm. films. The NFC is currently building a National Film Archive in Jos, where films made in the country will be preserved. The NFC has also successfully retrieved from various oversea agencies and laboratories film negatives and sound tracks held by such bodies but belonging to the FFU or States' Film Units. These retrieved negatives and sound tracks comprise part of the initial stock of the National Film Archive. The NFC also offers technical and sometimes financial assistance to Nigerian filmmakers and makes its facilities available to them.

The NFC produced ten documentaries between 1988 and 1989. One of them, *The Story So Far*, won a special award at the 1990 Pyongyang Film Festival of the Non-Aligned and Developing Countries held in North Korea. The NFC has also entered into bilateral agreements with three countries — Angola (1986), Ghana (1989) and Russia (1989) — to offer Nigerian filmmakers an opportunity for wider scope of operation. Its current project is a compilation of a comprehensive list of the following "(i) Available filmmaking facilities in the country, (ii) Active/trained filmmakers, including those employed by the various television stations, (iii) All film production companies in the country, (iv) A list of all cinema houses in Nigeria" (Ekwuazi, 1987: 44-45).

Beside the NFC facilities there is also a Rivers State Government owned color film processing laboratory for both 16 mm. and 35 mm. films in Port Harcourt. The old four regions and a few of the new states also have production facilities beside those inherited by the FFU from the CFU. There is also a privately owned 16 mm. color film laboratory, Latola Films, in Ikeja, Lagos.

The first attempt by the government to regulate the film industry in Nigeria was made in 1912 with the proposed "Theatre and Public Performance Regulation Ordinance, 1912," initiated nine years after the first film was shown to the public. The law failed to reach the Legislative Council of Nigeria because of public opposition. However, in 1933, the first Cinematographic Ordinance No. 20 was passed by the Council. The law became effective on April 1, 1934. The law, titled "An Ordinance for the Better Regulation of Cinematograph and Similar Exhibitions and Posters Advertising Such Exhibitions, and Purposes Connected Therewith" applied to both the Lagos Colony and the rest of Nigeria. The board created a Censorship Committee selected from the Board of Censors in 1934. The board governed the exhibition or showing of pictures or related optical effects by means of a cinematograph equipment and film designated for use with cinematograph equipment.

The 1933 Cinematograph Ordinance No.20 was amended in 1934, 1941, 1944, and 1945, and the 1963 Act was modeled after it. The law presently in operation in Nigeria is the Cinematograph (Film Censorship) Regulations Act of 1963. It was amended in 1964, with the regulations taking effect from April 1, 1964. Under this law, films dealing with sex, crime, religion, and controversial racial issues are liable to possible censorship. However, the owner of the censored film has a right to appeal for a further hearing. The 1963 Act replaced all former film censorship laws in Nigeria. The law is operated through the Federal Film Censorship Board. Parts I and III of the law apply throughout Nigeria while Part II applies only to Lagos (Ekwuazi, 1987: 151-183; Balogun, 1987: 17; Mgbejume, 1989: 57).

Though the Federal Government of Nigeria presently owns the bulk of film production facilities in the country it does not get involved in feature film production. The facilities are set up by the government as part of its policy of establishing a self-sustaining film industry in Nigeria. Its productions, as earlier noted, are essentially documentaries. Commercial feature film production is carried out by private film production companies set up by individual Nigerian filmmakers. The first of such private film production company established in Nigeria is Calpenny Nigeria Films Ltd, established in 1965 by Francis Oladele. Calpenny, in conjunction with Herald Productions (USA), Omega Films (Sweden), Film Three (West Germany), and Nigram Corporation (USA), produced *Kongi's Harvest* (Ossie Davis, 1970) and *Bullfrog in the Sun* (Jason Poland, 1971). Both films were adapted from works by Nigerian writers — *Kongi's Harvest* from a play of that title by Wole Soyinka and *Bullfrog in the Sun,* an adaptation of two of Achebe's novels, *Things Fall Apart* and *No Longer at Ease.* These works are not considered Nigerian films. Even though the casts of both films are principally Nigerian, they are not regarded as Nigerian films because they were directed by foreigners. Ossie Davis, who directed *Kongi's Harvest,* is an African-American, and was said to have directed the film with an African-American audience in mind; and this greatly affected his interpretation of Soyinka's play, and the film was not well received in Nigeria. As Hyginus Ekwuazi puts,

> The point is that Ossie Davis' *Kongi's Harvest* is a film that fosters the west's stereotype about the rest of us. Political demise, it avows, stems out of an endemic corruption; political power out of the barrel of a gun — and the military on the corridors of power, this translates into a coming and going that goes *ad nauseam.* In rhythm, style and texture, *Kongi's Harvest* is a film overtly aimed at a foreign audience, and the action-theme draws heavily from the stereotype in the conditioned imagination of this audience. (Ekwuazi: 24)

Soyinka who starred in the major role of Kongi in the film has denounced it as being unfaithful to the script he wrote for the screen adaptation of the play (Diawara, 1992: 125). However, the film was well received by African-American audiences, and a review of its premiere show in Washington D.C., published in the *Washington Post* of June 16, 1972, states that

> for many among the mostly black members of the audience, last night was an introduction to the African scene as viewed by Africans themselves. Over a wine, cheese and cake buffet after the showing, representatives of Washington's black intellectual and university community — their own dress revealing the spectacle of clothing in the film — predicted success for black film making. (Cited in Arologun, 1979: 30).

Whatever misgivings Nigerian film critics may have against *Kongi's Harvest*, its theme of abuse of power by post-colonial African leaders is still as relevant today in most African countries as it was when the film was first released in 1972. Lack of democracy, greed for and abuse of power create the unending cycle of coups and counter-coups with little to show by way of development. The second film produced by Calpenny, *Bullfrog in the Sun*, was not released in Nigeria because it included materials that dealt with the Nigerian civil war and the ill-fated Biafran Republic. Both novels upon which the film was based were pre-civil war novels but the director grafted the pre-civil war narratives onto those of the civil war. Since the film was shot immediately after the war, the Nigerian government considered it too early for such an emotional topic as a recently- concluded civil war to be used as material for a film. For this reason, the film was never shown in Nigeria.

Controversies also dogged *Son of Africa* (1971) dubbed by its producers, Fed Films Ltd, a Lebanese/Nigerian production company, Nigeria's first full-length feature film. As a matter of fact, the film can be described as a Lebanese film set in Lagos. The main actors, with the exception of Funsho Adeolu, were Lebanese, and "the theme of the film — the fight against currency molders — was not tackled from a Nigerian point of view" (Balogun: 50). The second production by Fed Films, *Golden Women* (1971), also starred mostly Lebanese women and it was not well received in Nigeria. Emmanuel Hart in a review published in the *Daily Times* of September 2, 1970, states that

> on seeing the preview of *Son of Africa* at the Federal Film Unit, Ikoyi, on Friday August 21, one question which I still cannot find an answer to is whether the title of the film should be *Son of Africa* or more appropriately 'Daughters of Lebanon' because the whole film is dominated by Lebanese belly dancers. (Cited in Balogun: 50)

Nigerian-directed feature films began to emerge from the middle of the 1970s with the simultaneous production, in 1975, of Ola Balogun's *Amadi*, the first full-length feature in a Nigerian language, and Sanya Dosunmu's *Dinner with the Devil*. Balogun, who is the most renowned Nigerian filmmaker, is a graduate of the *Institut des Hautes Études Cinematographiques* (IDHEC), Paris. He was once considered the most prolific African film director and has, in his over twenty-year career in the cinema, directed, by the last count, twenty films of which half are full-length feature films (Balogun: 55-68; Pfaff, 1988: 29). Balogun's first feature film, *Alpha* (1972), was shot in Paris with an international cast comprising mostly black diaspora actors. Before directing *Amadi* (1975), he had directed a series of ethnographic documentaries on Nigerian culture and tradition. They include *Fire in the Afternoon* (1971), recalling the festival celebrations in honor of the mythical heroine, Moremi, of Ile-Ife; *Thundergod* (1972), dedicated to the worship of Shango, the Yoruba god of thunder; *Nupe Masquerade* (1972), a traditional festival masque performances of the Nupe people of Nigeria; *In the Beginning* (1972), another documentary which focuses on the Yoruba myth of creation; and *Owuama* (1973), which deals with the traditional festival masque performances of the Kalabari people of Nigeria. Other non-ethnographic documentaries include *One Nigeria* (1969), in support of a united Nigeria at the outbreak of the civil war; *Les Ponts de Paris* (*The Bridges of Paris*, 1971*); Eastern Nigeria Revisited* (1973), a survey of the Eastern Region after the civil war; *Vivre* (*To Live*, 1974), dedicated to a friend and victim of a car accident; and *Nigersteel* (1975), a documentary on Nigersteel Company based in Enugu, the capital of the then Eastern Region of Nigeria.

Of all Balogun's feature films, the most popular within Nigeria are those written in the Yoruba language, and mythologies, all of which used actors/actresses of the popular Yoruba Traveling Theatre. They include films such as: the highly commercially successful, *Ajani-Ogun* (1976), a story of a young hunter, Ajani Ogun, who fights a vicious and corrupt politician; *Iya Ominira* (*Fight for Freedom*, 1977), adapted from a novel by Adebayo Faleti, a story of a tyrannical king banished from his kingdom by his subjects; *Aiye* (1979), the story of a struggle between the forces of good and evil in a Yoruba village; with the forces of good and evil respectively represented in the film by a *babalawo* (traditional healer and priest) and witche*s*. *Oru Mooru* (1982) is a moral fable structured very much like Amos Tutuola's novel, *The Palm-wine Drinkard*. The film tells the story of a poor villager, Lamidi, who, after having been duped several times on account of his credulity, is so depressed that he attempts to commit suicide. After several unsuccessful attempts he finally plunges into a lagoon to drown and finds himself in the land of the dead. Since it is not his appointed time to die, Death himself sends him to the palace of the

Queen of Joy, who endows him with enormous wealth and sends him back to earth. Unfortunately, he makes a fatal mistake of wanting even more money to show off in front of his friends, and this leads to his ruin. At a precise moment when Death is about to catch him, he emerges with horror from the coma of yet another unsuccessful suicide (Balogun: 67). Balogun's other feature films include the internationally well-received *Black Goddess* (1978), which won a prize from the International Catholic Office of Cinema, as well as Best Film Music prize at the 1980 Carthage Film Festival. The film deals with a mystical story of slavery and reincarnation. *Cry Freedom* (1981), shot in Ghana in 1980, is a liberation struggle film, adapted from a novel, *Carcasses for the Hounds*, by the Kenyan writer, Meja Mwangi. The film tells the story of a group of guerrilla fighters who rebel against colonial rule. *Musik-Man* (1976) was an unsuccessful Pidgin English adaptation of *Ajani-Ogun*; and *Money Power* (*Owo L'Agba*, 1982) won for leading actress, Clarion Chukwura, the prize of Best Female Actress at the Pan-African Film Festival at Ouagadougou, Burkina Faso (Pfaff, ibid: 21).

Most of Balogun's films are financed either by bank loans, income from his films or through direct investment by private business tycoons. Like other Nigerian filmmakers, his films are produced by his own production company, Afrocult Foundation. As a result of his non-reliance on government sources to fund his films, he has been one of the most vehement critics of his Francophone colleagues whose films are principally financed and produced by the French Ministry of Cooperation. He is on record for observing that

> film budgets provided by non-commercial sources such as governments have, in many cases, the disadvantages of opening the door to some form of political pressure and censorship ... and it may lead to favoritism and other forms of nepotism. There are obvious dangers in relying on foreign sources for film finance, the danger of paternalistic influence. I have seen some of my colleagues fall into inextricable contradictions ... how can you take money from the French government [in this case the French Ministry of Cooperation] to make films that denounce French colonial presence in Africa? (Cited in Pfaff: 23)

Apart from Balogun, another notable Nigerian filmmaker is Adamu Halilu, graduate of the Film Training School, Accra, Ghana, former General Manager of the old Northern Region Film Unit, and producer and film director at the FFU, Kaduna, in 1968. In 1982, he was appointed General Manager of the Nigerian Film Corporation (NFC). His films to date include, *Child Bride* (1971), which attacks the practice, carried out mostly in Northern Nigeria, of early marriages and pregnancies of girls, sometimes as young as eleven or twelve years. His first major feature film, *Shehu Umar* (1977), was the first Hausa language feature, and it follows the trail of Nigerian language films already blazed by Ola Balogun's *Amadi*. *Shehu Umar* was Nigeria's official entry at the 2nd World Black Festival of Arts and Culture (FESTAC 77) held in Lagos. It was produced by the NFC, and tells the epic story of an Hausa religious leader, *Shehu Umar*; it was based on an Hausa historical novel of the same title by the first Prime Minister of Nigeria, Alhaji Abubakar Tafawa Balewa, adapted for the screen by Umaru Ladan. Diawara has observed with respect to the film that

> even though *Shehu Umar* is important because of its use of Hausa tradition and historiography, and its glorification of Islam and the Hausa past, it risks letting the spectator down because of its length (140 minutes) and repetitious scenes. (Diawara: 122)

Despite its historical and artistic importance, *Shehu Umar* was not screened commercially in Nigeria, possibly because of government's sensitivity to Nigeria's diverse ethnic and religious composition. Another important historical film by Halilu is *Kanta of Kebbi* (1978), a co-production between Halilu's production company, Haske Films and the Sokoto State Government. The film tells the story of Mohammed Kanta, founder of the Kebbi Empire. Kebbi, situated in the present day Niger State was a vassal state of the powerful Songhai Empire, which covered most of the countries of the Savannah belt of West Africa. Mohammed Kanta revolted against the iron-rule of Askia Mohammed Toure (1492-1538), ruler of the Empire, and built an independent powerful Kebbi Empire. The film chronicles Mohammed Kanta's long reign, which was full of mysteries, predictions and magic rites, and constitutes a fascinating episode in West African history (Balogun, ibid: 71). Halilu's next film, *Moment of Truth* (1981), was also a co-production between Haske Films and the Sokoto State Government. It was adapted from a play produced by Sokoto State Television and entered for the National Television Productions Festival of 1975. The film tells the story of a woman who loses her only child through medical negligence. She attempts to take revenge on the doctor's only daughter but, at the last moment, common sense prevails. His last film, *Zainab*, was being shot when he was appointed General Manager of the NFC in 1982.

Adamu Halilu was a product of the John Grierson school of documentary, and most of his documentaries reflect the influence of this school — a basic narrative account of a particular social process geared towards mass enlightenment (Lovell, 1972: 28). This stylistic pattern can be discerned in his documentary films such as *It Pays to Care* (1955), *Hausa Village* (1958), *Northern Horizon* (1959), *Durbar Day* (1960), *Giant in the Sun* (1960), *Rinderpest* (1963), *Welcome Change* (1965), *Tourist Delight* (1967), *Back to Land* (1967), *Pride of a Nation* (1974) and *Black Heritage* (1977). Most of Halilu's productions were produced either by the NFC as in the case of *Shehu Umar*, or co-produced with the Sokoto State Government. However, this is an exceptional case because the bulk of Nigeria's feature films are produced by independent filmmakers who source their funds like other private commercial business undertakings in the country.

The next important Nigerian filmmaker, besides Balogun and Halilu, is Eddy Ugbomah. He studied Journalism and Drama in London, where he later studied Film and Television Production. Thereafter she worked with the BBC, and played small roles in films such as *Dr No*, *Guns of Batasi* and *Sharpville Massacre*. He also formed a black theatre group in London. His first film, *The Rise and Fall of Dr Oyenusi* (1977), was inspired by the story of a notorious Nigerian armed-robber who assumed the title of "Dr" Oyenusi. Since 1976, Ugbomah has shot eight full-length 16 mm. feature films. *The Mask* (1979) deals with attempts by a Nigerian agent to retrieve an ancient Benin Royal Mask of Queen Adesua, which was stolen by the British expedition force, which sacked the city of Benin in 1797. The film has been described as an unimaginative imitation of the James Bond series (Diawara: 123). His next film, *The Death of a Black President* (1983), was a representation of the historical events, which led to the assassination of General Ramat Murtala Mohammed, head of the Federal Military Government of Nigeria between July 1975 and February 1976. Murtala Mohammed is a highly venerated civil war hero, and his brief rule is often generally regarded by most Nigerians as a golden but brief episode in Nigerian history. He is considered one of the few truly trans-ethnic heroes in the country. Some of Ugbomah's other films include *Oil*

Doom (1980*)*, *The Boy is Good* (1982*)*, *Vengeance of the Cult* (1982*)*, and *Bulos 80* (1982).

Other Nigerian film directors worth mentioning include Jab Adu, director of *Bisi Daughter of the River* (1977), which launched the acting career of Patricia Ebigwei, now known internationally as Patti Boulay; then Wole Soyinka, director of *Blues for a Prodigal* (1984), a political satire on the corruption and administrative ineptitude of the era of President Shehu Shagari.

Presently, there are two types of cinematic practices existing side by side in Nigeria. The first practice to emerge is a product of western-trained directors and can be categorized as an elitist cinema due to its use of English as medium of expression, and its choice of urban milieux for setting. While films which belong to this elitist practice gain international recognition through presentation at international film festivals because of the connections of their western trained directors, the films are largely commercial failures in Nigeria. The second, popular cinematic practice referred to as Folklore Cinema, was actually launched by Ola Balogun, a product of IDHEC, Paris, when he directed *Ajani-Ogun*, a film in the Yoruba language adapted from a popular Yoruba Traveling Theatre play, in his search for a more popular form of cinema. It must be emphasized that it is not merely the use of a Nigerian language as a medium of cinematic expression that guaranteed the largely Yoruba dominated Folklore Cinema its popularity. Rather, this guarantee derives from an already well-established popular professional Yoruba Traveling Theater tradition that had its own star-system with well-managed commercially successful theater companies. A detailed historical account of Yoruba Traveling Theater and its companies has been undertaken by Biodun Jeyifo in his book, *The Truthful Lie*. This professional theater tradition was later transferred to the film industry.

Most of the films categorized under the practice of Folklore Cinema are actually stage-tested commercial successes. These stage successes, together with their immensely popular stars, ensure their popularity and commercial success in the cinema as well. Though, the base of Folklore Cinema was predominantly in the Yoruba speaking states of Nigeria, the films also enjoyed wide audience across the country. Folklore Cinema, as the name denotes, inherits its narrative form and themes from folk tradition, myth, legends, oral narratives of deified heroes/heroines, moral fables and traditional religious practices and rites. Therefore, the commercial success of Folklore Cinema derives from its use of Yoruba mytho-poetics in the form of traditional drama and cultic rites, festival rites and masquerade displays, rites of birth, adolescence, adulthood, old age and passage; music, song and dance, magical and supernatural agencies as subject matter or materials of filmic narration. Its use of narrative techniques of integrated performances embracing music, song and dance, fulfils Africa's concept of an integrated performance, rooted in religious beliefs and cultural practices. An African concept of a total narrative performance requires the incorporation of elements of narrative performances such as music, song and dance, and the inducement of audience participation by a narrative agent. The use of music, song and dance is to punctuate the performance, reinforce the mood of the narrative, and enhance audience participation. If the music is sad it makes characters within the narrative sad. If it is joyful, it induces spontaneous participation in the form of singing and dancing within the narrative. In the case of an oral narrative or dramatic performance, it induces spontaneous participation from the diegetic audience and characters and the witnessing spectator. For this reason, music that grows naturally from within the narrative is preferred to extradiegetic atmospheric music. Therefore, narration in Folklore Cinema is as complex as it is in African oral narratives, full of parallel tales and digressions in the form of delegated subjective narration, flashbacks, dreamstates, trances and possessions, ghosts and lots of photographically simulated manifestations of gods and other malevolent and benevolent spirits. It is these narrative incorporations that ensured the popularity and commercial success of Folklore Cinema and made it the most prolific and commercially self-sustaining and viable cinematic practice in Africa. Most of its productions have now been studied in detail by Onokoome Okome in his 1990 doctoral thesis presented to the University of Ibadan.

The Nigerian film industry is currently undergoing a lot of restructuring. Regular film production fizzled out in the late 1980s as a result of economic recession in the country. The introduction of IMF-inspired fiscal policies led to the devaluation of the national currency, the Naira, in a program tagged "Structural Adjustment Program" (SAP). The devaluation of the Naira made film production an extremely expensive venture to sustain. Filmmakers could not mobilize the necessary foreign currency needed to procure production and post-production equipment from Europe or North America. As a result, many abandoned the industry. For those who survived, necessity became the mother of invention, and they resorted to producing films by the use of video cameras. This innovation attained a professional status in the early 1990s and led to the birth of the video film industry in Nigeria. The industry is already attracting a lot of critical attention since the publication of the Jonathan Haynes' edited book, *Nigerian Video Films.*

Though the bulk of Anglophone African films are produced by Nigeria and Ghana, the East African nations of Kenya and Tanzania started to lay the foundation of their film industries by establishing national film corporations and film training centers. In Kenya, for instance, two government agencies, the Kenya Film Corporation (KFC) and the Kenya Institute of Mass Communication (KIMC), established with the help of the Federal Republic of Germany, has helped to establish the rudimentary production infrastructures, and train the personnel for a film industry. The KFC, like other corporations of its kind in Anglophone Africa, was an outgrowth of the old CFU. It operated MFUs for rural film shows like its counterparts in West Africa. The KIMC also had its own mini television studios and 16 mm. production facilities for the training of television personnel and filmmakers. The KIMC has also produced tourist-attraction documentaries such as *Waters of Mombasa, Passport to Adventure,* and *Immashoi of Masai,* all directed by Kenya's best-known director, Sao Gamba. Gamba also directed Kenya's first full-length feature film, *Kolormask,* a film about a Kenyan student who returns home with a white wife and finds his marriage threatened by cultural differences. *Kolormask* was entered for competition at the 1987 FESPACO and was criticized for being too exotic in its emphasis on documenting African culture. Kenya's first female director, Ann Mungai, trained at KIMC, has also directed a dramatized documentary, *Wekesa at Crossroad* and a full-length feature, *Saikati* (1992). Kenya also has a fledging Indian culture based cinema. Films by directors of Kenya Indian origin include *Mlevi* (1968) and *Mzembo* (1969) by Ramesh Shah, and *Rise and Fall of Amin Dada* (1980) by Sharad Patel (Diawara: 117; Bachy, 1987: 58).

Tanzania has an Audio Visual Institute donated to the country by the government of Denmark in 1974. The Institute has 16 mm. production facilities for the training of filmmakers and technicians. It has also produced instructional and publicity documentaries. In 1985, a Tanzanian co-production, *Arusi ya Mariama* (1983), directed by Nanga Yoma Ngoge and Ron Mulvihill (US), was awarded the prize for Best Short Film at the Pan-African Film Festival (FESPACO), Ouagadougou, Burkina Faso. The film deals with the conflict between tradition and modern forms of medical treatment. Zimbabwe has also established a Film Training Center with production facilities for training filmmakers and technicians with the assistance of the Federal Republic of Germany. So far, filmmakers trained at the Centre have restricted their productions mostly to newsreels, documentaries and short films. In the Sudan, film production started in the 1950s, when two black Sudanese students, Gadalla Gubara and Kamal Ibrahim, sent to study cinema in London, returned and helped to establish the Sudanese Film Unit in 1952. The Unit has produced mostly documentaries and educational films. Gubara, who received further training in California, has, since his return, directed a full-length feature film, *Tagoog* (1982), a love story set in the hills near the Red Sea. According to Bachy, the film was very well received. Another Sudanese who has directed a feature film is Anwar Hashim, and his film, *Oyon* (1984), set in Cairo, is a love story based on Sudanese student life in the city (Bachy: 57; Diawara: 116). Regarding film sponsorship and production policies in Anglophone Africa, most governments seem content to provide only the production infrastructures needed for the development of a film industry. Most are not interested in giving financial aid to filmmakers. The only form of aid available is allowing filmmakers free access to production facilities. They are also not interested in getting involved in commercial feature film production. Commercial cinema is considered to be an avenue for private investment. The only form of film production sanctioned by most Anglophone African governments is documentary or instructional film. In Francophone African countries, as we shall soon find out, most governments have set up film production agencies through which they provide funds for their filmmakers.

Film Production Structures and Sponsorship Policies in Francophone Africa

Post-Colonial Film Production in Francophone Africa

Film production in Francophone African countries is a post-independence phenomenon. Unlike the British and the Belgians, who had colonial film policies and established production facilities, and even made efforts to train indigenous filmmakers and technicians, the French had no similar policies for their colonies. Nor did they establish production facilities or trained indigenous personnel. The only intervention France made in the colonial era was the promulgation of a decree called "Le Decret Laval." The Laval decree was initiated by the French Minister of the Colonies, Pierre Laval, to control the content of films shot in Africa, and minimize the involvement of Africans in filmmaking. Diawara has observed that, though the decree was rarely applied, it was a panic measure taken by the French colonial government, with the advent of sound film in 1928 to contain the revolutionary impact, which the medium might have in the hands of African nationalists. The decree was directed at limiting the entrance of Africans into filmmaking, and restricting the filmmaking activities of French left-wing African sympathizers. Indeed, the first film censored under the decree was *Afrique 50* (1950), a documentary by the Frenchman, Robert Vautier. The film, which was clandestinely shot in the Côte d'Ivoire, is about the French repression of an African liberation movement, *Rassemblement Democratique Africain*. The second film censored under the decree was *Les Statues Meurent Aussi* (1955), a documentary by Chris Marker and Alain Resnais, both key players of the French New Wave. The film was produced by the famous African Publication House, *Présence Africaine*, and it examined the case of African statues taken out of their context and put in European museums. The violent montage technique used by the filmmakers to denounce the brutality of French colonialism has been praised by critics (Diawara, 1992: 22-23; Andrade-Watkin, 1992).

Faced with the Laval decree barring Africans from filmmaking activities on the continent, Paulin S. Vieyra, the first African graduate of *L'Institut des Hautes Etudes Cinématographiques* (IDHEC),

Paris, and his friends in *Le Groupe Africain du Cinéma*, had to resign themselves to making films about Africa and Africans in France. The first film by the group, *Afrique sur Scène* (1955), a film about Africans in France, was shot in Paris. This documentary film, directed by Vieyra, is now cited in African film history as the first film directed by a black African. Diawara has summed up the impact of the Laval decree on post-colonial French speaking African countries thus

> the Laval decree is an illustration of the French colonial system, which had no economic, political, or cultural policy encompassing the majority of its subjects and which was limited to assimilating few Africans such as Vieyra and *Le Groupe Africain du Cinéma* at the top. Thus in regard to the development of film in the colonies, where one may say that the British and the Belgian colonial film units failed because of racism and paternalism vis-a-vis the Africans, one can say that the French were opposed to an African cinema. (Diawara,1992: 23)

French attitude to the development of African cinema did change during the post-colonial era. France, alongside West Germany and the United States, donated film production equipment to the newly independent countries. Guinea-Conakry which rebuffed France's offer of a union with its African colonies and gained her independence in 1958, two years before the rest of Francophone African countries, got 16mm and 35mm production facilities as a gift from West Germany. Since Francophone African countries did not inherit any production facilities from France, most of them were faced, in the early sixties, with the difficulties of publicizing their governments' policies and programs to their illiterate population. As a result of mass illiteracy in the newly independent nations, radio and film offered the best possible means of disseminating government policies. Though most of the countries established radio stations, the film with its photographic quality was the preferred medium since it offered the people an opportunity actually to see government development projects and their implementations. However, most Francophone countries lacked film production structures, and the means to acquire them. They also lacked film technicians and, in most cases, directors. Under these circumstances, they welcomed any assistance that would enable them to acquire film production facilities and know-how. France, which understood the dire needs of her former colonies, stepped in to provide some of their immediate needs.

In 1961, the French government asked the four largest producers of newsreel in France, *Les Actualités Françaises*, *Eclair-Journal*, *Gaumont Actualités*, and *Pathé-Magazines*, to subsidize a fifth one, the *Consortium Audio-visuel International* (GAI), which would sign a contract with the former colonies to produce their newsreels, educational films, and documentaries. The CAI was, then, set up in Paris with post-production facilities, while the erstwhile colonies were provided with partial production equipment and technicians to man them. In this manner, the newsreels were shot in the erstwhile colonies, developed and edited with sound commentaries in Paris, and then, sent back to Africa for exhibition. The filmmakers and technicians were usually employees of *Les Actualités Françaises* and other organizations, which subsidized the CAI productions. This arrangement lasted from 1961 to 1977.

One of the key players in the development of film production in Francophone African countries, Jean-René Debrix, has explained the role played by France in assisting her erstwhile colonies publicize their national development efforts through the cinema as follows:

> keen to encourage the development of cinema in Africa, as long ago as 1961 the Ministry of Co-operation made a decision to intervene in the field of newsreels. The prime function of the cinema was seen as providing news coverage and acting as a vehicle for information, and it was felt that the first service to be rendered to the young independent African states should be to help raise the peoples' consciousness of their own national identity and unity: to enable them to see their own way of life and the rest of the world. (Debrix, 1982: 44)

By 1964, all the Francophone African countries had set up film production sections attached to their Ministries of Information as a result of their agreement with CAI. Some of the countries such as Niger, Côte d'Ivoire and Mali, invited internationally renowned film directors from Canada, France and Holland to make documentaries and educational films for them. Jean Rouch and Claude Jutra were invited on several occasions to make films for Mali and Côte d'Ivoire. Jutra made *Le Niger, Jeune République* (1960), a co-production by Niger and the *Office National Canadien du Film*, to celebrate Niger's independence. Canadian masters of the documentary, such as Norman MacLaren, Michael Brault and Claude Jutra, assisted Niger's pioneer filmmakers such as Moustapha Alassane and Oumarou Ganda in their first film projects. Both Alassane and Ganda also learnt their basic filmmaking techniques under Jean Rouch. However, the production arrangements with CAI, the preference for foreign directors and the emphasis placed on newsreel, documentaries and educational film production, helped to stagnate the creativity and opportunities available for the few trained indigenous directors for many years.

In broad terms, film production policies in Francophone African countries, reflect the economic policies of the countries concerned. Though most of the countries practice laissez-faire or liberal economic systems, a few of them such as Guinea-Conakry, Burkina Faso and Mali have nationalized certain sectors of their economy, like the film production sector, in keeping with their preference for a centrally planned economy with prominent state involvement. These economic policies are reflected in the film production sector of their economies. The majority of the countries which view nationalization of any sector of the economy as a repression of free enterprise have, in keeping with their policies of non-intervention in what they perceived as a private sector activity, refused to nationalize the film production sector of their economies. For this reason, countries such as Senegal, Niger, Cameroon, and Côte d'Ivoire, paradoxically countries that have produced the bulk of internationally available Black African feature films, are yet to set up their own film production facilities. However, as a result of the pressures from indigenous filmmakers, two types of state-sponsored financial support have emerged in the so-called liberal countries. The first type of state-sponsorship practiced in Senegal, Cameroon and Niger was characterized by government facilitating filmmaking with subsidies of one form or another. The other type of state-sponsorship practiced in Côte d'Ivoire, Gabon, and the Congo involves occasional provision of funds through state-owned national television stations.

Countries such as Guinea-Conakry, Burkina Faso (Upper Volta), which had more central planned economies with a lot of government involvement in the industrial sector, have nationalized production, distribution and exhibition of films in the bid to create national cinemas. All three countries have also set up film laboratories and editing facilities in an attempt to be self-reliant in film production. One needs to emphasize that the existence of production facilities alone does not guarantee the countries that have them more film output per year than those countries that have none. Diawara, for instance, has cited the case of Guinea, which has film production facilities but has actually produced fewer films in comparison to Senegal and Côte d'Ivoire, which have none. The reason for such discrepancies seems to lie in the patterns of actual financial assistance rendered to filmmakers by the various countries concerned. The success of those countries without production facilities depended very much upon the financial and technical assistance that they received from the French Ministry of Cooperation (Andrade-Watkins, 1992: 29- 33; Diawara, 1992: 57).

After the creation of the CAI in 1961, the French Ministry of Coopération established a *Bureau du Cinéma* at the Coopération in 1963, with Jean-René Debrix, former general director of IDHEC, as director. Before Debrix joined the Coopération, the emphasis of French cultural aid to its erstwhile colonies was in the area of literature, theatre, music and dance. Franco-African cultural exchanges were managed in the Coopération by the *Association pour le Développement des Échanges Artistiques et Culturels* (ADEAC). When Debrix took charge of activities at the newly created *Bureau du Cinéma*, his first priority was to change the emphasis of ADEAC from literature, music and dance to film. He succeeded in convincing people at the Coopération that the best way to assist Africans to regain their cultural identity was through the cinema. The *Bureau du Cinéma* also complemented the activities of the CAI in Francophone African countries. While the CAI placed emphasis on production of newsreels and documentaries, the newly created *Bureau du Cinéma* aimed at assisting independent African filmmakers in their film projects. The Bureau provided the filmmakers with funds, film equipment/technicians, and had post-production facilities at the Coopération for their use. For instance, the editing room of the Coopération, 20 rue de La Boétie, had professional editors such as Bernard Lefevere, Daniele Tessier, Paul Sequin and Andrée Daventure who worked patiently with the filmmakers. In his assessment of the contribution of the *Bureau du Cinéma*, toward the development of African cinema, its director, Debrix has observed

I think any objective observer would have had to acknowledge what has been done with integrity and, on the whole, with little cause for reproach. Between 1963 and 1975 around *185 films* were made in French-speaking black Africa, comprising features and shorts. Some 125 of these 185 films were produced with the technical and financial assistance of the Ministry [of Co-operation]. (Debrix: 44)

According to Diawara, the Ministry of Cooperation, through the *Bureau du Cinéma*, contributed to the growth of African cinema in two ways: the Coopération could either act as the producer of a film and provide the African director with the financial and technical means, as well as technicians, or the Coopération could wait until an independent director made the film, and then pay the director for the cost of production in return for some of the distribution rights of the film. In the first case, in which the Coopération assumed the role of producer from the beginning of the project, the filmmaker was required to submit a script with a detailed explanation of the sequences, which were carefully examined by a committee. The committee's role was limited to determining whether the script was cinematographically feasible or not. On the level of content, the directors were free to choose any subject they wanted. The only script rejected by Debrix on the basis of the subject matter was Sembène's *La Noire de …* (1966). Some of the early films which the Coopération produced directly include *Point de Vue 1* (1965) by Urbain Dia-Moukori (Cameroon), *Concerto Pour un Exilé* (1967) by Désirée Ecaré (Côte d'Ivoire), *Cabascado* (1968) by Oumarou Ganda (Niger) and *Diankhabi* (1969) by Mahama Traoré (Senegal) (Diawara: 26).

In the second case, in which the Coopération bought the right of a film that was finished or almost finished, the filmmaker acted as his or her own producer and procured funds from varied sources. However, since there is often a lack of enthusiasm for film production funding because the cinema is not considered a priority, African filmmakers have often found it difficult to secure the necessary funding for their film projects. As a result, offers of payment of production costs or provision of funds for on-going projects by the Coopération were often gratefully accepted in return for the Coopération's rights of distribution. Some of the first films to benefit from the Coopération's aid in this way include Sembène's *Borom Sârret* (1963*), Niaye* (1964*), La Noire de* (1966)

(Senegal) Moustapha Alassane's *Aoure* (1962), *La Bague du Roi Koda* (1964), *Le Retour de l'Aventurier* (1966) (Niger) and Timité Bassori's *Sur la Dune de la Solitude* (1964) and *La Femme au Couteau* (1968).

According to Diawara, the aid provided by the Coopération gave many Francophone African directors the opportunity to realize their dreams as filmmakers. Within the first five years of the creation of the *Bureau du Cinéma*, it contributed to the production of thirty-nine films, most of which were shorts. By 1985, 185 shorts and features were made in Francophone African countries, four-fifths of which were produced with the financial and technical assistance of the Coopération. Most of the renowned and internationally acknowledged Francophone African directors such as Ousmane Sembène, Med Hondo, Moustapha Alassane, Souleymane Cissé, and Cheik Ouman Sissoko made their directorial debut under the tutelage of Debrix at the *Bureau du Cinéma*, even though directors such as Sembène have now stopped asking the Coopération's help, and have even accused its members of paternalism and imperialism.

In 1979, France temporarily stopped producing African films because most of them were becoming very critical of Francophone African governments. Also, African leaders who were worried about the influence of African films on their population put a lot of pressure on the Giscard government to suspend aid to African filmmakers. Since France has very strong links with those of her erstwhile colonies in Africa, the Giscard government felt that films that were critical of African governments were destroying the friendly relations France had with African leaders. One of the films affected by the suspension of aid was Souleymane Cissé's prize-winning film, *Finye* (1982). The Coopération had originally agreed to bear the post-production cost of *Finye* in return for the rights to distribute it on the non-commercial circuit. If all had gone according to plan, *Finye* would have been completed in 1980. But the suspension of aid made it impossible for Cissé to complete production. The Coopération's financial and technical assistance policy, as it affected the production of *Finye*, reflected the ambivalence that underlies French production of African films. French post-colonial film policy toward Africa as reflected in the activities of the Coopération is tied to the fortunes of the political party in power in metropolitan France. The case of *Finye* illustrates this point. *Finye* is a political film that depicts the corruption and inefficiency of military regimes in Africa. The film chronicles the clash between such regimes and students' movements, as well as the friction between tradition and modernity. Its theme, as earlier noted, was considered to be critical of post-colonial African leaders, most of whom were military dictators. Since the Coopération could not convince radical filmmakers like Sembène or Cissé to make films which were less critical of post-colonial states, it decided to suspend aid to the whole of Francophone African film production.

When the socialist government of Françoise Mitterand assumed power in 1980, it decided to resume aid to the "progressive" African directors. One of the very first films to benefit from this resumption of aid was Cissé's *Finye*. The socialist government also ordered a reappraisal of the whole structure of the Coopération's aid to African cinema. The new French policy initiated by Mitterrand's technical adviser at the Coopération de-emphasized the old regime's patronage of a few filmmakers in favor of financial and technical aid channeled through the inter-African Francophone bodies such as *Organization Commune Africaine et Mauritienne* (OCAM). As a result of this new attitude, more funds and technical equipment were made available to the OCAM; also sponsored was the Film School, the *Institut Africain d'Education Cinématographique* (INAFEC), in Ouagadougou, Burkina Faso. The Coopération additionally decided to support such branches of OCAM as *Consortium Inter-Africain de Distribution Cinématographique* (CID) and *Consortium Inter-Africain de Production du Film* (CIPROFILM) (Diawara, 1992: 29).

The reforms were equally extended to the distribution of Francophone African films. The administrators at the Coopération decided to go beyond the old regime's policy of confining African films to academic circles, *cinémathèques*, and festivals, and to exhibit them in commercial French movie theatres, and air them on French television. The first film to enjoy the benefits of the reformation of the Coopération's policy was *Finye*. Cissé was reportedly given ten million francs (about twenty thousand US dollars) to advertise it. As a result of this publicity, the film was selected to compete at the 1982 Cannes Film Festival. In 1983 the film was shown commercially for six weeks in Paris. Over 400,000 viewers reportedly saw *Finye* (Pfaff, 1988: 54; Diawara, 1992: 29).

The film, then, won the Grand Prizes at both the Carthage and Ouagadougou Film Festivals.

French aid to African cinema has come under attack both in France and Africa, and also from concerned historians of African cinema. In France, the attack can be categorized into two forms: those launched by bureaucrats of the in-coming socialist administration of Mitterrand and those launched by ordinary French citizens. The bureaucrats of the socialist government criticized the out-going government of Giscard for giving direct aid to independent African filmmakers and thereby provoking a political crisis between France and some African countries. They also argued that French aid from the Coopération under the Giscard government did not promote the foundation of an African film industry. French aid, they insisted, should have been directed through OCAM sponsored organizations, and independent directors should, then, have been recommended for French aid either by their government, or by OCAM. The new bureaucrats further contended that the Coopération under Giscard was less respectful of the independence of African countries between 1963 and 1979.

French aid to independent African directors was also criticized by ordinary French citizens who felt that the exclusive focus on the aid to Francophone African countries was too narrow and unfair to other deserving artists around the world. They maintained that it was time for the Coopération to think globally in terms of aiding Third World countries in general rather than placing emphasis only on erstwhile colonies (Andrade-Watkins, 1992: 34-40; Diawara, 1992: 30).

Victor Bachy has also opined that French aid to independent African directors was being used by France as a neo-colonial tool for perpetuating the dependency of African countries on France. He further contested that those countries like Guinea-Conakry, which charted independent industrial policies were deliberately excluded from French aid, thereby making it possible for countries like Senegal and Côte d'Ivoire which had no production facilities but enjoyed French aid, to produce more films than the former (Bachy, 1987: 17). Ferid Boughedir also argued that French aid to independent African filmmakers was an indirect way of protecting the monopoly of French distributors like *Compagnie Africaine Cinématographique Industrielle Commerciale* (COMACICO) and *Société d'Explotation Cinématographique Africaine* (SECMA). These two distributing companies owned sixty to eighty per cent of the cinema chains of the Francophone African countries. Boughedir further insisted that by aiding African directors, France kept them from protesting the takeover of their domestic markets by foreign distributors. The Coopération's aid made it possible for the directors to recoup their production costs thereby protecting them from worries associated with recovery of production cost (Boughedir, 1982a: 36).

Francophone African filmmakers have themselves felt sure that French aid to African cinema was tied to paternalism and the deliberate promotion of negative African film aesthetics. For instance, they accused Debrix of imposing his own aesthetic view of Africa as a way of judging African films. African directors cited his open admiration for Daniel Kamwa's *Pouse Pouse* (1975), as an instance of what they considered Debrix's paternalistic and ethnocentric patronage of African cinema. *Pouse Pouse*, a comedy about the payment of dowry in Cameroonian society, is considered by many African directors as naive and iconoclastic towards African tradition, and less critical of French cultural imperialism in Cameroon. Moreover, the film is loosely edited, which makes it inartistically repetitious. That Debrix preferred such a film, and deliberately promoted it over films of Sembène, Cissé, and Hondo, peeved leading African directors who accused Debrix of despising African films, and of being opposed to the ideological and artistic maturity displayed in them. Sembène, recollecting the experiences he had with the French *Centre National du Cinéma* (CNC) during the production of his film *Le Mandat* (1968), went beyond criticizing Debrix as paternalist and ethnocentrist, to attacking French aid to African cinema. Before Sembène's experience with the CNC, the CNC's aid was restricted to French directors of the New Wave, such as Jean-Luc Goddard, François Truffaut, and Chris Maker. However, André Malraux, the French Minister of Culture, in 1968, granted special permission to Sembène to compete for the CNC's aid. Having won the aid, Sembène was required to take a French producer, Robert Nesle, who controlled the budget. According to Diawara, Sembène's experience with his producer was such that he decided, following the completion of *Le Mandat*, not to accept any aid from France in the future, and to produce his films in Africa with African financial support (Diawara: 32). The first conflict

Sembène had with Nesle was over choice of color for the film. Sembène wanted to shoot it in black and white because he was worried about the sensational effect a color film could bring to his story. He was also unsure about the way people would look in a color film under African skies. The next conflict he had with Nesle originated from refusal to include sexual and erotic scenes in the film. Sembène took Nesle to court to settle the matter. In view of this experience,

Sembène has observed that

> co-production with the West is often tainted with paternalism, and it is an economic dependency, which, as such, gives the West the right to view Africa in a way that I cannot bear. Sometimes, one is also coerced into consenting to commercial concessions. In a word, Europeans often have a conception of Africa that is not ours. (Cited in Diawara, 1992: 32)

Sembène also decided to stop co-production with the Coopération because, being a non-profit organization, it attracts people of various ideological inclinations, who want to use African films to illustrate their opinions of the continent. Thus the same film is often used to illustrate notions of African tradition and modernity, patriarchy and feminism, revolt and feudalism. Sembène felt that the unrestricted distribution rights which the Coopération had over his earlier films was both exploitative and open to manipulation of his views.

Souleymane Cissé, on his part, argues that the Coopération's pattern of distribution outlets — schools, cinémathèques, festivals, and cultural centers — reduces African films to sociological or anthropological documents; or what he generally refers to as the confinement of African films to "cultural ghettos." He would prefer a situation in which the Coopération reduces its rights by distributing the films only in French embassies and cultural centers in Africa, while pushing for commercial distribution in Europe (Diawara: 33).

The dependence of Francophone African cinema upon France has generated a major trend in the sponsorship pattern of French aid, worth noting. The trend manifests in the fact that the fortune of Francophone African cinema is tied to the cultural (cinematic) policy of the political party in power in metropolitan France, and the nature of sponsorship it preferred to operate through the Ministry of Coopération's *Bureau du Cinéma*. Within Africa itself, two main trends could be discerned in the current development of Francophone African cinema. First, a few countries like Guinea-Conakry, Mali and Burkina Faso (Upper Volta), which had established production facilities, did not seem to have as yet put in place the required financial support for aspiring and practicing filmmakers. The reason for this could be because most African governments did not yet consider the film industry as a priority sector of the national economy. Second, there was the trend in countries like Senegal, Côte d'Ivoire, Cameroon, and Niger, which did not have production facilities but have put in place the necessary financial arrangements that ensured that their filmmakers had access to state sponsorship of their projects. The remaining part of this section concentrates on a few chosen national cinemas such as of those of Senegal, Cameroon, Côte d'Ivoire, Burkina Faso and Guinea-Conakry, to illustrate the two trends in the development of cinema in Francophone African countries.

Senegal was the first Francophone country to sign a production agreement with the *Consortium Audio-visuel International* (CAI) in 1961, which led to the creation of *Les Actualités Sénégalaises* as an affiliate body of the CAI. The agreement required CAI to provide Senegal with a cameraman/reporter to cover the events in the country. The filmed events were sent to Paris, the headquarters of the CAI, to be developed and edited, along with other African and world events covered by the CAI. The editing and added commentaries were carried out according to the specification of the Ministry of Information of Senegal. The same arrangement operated in Côte d'Ivoire, Dahomey (now Republic of Benin), Togo, Madagascar and Burkina Faso. The arrangement very much resembled the British colonial government's raw film stock program which were shot by its bureaucrats in the colonies, and then sent to London for processing and post-production finishing touches. The only difference was that the French program was a post-colonial arrangement and the people involved were the elites of newly independent African countries.

Initially, the CAI made two newsreels a month for *Les Actualités Sénégalaises*. This was increased to a newsreel per week in April 1962, because of the growing demand for news. Soon, even the one newsreel per week proved insufficient, because it could not cover all the activities that were considered newsworthy by the different ministries. There was also the growing need for educational films and documentaries for which the newsreels could not substitute. As a result, *Les Actualités Sénégalaises* made plans to create a *Service de Cinéma* that would be involved in the production of documentaries and educational films. At this period too, the first set of African graduates from the French Film School, the *Institut des Hautes Études Cinématographique* (IDHEC), Paris, Paulin S. Vieyra and Blaise Senghor, were anxious to make films in their country, now that they had gained independence. Under the direction of Vieyra, several short films were financed by the *Service de Cinéma*. They included films on special topics, ordered by the various arms of government. Films directed by Vieyra, under this arrangement, included *Une Nation est Née* (1961), on the anniversary of Senegal's independence, *Voyage Présidentiel en URSS* (1962), a newsreel coverage of presidential visits to Senegal, *and* Lamb (1963), a documentary on wrestling, a popular sport in Senegal. Blaise Senghor also directed a short film, *Grand Magal à Touba* (1962), a documentary on Islam in Senegal. Until the late 1960s, when Ousmane Sembène appeared on the scene, Senegal did not give its nationals the chance to direct feature films or major documentaries. For instance, in 1960, *Les Actualités Sénégalaises* hired Ives Ciampi, a Frenchman, to direct *Liberté 1*(1960), a Franco-Senegalese feature production, based on the conflict between tradition and modernity. The film was a major failure. Another Frenchman, Jean Claude Bonnardot, was also commissioned to direct a major documentary, *Sénégal, Ma Pirogue* (1962) (Diawara: 59).

To understand why Frenchmen were being commissioned to direct features and major documentaries while there were trained Senegalese directors like Paulin S. Vieyra and Blaise Senghor, one must take into cognizance the colonial mentality of the first generation of African leaders, most of whom are still in government or positions of authority in the continent, and who were products of the colonial school system that taught them that Africans were inferior beings. For this generation of leaders, among whom towered the philosopher-statesman and retired first president of Senegal, Leopold Sedar Senghor, expertise was not something acquired through training, but rather the exclusive natural possession of the white ex-colonial master. In addition, one must also recollect the Laval decree, promulgated during the colonial era in 1934, and the colonial mentality it imposed on the newly independent Senegal. In a sense, France considered

Francophone African countries as nominally independent countries where French authority still reigned supreme.

Besides, *Les Actualités Sénégalaises* was an affiliate of a French conglomerate, CAI. And just as *Les Actualités Sénégalaises* depended on the CAI for the production of its newsreels, and on French directors for the making of features, so too did the *Service de Cinéma* depend on French facilities for production and post-production activities. When the *Service de Cinéma* was conceived to remedy the urgent need for documentaries and educational films, the project did not include the procurement of production facilities, which would have, in the long run, saved Senegal a lot of money. As a result, the *Service de Cinéma* acted only as a bank through which individual ministries financed film projects meant to publicize the activities of their ministries. The *Service de Cinéma* continued to depend upon France for the provision of filming equipment and post-production activities. In its double role as a financier and an agent, it co-produced with the *Bureau de Cinéma* of the French Ministry of Coopération and CAI, the films of Senegalese directors, such as Sembène, Babakar Samb, Paulin S. Vieyra, and Mahama Traore. In essence, the emergence of Senegalese cinema, in the late sixties, owed more to the patronage of France than to the availability of production facilities in Senegal.

In the early seventies, the *Association des Cinéastes Sénégalais* began to rethink the role of the *Service de Cinéma*. This reassessment was the result of an on-going general reassessment of African culture and tradition, both inside and outside the continent, after majority of African countries began to gain independence from the early 1960s onwards. The general reassessment of African cinema was launched in the mid-sixties when radical, non-conformist filmmakers like Sembène and Med Hondo began, consistently, to attack the monopolistic practices of the *Compagnie Africaine Cinématographique et Commerciale* (COMACICO) and the *Société d'Exploitation Cinématographique Africaine* (SECMA) in the media.

African filmmakers also argued the case of African cinema in international forums such as the *Colloque de Gene* (1965), the Premier Festival *Mondial des Arts Nègres de Dakar* (1966) and the *Table-Ronde de Paris* (1967). All these activities built up to the conception, in Algiers (Algeria) 1969, of what was to become known as the *Fédération Panafricaine des Cinéastes* (FEPACI) or the

Pan-African Federation of Filmmakers, later inaugurated at the 1970 Carthage film festival in Tunisia.

When the *Association des Cinéastes Sénégalais* saw how North Africans had well-defined policies of production, distribution and exhibition, it began to put pressure on the government to improve the conditions of film production in Senegal. In the end, what they won amounted to only cosmetic changes. The government created a new body, the *Société Nationale de Cinéma* (SNC), within the Ministry of Culture, to oversee the sponsorship of Senegalese filmmakers. Filmmakers, once again, were asked to submit scripts, as was the tradition in the *Bureau de Cinéma* of the French Ministry of Coopération, on topics ranging from juvenile delinquency and urban problems to literacy campaigns. The best scripts were selected by a group of readers chosen by the president of SNC. In this manner, six feature films were produced and/or co-produced by the SNC in 1974. They included, *Xala* by Sembène, *Le Bracelet de Bronze* by Tidiane Aw, *Baks* by Momar Thiam, *Njangaan* by Mahama Traore, *L'option* by Thierno Sow, and *Boram Xam Xam* by Maurice Dore, a French psychiatrist based in Senegal. The SNC also worked with the *Association des Cinéastes Sénégalais* in the discovery and encouragement of young filmmakers. It was in this way that new and talented directors like Moussa Bathily, Ben Diogaye Beye and Cheikh N'Gaido Ba made their debut in filmmaking. Bathily, a former assistant director to Ousmane Sembène, has since become the master of the documentary form with such prize-winning films like *Tiyabu Biru* (*The Circumcision*) (1978), and *Le Certificat d'Indigence* (1981), a documentary on hospitals and corruption in the medical profession in Dakar. Cheikh N'Gaido Ba now leads the *Collectif l'Oeil Vert*, a radical non-conformist association of young filmmakers committed to the need for reformation within FEPACI organizational structures (Diawara, 1992: 60).

As earlier noted, apart from providing financial assistance to practicing and aspiring filmmakers, the SNC did not embark on a policy of procurement of production facilities. In essence, the old order remained in place — Senegalese films continued to be processed, edited and sound-synchronized in studios in Paris. However, after the brief success of 1974, the SNC began to be plagued with serious problems, most of which could be traced to the government's discomfort with the critical tone of most of the films produced by the agency, but also because most of its films were commercial failures. Of all the films it produced in 1974, for instance, only three, Xa*la*, *Le Bracelet de Bronze*, and *Njangaan*, were commercial success. Besides, the contents of *Xala*, an indictment of the impotence of Senegalese political leaders, and *Njangaan*, an indictment of Senegal's main religion, Islam, unsettled many in government and religious circles. Furthermore, apart from the fact that the SNC used government money to produce films which made political leaders uncomfortable, there also developed a conflict with another government agency, the *Société d'Importation de Distribution et d'Exploitation Cinématographique* (SIDEC).

While the SNC accused the SIDEC of not promoting and distributing its films, the SIDEC countered that the SNC was interfering with the distribution of films in the country. The conflict could easily have been avoided either by initially creating a single body to handle both services or by merging both agencies, when the problems cropped up, and putting it under the control of a single ministry. Instead, the government created a situation in which the SNC was under the control of the Ministry of Culture, and SIDEC, at the Ministry of Commerce, was charged with the importation and distribution of foreign films. In the end, to save itself the embarrassment of SNC sponsored films, the government dissolved SNC in 1976. After the dissolution of the SNC, recent government assistance to filmmakers was restricted to guaranteeing bank-loans for directors. In addition, *Actualités Sénégalaises* and *Service de Cinéma* also resumed the production of short films and documentaries. Presently, film production has dropped immensely in Senegal as a result of the drop in state film sponsorship. Senegalese directors, such as Safi Faye and Moussa Bathily, depend more and more on the French Ministry of Coopération, and Swedish and German television stations to produce their films.

One other country, which operates a sponsorship policy similar to that of Senegal, is Cameroon. Cameroon has set up a body for film production called *Fonds de Développement de l'Industrie Cinématographique* (FODIC). FODIC derives most of its funds from tax revenues from film import and exhibition, and uses such funds to finance Cameroonian directors. However, FODIC, like its Senegalese counterpart, the SNC, was not intended to be a film corporation with its own production facilities. Rather, it was a funding agency for Cameroonian cinema. Before Cameroon set up

FODIC, its pioneer filmmakers, such as Jean-Paul N'Gassa, an IDHEC graduate, and Cameroon's best known directors, Daniel Kamwa and Jean-Pierre Dikongue-Pipa, enjoyed the sponsorship scheme of the *Bureau de Cinéma* of the French Ministry of Coopération. Daniel Kamwa's *Pousse Pousse* (1975) was a favorite film of Debrix. According to Bachy, over seven hundred spectators have seen *Pousse Pousse* (Bachy, 1987: 31).

Cameroon's next best known director, Jean-Pierre Dikongue-Pipa, gained international acknowledgement with his first major feature film *Muna Moto* (1975), produced by the Coopération and CAI. This film has won several international awards, including, the First Prize at the *Festival International du Film de l'Ensemble Francophone* (FIFEF), held in Geneva in 1975, the Georges Sadoul's Prize in France, jointly awarded to Safi Faye's *Kaddu Beykat* (1975) and Sidney Sokhana's *Nationalité Immi*grée (1975), First Prize at the fifth Pan-African Film Festival in Ougadougou, Burkina Faso and Second Prize at the Carthage Film Festival. In its present state, Cameroonian cinema, like those of most Francophone African countries, has existed only by the grace of French sponsorship. Production equipment and post-production activities are still carried out in Paris (Pfaff, 1988: 70-76, 185-192).

The next set of Francophone African countries, which have no production facilities, but do have internationally acknowledge directors, are countries such as Côte d'Ivoire, Gabon and Niger. These countries also have sponsorship schemes similar to those of Senegal and Cameroon. The only difference is that most of them acquired television facilities immediately after their independence, and film sponsorship in these countries is tied to the national television stations. For instance, unlike most other Francophone African countries, which did not acquire television facilities until the mid-seventies, the Côte d'Ivoire and Gabon had television facilities as early as 1963. A year after the establishment of Ivoirien television, Timite Bassori, a graduate of IDHEC, directed *Sur la Dune de la Solitude (On the Dune of Solitude)* (1964), a recreation of the famous mermaid legends of West Africa. Most IDHEC-trained directors, like Henri Duparc and Desiré Ecaré, and Kramo-Lacine Fadika, trained at the Louis Lumière Film School, and have also worked for the Ivoirien television, or for the *Société Ivoirienne de Cinéma* (SIC), created in 1962. Before the creation of the SIC, Ivoirien documentaries and educational films were produced by the

CAI. On his return from Paris, Bassori was employed by the SIC, where he directed half-hour length documentaries such as *Les Forestiers (The Foresters)* (1963), *L'Abidjan-Niger* (1963) on the Abidjan-Niger railway and *Amédée Pierre* (1963). Bassori also collaborated with Claude Vermorel in the production of the film series for television, *Yao,* a pre-colonial adventure story of an African hero, Yao. He also worked with Christian Jaque during his direction of *Le Gentleman de Cocody* (1966). Bassori's only full-length feature to date is *La Femme au Couteau (The Woman with a Knife)* (1968). In the seventies, he made a series of short documentaries based mainly on social commentaries on the Ivoirien society. They include, *Abidjan, Perle des Lagunes (Abidjan, The Lagoon Pearl)* (1971), *Bondoukou, an 11 (Bondoukou, year 11)* (1971), *Ondienne, an 12 (Ondienne, year 12)* (1972), *Kossou 1* (1972), *Kossou 2* (1974), and *Les Compagnons d'Akati (The Akati Fellows)* (1974) (Diawara, 1992: 62-67; Pfaff, 1988: 34-41).

Like Bassori, Henri Duparc, after his studies at IDHEC, was employed by the SIC. His first major feature film, *Mouna ou le Rêve d'un Artiste (Mouna, Or An Artist's Dream)* (1969), a low-budget film shot in ten days, was produced by the SIC. While working for the SIC, he also directed, as was the case with Bassori, several documentaries aimed at highlighting the economic and tourist potentials of Côte d'Ivoire. They include *Recolte du Coton 1 (Growing Cotton)* (1968), *Recolte du Coton II (Growing Cotton, part II)* (1968), *Achetez Ivoirien (Buy Ivorian Products)* (1968), *Tam-tam Ivoire (Ivoirien Drum)* (1968), *Profil Ivoirien* (1969), *J'ai Dix Ans (I Am Ten Years Old)* 1970) and *Carnet de Voyage (A Traveller's Notes)* (1969-70). His first full-length features include *Abusuan* (1972), which depicts the problems of Africa's extended family system, and *L'Herbe Sauvage (Weeds)* (1977), which deals with the anxieties of a housewife over her husband's infidelity (Pfaff, 1988: 88-93).

Desiré Ecaré started his directing career in Paris shortly after graduation from IDHEC in 1966. His debut effort, *Concerto pour un Exile (Concerto for an Exile,* 1968), was essentially a student low-budget production that used mostly non-professional black students resident in Paris, as actors, to act out their experiences of life in exile. The film also starred fellow Ivoirien director, Henri Duparc, and Ecaré's Finnish wife, Marjietta, who was herself a graduate of IDHEC. The technical crew consisted of friends, and the *Bureau du Cinéma* of the French Ministry of Coopération provided additional aid for the project. The film won a number of international awards at the Hyeres (France), Oberhause (Germany), Carthage (Tunisia), Tashkent (USSR), and Cannes film festivals. It also enjoyed television broadcasts in Germany and the Scandinavian countries, and featured at the San Francisco Film Festival (Pfaff, 1988: 95-103).

Ecaré's next film, *A Nous Deux, France* (*For us both, France,* 1970), depicts the artificiality of the so-called Francophone African "évolués" staying in Paris. It was produced by *Les Films de la Lagune* and Argos Films. It was premiered in Abidjan on June 16, 1970, during the course of a gala evening sponsored by the *Société Ivoirienne de Cinema* (SIC). Ecaré returned to Côte d'Ivoire in 1972, and, because of the limited opportunities in the cinema in Abidjan, he was employed as counselor first, at the Ministry of Tourism, and, subsequently, at the Ministry of Culture, where he examined the impact of the tourist industry on Côte d'Ivoire's cultural heritage. His major feature since returning to Côte d'Ivoire, *Visages de Femme* (*Faces of Women*, 1985), depicts the changing conditions of women in modern Côte d'Ivoire. It was a major success and was selected as part of the films billed for the Critic's Week at the 1985 Cannes Film Festival, where it received the International Critic's Award, as well as the CITC Prize, awarded by the International Council of Television and Cinema (*Conseil International de la Television et du Cinéma*).

Currently, Ivoirien television plays a major role in the production of films by Ivoirien directors. In 1963, a year after the inauguration of *Société Ivoirienne de Cinema* (SIC), the Côte d'Ivoire installed television facilities which included 16mm film laboratory and studio. Most of Bassori's documentaries were produced and broadcast on Ivoirien television. In 1964, the Ivoirien television produced George Keita's film, *Karogo*, a two-hour feature based on the myth of Queen Pocou, a legendary heroine who sacrificed her two sons to appease the gods. In 1979, after SIC was abolished by the government for being commercially unviable, and for making little contribution to the training of filmmakers and technicians, a new agency, the *Centre de Production des Actualités Audio-visuelles et du Perfectionnement Permanent* (CPAAPP), was created to make film production a subsidiary of Ivoirien television. The CPAAPP is charged with the production of documentaries, serials and newsreels highlighting the activities of the various agencies of government that need films to propagate their policies and programs. The agency has facilities in 16mm, black and white production, and shooting equipment for 35mm.

Gnoan M'bala happens to be one of the Ivoirien filmmakers who have fully exploited the television facilities to produce his films. He studied film production in Paris and Sweden. Upon his return home in 1970, he chose to work for the television instead of the SIC, which had hitherto employed filmmakers like Bassori and Duparc. He proceeded to direct short fiction television films, which, according to Diawara, were well received, in the Côte d'Ivoire and by international film critics and historians. His narratives, which revolve mostly around comic and satiric situations, deal with cases of deception, mistaken identity and the general naiveté of people. They include *La Biche* (1971) in which a black woman invites herself to the home of a mixed couple where she passes for the cousin of the husband, who is black, and becomes his mistress without the wife, who is white, knowing it. In another film, *Amenie* (1972), a peasant who moves to Abidjan fools people by passing for a wealthy diplomat. *Amenie* is considered M'bala's best work to date. His other films include, *Vasily* (1974), *Le Chapeau* (1976) and *Ablakon* (1983) (Diawara, 1992: 65-66; Bachy, 1987: 17-48).

Thus far, the film sponsorship and production structures of the liberal Francophone countries have been tied very much to French aid. In most of the countries such as Senegal, Niger, Cameroon and Togo, where there are no production facilities, and the introduction of television broadcasting was a mid-seventies phenomenon, film production depended solely upon French aid in form of provision of funding, sponsorship, shooting equipment, technicians and post-production facilities. Countries, such as Senegal and Cameroon, later set up production agencies like SNC and SIDEC (Senegal) and FODIC (Cameroon), where activities were restricted to financial sponsorship, and they continued to depend upon France for shooting equipment and post-production facilities. Other countries such as Côte d'Ivoire and Niger shifted film production and sponsorship to their national television institutions. Nigérien television for instance, produced Moustapha Alassane's *Kankamba* (1982), Mahamane Babake's *Si les Cavaliers* (1982), Moustafa Diop's *Le Medicin de Gafire* (1983), and also co-produced Med Hondo's *Sarraounia* (1986). But, even in Côte d'Ivoire and Niger, post-production activities still have had to be carried out in France, which also provides most of the shooting equipment and film technicians.

In Burkina Faso, Mali and Guinea-Conakry, the situation is slightly different, probably because these countries, at one time or another, revolted against the French hegemony. Guinea broke ranks with the rest of the French colonies, became independent in 1958 and adopted a socialist political economy, to the consternation of France. Burkina Faso and Mali have also experimented with socialism. The change in name, from Upper Volta to Burkina Faso in 1984, during the brief popular revolutionary government of Captain Thomas Sankara, is often considered as part of its efforts to defy the French hegemony by looking beyond France, towards Eastern Europe for a socialist model of economic development. When Burkina Faso became independent in 1960, the new government planned to build its own production facilities for 16mm film and a television station. To this end, in 1961, the Ministry of Information built studios that were supposed to become montage and sound-synchronizing rooms. However, because the CAI was preparing in 1962 to sign contracts with most Francophone African countries in order to handle the production of their newsreels, Burkina Faso did not get the necessary co-operation from France, which considered the Burkinabe facilities a duplication of CAI's in Paris. According to Bachy, in 1963, France helped Burkina Faso to build a television station "which only works three hours a day, four days a week, airing programs provided by France. Only the news events are filmed in Upper Volta" (cited in Diawara, 1992: 73).

Post-independence Burkina Faso also lacked trained directors. Unlike in Senegal and Côte d'Ivoire, where indigenous directors, trained in the late fifties and early sixties, took charge of their national cinemas, in Burkina Faso, there were no trained staff for a national cinema. A French director, Serge Ricci, dominated the national production of newsreels, documentaries, and educational films, from 1960 to the early 1970s, and made several 16mm medium length documentaries for the government. They included films on independence movements, *Fiere Volta de nos Aieux* (1961), on economics, *Espoir d'un Nation* (1961), *Operation Arachide* (1962) and *Culture Atelée et Fertilisation* (1964), on health education, *Les Grands Marigots Magents les Yeux* (1964), *Comment Mourrir Mes Enfants*

(1966), and three films on geography. Burkina Faso's first indigenous filmmaker, Sekou Ouedraogo, trained as a cinematographer under the guidance of Ricci. He later made two documentary films on regional fairs, *Foires Regionales Voltaiques* in 1969 and 1970.

The most significant event in the history of Burkinabe cinema, and, to a large extent, that of most Francophone African countries, is the nationalization of film distribution and exhibition of the then Voltaique government in 1970 and the creation of the *Société Nationale d'Importation-Distribution* (SONAVOCI), to control film distribution and exhibition which had hitherto been monopolized by the French distribution chains of *Compagnie Africaine Cinématographique Commerciale* (COMACICO) and *Société d'Exploitation Cinématographique Africaine* (SECMA). This action was to have reverberating effects throughout Francophone African countries. That same year that the Voltaique government took action, 1970, Mali followed suit with the nationalization of its film distribution and exhibition through the creation of *l'Office Cinématographique National du Mali* (OCINAM). In 1974, Senegal and Benin established their own distribution companies, the *Société d'Importation de Distribution et d'Exploitation Cinématographique* (SIDEC) and the *Office Beninois de Cinéma* (OBECI) respectively. Madagascar followed in 1975 when it nationalized its film distribution and exhibition and created the *Office du Cinéma Malgache*. The response of COMACICO and SECMA to this spate of nationalization is examined shortly. A year after the creation of SONAVOCI, *Fonds de Développement du Cinéma Voltaique* was set up to promote national film production. Though SONAVOCI did not invest in production facilities, it financed the production of several shorts and full-length feature films. Besides financing the documentaries of Serge Ricci between 1971 and 1973, in 1972, *Fonds de Développement du Cinéma Voltaique* financed the first indigenous feature film, *Le sang des parias*, directed by Djim Mamadou Kola. The seventies also witnessed the emergence of Burkinabe directors such as Hilaire Tiendrebeogo, director of the health education documentary, *Histoire de la Tuberculose* (1973), and Augustin R.T. Taoko, Gaston Kolko and Idrissa Ouedraogo.

In 1976, the government of Upper Volta created the *Centre National du Cinéma* (CNC) and appointed Gaston Kaboré, Burkinabé best-known director, as head of the agency. The CNC has so far produced shorts such as Ouedraogo's *Yikyan* (1978), Sanou Kollo's *Beglro Naba* (1979) and *Dodos* (1980). As head of the CNC, Kaboré assumed the role of principal government filmmaker, a role which had hitherto been played since the 1960s by Serge Ricci. In this capacity, Kaboré directed a series of documentaries highlighting government programs and enlightenment campaigns. They include *Stockez et Conservez les Grains* (*Stock and Keep Grains*, 1978), *Regard sur le VIème FESPACO* (*A Look at the Sixth FESPACO*, 1979) and *Utilisation des Énergies en Mileu Rural* (*The Use of New Energies in Rural Environment*, 1980). Kaboré's first feature film, *Wend Kuuni, le Don de Dieu* (*Wend Kuuni, the Gift of God*, 1982), set in precolonial Africa, deals with issues such as marriage and the concept of family, sex and love. According to Diawara, what is interesting about this film is that

> the manner in which the definition of these issues (themes) changes in the evolution of the narrative deconstructs the stereotypical view of precolonial Africa as a stagnating place or primitive paradise. (Diawara: 75)

Wend Kuuni, released on September 1982 in Burkina Faso, has enjoyed both local and international acclaim. In Burkina Faso, alone a total of 200,000 people viewed it upon its release, and this is in a country which has only fourteen movie theatres and a population of less than seven million. The film was also shown simultaneously in three commercial movie theatres in Paris where it enjoyed widespread critical acclaim.

Though SONAVOCI, *Fonds du Développement du Cinéma Voltaique* and the *Centre National du Cinéma* (CNC) did not set up production facilities, a Burkinabe businessman, Martial Ouedraogo, in appreciation of his country's international reputation as the unofficial headquarters of Pan-African Cinema, invested more than $300,000 in film equipment, including 16mm and 35mm cameras, laboratories, editing tables, sound track facilities, and props. His production company, *Société Africaine de Cinéma* (CINAFRIC), is a profit venture set up to assist indigenous continental and foreign directors filming in the continent. The wide range investment, made by CINAFRIC in film equipment and studios, has earned it the title, "Hollywood on the Volta." Since starting business in 1981, CINAFRIC has produced two feature films, Sanon Kollo's *Paweogo* (1981) and *Les Courages des Autres* (1982) by Christian Richard, a French professor of film at the

Institut Africain d'Education Cinématographique. Curiously enough, the new film production company was denied patronage in its early days, as CNC financed films such as Gaston Kaboré's *Wend Kuuni* and Paul Zoumbara's *Les Jours de Tourments* (1983) were sent to Paris for post-production finishing touches when the same facilities were available in Ouagadougou. CINAFRIC has since signed on several African directors, including Ousmane Sembéne.

In sum, the production policy and financial sponsorship of the cinema in Burkina Faso was certainly geared toward the creation of a self-reliant cinema with its own production facilities. Shortly after independence, the country initiated plans to procure its own production facilities but the effort was frustrated by contractual obligations to the French production outfit, CAI. Despite this initial disappointment, Burkina Faso (Upper Volta) was the first Francophone African country, apart from Guinea-Conakry, which broke ranks earlier on with France by gaining independence in 1958, to confront the monopolistic hold of the French film distribution and exhibition chains, COMACICO and SECMA which control Francophone African film distribution and exhibition. The nationalization of the Burkinabe subsidiaries of these multinationals in 1970 signaled the beginning of confrontations between COMACICO, SECMA and those countries dedicated to the development of self-reliant national cinemas. Though Burkina Faso could not establish its own production facilities because it lacked the technological ability and manpower to do so independently of French support, the nationalization of film distribution and exhibition made it possible for the country to secure enough funds to finance indigenous film production even though post-production work still had to be carried out in France.

The situation in Guinea-Conakry was quite different and much more complex. In response to the on-going Algerian liberation war and the growing demand for independence in sub-Saharan French colonies, General De Gaulle held a referendum of French colonies in September 1958, in which they were offered an option to stay French or become independent but in a loose association or alliance with France. Guinea was the only country that rejected either possibility and Sekou Touré declared independence from France in October 1958. In response to Sekou Touré's action, De Gaulle pulled out French technicians and stopped all French aid to the country. To compound matters further, Touré decided to ally himself to the eastern bloc countries instead of the western democracies (Martin, 1982: 57). As a result of this total break in relations with France, the country started very early to develop its own national cinema. The newly independent Guinea nationalized film distribution and exhibition, and created a state agency, *Sily-Cinéma* — the same year it became independent — to control film production, distribution, and exhibition in the country. Fearing that other Francophone African countries would follow Guinea's example, COMACICO and SECMA placed an embargo on supply of American and western European films to Guinea, to serve as deterrence. As a temporary measure, the country turned to eastern European countries for supply of films. However, since most Guineans were used to Hollywood and western European films, Guinea had to make some concessions to COMACICO and SECMA. A compromise was worked out whereby the twenty-eight movie theatres in the country were divided equally between *Sily-Cinéma* and the French multinationals. The arrangement allowed COMACICO and SECMA to run fourteen movie theatres in exchange for access to their films. In 1970 when Upper Volta (Burkina Faso) decided to confront the monopolistic practices of SECMA and COMACICO, the settlement between both parties took the form of that entered into between Francophone African countries and *Société de Participation Cinématographique Africaine* (SOPACIA) owned by the French holding company, *Union Générale Cinématographique* (UGC), that bought the shares of COMACICO and SECMA in 1973 (Boughedir, 1982a: 34-41; Diawara, 1992: 68-69).

As a result of French boycott of the country, Guinea could not enter into agreement with CAI, as other Francophone African countries did shortly after their independence in 1960. Instead, with the help of Eastern Bloc countries like the former Soviet Union, Yugoslavia and Poland, facilities in 16mm black-and-white film production were acquired by Guinea. With these facilities in place, the country was able to produce one newsreel every week in the early 1960s while the other countries that signed contracts with CAI were being supplied a newsreel per month because of the time it took the headquarters of CAI in Paris to complete post-production work and dispatch films back to Africa. Since Guinea, at this time, lacked trained indigenous directors, most of the early propaganda films produced by *Sily-Cinéma* between 1960 and 1966 were directed by foreigners. However, by 1966 six directors trained in the Soviet Union and the United States returned home to take charge of affairs in *Sily-Cinéma*. Bob Sow was made head of film distribution and exhibition while Mahamed Lamine Akin headed the production section of *Sily-Cinéma*.

Between 1966 and 1970, the majority of the films produced by *Sily-Cinéma* were documentaries, educational and propaganda films. This initial orientation was probably a product of the state's conception of cinema as an instrument for the dissemination of government policies and developmental programs. The films were directed by indigenous directors such as Costa Diagne, Mahamed Lamine Akin, Gilbert Minot, Sékou Camara, Barry Sékou Omar and Moussa Kemoko Diakité. The films directed between 1966 and 1968 included Diagne's *Peau Noire* (1967), *Huit et Vingt* (1967) and *Hier, Aujourd'hui, Demain* (1968), in the latter of which Diagne masterfully uses flashes, back and forward, to allude to Guinea's past, present and future. The film won the Joris Ivens prize in 1968 at the Leipzig film festival. Other films of the period included Akin's *Le Sergeant Bakary Woulen* (1966), *Mary Narken* (1966) and *Dans la Vie des Peuples, il y a des instants* (1966), while Omar directed *Et Vint la Liberté* (1966) (Diawara, 1992: 71).

In the late sixties and early seventies, both Gilbert Minot and Moussa Kemoko Diakité dominated the documentary scene. Minot made *Le Festival Pan-Africain d'Algiers* (1968), on the Algerian film festival, and several other short documentaries in the early seventies on presidential visits made by William Tolbert of Liberia, General Yakubu Gowon of Nigeria and Amilcar Cabral of Guinea-Bissau to Guinea. Diakité made *Rizi-culture dans le Bogate* (1969), a documentary on agriculture, *L'Université Campagne* (1975), on education, and a documentary on the funeral ceremony of Kwame Nkrumah who died in exile in Guinea in 1972. *Sily-Cinéma* also produced a series of didactic short fictional films during this period. They included Moussa Camara's *Amie Perdu* (1968); *Un Amour Radical* (1972) and *Un Grand Père dans le Vent* (1973) co-directed by Moussa Camara and Alpha Adama. Since most of the films produced by *Sily-Cinéma* in the sixties and seventies were didactic and nationalistic, they were shown mostly in Guinean movie theatres and on its national television, which was established in 1977. In the early 1980s however, *Sily-Cinéma* made international news when it co-produced *Amok* (1982) with Morocco, and produced *Naitou* by Diakité. The film, *Amok*, is based on the 1973 Soweto massacre, and it was directed by the Moroccan, Ben Barka, and starred the famous South African singer, Miriam Makeba. Guinean technicians, using *Sily-Cinéma* equipment, filmed the work, and Dan Soko Camara, who was assistant director to Ben Barka during the shooting of *Amok*, later went to direct his own film, *Ouloukoro* (1983). The next film that brought *Sily-Cinéma* international attention was Diakité's *Naitou*. The film was a musical about a young girl, Naitou, whose mother is killed by a jealous rival wife. After killing Naitou's mother, the rival now Naitou's stepmother, mistreats her and prevents her from taking part in an initiation ceremony for girls of her age-grade. The stepmother is finally punished by an old lady who symbolizes justice. The film's originality lies in its being narrated through dance and music by the Ballet National de Guinée. It won the UNESCO prize at the Ouagadougou film festival in 1983 (Diawara, 1992: 72).

Despite attempts by Guinea to establish a national self-reliant cinema, the country's efforts met little success. First, the placing of emphasis upon documentary and educational films meant that Guinean movie theatres continued to be dominated by Hollywood, European and Hong Kong films. Furthermore, though the country had 16mm production facilities, the rushes of Guinean films still had to be sent abroad for post-production processing, because the lack of proper maintenance had resulted in the breakdown of most equipment. Curiously, too, the 35mm film laboratory, which West Germany started installing since 1966, is still uncompleted today. Therefore, like most other Francophone African countries, attempts by Guinea to develop a self-reliant national cinema, without the necessary industrial base to sustain such an industry, met with little success. Even attempts to nationalize the distribution and exhibition arm of the industry witnessed little success due to the blackmailing and arm-twisting tactics of the French multinational distribution and exhibition chain, SOPACIA which replaced COMACICO and SECMA. With its powerful connections within the French political structure, and strong international working agreements between SOPACIA's parent company, *Union Générale Cinématographique* (UGC) and the American Motion Picture Export Company of America (AMPECA), no Francophone African country stood the chance of successfully confronting SOPACIA or building a national cinema without the necessary industrial base (Boughedir, 1982a: 32-41).

The Effects of British and French Colonial Policies on Film Production in Anglophone and Francophone African Countries

Britain and France had divergent film policies as part of the cultural package of their overall colonial policies, both during and after the colonial era in their respective colonies in Africa. To a large extent, the film policies of each of the colonial powers, both during and after the colonial era, reflect the overall nature of the so-called policies of "association" and "assimilation", adopted by Britain and France, respectively, toward their colonies. From the appraisal given thus far, these policies account for much of the divergent film production organizations, policies and sponsorship currently noticeable in both Anglophone and Francophone African countries. Frank Ukadike has observed in respect of this development that

> different patterns of film production within Anglophone and Francophone regions derive from the contrasting ideological pursuits of the colonial French and British governments. For example, while the French pursued a so-called assimilation policy, British involvement with its colonies was pragmatic business. Similarly, observers point out that while the French "gave" feature films to its colonies, the British "gave" theirs documentary. France seemed to adopt a cultural policy that encouraged production in the Francophone region, whereas the Anglophone region (where film production did not pass the economic priority test) resolved to cling to the British tradition of documentary filmmaking. (Ukadike, 1991:75)

There are three interrelated aspects to the question of the impact of British and French colonial policies on current production policies and outputs in both Anglophone and Francophone African countries. These are the question of the policy of association versus assimilation; that of the often stated Anglophone African inheritance of documentary tradition versus Francophone African inheritance of feature film tradition; and the question of the post-colonial cultural policies of both colonial powers in Africa. In his assessments of these issues, Ukadike merely restates unqualified assertions which have been made earlier by film historians and critics such as Angela Martin (1982: 30) and Manthia Diawara (1986: 63), that the policies of association and assimilation and the legacies of documentary and feature film practices left by the erstwhile colonial powers explain the divergent nature of film practice in Anglophone and Francophone African countries. On the contrary, one can argue that this explanation is too simplistic an account of why film production progressed more steadily in Francophone than in Anglophone African countries.

The impact of the British colonial policy of association (indirect rule), and the French policy of assimilation, on African cinema can only become clear if the policies themselves are fully explained and the impact of their agencies on African cinema accounted for. In his article "Indirect Rule — French and British Style," Michael Crowder has fully explained the impact of both policies on African culture and traditional political institutions. For instance, he has observed about the policy of association that the British believed that it was their task to conserve what was good in indigenous institutions and assist Africans to develop along their lines. Thus the relation between the British political officer and traditional ruler was in general that of an adviser who only in extreme circumstances interfered with the traditional ruler and the native authority under him. However, where the traditional ruler governed small political units, and in particular, where his traditional executive authority was questionable, the political officer found himself interfering in native authority affairs more frequently. In principle, the borderline between "advisory" and "supervisory"in the activities of the political officer was not always clear. Crowder further argues that, though indirect rule depended primarily on a traditional ruler as executive, its aim was not to preserve the institutions of monarchies or chieftaincies, as such, but to encourage local self-government through indigenous political institutions, whether these were headed by the single authority of a king, by a council of elders or by an appointed chief (Crowder, 1978: 199). In his explanations of the differences in relation between British and French political officers and African traditional rulers, Crowder has observed that

> the British system depended on the advisory relationship
> between the political officer and the native authority, usually a
> chief, [king or emir], leading a local government unit that

corresponded to a pre-colonial political unit. The system placed the chief in an entirely subordinate role to the political officer. But it is important to stress that the chief, in relation to the French political officer, was a mere agent of the central colonial government with clearly defined duties and powers. He did not head a local government unit, nor did the area, which he administered on behalf of government necessarily, correspond to a pre-colonial political unit. (Crowder, 1978: 200)

In the interest of conformity, the French divided up both the Federations of French West Africa and French Equatorial Africa administratively into cantons, which frequently cut across pre-colonial boundaries. The *Chefs de Caton* did not remain traditional rulers of their old political units, but of the new cantons, though sometimes the two coincided. Most importantly, the *Chefs de Canton* were not necessarily those who would have been selected according to customary practice. More often than not, they were those who had shown loyalty to France, or had obtained proper French education. In his assessment of the role of traditional African rulers in French colonial administrative set-up in Africa, Jean Suret-Canale has observed that

a sense of ambiguity permeated their whole position. On the one hand, it was extolled as testimony of respect for "customs" and "African institutions"; on the other they were always being reminded that they existed only by the grace of the colonizer and were nothing but tools in his hand. A second contradiction concerned the chief's function: on the one hand, he was the representative, the executive, of administrative authority and, on the other, he was the representative of the African community, who recognized no other. He found himself between the hammer and the anvil. There was no statute or guarantee to protect him. He was simply mentioned in circulars which, in themselves, created no obligations until 1934-6. (Suret-Canale, 1964: 322)

The British, on their part, were scrupulous in their respect for customary methods of selection of traditional rulers. The difference between both countries' approach has much to do also with the difference in national character and political traditions. While Britain operated a parliamentary constitutional monarchy, France had been a republic most of the time since the 1789 revolution. As Crowder puts it, the administrator from republican France, particularly in the inter-war period, had little time for the notion of chiefs holding power other than that derived from the administration itself. This provides a marked contrast with the average British administrator, who believed sincerely that, for Africans, their own traditional methods of government were the most suitable, provided they were shorn of certain features that did not correspond to his sense of justice. Coming from a country which still maintained a monarchy, the British officer respected his chief as separate but equal, though certainly not somebody with whom he could establish personal relations. It was the educated African before whom he felt uneasy. Indeed many political officers openly express their contempt for the 'savvy boy' or 'trousered African.' (Crowder, 1978: 206)

The definition of the term "assimilation" is quite problematic. M. O. Lewis, for instance, has drawn attention to the many definitions of assimilation in use. They include (i) assimilation as the dominant colonial policy of France, i.e. its dominant and continuing characteristics; (ii) assimilation as the policy abandoned in favor of association; (iii) assimilation as opposed to autonomy, i.e. integration versus devolution; (iv) assimilation as a legalistic definition, i.e. representation in the mother of parliaments; (v) assimilation as civilization; (vi) assimilation as representing racial equality, as against British tendency to the color bar; (vii) assimilation as a highly centralized form of direct rule of colonies (cited in Crowder,1978: 204). It is difficult to choose any of these seven definitions of assimilation as the most satisfactory one; they all probably combine to give a wide-ranging picture of the term. Besides, it must be noted that the policy of assimilation was only fully experimented in Senegal, which was then politically assimilated to France through the representation of Senegal in the French *Chambre des Deputés* in Paris. As a result of this assimilation, a *Conseil Général* was created for Senegal, modeled on the *Conseil* Department of France. In addition, municipal councils were structured after the French model, and the policy included the personal assimilation of Senegalese in the communes by according them the status of French citizens, though they were allowed to retain their *statut personnel.* This explains why the erstwhile president of Senegal, Léopold Sédar Senghor, served as a French deputy in Paris. The policy of assimilation in Senegal also included the extension of French educational facilities as part of the French *mission civilisatrice*.

When the French found out that the wholesale application of the policy of assimilation would be too expensive to operate, they opted for the Lugardian policy *of politique d'association*. But even after France had adopted the policy of *politique d'association*, its overall outlook continued to be a much more moderated policy of assimilation, rather than a carbon copy of the British policy of association. First, the goal of creating French citizens out of Africans was not totally abandoned; rather, it was now approached more pragmatically than before. Second, there remained in place a high degree of administrative centralization which was not compatible with a true *politique d'association*. Third, the education curriculum continued to be modeled on the French system. Unlike the British who encourage the teaching of vernacular languages, especially in primary and infant classes, children in Francophone Africa were made to speak French right from the day they entered school. Fourth, due regard was not given to the individual character of a region; rather, the same administrative organization was imposed throughout French territories. As a result, French political officers were subjected to posting from one territory to another sometimes every other year. This gave them little opportunity to learn local languages or understand local customary practices. In contradistinction to the French practice, British political officers remained in the same territory for a long period of time and, in the case of Nigeria, in the same region; and promotion depended in part on the ability of the political officers to learn indigenous languages (Crowder, 1978: 205; Armes, 1987: 19-20).

The French of course encouraged the formation of a native elite, which was absorbed into territorial and federal administrative services, although this was not carried out on a very large scale. But the general French attitude toward educated Africans was that, once you have gone through French tertiary education system, you were considered cultured enough to be accepted as a French citizen. As Lucy Mair states,

> the assumption which governs the whole attitude of France towards native development is that the French civilization is necessarily the best and need only be presented to the intelligent African for him to adopt it. Once he has done so, no avenue is to be closed to him. If he proves himself capable of assimilating

French education, he may enter any profession, may arise to the dignity of Under-Secretary for the colonies, and will be received as an equal by French society. This attitude towards the educated natives arouses the bitter envy of his counterpart in neighboring British colonies. (Cited in Crowder, 1978: 205)

The British, on the other hand, in the twenties and thirties actively discouraged the formulation of a class of Europeanized Africans, particularly at the level of the central colonial administration. It is difficult to say which of the two political policies, the British policy of association and the French policy of assimilation, was better. Both had profound positive as well as negative impact on African culture and tradition; and ultimately, both forms of acculturation helped to fashion contemporary African personality.

For instance, while the French policy of assimilation was more accommodating towards African elites, it also promoted French culture at the expense of the African culture. As a result, most Francophone African intellectuals were greatly alienated from the African culture and tradition, since the education curriculum of Francophone African countries was structured, with little moderation, on the French model. Most Francophone African intellectuals experienced cultural re-awakening only after encountering racism in Europe between the 1920s and 1930s. The level of cultural alienation and re-awakening experienced by these intellectuals partly explains why it was Francophone African intellectuals that championed the Negritude Movement, and Anglophone African intellectuals have traditionally been the greatest critics of Negritude, because they were not as alienated as their Francophone African counterparts, from the African culture and tradition. As a result, Anglophone African intellectuals were often astonished as to why anyone needed to propagate his or her culture and racial attributes. Most of these Anglophone intellectuals were often so assured of their African background, coming as they did from countries where the British did everything to preserve the African culture and institutions, that they were often astonished when Francophone African intellectuals, in a moment of cultural awakening, began to valorize African culture and racial attributes (Soyinka, 1976: 126-139; Irele, 1981: 67-86; Appiah, 1992: 1-73). There is the need to take cognizance of the fact that France's *politique d'association* continued the cultural assimilation of African elites after the colonial era; and that French sponsorship of

Francophone African cinema is but just one aspect of France's overall neo-colonial policies towards its erstwhile colonies. In fact, it can be argued that France only recognizes its erstwhile colonies in Africa as nominally independent countries, and continues to treat them as *de facto* French provinces and this partly explains why French garrisons still abound in most Francophone African countries.

The British, on the other hand, were hostile to African elites during the colonial era, even though the same colonial power did set up the schools and universities that trained indigenous manpower, in anticipation of decolonization. While helping to build up an African elite through education, the British, paradoxically, erected structures that barred the same elites from enjoying the material benefits, and social status of the elite class. For example, through the color bar, African elites were not only barred from social clubs, they were also denied equal status with their white colleagues at work places. This partly explains why nationalist movements sprang up earlier in Anglophone African countries than in Francophone Africa, where the indigenous elites were incorporated partially into the French national and colonial elite class. It must be noted, that notwithstanding their negative attitude towards the indigenous elites, the British did everything to protect and preserve traditional African culture, institutions, ethics and value systems. British political officers were also made to learn the languages and customary values of the ethnic groups under their jurisdiction. Many of them undertook ethnographic studies, translated the Bible into local languages, and folktales from local languages into English. All these came well before linguistic studies became instituted as academic disciplines in the newly established universities in Anglophone Africa.

Although the phenomenal growth, both in quantity and quality, of Francophone African cinema is not comparable to that of its Anglophone African counterpart, one cannot convincingly argue that France's colonial policy of assimilation was responsible for the difference. While the policy of assimilation favored the creation of a Franco- African elite, it did not favor the development of a self-reliant Francophone African cinema, because France, during the colonial era, did not pursue any consistent policy that potentially favored such a development. French agencies established to promote the development of Francophone African cinema — the

Consortium Audio-visuel International (CAI) and the *Bureau de Cinéma* of the French Ministry of Coopération — were post-colonial creations. Even then, production facilities continued to revolve, like the French colonial policy of assimilation, around France. There was no attempt to decentralize the production facilities and activities of CAI which was charged with the production of newsreels and documentaries for the newly independent Francophone African countries.

The African subsidiaries of CAI engaged only in photography; film processing, editing and sound commentaries were carried out in Paris. Most of the film technicians were also Frenchmen. While most Anglophone African countries had film production facilities since the late forties, trained personnel to man them, and had acquired television broadcasting facilities in the 1960s, to complement the documentaries and instructional films exhibited through the Mobile Film Units (MFUs) in the rural areas, most Francophone African countries acquired television facilities only in the seventies; and without the added facilities of film production or the establishment of Mobile Film Units, the few movie theatres that were available, were restricted to the urban centers. This situation cannot be said to have helped to create an enduring film culture during the colonial era, as was the case in Anglophone Africa, where rural dwellers were enjoying film shows since the late forties. The current Francophone African film culture is, therefore, a post-colonial development, and it is mostly an urban phenomenon. It was unlike the case in Nigeria for instance, where smart businessmen, who were quick to note the effectiveness of the Mobile Film Units (MFUs), later started using MFUs to exhibit Hollywood westerns in order to promote the sale of consumer goods in the rural areas. This practice did not only lead to the proliferation of private businessmen operated MFUs, it also enabled rural dwellers to enjoy "free cinema" while being commercially induced to buy European manufactured goods.

With regard to current notable development of Francophone African cinema, one should recognize that the French did not really abandon the policy of assimilation even after they adopted the *politique d'association*, both during the latter part of, and after the colonial era. Over the years, the French have built a strong Franco-African alliance between French elite and their African counterparts. This alliance even developed into political cells and cliques. As earlier observed, the sponsorship of Francophone African cinema was but one facet of the grand neo-colonial political strategy that entrenched France as both the political/military protector of its erstwhile colonies, and French multinational corporations as the major controllers of the Francophone African consumer market. The French financial and technical sponsorship of Francophone African cinema was tied to both the politics and policies of the political party in power in France, and the political/ideological preferences of its ruling cliques or cells in Francophone African countries. For instance, the temporary suspension of French aid to Francophone African filmmakers in 1979 was tied to the fact that, by this time, there was a major shift in emphasis from preoccupation with themes of colonial rule and exploitation, to focusing attention upon the failures of post-colonial states and post-colonial rulers. This shift in thematic emphasis invariably brought into full focus the corruption, greed, nepotism, ethnicity and gross administrative inefficiency of the emergent political class.

With films such as Sembène's *Borom Sârret* (1963), *Mandabi* (1968), *Xala* (1974), and Soulaymane Cissé's *Baara* (1978) and *Finye* (1982), focusing attention on the growth of both urban and rural poverty, and tracing this poverty and social degeneration to the corruption and administrative ineptitude of post-colonial rulers and governments, various Francophone African governments started worrying about the social impact of films with strong political undertones. When Francophone African governments applied pressures on the Giscard government, it suspended aid to Francophone African filmmakers in 1979 in order to maintain the special friendly relations between Francophone African leaders and the French government. Aid was resumed only in 1980 at the onset of the Mitterrand socialist government, signifying an ideological shift in Franco-African political relations in favor of progressive filmmakers such as Sembène, Hondo and Cissé.

The second argument often advanced for the notable development of film production in Francophone African countries, in comparison to its Anglophone counterparts, is the rather simplistic view that the French bequethed its erstwhile colonies, a heritage of feature film production, while the British left theirs a documentary and instructional film production tradition. As earlier argued, this is not true because the French involvement with the development of Francophone African cinema is a post-colonial phenomenon, and even at that, France did not establish film production infrastructures in its erstwhile colonies. In addition, the post-colonial film production arrangement put in place by France was meant to encourage the production of documentaries showing the development policies and programs of its newly independent colonies. French sponsorship of Francophone African cinema took the form of the provision of money to finance film production, film equipment and technicians to work with filmmakers, and the provision of post-production facilities in Paris for film processing, editing, sound-synchronization and film promotion. It was these services that accounted for the notably high quality of Francophone African films, in comparison to those from Anglophone Africa, not inherited forms of film production. Furthermore, it is not true, either, that Francophone African filmmakers had specialized in feature film production, while their counterparts from Anglophone Africa had specialized in documentary and instructional film production. Many Francophone African filmmakers such as Pauline S. Vieyra, Soulaymane Cissé, Moussa Bathily, Timite Bassori, Henri Duparc, etc., also have acclaimed documentary and instructional film practices to their credit. It is therefore not correct to suggest that Francophone African filmmakers inherited a tradition of feature film production from France, as a result of which they have produced the best quality of African films available in international film circuits.

The question to ask at this juncture is whether other African countries, the Anglophone countries included, produce films at all. If they do, the next question will be: why are they not available in international film circuits? Why is it that only films from Francophone African countries continue to dominate international film circuits, as representatives of African cinema? The answers to these rhetorical questions will be that, indeed, films are produced in other African countries, including Anglophone African countries, but that filmmakers from these countries neither enjoy state sponsorship of film production, nor the financial and technical backing of a post-colonial power like France, whose patronage includes the promotion of Francophone African films in Paris, from where they enjoy privileged entrance into the international film circuit, thereby perpetuating the myth that only Francophone

African countries produce good quality films. It costs money to travel to international film festivals to promote one's film(s). And in the absence of any financial backing, either of the sort France makes available to Francophone African filmmakers, or national sponsorship by Anglophone African governments, there is no way one can ascertain whether good quality films are produced in Anglophone African countries or even other African countries.

It is also not true that Anglophone African filmmakers have specialized in documentary and instructional film production. Filmmakers such as Ola Balogun, Adamu Halilu, Eddie Ugbomah, Ade Folayan, Oyewole Olowomoruoje, and Wole Soyinka, all of Nigeria, have directed films of quality comparable to some of the internationally widely acclaimed films from Francophone African countries. Balogun's *Black Goddess* (1978) and *Money Power* (1982) have won international film prizes. Nigeria is also the home of the first truly indigenous cinema, currently referred to as Folklore Cinema, because of its outgrowth from Yoruba Traveling Theatre. Folklore Cinema, or what one prefers to call New Nigerian Cinema, is a truly indigenous cinema with its own crude form of star-system and production companies, which used mostly all-Nigerian production staff and production facilities within the country. The closest correlatives of New Nigerian Cinema, in the context of the broad category of Third World Cinema, would be the much more established Hindi Indian Cinema or Hong Kong (Kung fu) Cinema. Indeed, one of the main criticisms of New Nigerian Cinema is its predilection for borrowing from Hindi, Hong Kong (Kung Fu) Hollywood and European cinematic practices in its bid to survive as an emergent national cinema.

The free borrowing spirit of New Nigerian Cinema has not yet been extended fully to adaptations or even reproductions of Hollywood releases, possibly because of the technological and narrative sophistication of these films. At present, Hollywood techniques like chase sequences and narrative suspense, built around plot and atmospheric/mood music, are freely adopted in New Nigerian Cinema. Beside this obvious commercial bias, the cinema is also financially self-reliant because its production capital is derived from savings from the various families' traveling theatre companies that have metamorphosed into film production companies. One of its other survivalist features is that most of the companies assist one another when major film projects are in execution. Indeed, Nigeria's adoption of the IMF imposed Structural Adjustment Program (SAP), in the mid 1980s, eventually killed the burgeoning film industry. Before then, the life-styles of producers, directors and the film "stars" were already betraying the financial success of New Nigerian Cinema. It is also instructive to note that, though New Nigerian Cinema is predominantly Yoruba-derived, like its theatre progenitor, its audience range extended beyond the Yoruba speaking states of Nigeria, and its mode of exhibition has, in addition to the established movie theatres, been itinerant, as in its traveling theatre days, when shows were presented in school halls, churches, town halls, or any secure and enclosed space or compound.

Apart from the fledging New Nigerian Cinema, Ghanaian directors such as Sam Aryetey, Kwate Nee-Owoo, King Ampaw and Kwaw Ansah have also made feature films of notable quality. Ansah's film, *Love Brewed in the African Pot* won the Oumarou Ganda Prize at the Seventh Pan-African Film Festival at Ouagadougou, and it was a commercial success in Kenya, Zambia and Sierra Leone, besides Ghana. Indeed, it was one of the most widely seen African films within the continent so far.

In view of all the overwhelming facts of the complex and multifarious nature of African cinema, it is not only wrong but simplistic to suggest, as Martin (1982: 30), Diawara, 1986: 63) and Cham (1987: 13) have done, that Francophone African cinema is much more developed than its Anglophone counterpart. It is equally wrong and simplistic to suggest, as these critics sometimes do, that Francophone African filmmakers have produced more internationally acclaimed feature films because they inherited feature film production culture from France, while their counterparts from Anglophone Africa have specialized in documentary and instructional films because they inherited these forms from the British. While conceding the latter case — that Anglophone African countries inherited production infrastructure and documentary and instructional film practice from the British — these facts alone do not account for the nature of the current production patterns in the countries concerned; nor is it true that there is generic imbalance with regard to the forms in question.

On the contrary, Francophone African cinema's current domineering representation of the continent in international film circuits is as a result of two interrelated factors: the post-colonial technical, financial and promotional sponsorship from France, and the financial sponsorship of filmmakers' projects by the various national governments. Both forms of sponsorship, with the possible exception of Guinea-Conakry and Burkina Faso, have often neglected the setting up of production facilities in Africa, to promote the growth of national cinemas. In the case of France, the sponsorship policy is a continuation of the country's grand neo-colonial strategy that aims to preserve and secure France's hegemonic geo-political, military, economic as well as cultural influence in its erstwhile colonies, so that its consumer markets are firmly secured for French multinational corporations.

Britain, on the other hand, stopped all forms of technical and financial sponsorship of African cinema in the mid-fifties, even before most of its colonies were granted independence. In keeping with its colonial policy of association, Britain also granted its colonies independence, and physically left Africa, content to use the enormous economic clout of its multinational corporations and historically-established links with powerful traditional rulers and Sandhurst-trained military officers, to control the governments of its erstwhile colonies, protect its interest, and influence policies without being physically present. While Francophone African countries have contented themselves with depending on French production facilities and technical support, Anglophone African countries, lacking such support by a post-colonial power, have had to embark upon the procurement of production facilities and mass training of indigenous personnel to manage them. As a result, most film productions in Anglophone African countries are handled by trained indigenous technicians. In most Francophone African countries, French technicians are still in charge of cinematography, film development and processing, editing, and other technical related activities. But having set up these production facilities, Anglophone African governments refused to grant direct financial aid to their filmmakers. Most of them consider commercial cinema productions as a realm of private business investments, and are content to render commercial services to filmmakers who wish to use the national production facilities, film equipment and technicians. It is a purely business affair. For this reason, most filmmakers have had to hire film equipment from private sources, or from the national film corporations in addition to securing the services of either private, national film corporations or television cinematographers and technicians, if the production company does not have its trained technical and cinematographic staff.

In addition to securing the services of technical and cinematographic staff, production companies have had to secure funding, in the form of bank loans, personal savings or financial assistance from family sources or friends, for their projects. These financial constraints explain why, in Nigeria, only New Nigerian Cinema, with its savings from its traveling-theatre-company-days, has a prolific and self-reliant practice. Other directors working outside the structure of New Nigerian Cinema suffer a lot of financial constraints. Ironically, it is in the area of direct financial aid to filmmakers — however irregular — that Francophone African governments have surpassed their Anglophone counterparts. These factors have direct bearing upon the production output of filmmakers from both Anglophone and Francophone African countries.

Summary

This chapter has examined the historical context within which film production flourished in colonial and post-colonial Anglophone and Francophone Africa. The view that Francophone African filmmakers inherited a feature film production culture from France while those of Anglophone Africa inherited documentary practice has been questioned. On the contrary, one has argued that France's sponsorship of African cinema is a post-colonial phenomenon. Arguably, Francophone Africa has produced renowned filmmakers who have distinguished themselves in both documentary and feature productions. But to posit that this is so because Francophone African countries inherited the tradition of feature film production from France is another matter altogether. One has equally argued that Anglophone filmmakers have, equally intermittently, given good accounts of themselves in feature film practice, in addition to the legacy of the Griersonian school of documentary tradition, introduced into the linguistic zone, through the British Colonial Film Units. In addition, the role of the colonial Mobile Film Units in establishing a popular film culture in Anglophone Africa has been examined. Equally acknowledged is the impact made by the short-lived predominantly Yoruba-derived New Nigerian Cinema. Though this cinema was Yoruba-derived, like its theatre progenitor, its audience extends beyond the Yoruba speaking states of Nigeria. Its mode of exhibition has, in addition to the established movie theatres, been itinerant like its traveling theatre days when shows were presented in school halls, town halls, churches, or any secured and enclosed space or compound. Finally, the impact of both the colonial and post-colonial administrative and film policies of Britain and France has been examined, as well as the consequences of these policies on current film production outputs in Anglophone and Francophone African countries.

POST-COLONIAL AFRICAN HISTORICAL TEXTS AND COLONIALIST COUNTER-DISCOURSE IN AFRICAN CINEMA

Introduction

In this chapter, the historical background to the response of Africa cinema to colonialism and colonialist African cinema/discourse is examined. This is followed by analysis of how African filmmakers represented Africans and their European colonizers in films set in the colonial era. My argument is that though post-colonial African historical texts respond to the history of the whole colonial enterprise in their narratives, they are inspired, first and foremost, by the desire to refute the images of Africa and Africans identifiable with the discursive tradition of colonialist African cinema/discourse. In this regard, they present a version of history and historical events that is counter-discursive in nature. From distinctions between colonial African instructional cinema and colonialist African cinema, my analysis of the post-colonial African historical texts set in the colonial era will make clear that they are inspired counter-discursive responses more to the latter tradition than the former.

Coincidentally, the first generation of African filmmakers, whose works are to be analyzed, grew up under colonial authority. Their version of historical events is informed either by direct personal experience, through information derived from those directly affected by the events recounted, news media and government documented sources, or through the sheer experience of generally growing up under colonial authority. Ousmane Sembène, for instance, fought in the Second World War and the events he recounts in *Camp de*

Thiaroye bear the resonance of personal experience. To round off this chapter, I will analyze Med Hondo's *Sarraounia* (1987), and Ousmane Sembène and Thierno Faty Sow's *Camp de Thiaroye* (1988).

The Historical Background of Post-colonial African Historical Texts

For purely historical reasons, the foundation of early African scholarship has, in general, been built upon the tradition of colonialist counter-discourse. The reason for this is not far fetched. Africa has been subjected to two waves of European colonialism — the first, which occurred during the Roman Empire, covered much of North Africa, and the second which began in the fifteenth century was accompanied by the slave trade. In both cases, colonialism had made it possible for the production of a body of knowledge about Africa colored by European authority and awareness of its social position on the continent: a body of knowledge which moreover, reflecting this uneven Afro-European power relations, defined Africans as inferior beings and their customary practices as perversions of European ideals.

The first generation of Africans to acquire western education — or people of African descent with such education who settled in the continent after the abolition of the slave trade — were the first set of people to encounter this body of knowledge. It was they, too, who initiated works, which they intended to correct the negative image of Africa and Africans, which they encountered in the process of acquiring western education. In Africa, the tradition of colonialist counter-discourse was initiated by scholars of African descent such as Alexander Crummell, Edward Wilmot Blyden and W. E. B. Du Bois, all of who settled and naturalized in Africa. According to Kwame A. Appiah,

> at the heart of Crummell's vision is a single guiding concept: race. Crummell's 'Africa' is the motherland of the Negro race and his right to act in it, to speak for it, to plot for its future, derived - in his conception — from the fact that he too was a Negro. More than this, Crummell held that there was a common destiny for the people of Africa — by which we are always to understand the black people — not because they had a common historical experience or faced a common threat from imperial

Europe, but because they belong to this one race. Crummell was one of the first people to speak as a Negro in Africa: and his writings effectively inaugurated the discourse of Pan-Africanism. (Appiah, 1992: 5)

Though Crummell's works were written in response to European nineteenth century racist theories, he had to invoke concepts of race in order to theorize the oneness of people of African descent, a process which involved the inversion of racist theories but which Appiah qualifies as racist because of its dependence upon biological concepts of race. The only exception Appiah ascribes to Crummell's works is that Crummell did not conceive of race as a basis for the institution of racial discrimination or inflicting harm but as a general term of racial solidarity among people of African descent (Appiah: 25). The same trend of thought also informed the works of Edward Blyden. Blyden, in his work, *Christianity, Islam and the Negro Race* argues that

there is not a single mental or moral deficiency now existing among Africans — not a single practice now indulged in by them — to which we cannot find a parallel in the past history of Europe, and even after the people had been brought under the influence of a nominal Christianity. The Negro of the ordinary traveler or missionary — and perhaps, of two-thirds of the Christian world — is a purely fictitious being, constructed out of the traditions of slave-traders and slave-holders, who have circulated all sorts of absurd stories, and also out of prejudices inherited from ancestors, who were taught to regard the Negro as a legitimate object of traffic. (Blyden, 1888: 58)

V. Y. Mudimbe in his study of the works of Blyden drew conclusions similar to those that Appiah drew in respect of Alexander Crummell. Mudimbe argues that Blyden rejected in his works European nineteenth century racist theories according to which Africans represented the starting point in man's evolutionary process while Europeans represented the highest point of evolution. As Mudimbe puts it, Blyden's

political ideology arose from a response to racism and to some of the consequences of imperialism. It represents an emotional response to the European process of denigrating Africa and an opposition to the exploitation that resulted from the expansionism of Europe from the fifteenth century. At the same time, in order to prove its own significance, his ideology strongly asserts the thesis of pluralism in the historical development of races, ethnic groups, and nationalities. Consequently, Blyden can reject the evolutionary assumption of "identical but unequal races" which provides grounds for the theme of the "white man's mission" and thus justifies imperialism and colonization. In its place, he put a different assertion: "distinct but equal." (Mudimbe, 1988: 132)

These scholars wrote their works in the midst of the ongoing European colonization of Africa. In this respect, their works were a protestation against both the ongoing colonial enterprise and its intellectual product, colonialist African discourse. Therefore, their works not only laid the foundation of both pan-Africanism and the intellectual practice of colonialist counter-discourse but also anticipated the political and cultural nationalism that preceded the struggle for independence in most African countries. Subsequent generations of black scholars and statesmen such as Joseph Casely-Hayford, Nnamdi Azikiwe, Kwame Nkrumah, Julius Nyerere, Leopold Sedar Senghor, Aimé Césaire, Frantz Fanon, Walter Rodney, Cheikh Anta Diop, and Wole Soyinka, later built upon this intellectual tradition in their own individual ways. For instance, it is now common knowledge that both the concepts of African personality and its Francophone correspondence, Negritude, owe their roots to the broader concept of Pan-Africanism as defined by Crummell, Blyden and Du Bois (Irele, 1981: 89-116). According to Noureddine Ghali,

the concept of "negritude" was developed by a group of French-speaking black intellectuals studying in Paris in the 1930s and 1940s; among them was Leopold Senghor, later to be first president of Senegal after the close of formal colonial rule. It denoted a view of black people as peculiarly gifted in the art of immediate living of sensual experience, of physical skill and process, all of which belonged to them by birthright. It was an attempt at the time to combat the racist view of African civilization as a null quantity, and the ideology that French colonial rule was providing otherwise worthless, culture-less beings with the opportunity to assimilate themselves to French culture, and thus take on a cultural dignity otherwise unavailable to them. (Ghali, 1987: 52)

Anglophone African intellectuals have traditionally vigorously criticized the negritudinist notion that the European contribution to global culture is technological and rational while that of Africa is governed by intuitiveness, emotionality and sensuality (Soyinka, 1976: 126-139). But as Irele has demonstrated in his analysis of the concept of African personality, Negritude is a version. Although both concepts are articulated differently by black intellectuals of the Anglophone and Francophone linguistic divide, both owe their origins to the broader concept of pan-Africanism as articulated by the first generation of black scholars in the diaspora. As Irele puts it,

> Negritude is a version, a distinctive current of the same cultural nationalism expressed in different ways among black people and at various times in their reaction against white domination. Negritude is, in a word, the Francophone equivalent, of the term 'African personality' in its original meaning as used by Blyden and in its association with the pan-Africanism of Sylvester Williams and W. E. B. Du Bois. The two concepts thus stand in a reciprocal relationship as being, each in its own way, a formulation of vision of the race founded upon an idea of Africa. (Irele: 91)

Apart from the fields of philosophy, history and social theory, other field where the tradition of colonialist counter-discourse has been firmly established is that of African literature. Emmanuel Obiechina, in his examination of the initial creative impulse underlying the practice of early modern African literature has argued that it can be linked to the desire to correct negative images of Africa and Africans, which African writers encountered in European literature. As he puts it,

> the position, stated bluntly, is this: foreign writer on West Africa express in their writing prejudices and preconceptions which distort their picture of West African life. *Sometimes the writer is aware of these distorting elements and boldly works them into the technique and texture of his narrative; in other circumstances they may operate on him as an unconscious projection of his reaction to something strange and disturbing.* In either case, the result is different from the view of West African life held by West African writers who see it from the inside. This is why novels by foreigners are a factor operating on the indigenous writer and impelling him, consciously or unconsciously, to counter through his own writing the outsiders' view (my emphasis). (Obiechina, 1975: 17-18)

Chinua Achebe's critical and creative responses to colonialist African literature in general, Joyce Cary's *Mister Johnson* and Joseph

Conrad's *Heart of Darkness* in particular, are now famous instances of colonialist counter-discursive responses in African literature (Achebe, 1988: 1-3). Obiechina's study, however, acknowledges that colonial African literature written by Europeans was not a unified discourse. While he cites the works of European authors such as Joyce Cary, Joseph Conrad, Graham Greene, and Elspeth Huxley, as belonging to the tradition of colonialist African literature, he nevertheless singles out the works of Margaret Field, especially *Stormy Dawn*, written within the same period, as an exception to that tradition (Obiechina: 24-25). Though Obiechina does not treat in detail the relation of power and authority to the institution of colonialist African literature, there is an implicit acknowledgement of this fact in his argument that some European writers are aware of the intrusion of the distorting elements of prejudices and preconceptions into their works but *boldly* work them nonetheless into the technique and texture of their narratives. Of course, though early modern African literature responded to colonialist African literature, African writers have since graduated from both critical and creative responses of the early phase of their works to pre-occupation with the post-colonial state and society.

Similar colonialist counter-discursive trends such as those cited are also noticeable in the cinematic practices of the first generation of African filmmakers. Products of this initial creative responses to colonialist African cinema/discourse can be found in works such as Ousmane Sembène's *La Noire de* (*Black Girl*, 1966), *Emitai* (1971), *Ceddo* (1976), Ousmane Sembène and Thierno Faty Sow's *Camp de Thiaroye* (1988), Med Hondo's *Soleil O* (1969), *West Indies* (1979), and *Sarrounia* (1987), Ola Balogun's *Black Goddess* (1978), and *Cry Freedom* (1981), Eddie Ugbomah's *The Mask* (1976), Adamu Halilu's *Shehu Umar* (1976), and Kwaw Ansah's *Heritage Africa* (1988). Though these filmmakers have since moved on to concentrate upon post-colonial themes, the colonialist counter-discursive phase of their works recalls earlier historical works by black scholars and literary writers in response to the existing canon in Euro-America scholarship and filmic practice. The question of the success of such colonialist counter-discursive practices is a matter open to disputation and one, which is not central to this study. What is of interest to me is the version of history and historical events put forward by African filmmakers vis-à-vis other discursive traditions referenced in the colonial period, and the relevance of this to the nature of African and European subjectivities, represented in historical colonial encounter texts. The point should be stressed that since these historical colonial encounter films present an African version of historical events, the spectatorial textual positioning of the African viewer differs markedly in respect of the colonialist African texts to which they respond. Writing on the subject of the spectatorial positioning in post-colonial African films of the historical colonial encounter genre, Manthia Diawara has argued that

> these films position the spectators to identify with African people's resistance against European colonialism and imperialist drives. These stories are about colonial encounters and they often pit African heroes and heroines against European villains. They are conditioned by the desire to show African heroism where European history only mentioned the actions of the conquerors; resistance where colonial version of history silenced oppositional voices; and the role of women in the armed struggle. For the filmmakers, such historical narratives are justified by the need to bring out of the shadow the role played by the African people in the shaping of their own history. (Diawara, 1989: 116)

In the remaining part of this chapter, I will analyze selected texts such as Med Hondo's *Sarrounia* (1987), and Ousmane Sembène and Thierno Faty Sow's *Camp de Thiaroye* (1988).

Background Notes On Med Hondo

Abid Mohamed Medoun Hondo, better known as Med Hondo, is the son of a Senegalese father and a Mauritanian mother. He was born on May 4, 1936, in Ain Ouled Beni Mathar, in the Atar region of Mauritania, where the Tuareg, a desert dwelling nomadic ethnic group of Arab ancestry who live around oases in the Sahara desert, took his forefathers as slaves. In 1954, Med Hondo was sent to Rabat, Morocco, where he trained for four years as a cook at a hotel management school. He later traveled to France at the end of his training in search of a job in 1959. For a while he was unable to find a job related to his training due to racism in French society, and like most black migrant workers of his time he had to earn a living by working as a dock-worker and a farm hand before he eventually got a job in a Marseille restaurant. His boss, who was ashamed of hiring a black chef, confined him to the back of his kitchen until he noticed that Hondo's chef cap was providing an exotic air to his restaurant. He later worked in a restaurant in Vittel, a thermal health resort in eastern France, before moving on to Paris in 1962 where he worked for a while as a Swiss cheese delivery man before he was employed as a waiter at the posh La Rein Pédauque restaurant.

In 1965, out of his desire for self-expression, he began to take drama courses under the late Françoise Rosay, a well-known French stage and screen actress. On completion of his training as an actor, the limited range of roles available to him as a black actor soon made him disillusioned with the idea of taking up a professional acting career in mainstream French theatre. In an interview, which he granted Françoise Pfaff in 1976, he states that

> I became involved in drama because I felt a need to express myself and because I had a great deal of naiveté. As I saw actors on the stage, they reminded me of the griots and the palaver trees under which African people debated their problems. I thought that by way of the theatre I could tell what I had been enduring and what I felt. My assumptions were proved to be wrong. While studying drama I had to learn parts from plays by Molière, Racine and Shakespeare. They did not illustrate the experience I had sought to express. Moreover, there were few parts black actors could play on the French stage. Classical theatre did not answer my needs. (Pfaff, 1988: 158)

In 1966, he founded a black repertory theatre known as Shango, named after the Yoruba god of Thunder, in order to explore the themes of black diaspora experience in France. His theatre company comprised of Africans and African diaspora actors and actresses, especially those from the United States and the French West Indies. The troupe undertook a tour of France with plays by the Martinican poet and playwright Aimé Césaire, African-American authors such as Imamu Baraka (Leroi Jones) and many by African and South American playwrights. They played in small theatres and cultural centers but the public showed little interest in their productions. He later merged his troupe with *Les Griots*, a theatre company headed by the Guadaloupean actor and director, Robert Liensol. The new company became known as Griot-Shango, and it continued to produce works by black authors such as Réné Depestre (Haiti), Guy Monga (Congo) and Daniel Boukman (Martinique). Med Hondo made his entrance into film by working as an actor and assistant director in various productions. Among the films he acted in are: *Un Homme de trop* (*Shock Troops*, Costa-Gavras, 1967); *Tante Zinta* (Robert Enrico, 1968), and *A Walk with Love and Death* (John Huston, 1969).

Med Hondo made his debut as a filmmaker with two black and white shorts, *Balade aux sources* (*Ballad to the Springs*, 1969) and *Partout ou Peut-être Nulle Part* (*Everywhere, or May Be Nowhere*, 1969). He gained international recognition as a filmmaker with his first full-length feature, *Soleil O* (*O Sun*, 1969). *Soleil O* is a black and white film made over a period of five years on a low budget of $125,000. The film owes its title to an old song that African slaves used to sing on their way to the West Indies. The film's main protagonist is an anonymous African accountant, a symbolization of black migrant workers in France, whose experience of racism drive him to the edge of mental breakdown. The film uses a series of narrative flashbacks and a trance scene towards the end of the film to relate the experiences of black migrant workers in France to French colonialism in Africa and the role of world revolutionary figures such as Patrice Lumumba, Che Guevara, Mehdi Ben Barka and Malcolm X in containing the spread of imperialism in the world. Two years after *Soleil O*, Hondo made his first color features, *Les Bicots-nègres vos Voisins* (*Arabs and Niggers, Your Neighbour*, 1973). Like *Soleil O*, the film deals with the routine experiences of Black and Arab workers in France. Between 1974 and 1978, Med Hondo spent several months with the Saharouis and in the course of those months made two full-length color documentaries about the Polisario struggle for independence in Western Sahara. These films are: *Nous Aurons Toute la Mort Pour Dormir* (*We'll Have all the Time We're Dead to Sleep*, 1977) and *Polisario un Peuple en Armes* (*Polisario, A People in Arms*, 1979).

The documentaries on the Polisario movement were followed by another feature film, *West Indies, Les Nègres Marrons de la Liberté* (*West Indies, the Black Freedom Fighters*, 1979). The film is based on *Les Négriers* (*The Slavers*), a play by Daniel Boukman, which Hondo had produced thrice on stage. By African standards, *West Indies* was a big budget film since its production cost reached $1.3 million, including a set with a slave ship built by set designer Jacques Saulnier and costing $200,000. To finance the project, Hondo raised a substantial part of the money from investors in Senegal, Mauritania and Côte d'Ivoire after refusing a $1.5 million offer from MGM because they wanted him to use noted black American actors instead of a lesser known Caribbean cast. He also sought and received technical support from Algerian television as well as obtaining $85,000 from the French National Cinema Center (CNC). In the end, with both professional and amateur actors, seventy dancers, most of whom were Caribbean performers, ballets choreographed by the black American choreographer, Linda Dingwall, and a musical score composed by the Martinican composer, Frank Valmont, Hondo made what may be considered Africa's first musical on film.

When *West Indies* was released in 1979, it was shown simultaneously in eight Gaumont movie theatres in Paris where it proved to be a commercial failure. However, the film has fared very well in the festival circuits, where it won a lot of awards. *West Indies* chronicles black experience from the slave trade to the present day neo-colonialism, through a symbolic representation by way of the slave ship of French imperialism in both Africa and the West Indies. His next major project after *West Indies* was another historical film, *Sarraounia*, a $2.5 million feature film based on Abdoulaye Mamani's text, *Sarraounia*, which was itself a literary transcription and documentation of the oral Azna epic of Sarraounia, a warrior queen who in the late nineteenth century resisted French colonialism in the present day Niger Republic. Med Hondo, like Ousmane Sembène, considers himself to be a "committed filmmaker," a term used to affirm their commitment to the production of works that would explicate the historical circumstances surrounding present day black experience both on the continent and in the black diaspora (Pfaff, 1986; Ranvaud, 1987; Reid, 1986). In the remaining part of this chapter, I will be analyzing *Sarraounia*

A Critical Reading of Med Hondo's Sarraounia

The events recounted in *Sarraounia* are based on what actually occurred in the Hausa-speaking region of what is today the Dongondoutchi district of Niger Republic. By this I mean that both Mamani's work and the film itself do not contradict, in broad terms, the actual historical account from which they draw inspiration. Ousmane Tadina, who has carried out a thorough

study of both the French account of the events and those
recounted by Abdoulaye Mamani in *Sarraounia*, states that

> Mamani's work does not contradict the historical accounts from
> which it draws inspiration, but it should not be confused with
> history, which remains a scientific discipline that proposes to
> discover the truth, to attain a certain level of objectivity. Thus,
> *Sarraounia* is essentially a product of the literary imagination, not
> an historical or ethnographic document. (Tandina, 1993: 29)

Tandina's account of the broad narrative thrust of Mamani's text is
not deviated from in the film. Mamani also co-wrote the screen
version with Med Hondo. In the historical account itself, on 2nd
January, 1899, a French colonial expedition force made up of black
mercenary soldiers, commanded by Captain Voulet and Lieutenant
Chanoine, set off from Segou, in present day Mali, to occupy
Zinder, a town in present the day Niger Republic. The Sultan of
Zinder had executed of a young French captain leading an
expedition force to Chad through Niger Republic. The Voulet-
Chanoine expedition column crossed the country of the Zarma and
that of the Gourma before entering into the Dallal Mawri, a large
valley — over what is now considered to contain a large
underground stream — of thick forest vegetation outlying Lugu,
the seat of the Azna Kingdom. On 17th April, 1899, the French
expedition force laid siege to the village of Lugu where they
encountered a fierce resistance from the Aznas led by their warrior-
queen, Sarraounia. Of course, the French, through superiority of
arms, eventually succeeded in occupying her palace, but instead of
surrendering, Sarraounia withdrew into the forest around Lugu and
embarked upon guerrilla and psychological warfare that wore down
the morale of the French expedition force, especially that of the
tirailleurs who were terror-struck by the name of Sarraounia and her
famed sorcery and fetishes. In the end, Voulet and Chanoine were
forced to withdraw from Lugu after a mutiny by the *tiarilleurs*.

According to Michael Crowder, the Voulet-Chanoine
expedition force was bedeviled from the start by troubles because
they permitted pillaging and cruelties on a scale that exceeded
anything yet witnessed in the French colonial conquest in West
Africa. Reports of the cruelties themselves were taken to France by
Lieutenant Peteau, a member of the expeditionary force who was
sent back by Voulet because of disagreement between the two. As
a result of the report by Peteau, the French authorities sent

Lieutenant-Colonel Klobb to take over command from Voulet, who assassinated him. The death of Klobb led to another mutiny by the *tirailleurs* who placed themselves under the authority of Lieutenant Pallier, the next most senior officer. When Voulet tried to assert his command over the *tirailleurs*, they murdered both him and Chanoine. The many crimes committed by the Voulet-Chanoine expedition column included murdering their superior officer; sacking the town of Sansanne Haoussa, already under French control; taking the inhabitants of captured villages as "captifs"; killing twenty-five women and a number of children as an example to the population of a village which had wounded some *tirailleurs*; requesting soldiers to bring hands of corpses as proof of the fact that they killed the enemy; and the sacking of Birni Nikoni, a town of 10,000 people, where many women and children were massacred (Crowder, 1968: 106-114). Many of these crimes are replicated in the film, *Sarraounia.*

Tandina, in his analysis of Mamani's text, has correctly argued that it can be classified alongside other African epics dealing with the theme of leadership, communal resistance and heroism like, D. T. Niana's *Soundjata* and Thomas Mfolo's *Chaka*, all of which deal with the theme of resistance by African traditional rulers to the incursion of European colonial forces into their Kingdoms. Traditional court historians, the griots, first documented the stories of colonial resistance by these leaders, through praise-songs, before their present authors translated them. In this respect, the question of authorship of these texts is often quite problematic since they were handed down through generations of griots. Considering the general question of the definition of African epic, Tandina has noted that

> although it remains difficult to define the African epic with precision, we can say that it resolves around a battle, a political event of major importance, a confrontation between noblemen. It is a song of glory. Created after the fact by specialists, it can be either sung or recited. The hero is idealized and even his faults are transformed into virtues. In endowing the hero with superhuman qualities, the performer introduces incredible details not only to embellish the story, but also to add lustre to the hero's reputation. In fact their victories and their death reflect the intervention of outside forces as much as (if not more than) the effects of their own physical and mental powers. (Tandina: 24)

The portrayal of the main protagonist, Sarraounia, in the film, meets the characteristics that Tandina has described in respect of characterization in the epic genre of African literature. The film itself can be classified as belonging to the epic genre in African cinema. Other films which fit such a classification are Adamu Halilu's *Shehu Umar* (1977) and *Kanta Kebbi* (1978), both of which deal with epic stories and exploits, incorporating elements of colonial resistance, by traditional rulers in Nigeria. Sarraounia is of noble birth and her ascension to throne of the Azna Kingdom displayed all the noble qualities identifiable with the genre. But as in the idealized characterization of the literary epic, Sarraounia, in the film version, is also very much an idealized heroine. This point will be explored further in some detail when the question of the representation of character-subjectivity in the film is examined. It is sufficient for now to note that though the film pays detailed attention to the crimes of the Voulet-Chanoine force, its central narrative point of view is the celebration of the warrior-queen, Sarraounia, and the noble resistance, which she led against French colonialism in the late nineteenth century.

By African standards, *Sarraounia*, like Hondo's earlier features, was a big budget film. Its production costs amounted to $2.5 million and its large cast included, apart from the lead roles, some 800 extras. The film was shot on location in Burkina-Faso over a period of twelve weeks and was produced by Hondo's production company, Films Soleil O, in conjunction with the Ministry of Information and Culture of Burkina Faso and the French Ministry of Culture and External Cooperation. Its large cast and production staff was drawn from several Francophone African countries, including Niger, Burkina-Faso, Cameroon, Benin, Gabon and Mauritania.

Sarraounia is a very complex film. In term of narrative structure, it switches both backward and forward, through time and space, as it tries to articulate the events culminating in the European colonization of Africa. It begins with a prologue showing the march of the Voulet-Chanoine colonial expedition force into the Savannah grassland, and ends with an epilogue depicting Sarraounia giving a long speech on religious and ethnic tolerance and the need to fight and preserve one's freedom, a speech which is appropriately crowned by her praise-song rendered by a company of her griots, who also implicitly acknowledge the contributions of both old and modern griots, i.e., filmmakers, to the preservation of African history. The prologue prefaces a narrative flashback sequence, which deals with the childhood of Sarraounia. The childhood sequence takes us into the secrets behind Sarraounia's famed reputation in warfare and sorcery. She was brought up by a maternal fetish doctor/warrior uncle who not only taught her both traditional medicine and the art of warfare but also instilled in her, at a very young and impressionable age, a sense of her extraordinary infancy, not having been nurtured as an infant by a woman's milk but that of a mare due to her mother's death after her birth. The uncle also made her aware of her social status as the future Queen of the Aznas, destined to be lord over both men and women. This was her past story. Her present story as the crowned Queen of the Aznas begins with her victory over an invading army of Fulani jihadists of Sokoto. After this victory, she marries her general, Baka (Ben Idriss Traore). The marriage ceremony itself is not shown; however, the marriage is short-lived because of her peculiar upbringing and Baka's pride, which cannot stand the praise-songs of her griots.

With Baka's desertion, the narrative switches back to the story of the partition of Africa. The story of partition is narrated through a combination of a voice-over narration of the events surrounding the partition and a symbolic partition represented through a sculptured map of the continent superimposed on a flame, which cracks up into individual countries with blood issuing out of the forcibly created boundaries. This symbolic representation graphically recounts the bloody tale behind the partition of Africa and the actual colonialism, which attended it. This symbolic sequence ends with a cut to a full frontal view of the Voulet-Chanoine force. When the narrative switches back to Sarraounia, we find her in a restless worried mood. She has heard of the destruction, looting and rape in the wake of the invading army but rather than surrender without resistance and be subjected to the attendant atrocities of the army or collude with them as others are doing, she prepares her subjects for resistance. In the meantime, Sarraounia's Islamized neighboring kingdoms debate among themselves whether they should assist her or allow the French to destroy the "witch" and "infidel." The Sultan of Sokoto, which is under British authority, goes beyond sitting on the fence. When he learns of the impending French attack, he promptly dispatches an envoy (Hama Gourounga) to Captain Voulet (Jean-Roger Milo) to guide him to Sarraounia (Ai Keita), as a way of punishing her for refusing to convert to Islam with her subjects. Captain Voulet who suspects him of being a British spy detains the envoy.

When the French High Command in Niger learns of the impending attack, it dispatches a letter through a Corporal to Voulet, who not only ignores his superiors' letter but also executes the messenger as a spy. He subsequently declares himself independent of the French authorities and sets himself a personal target of building an empire to enrich himself and the *tirailleurs*, whom he coerces to join him, with an additional sweetening promise of share in all loots. Receiving no reply to their first letter, the French authorities next dispatch Colonel Klobb (Jean Edmond) to take over the Voulet-Chanoine force. In the meantime, in a cut to the palace, we find preparations being made to defend Lugu. Back at Voulet's camp, the French officers attend a formal dinner where they brag about bestial exploits such as tying a black woman down on a table for a horse to have sexual intercourse with and comparing the gentleness of Oriental women in bed with the roughness of "nigger women." While the French officers dine and wine and gaily brag about their exploits, their mercenary soldiers, in a contrastive montage, are in a sad mood, singing a dirge in anticipation of their impending death. The dinner party itself is cut short midway by a thunderstorm that strikes terror into the black mercenaries, who reason that Sarraounia sent the N'Komo after them. Consequently, many flee out of fright, while their slave-captives seize the opportunity of the storm to desert to Sarraounia. Those caught fleeing are made to flog themselves the following day as a warning against future desertion.

The Prince of Matankari, a neighboring *emirate* whose father colluded with the invading army by quartering them, deserts his father and switches allegiance, with his followers, to Sarraounia. Sarraounia's ex-husband and general, Baka, learns of the impending attack and rallies to her support. When the forces finally join battle, Voulet's men are beaten back twice before they succeed in occupying the palace after bombarding it with cannons. As the defensive walls around Lugu are torn down, the defenders withdraw into the outlying forest and adopt a scorched earth policy as they go. Voulet successfully occupies Sarraounia's palace and earns his loot, but the Queen herself proves an intractable mirage encountered only momentarily in unceasing waves of guerrilla attacks. With her tactics and psychological warfare, Sarraounia gradually wears down the soldiers, who become terror-stricken and thoroughly demoralized. Voulet and his officers themselves become so over-excited in their response to the terror stricken soldiers who are taunted by an elusive vision of Sarraounia, that between them and the soldiers, it is almost impossible to distinguish the sane from the insane. In the end, seeing that Voulet will never withdraw for reasons of prestige, the soldiers are forced into mutiny and he has to withdraw from Lugu. But as they withdraw in broken and disorganized columns after burning down the remaining houses, the French officers take vengeance on the *tirailleurs* by murdering their wounded colleagues along the way. When Klobb eventually catches up with Voulet, the latter assassinates him. In the mutiny that follows, Voulet and his aide, Coulibaly (Tidjani Ouedraogo), are killed by the *tirailleurs*; and in the general pandemonium, that follows, Chanoine (Feodor Atkine) is stabbed from behind by a group of women. Lieutenant Joalland (Roger Mirmont) then takes over command of the forces. The film ends with Sarraounia's speech on religious and ethnic tolerance — some of the causes of political friction in post-colonial African societies — and the need to fight to preserve one's freedom and independence. The speech is immediately followed by a praise-song in honor of Sarraounia, which also acknowledges the role of griots in the preservation of African history.

Throughout the narrative, there is not much deviation from the historical accounts. All the crimes detailed in the historical reports are accounted for before the encounter between the Voulet-Chanoine force and Sarraounia. The only noticeable change is that made in the ranks of the French officers: Lieutenant-Colonel Klobb is now Colonel Klobb and Lieutenant Chanoine is now Captain Chanoine. In the historical account, Lieutenant Pallier took command of the force after the death of Voulet and Chanoine while in the film, Lieutenant Joalland takes command. Apart from these few alterations, which do not alter the course of the events, there is great fidelity to the historical accounts.

Sarraounia explores a lot of themes, many of them dealing with the nature of conflicts both within Africa and between the competing European powers during the period of colonial conquests. They include the themes of honor and courage on the part of those who chose the path of resistance, and collaboration and cowardice, on the part of those who chose to collude with the invading forces. Other equally important themes include the theme of ethnic division and indecision within Africa during the period of colonial conquest and that of rivalry among the colonial powers, specifically British and French. Within these thematic divides, Sarraounia represents the forces of colonial resistance. Beside her, we can also add figures such as her general, Baka, the Prince of Matankari and her courageous subjects. On the other hand, we can count among the collaborators the Sultan of Sokoto (Sekou Tall), the *Serkin* Arewa (Djibril Sidibe) and Amenokal (Rajoun Tapsirou), the leader of the Awellimiden Tuareg. Each of them has varying reasons for collaborating beyond the problem of ethnic rivalry. For the Sultan of Sokoto, it is for religious reasons. He considers Sarraounia an affront to his ambition of building an Islamic theocratic state. The case of the *Serkin* Gobir (Baba Traore) is one more of political indecision than religious fervour while *Serkin* Arewa collaborates out of pure cowardice. Amenokal's case is purely economic. He considers Sarraounia a hindrance to his slave raids into black Africa.

One of the sequences, which explore the theme of honor and courage, is that which deals with Sarraounia's exhortation speech to her fighters before the first battle with the Voulet-Chanoine force. What is significant about this speech is not so much the way it is represented in terms of narration: it is shot in a straight anti-clockwise moving tracking shot, without diegetic audience commentaries upon her speech, without interruptions in form of break in speech or cut away for reaction shots, and ends in a pan away from her, at the end of her speech, to her ex-husband and general, Baka, arriving at the scene. The strength of this speech lies in its themes of honor and courage. This 360° shot is almost unheard of in Western cinema. It breaks not only the 180° rule but also does so twice. The shot roots Sarraounia's speech in its rightful place and puts her differently in place, in contrast to the lateral tracking that is used for the French. I shall paraphrase the speech and comment upon it because it carries a lot of cultural significance related to African culture. The speech begins with Sarraounia telling her subjects that they are fighting for the honor and dignity of the Azna people, that she gave them the pride of being Aznas, and that even though she has not borne an heir to the throne, she will leave them a name which is equally valuable and long lasting. She also tells them that the Fulanis die to go to heaven but they (the Aznas) choose to die to leave a respectable name. Further, that they who die without a good name die forever, but when they die for the preservation of their honor, their musicians and their children will preserve their names through praise-songs. She concludes by telling them that they choose to fight to uphold their dignity and leave a good name, that they are fighting those who want to dominate and humiliate them.

What is being emphasized in this speech, beyond the question of honor and patriotism, is the very high premium which Africans place on names, especially family names, and the need to reproduce to ensure the continuation of one's lineage. In African societies, even in modern times, people who have engaged in anti-social activities likely to soil their family names have been known to be publicly disclaimed by such families in order to preserve the honor and dignity of the family name. The same goes for cowards who refuse to fight for the preservation of the freedom and independence of their communities. They are often scarred for life and the lineage of such people is branded through ceremonial satirical songs. The same goes for families noted for thievery or the infidelity of their women. No respectable family wants to be linked in marriage to such publicly disgraced families. Despite the growth of philistinism in modern African societies, the average African family still lives by this social norm. Also, even though corruption is rife in post-colonial African societies, there are many people in public services who will never partake in it for the sake of the honor of the family name. As a result of this strong attachment to names, careful choices are made when choosing names for children since the names not only carry significant meaning but Africans believe that people live-out the meaning of their names. The significance of these names will be examined when the question of elements of symbolism as reflected through the naming of African characters in the film is dealt with.

With respect to Sarraounia's speech, the honor at stake is not only the name of the ruling house but also that of the entire ethnic group. It is relevant to note that there are certain ethnic groups within Africa noted for their cowardice. Thus through her exhortation speech, Sarraounia not only affirms the dignity of her crown and ethnic group but also takes satirical swipes at the religious fanaticism of the Fulani jihadists who place a foreign religion above the dictates of patriotism. The question of the sanctity of family names is also reflected elsewhere in the film, as in the conflict between the Prince of Matankari and his father, *Serkin* Arewa. When the prince of Arewa is cursed and disinherited by his father for joining forces with Sarraounia who is a pagan, the prince remarks, "Good, none of us would ever want your disgraced throne," a reference to his father's cowardice which has soiled the name of the ruling house of Arewa.

The theme of ethnic rivalries and divisions, reflected at the level of relations between traditional rulers and courts is also played out within individual kingdoms. This can be witnessed in the scene of the debate in the court of *Serkin* Gobir, where the issue of assistance to the besieged Sarraounia is tabled. The scene opens with the *Serkin* tabling before his traditional council news of the atrocities of the invading army. He specifically informs the council that the army had destroyed whole cities, taken women by force to satisfy their lust, and finally, that silos full of grains have been plundered. From the way he presents the information, one can deduce that he is trying to elicit a response favorable to offering help to Sarraounia. However, in the debates, which follow, we find that what we are faced with is a divided house, with the division reflecting the larger division in Africa as a whole between those forces in favor of resistance as against those supporting collaboration or neutrality. The debate ends in stalemate. In terms of narrative structure, the forces of resistance and neutrality are arraigned against each other on screen right and left respectively. The opinions in each camp are articulated by leading figures within the kingdom. The debate itself is narrativized along the structure of dialogue scenes, in shot/reverse shots. However, the forces in favor of resistance seem to have longer lines to deliver and this make their argument much more forceful than those of the opposing camp. As in most other scenes of similar structure in the film — e.g. the conflict between the Prince of Matankari and his father, *Serkin* Arewa — the strength of the arguments of the two opposing camps pitched against each other lie more in the power and quality of verbal discourse than in the manner of their spatial articulation. Most of the leading speakers are shot in medium close-ups with rapid cuts, which do not permit character accessibility.

There are no cut aways to approving or disapproving commentaries in the background.

This scene is also significant in other respects. Apart from dealing with the issue of ethnic rivalries, it is also the only scene within the film that fully explores the structure of traditional African public discourse. For instance, when the king is informing the council about the atrocities of the invading army, there are a lot of commentaries and exclamations going on the background. This accurately reflects the nature of most traditional African public discourse. Important public speeches are often punctuated with approving or disapproving commentaries or plain exclamations, depending on the nature of speech or occasion. For instance, not every public speech is similarly punctuated in this film. The speeches that need punctuation are those structured around the rhetoric of public debates. This explains why those by Sarraounia are not similarly punctuated. The scene at the *Serkin* Gobir's court is one such occasion, which requires punctuation through public commentaries, though in this instance, the *Serkin*'s indecision is also reflected in his inability to take a firm stand at the end of the debate. Thus apart from exploring internal divisions within various kingdoms, the scene also deals with the manner in which traditional African public affairs are conducted. The debate in this scene recalls similar ones such as that of the scene of the village council meeting in *Daybreak in Udi*, the public debate among the *tirailleurs* that preceded the hostage scenes in *Camp de Thiaroye*, and the ones that preceded the *tirailleurs*' mutinies in *Sarraounia*.

Other themes dealt with in respect of the European colonial conquest in Africa are those which explore the cruelties and crimes of the entire enterprise, specifically that of the French as exemplified by the Voulet-Chanoine expedition force, and the theme of rivalry among the competing European powers, e.g. that between the British and the French. A series of images vividly captures the cruelties and atrocities of the Voulet-Chanoine force. The first is recorded in the ruins of an already plundered village littered with corpses. This scene is also a record of the first encounters between the troops and the people of the region. The image being referred to is that captured by a long leftward tracking shot, showing corpses amidst the burning debris that rests momentarily on a lone child nestling its dead mother. This image, in all its vividness, graphically states that not even nursing mothers are spared by the troops. Another series of images is captured in the sequence dealing with the village whose traditional ruler pleads to be spared destruction by welcoming the invading force with gifts and an offer of quartering. In the mayhem, which follows after Voulet and Chanoine interpret the traditional ruler's reception as a smoke screen for treachery and pride, almost the entire village population is wiped out. But the images with the most lasting effects recorded in the sequence are those of Voulet smiling approvingly as a captured woman is being raped by his soldiers, and the image of captured men of the village, buried up to their necks, being beheaded by horse-riding soldiers in what looks like a macabre polo sport. This series of images together with those of mutilated corpses hung on trees, (especially that with an old-man mumbling away absent-mindedly beneath his hung relatives), images which vividly recall those blacks hanging from trees in the old South of the United States, and the habit of requesting the severed palms of war victims, as evidence of having killed the enemy, graphically capture the atrocities of the Voulet-Chanoine force.

The theme of British/French rivalry during the period of colonial conquest in Africa is explored in the scene showing the arrival of the Sultan of Sokoto's envoy at Voulet's camp. The Sultan, out of personal disdain for Sarraounia's refusal to convert to Islam with her subjects, sent the envoy to lead the Voulet-Chanoine force to Lugu, the seat of Sarraounia's kingdom, as punishment. But Voulet, wary and suspicious of the offer of assistance from a British subject, concludes that the envoy is a British spy and orders his execution. Only the timely intervention of his aide, Coulbaly, spares the man's life.

Apart from recounting the crimes of the Voulet-Chanoine expedition force, and eulogizing the resistance of Sarraounia and the Aznas, the film is also significant with respect to representing the nature of colonial conquest in Africa. We know, for instance, from the composition of the Voulet-Chanoine force that the army, which conquered Africa, was made up of African mercenary soldiers who were enlisted through a promise of sharing in colonial loot. In fact, from the composition of the force, one can reconstruct the entire history of post-colonial modern African armies, by tracing their present mercenary mentality, reflected in their corruption and lack of respect for democratic institutions, to the psychological make-up of its colonial precursors. Decades after independence, the armed forces in most post-colonial African countries are still constrained by the mercenary ethics that underlay their constitution.

Sarraounia contains several symbolisms and imagery, most of which help to locate and authenticate the work as a product of traditional pre-colonial African society. These symbolic elements are reflected both in the naming of African characters in the film and in the connotations which each name carry. Others are realized in the imagery invoked through figurative speech. For instance, most of the African names effectively help to locate the locale of action within the ambience of traditional Niger society, specifically among the Azna people. Thus names like Dawa, Baka, Gogue and Boka carry significant meaning in Hausa, the dominant language of the region. For example, Tandina has noted that

> in Hausa, *dawa* refers to the bush. When applied to a person, it signifies "master of the bush" and is often accompanied by the title "Mai." Baka means "bow" in Hausa; in *Sarraounia* [the literary text] it designates the leader of the warriors. Gogué is a stringed instrument; in Mamani's text, it becomes the name of the person who plays a stringed instrument. Boka is the equivalent of "sorcerer". Such names thrust us into the midst of Azna society. They tell us about the various professions and how these professions are organized. A particular person is in charge of each kind of activity. Some of the names (e.g., Dawa and Boka) also inform us about another important dimension of Azna society — religion, which is defined as a "religion of earth and nature." The person in charge of the earth, the Mai Dawa, has the task of dominating and taming nature. (Tandina: 29)

In the film, Dawa, Sarraounia's uncle, is represented as a master fetish-doctor who knows the secrets of various herbs and the cure for various ailments, in addition to being a retired warrior fully knowledgeable in war-tactics which he teaches Sarraounia. Baka, in the film, is an army general; a symbolization of his name which literally means a warrior. Mai Gogué (Abdoulaye Cisse) in the film is an accomplished poet-musician and court-historian. In Hausa language, "Mai Gougé" literally translates to mean one who plays the instrument called Gougé. Boka, on the other hand, is the court fetish-doctor. He is the one whom Sarraounia consults to seek the protection of the ancestors. All these not only designate professional origin but also mastery of one's profession.

Apart from characterization, a lot of symbolic elements are also invoked in the film through figurative speech, especially that of Sarraounia. Most of these symbols are trademark invocations of traditional African public discourse. The masters of this highly stylized form of speech are the griots, from whom other strata of society learn the art of public orature. For instance, in the exhortation speech, which Sarraounia gives in her palace, as preparations are being made for its defense, she refers to the invaders as "white locusts," a signification of plague by a swarm of insects. Their mercenary soldiers and collaborators are referred to as "wretched cringing dogs," again a signification of domestication and blind obedience. In literal terms, the soldiers are characterized as plain ignoramuses lured by promises of loot and lust for women. In general, while negative symbols are used to characterize the nature of the invading force and its collaborators, positive ones are applied in the characterization of Azna cultural symbols. For instance, the totem of the Azna kingdom is the panther, an animal that symbolizes agility and power. When this image is linked with the warrior caste, the panther image signifies pride and skill, and when applied to Sarraounia, it connotes royalty, skill, and bravery. The image of the panther is invoked through Gogué's song:

> I love you because you are my lover at night.
> I fear you because you are the greatest sorceress.
> I respect you because you are my queen.
> I adore you because you are my lord.
> I praise you because you are the strongest.
> You are the eye and the honor of the Azna.
> Sweet Sarraounia with talons of steel.
> You break your enemies as surely as
> The panther breaks the bones of his prey ....

This eulogy does not mean that Gogué is addressing Sarraounia as a lover. In his review of the film, James Leahy seemed to suggest that Baka quitted the services of Sarraounia he was envious of her new lover, the royal griot: "After the victory celebrations, her general and former lover, Baka quits her service, jealous of the *griot* (poet/musician) who now loves her." (Leahy, 1988: 8). In fact, the lyrics of the praise-song are paying homage to the multiple roles of Sarraounia as potential mother, great-sorcerer, queen and lord of the Aznas, who also is capable of being tough, swift and destructive toward her enemy-prey like a panther is notorious of. Images of benevolence and malevolence are used interchangeably in the lyrics. Baka deserts Sarraounia because as a proud warrior, he cannot bear the daily bombardment of praise-songs in honor of his wife. It is instructive to note too that pride and arrogance are trademarks of the warrior caste in Africa. They are natural born soldiers who later graduate into building their own kingdoms. When Baka deserts Sarraounia, he goes to do just that. He returns later on in the film to help defend Sarraounia because Lugu is his ancestral home and, he is still, after all, the general of the Aznas. Even if his kingdom were fully independent of Sarraounia's authority, he would still owe allegiance to his ancestral roots and still be obliged to defend it. Symbolism and imagery are therefore used in the film as additional figurative element of characterization. They help to create a contrastive framework which designates the invaders and their collaborators as evil and destructive, and Sarraounia as brave and courageous.

Beside symbolism and figurative speech, which are used to authenticate and historicize the text as a product of a particular age, African religious practices and belief-systems, are also foregrounded in the text. Of particular interest in this regard are the role of witchcraft, sorcery, and ancestral worship in African belief-systems. These are societies of rainmakers who are thought to be capable of invoking thunder on their enemies as part of psychological warfare. These fetish doctors are also thought to be capable of directing thunderbolts to their enemies in the privacy of their rooms. It is the awareness that Sarraounia possesses this knowledge that breaks the morale of the *tirailleurs*. They reason that the N'Komo woman is capable of delivering elemental forces of destruction at them whenever she pleases. Being a product of such a belief-system helps to reinforce a psychological frame of mind, predisposed towards actualization of the suggested effects. In fact, psychological warfare is Sarraounia's major weapon for defeating the invading army. Once the backbone of the force made up of predominantly African mercenary soldiers is broken, the French are forced into retreat. The significance placed on ancestral worship is also highlighted in Sarraounia's invocation of the name, Dogua, the name of the ancestral head of the Aznas, for protection. For instance, during the evacuation of the palace, even though Sarraounia's personal belongings are left behind, the camera momentarily captures items of ancestral worship being carried away into safety under the watchful guidance of the elders of the kingdom. The application of psychological warfare in the film climaxes in the incidents leading to the withdrawal of the troops from Lugu. Most of these incidents are extremely hilarious in the manner in which they set up the French officers for ridicule, besides offering momentary comic relief to the unfolding tragic events in the text.

The first of these incidents occur in the sequence where attempts by one of the French officers to defile an object of ancestral worship, as part of his attempts to demystify the effects of N'Komo on the *tirailleurs*, backfire. The sequence begins with the officer, leading a group of soldiers, stumbles upon the ancestral shrine of the kingdom. On seeing an ancestral mask hanging by the doorway, the soldiers begin to beat a retreat. The officer rebukes them, calling them cowards, for getting scared of the mask. He walks towards the mask, puts aside his army cap and wears it; making a cockerel sound and hopping about playfully toward the soldiers who respond to his play-act by laughing. Suddenly, he begins to scream and tears frantically at his face as if the mask has become stuck to his face. As he falls down crying, the soldiers flee shouting 'N'Komo' and remarking that a mask on an albino (white body) signifies an abomination. Albinos are extremely light-skinned children begotten by Africans. They are dedicated to the gods of the community where they are born as shrine slaves and objects of ritual sacrifice. As the officer reels on the ground crying, there follows a series of cut away to reaction shots where we find old women priestesses who guard the shrine, fleeing in horror. In another cut away, we find the sultan's envoy tied to a stake close to the scene shouting "Bi similah!" in prayer for protection. When the officer finally tears the mask from his face, we find it full of red soldier ants, a furious tropical African specie notorious for their extremely hurtful sting. In terms of a narrative explanation of why the mask was loaded with soldier-ants, Dr. Henric (Didier Sauvegrain) tells us that the ants had been attracted to the mask by the scent of blood. But whatever the explanation, it seems like retributive justice for the officer's derisive treatment of traditional African object of religious worship. And in a film where the French officers are supposed to put up a face by playing gods from the sky sent, according to Voulet, to rule over the blacks, it certainly is a literal de-masking of a god when the soldiers see their officer crying like a child.

The next incident takes place in the sequence preceding the troops' withdrawal from Lugu. The sequence begins with a leftward tracking shot, in the scene where the soldiers debate the possibility of a mutiny to force Voulet to withdraw from Lugu. Though the mutiny is precipitated by the loss of war booties, their ulterior motive is fear of Sarraounia's N'Komo. When Coulibaly walks into the impending mutiny and tries to dissuade the soldiers from doing so, they set upon him, and he flees for his dear life and alerts Voulet who is drawing up an ordinance map for an attack on Sarraounia. While Coulibaly breathlessly reports to Voulet about the ongoing mutiny, the latter calmly instructs the former to get some of the loot taken from Sarraounia's palace so that he can use it to bribe the soldiers. This thin veneer of calmness with which Voulet receives the news of the mutiny will later contrast with his near deranged demeanor towards the end of the sequence. In the debate that takes place before the arrival of Voulet on the scene, we find that far from accepting Corporal Traore's arguments that they betrayed Samory Toure — the king of the Mali Empire who was deposed and exiled by the French — because they deserted him, the soldiers are only interested in forcing Voulet to withdraw from Lugu for fear of N'Komo.

When Voulet arrives on the scene, he tries some of the old tricks, which he had used to secure their loyalty in the past — e.g. promises of larger rewards — and finds that the soldiers are not ready to compromise. Tinga, one of the princes who enlisted in French colonial force after he had been disinherited, captures the soldiers' level of anxiety about Sarraounia's N'Komo when he informs Voulet that her fetish is evil: "It eats our hearts in our chest. It's already made some of us impotent, sir!" Gradually the events build up into a climax when Voulet, in desperation to win back the confidence of the troops, decks himself up as a woman in Sarraounia's clothes and jewelry and tries to simulate an erotic scene, in order to rekindle the soldiers' lust for women. In a crane shot taken from above the head of the soldiers, we find Voulet standing rather inappropriately behind the soldiers instead of being in front of them, invoking a wide variety of booty and women to tempt them and win back their confidence, in an act which he himself likens to self-clowning since the soldiers do not pay attention to him. As he tries to end his improvisation, he experiences temporal loss of self-control not dissimilar to that which the officer who wore an ancestral mask had in the earlier mentioned incident. It begins as an entrapment within the costumes of Sarraounia, which he had just used as a figurative mask for improvisation.

After dismissing the soldiers and agreeing to withdraw, he begins to kick at the dust in front of him in an uncontrollable frenzy. Gradually, he experiences temporal loss of self-control. Chanoine then moves to him and calms him down by removing from his neck Sarraounia's piece of jewelry, which is narrativized as the object responsible for his entrapment and temporal loss of self-control. As he is being de-robed of his improvisatory accoutrements, Voulet remarks: "I'm alright, Julian, I'm French!" This remark is an important act of self-absolution in traditional African belief-systems. Of course, Voulet does not realize the significance of his utterance, but an African spectator knowledgeable in African belief-systems will know that his utterance amounts to an act of self-absolution. In traditional African belief-systems, if a stranger feels the malevolent forces of his host community are punishing him unjustly, he can invoke, verbally, the principle of self-absolution to protect himself, and the mere pronouncement of this principle can help neutralize the malevolent forces. Besides providing momentary comic relief, the literal de-masking of the French officers also help to remove the thin veneer of the superiority complex which the officers had put up till now and exposes them in their plain human idiosyncrasies. These two sequences also marked the beginning of total breakdown in discipline and morale among the troops.

Beside belief-systems, symbolic elements of worship and social ranking, the question of name and naming, and the rhetoric of traditional African public discourse, the other most noticeable elements of authentication of pre-colonial African culture in the film are architectural structures and costumes. The rectangular mud buildings with flat mud roofs and mud walls enclosing large courtyards dotted with individual huts are authentic architectural structures of the Savannah belt in pre-colonial West Africa. Even in these days of modern apartment-blocks, flats, mansions, etc., this age-old architectural practice still predominates in the older sections of most cities located in the Savannah belt. The costumes are also authentication of what was worn by most people of the region at the time. The only exception in this regard is the flash-forward scenes towards the end of the film where we find youths dressed in contemporary youth clothing. This flash-forward is of course meant to relate the past events to the present. After Sarraounia and her historical train had moved off screen, the scene reverts to an ordinary contemporary youth playground, a figurative way of linking past events to the present with an underlining catch that the youth of today needs to learn from the lessons of history so as to avoid the mistakes of their forefathers. Besides this last scene, the costumes worn by most people in this film are what people still predominantly wear across West Africa today. This traditional clothing comprises: *agbada*, *buba* and *shokoto* with hand woven caps, etc., for men and *buba*, *wrapper*, etc., for women. Modern designs of these clothing are of course much more varied and glamorous nowadays. Traditional clothing, and, office wear which is made up of mostly Western clothing and designs, form the thoroughfare of contemporary West African fashion.

All these elements of cultural authentication help to build up an idyllic image of pre-colonial Africa as a self-sufficient society built on subsistence farming, trade and animal husbandry. The jostling for spheres of influence by traditional African rulers, represented through inter-ethnic rivalries, also indicates that a process of nation building was on across Africa at the onset of colonial conquest. The Sokoto Caliphate which stretched beyond the boundaries of the modern day Federal Republic of Nigeria, the Benin Empire of Oba Ovonramwen Nogbaisi, the Oyo kingdom, and Kanem Borno Empire, all of which form parts of present day Nigeria, was an indication of this going process. The Ashanti kingdom of Ghana and the Mali Empire of Samory Toure also covered land areas far larger than most of the modern states constituted by European powers in the nineteenth century. Most of the traditional rulers of the kingdoms cited and indeed many others across Africa still rule their subjects beyond the boundaries of modern African states. Perhaps, this is why the film represents the current boundaries of African countries as forcible creations carved up in blood.

With respect to characterization, the persona of Sarraounia is accorded privilege status. Most actions revolve around her personality and narrative details related to her childhood and Spartan up-bring is furnished in the narrative flashback sequences. Despite the early loss of her mother, the image of the young Sarraounia, which comes across in the flashback sequences, is that of a person who had a happy childhood. When the flashback begins, we find her playing in the company of her age-mates. But in keeping with her characterization as a born warrior, she is cast in a role of leader among them, and the game they are playing is appropriately the war game of throwing a spear, a figurative foreshadowing of her future role as warrior-queen. Her teenage years are spent mostly in the company of her uncle who teaches her the art of governance, traditional warfare and herbal healing methods. But the rigid masculine role into which her uncle casts her through verbal indoctrination and physical training later creates in her a major character flaw. This character flaw is reflected in her inability to sustain a marital affair with Baka. Besides this flaw however, the overall image of Sarraounia, which emerges in the film, is that of a resolute ruler determined to protect and preserve the freedom and liberty of her people from both internal colonialism of the sort posed by the authority of the Sultan of Sokoto and external colonialism represented by the French colonial expedition force.

Her reputation in sorcery and warfare bestows upon her the image of a dangerous and uncontrollable woman, a *femme fatale* whose name strikes terror in the minds of her enemies. The Sarraounia persona is not a strange one to the African continent. In fact, Africa had always had very powerful women. Her persona therefore recalls such other equally powerful historical figures that ruled with iron hands and were fiercely independent like Queen Amina of Zaria and Queen Ida of Benin. Female warrior figures, which readily come to mind, are the dreaded, ferocious single-breasted women soldiers of the Dahomey kingdom referred to in history as the Amazons. Sarraounia is also the only African character granted spectatorial spatial closeness and narrative authority throughout the film. She is constantly shot in medium close-ups, most of the times to highlight her facial beauty and femininity that contrasts sharply with her image of sorcerer and irrepressible warrior. At other times, especially in the sequences preceding the attack on Lugu, this spatial closeness helps to exteriorize her internal anxieties about the impending attack by the

Voulet-Chanoine force. All the other African characters, including the traditional rulers, are not granted spatial closeness. They are shot flatly, without depth, mostly in medium long shots trained at theatricalized ensemble acting that gives no room for individualized characterization. Occasionally, when they are shot in medium shots, it is accompanied by quick cuts that prevent intimacy of any sort.

The only other character granted comparable but unequal spatial closeness in the film is Captain Voulet. For instance, in the withdrawal sequence, he is captured in a rather long reflective mood which begins, first, as his voice-over commentary upon the disorganized and disorderly column withdrawing from Lugu, which towards the end of the film contrasts radically with the orderly and disciplined column which we saw at the beginning of the film. The voice-over commentary is later anchored through a cut to a medium close-up of Voulet in a thoughtful mood. Incidentally, this is the only case of individualized character-narration — effected in this case, through mental process subjective reflection — in the film. As a result of the spatial closeness effected through Voulet's reflective (almost regretful) mood, towards the end of the film, he cuts the image of a tragic figure overrun by personal greed for power and fame. However, in terms of the relation of narrative authority through spatial positioning with respect to other characters in the film, especially in dialogue scenes involving him and Chanoine or Coulibaly, he is shot in the classical dialogue format of shot/reverse shot which does not transit into dollying into medium close-ups which would otherwise privilege him over the other character with whom he is involved in dialogue. The only character granted this form of spatial privilege is Sarraounia. This occurs in the dialogue scene involving her and her fetish doctor, Boka, when she goes to inquire about the outcome of the impending attack, and in the scene of her first encounter with Baka when he returns to help defend Lugu.

As a result of this spatial generosity and non discriminating spatial articulation in relation to the characterization of the main protagonist and antagonist in the film, Sarraounia and Voulet respectively, character-subjectivity in *Sarraounia* is realized more through the quality and tone of verbal discourse and narrative actions than through spatial articulation. For instance, we get a sense of Voulet's cruelty and murderous predisposition not through spatial distortions or make-up meant to highlight his deviousness but through his verbal denigration of Africans and devaluation of African lives through narrative actions. Likewise, we get a sense of Sarraounia's greatness and heroism, more, through her fiery exhortatory speeches, magical powers and participation in battle scenes, than through forms of spatial articulations.

In an interview which he granted James Leahy in 1988, Hondo, relating his editing style in the film, states that "I always try to use dialectical montage, to put the spectator in a dangerous situation, to keep the spectator questioning, awake" (Leahy, 1988:10). This form of dialectical editing stands out in the way in which sequences are juxtaposed in *Sarraounia* to create levels of contrast, irony, and critical awareness in the spectator. For instance, the sequence dealing with the representation of the nineteenth century division of Africa among the European powers, recounted through voice-over narration and the symbolic splitting of a sculptured map of the continent, ends with Moslems hastily fleeing a prayer ground. This is immediately followed by a cut to a full frontal view of Voulet and Chanoine at the head of the expedition force. This juxtaposition uses the current image to explain the hasty evacuation of the prayer ground in the last sequence as well as prefiguring what follows. In the next sequence that follows this one, we find an anxious Sarraounia moving restlessly about in her palace. We will later learn that the cause of her anxiety is the news of the invading army of the preceding sequence. In another sequence, the traditional ruler of a besieged village who thought he could spare his village's destruction by offering to play host to the invading force, has his efforts crowned, ironically, with the destruction he sought to avoid. Later in the film, when Serkin Arewa tries to convince his son, the Prince of Matankari, that by playing host to the invaders they will spare their families the horrors of war, the earlier failed attempt of such an overture presents a contrastive nullification of Serkin Arewa's optimism. Furthermore, during the war of attrition between Sarraounia and the Voulet-Chanoine force, the editing pattern becomes much more dialectical as it relates alternating montages of activities within both camps. A classic example of this form of editing is shown in the scene of both camps set in the forest outlying Lugu. The first of these alternating montages begins with a tracking shot, following Voulet and his troops, from screen left to right, as they search the outskirts of the forest fully aware of their vulnerability within the area. In an alternating montage, deep inside the forest, we find Sarraounia, followed by another tracking shot, this time, one moving in opposite direction, from screen right to left, as she challenges Voulet and his force to dare move into the forest.

Through this combination of alternating montages related through a complex form of narration incorporating omniscient narration, narrative flashback, voice-over narration, and subjective reflection, *Sarraounia* unveils a multiplicity of contesting voices and levels of meaning, all tied to the divergent opinions of various groups within the text, and all bearing upon the theme of resistance to colonialism advanced in the film. These contesting voices and opinions about the emergent conflict of external colonial invasion, are also reflected, at the linguistic level, as I earlier noted, in the internal division and jostle for power within Africa by rival ethnic groups. However, whereas before the advent of colonialism the struggle for power and influence within the region raged between the Djoula (spoken in Sarraounia's kingdom), Peuhl (spoken by the Fulani) and the Tamashek (spoken by the Tuareg), with the advent of colonialism, other levels of power, represented by the French and the British, impose a new linguistic order. In addition to the contending indigenous languages, the seeds of new linguistic hegemonies are signified in the emergence of French and British colonial authorities. The emergence of these colonial authorities also signifies the advent of new linguistic realities — for example, that represented in the colonial and post-colonial eras, by the constitution of new subjects caught in the ambivalent split between indigenous languages and imperial languages, on the one hand, and their corruption such as French, Pidgin French, English, Pidgin English on the other.

In sum, as earlier noted, the image of Sarraounia, as constructed in the film, is very much in close keeping with the narrative traditions of the epic. She is an idealized heroine whose character flaws are overlooked in an attempt to foreground her heroic resistance to French imperialism. Furthermore, her story covers only an aspect of the overall events leading to the constitution of the modern state of Niger by the French. Her resistance, in effect, did not alter the course of history. It is celebrated here as an invocation of an existing ancient African tradition of resistance to all forms of foreign domination.

Background Notes on Ousmane Sembène

Ousmane Sembène was born on 1st January, 1923, in Ziguinchor, a town in the Casamance region of Senegal. He spent most of his childhood under the tutelage and care of his maternal uncle, Abdou Rahmane Diop, a devout Muslim and Koranic school teacher from whom he learnt a lot about oral African history, culture and tradition. Following the death of his uncle in 1935, Sembène was put under the care of a relation who lives in Dakar. Here, for a while, he pursued his elementary school education, which he later abandoned toward the end of his studies because of disagreements with his headmaster. At the age of fourteen, he began to try his hands in various trades, working first as a mechanic and as a carpenter before undertaking apprenticeship in masonry. During this period also, he began to show interest in artistic endeavors by participating in local amateur theatrical activities, and concerts, as well as attending performances by professional griots, local historical raconteurs, from whom he learnt a lot about African legends and great historical epics, and traditional storytelling techniques which have immensely influenced both his literary outputs and his films.

At the age of nineteen, Sembène joined the French colonial army at the outbreak of the Second World War and fought for four years in campaigns both in Africa and in Europe. After his discharge from the military in 1947, he participated in the Dakar-Niger railroad strike for better wages and improved working conditions. The strike, which lasted from October 1947 to March 1948, later furnished him with materials for his first major novel, *God's Bits of Wood*. His participation in the strike also signaled the beginning of his political and labor union activism, both of which he devoted a lot of attention and active participation during his stay in France. After the strike, Sembène immigrated to France where he worked as a factory worker at the Citroen motor factory near Paris before moving on to Marseilles where he became a labor union leader while working at the Dockyard. He subsequently actively participated in both the political and cultural debates that followed the emergence of the Negritude Movement, as well as participating in the First International Congress of Black Writers and Artists held in Paris in 1956. Sembène is however one of the very few black Francophone writers who right from the beginning of the Negritude Movement criticized its key concepts (Ghali: 52). In 1957, he wrote *O Pays, Mon Beau Peuple!* (Oh My Country, My Beautiful People), a novel about a Senegalese war veteran who, with his French wife, returns to his native village and subsequently embarks upon self-help development projects through organization of the peasants and application of modern agricultural techniques to farming. This was followed by the publication in 1960 of his major work, *Les Bouts de Bois de Dieu* (*God's Bits of Wood*), an epic novel based on his personal fictional account of the 1947 Dakar-Niger railroad strike. Since then, he has published a collection of short stories, *Voltaique* (*Tribal Scars*, 1962) and novels such as *L' Harmattan* (1964), *Le Mandat* (*The Money Order*, 1965), *Vehi Ciosane ou Blanche-Genese* (*White Genesis*, 1965), and *Xala* (1974). Sembène has made some of these novels such as *Le Mandat* and *Xala* successful into films.

The year 1961 was a watershed in the writing career of Sembène. By that year, he had come to the conclusion that no matter how popular his novels were, only the elite who can read and write would have access to them since the majority of the populace in his country, as indeed elsewhere in Sub-Saharan Africa, were illiterates. His search for a popular form that will bear the same themes of colonial atrocities and exploitation by the French and the neo-colonial corruption and bad governments by African elite — themes which have pre-occupied him in his novels — led him to opt for the cinema. In an interview, which he granted Teshome Gabriel in 1975, Sembène explained the events that led to his decision to opt for filmmaking thus:

> before becoming a filmmaker, I'd already written several books. I think that I am a committed writer, and I'm not ashamed to say so. My commitment is to raise awareness and bring the people to change their situation. I live in Africa, and no matter what happens tomorrow, I will not go into exile. But the problem when I was writing books was that, I was only known by the elite minority. When I talked with the masses, some had heard about me or they had seen my picture in the newspaper but other than that, that is all they knew about me. And so the problem for me was to get involved in an art like cinema, which has a larger audience. (Gabriel, 1979: 112)

In 1961 Sembène was awarded scholarship by the USSR government to study film in that country. This enabled him to study filmmaking for two years at the Gorki Studios in Moscow, under such distinguished teachers as Mark Donskoi and Sergei Gerasimov. In his return to Africa in 1963, filmmaking began to take predominance over his writing career. On the year he returned, the government of Mali commissioned him to make a short documentary, on the Songhai Empire, *L' Empire Sonhrai*. Next, he shot his first feature, *Borom Sârret* (1963) — a film that deals with the misfortunes of a cart driver in Dakar — produced by his production company, Domirev. In 1964 Sembène adapted *Vehi Ciosane ou Blanche-Genese*, a novel that he published the following year, into film. The adaptation however seemed not to have succeeded because the resulting thirty-five minute film, *Niaye* (1964), was never released. His first successful feature length film, *La Noire de* (Black Girl, 1960) - which deals with the sufferings and eventual suicide of a young African maid in France - is also presently considered Black Africa's first feature length film. This has since been followed by highly rated works such as *Mandabi* (The Money Order, 1968), *Taw* (1970), a documentary on youth unemployment in Dakar, shot for the National Council of the Church of Christ, and *Emitai* (1972) which deals with Second World War revolt by the people of Diola of the Casamance region, against French colonial authority. Next, *Xala* (1974), a social satire on modern African elite and the neo-colonial state, and *Ceddo* (1977), which deals with efforts made by Africans to contain the spread and influence of Arab and Islamic culture in Africa during the early days of European advent on the continent, then followed. In 1988, Sembène and his co-director, Thierno Faty Sow, revisited events of the Second World War in *Camp de Thiaroye*, a film which deals with the December 1944 French massacre of West African infantry men in Dakar who were awaiting their discharge from the army at the end of their tour of duty. This was followed by, *Guelwaar* (1992), which critiques the politics of foreign aid in Africa. His latest film, *Faat Kine* (2000) deals with the issue of women's quest for self-realization and independent agency in male dominated modern African society, an issue, which Sembène has consistently exploited, in detail in works such as *La Noire de*, *Mandabi*, and *Xala*.

A Critical Reading of Ousmane Sembène and Thierno Faty Sow's Camp de Thiaroye

The events represented in *Camp de Thiaroye* are intricately tied to the overall political conflicts and intrigues that emerged during the Second World War between the supporters of General de Gaulle and his Free France Army, and the adherents of the fascist Vichy regime of Marshal Pétain. The Vichy regime had concluded an armistice with Germany in 1940 after the occupation of France, whereby the rump of France, Southern France, was left under French rule, with the understanding that her Empire would be neutral during the Second World War. As a result of this armistice, between 1940 and 1942, the French West African regime of Pierre Boisson, based in Dakar, appointed by the Vichy regime, was hostile to the Free France Army of de Gaulle and the Allies. Though German and Italian nationals were barred from French West African territories, so too were agents of General de Gaulle. But as French society was divided over the armistice in France, so too were overseas French administrators. The supporters of de Gaulle therefore continued surreptitiously to recruit troops in the region, through agents in neighboring Anglophone West African countries, despite Boisson's objections and sabotage of their efforts.

While French West Africa was partially neutralized due to Boisson's adherence to the terms of the armistice, the governments of French Equatorial Africa, led by Felix Eboue, the Guyanese Governor of Chad, revolted against the Vichy regime and rallied around de Gaulle. Through Chad, the pro-Vichy administrations in Cameroun and Gabon were quickly overthrown and pro-de Gaulle men installed. Soon afterward, Congo-Brazzaville switched over allegiance to de Gaulle and Felix Eboué was appointed Governor General of French Equatorial Africa with its base at Brazzaville. This switch in allegiance gave de Gaulle the much needed land-base for his Free France campaign. From his land base in Brazzaville, de Gaulle mobilized the whole of French Equatorial Africa through its northern access in Chad, with the help of the Allies in British West Africa, for the liberation of North Africa and the eventual push into mainland France itself.

While many French troops stationed in French West Africa were loyal to the Vichy regime and refused to participate in the liberation efforts of France, there were many West African volunteers who joined forces with de Gaulle in French Equatorial Africa and fought through North Africa into France. Most of the repatriated *tirailleurs*, Francophone African infantrymen, who were massacred in December 1944, were made up of both West African infantrymen and those from French Equatorial Africa. The acrimony that is reflected in *Camp de Thiaroye* between those that fought for the liberation of France like the *tirailleurs* and their commander, Captain Raymond, and the French troops based in Dakar who initially honored the armistice and who refused to fight, is borne of the conflicts between the supporters of General de Gaulle and those of the Vichy regime (Crowder, 1978: 268-281, Pedler, 1979: 46-65). The fact that the national film corporations of Senegal, Algeria and Tunisia funded the production, is itself, a tribute to the earlier mentioned co-operative efforts that led to the liberation of North Africa during the Second World War. While *Camp de Thiaroye* attacks the collaborative Vichy regime in Dakar and France, it does not spare de Gaulle either, because most of the massacres carried out by the French troops among the Diola people of the Cassamance region of Senegal during the Vichy regime — where both Sembène and the Sergeant-Major in the film, Diatta, come from — continued after the liberation of France and de Gaulle's assumption of power (Leahy, 1989: 271). The same is true of the massacre at Thiaroye Camp upon which the film is based. I have had to examine the background of events in French West Africa because they are necessary for a thorough comprehension of the tone of debates in *Camp de Thiaroye* between the resident French colonial force and the *tirailleurs* who fought for the liberation of France.

Camp de Thiaroye is an historical representation of the events that built up to the massacre on 1st December, 1944, of a group of repatriated *tirailleurs*, who were awaiting their discharge having completed their tours of duty. In November, 1944, a batch of such troops disembarks in Dakar, the capital of Francophone West Africa during the colonial period, and is camped at Thiaroye, the colonial army camp for the demobilization of troops that have completed their tour of duty prior to repatriation to their countries of origin. Some of these soldiers fought gallantly for the liberation of the mother country. Like the Allies whom they fought alongside, they suffered heavy casualties in battles, were taken prisoners of

war and many died from cold and hunger. One of them, Pays, was
a prisoner of war at Buchenwald where he lost his power of speech
due to torture. Others like Sergeant-Major Diatta, fought with the
Free France 1st Army from North Africa to the liberation of Paris
due to the compulsory extension of his enlistment period. In the
midst of all this suffering, they were additionally subjected to racial
discrimination, and at the end of their tour of duty, many of them
were in tattered army uniforms and the American military had to
donate uniforms to them before they are repatriated home.

On arrival at the port of Dakar, their liberal French
Commander, Captain Raymond, hands them over to the
commander of the resident French colonial force in Dakar, Major
Auguste, who in turn hands them over to Captain Labrousse, the
commandant of Thiaroye Camp. At the port, there is a great turn
out of relations and French citizens in Dakar, to welcome the
returning heroes. One of the highlighted relations at the port is that
of Sergeant-Major Diatta, made up of his maternal uncle, wife, and
their daughter, Bintu, chosen by his mother and his uncle as
Diatta's wife. Noting that his parents did not turn up to welcome
him, Diatta asks if all is well and his uncle informs him that their
village, Effok, was destroyed by the resident French troops and his
parents were among the casualties. Captain Raymond, who is
unaware of the sad news, joins Diatta after introducing himself to
Major Auguste and Captain Labrousse, in order to greet Diatta's
relations. Diatta introduces him to his uncle but when Raymond
attempts to shake hands with the uncle, he barely accepts
Raymond's handshake. When they arrive at the camp, his uncle's
wife and daughter, Bintu, pay him a visit. When they discover that
Diatta is married to a French woman and that the couple has a
daughter, they leave him in annoyance, protesting the morality of
his action.

The camp itself, where they are quartered is little better than a
concentration camp. It is built on an open stretch of land fenced
round by barbwires with four watchtowers located at four cardinal
points of the square-shaped camp, guarded continuously by troops.
To Pays who, had been a prisoner at Buchenwald, being kept in a
compound fenced round by barbwires with guarded watchtowers,
bring back nightmarish memories of tortures and executions at
Buchenwald. On their arrival at the camp, the first place he
wanders to is the barbwire fence, which he feels with his hand. He

is led gently away and assured by his co-patriot, Lance-Corporal Diarra that they are back in Africa. On-lookers at the scene comment that Pays lost his mind due to torture at Buchenwald. Throughout the film, he will be treated as a mental case and his advice will be disregarded. Camp life itself is restrictive. The food is poor and they have to protest before meat is included in their meal.

Obtaining his first pass, Diatta visits a local brothel cum pub, "Le Coq Hardi," in the European quarter of the city. At first he is well received because they think he is a black American with plenty of dollars to spend but when Diatta requests Pernod in French instead of Whisky, they realize he is a "native" and the woman who runs the brothel throws him out despite his protestation that he wants to have only a drink. Once out on the street, a local detachment of American military police on patrol, led by a black American, beat him up and arrests him because of his American uniform, thinking that he is an impostor. When the news of the incidence is received at Thiaroye Camp, Diatta's men, led by Lance-Corporal Diarra, take an America Sergeant visiting "Le Coq Hardi" hostage to secure his release. The French military is horrified when it learns that the soldier taken hostage is a white American, but since the American military is not aware where their man is kept, they have to release Diatta to secure his release. However, when the American military learns that Diatta has just returned from the war front, the black American military police goes to apologize to him and the case is closed.

Just as the camp is about to return to its daily routine of waiting for their discharge, another crisis emerges when the French military authorities in Dakar refuse to pay the troops the correct monetary exchange rate of 1000 French francs to 500 CFA francs. The military authorities insist they can only grant them an exchange rate of 1000 French francs to 250 CFA francs, suggesting moreover that the soldiers may have gotten their money by looting the corpses of their dead comrades in the battlefield. In addition, they also try to avoid paying the soldiers their allowances and gratuities by tricking them that they will be paid only when they arrive at their countries of origin. However, the troops, recollecting that that was how they were tricked in Paris by shifting the responsibilities for the payment of their discharge entitlements to Dakar, reject the authorities' offers. At a meeting called to discuss the matter by the Governor of Dakar and General Commanding

Officer of Francophone African colonial forces, Captain Raymond informs the officers that the troops were paid only part of their salaries in Morlaix before their departure for home — which is the money the military authorities are suggesting they stole by stripping corpses — that he sent a memorandum to the General who is himself presiding over the meeting. He also reminds them that the troops' counterparts in France have been paid all their entitlements. When Major Auguste and Captain Labrousse question the wisdom of paying "natives" such a large amounts of money, Captain Raymond argues that justice demands that they should honor their promises and pay the soldiers all their entitlements, adding that even though wars demand periods of austerity, France would not be rebuilt by swindling a thousand "natives."

The General, who refuses to heed Raymond's advice, goes to Thiaroye camp and tries to invoke military discipline to force the troops to accept his terms of payment. Disappointed that the General is determined not to pay them their gratuities, and that he has them only half the exchange rate for their money, the soldiers' revolt, takes the General hostage, and take over control of the camp. When Captain Labrousse and Major Auguste fail to secure the General's release, they send for their commanding officer, Captain Raymond. He too fails to secure the release of the General. In the end, the General tricks the soldiers by agreeing to pay them the correct exchange rate and their gratuities. The soldiers release him amidst jubilation.

Pays, who smells treachery behind the General's capitulation to their demands, take up his position as a sentry in one of the watchtowers. Once the General is out of the camp, he orders Captain Labrousse to withdraw all local support staff at the camp and level it out. The soldiers, unaware of the deadly maneuvers around them, celebrate their victory. Shortly after they have retired to bed Pays, from his post at the watchtower, sights motorized artillery moving into position around the camp. He hurries down and warns the soldiers that they are about to be bombarded. They misunderstand his gestures by thinking that he is saying that they are surrounded by German troops. He is angrily dismissed and they retire again to their blocks. At 3.00 am on 1st December, 1944, the camp is leveled by a barrage of bombardments. When the massacre is over, at daybreak, Captain Labrousse and Major Auguste report to the General that his orders have been executed. The General, in turn informs them that the Governor-General of Francophone Africa and the Colonial Minister approved his action. Meanwhile captain Raymond who is to return to France with another batch of *tirailleurs*, and quite unaware of the massacre, waits in vain for Diatta who promised to send coffee through him to his wife and daughter in Paris. Diatta's uncle and his daughter, Bintu, who bear the coffee to the port on the understanding that he would join them there, also wait in vain. The film ends on a freeze frame of Bintu shedding tears with the bag of coffee and a little baby doll fetish meant to scare away Diatta's wife, in her hands.

The plot of *Camp de Thiaroye* is a straightforward simple one, with conflicts emerging from time to time as the story unfolds. There are a number of sequences in the film that help to define the nature of relationship that existed between French colonial authorities and their African subjects during the Second World War. I will be examining some of these sequences in order to determine the nature of subjectivity constructed in respect of both African and European characters in the film. The sequences are: the opening sequence; arrival at Thiaroye camp and revelations about the cause of Pays' loss of speech; protest over inedible food; visit by Diatta's uncle, Bintu, and Captain Raymond's return of Diatta's novel; protest over refusal by the French military authorities to grant the soldiers the correct exchange rate and accusations regarding the source of the soldiers' money; and the taking of the General as hostage and the consequent massacre of the unarmed soldiers.

The opening sequence begins with an establishing shot of the port of Dakar packed with French citizens and relations of the returning soldiers. In the foreground of screen right we see two soldiers bearing a wounded colleague on a stretcher through the ship's gangway to an ambulance close to it at screen right. In front of the gangway is a truck waiting to take wounded soldiers to Thiaroye camp. In the mid frame space is an Army Band playing, with an Army jeep and a staff car adjacent to them. In the furthest background at extreme screen right, behind the Army Band, is a group of African relations of the soldiers; and at screen left, separate from the Africans, are French citizens. Next, there is a cut to a medium long shot of the frontal view of the ship's gangway taken from the foot of the gangway. We see the two soldiers bearing the stretcher, followed closely behind by two wounded soldiers and Captain Raymond. In a cut to a cross-section of the crowd, we notice that the French citizens are made up of mostly women and children, with many of them chanting "Long live France, Long live de Gaulle!" in honor of his role in the liberation of France. At the end of the focus on the crowd, there is a cut to captain Raymond reporting to Major Auguste and captain Labrousse. Captain Labrousse, looking at the disembarking soldiers, complains at the irregularity of their kits, and Raymond informs him that if the American military had not donated uniforms to the soldiers, they would have arrived in rags. This sequence is significant for three reasons. First, colonial public space is divided along racial lines. The Africans and the French citizens occupy different arches of the reception venue. Second, the ironical injustice suffered by African infantry men who went to fight for the liberation of France from German occupation, and who, upon completing the task, would have returned home in tattered uniforms if the American military had not donated uniforms to them. It is ironical because one would have expected that as a people under foreign occupation, the French would, irrespective of the status of their liberators, in this instance, the Africans were French subjects, appreciate their assistance rather than treat them shabbily. The film stresses the point that the treatment meted out to the African infantry men was a deliberate one because, whereas, the French military refused to supply those returning from the warfront with uniforms, at the end of the film, those replacing the demobilized soldiers are supplied uniforms. Third, the tragic experiences of individual soldiers are narrated. For instance, we know that Pays became deaf and dumb from torture in Buchenwald, and Diatta will soon learn that his parents were killed in an operation carried out by the French colonial force in Senegal.

Of the disembarking soldiers, apart from a momentary focus on the deaf and dumb Private Pays and Lance-Corporal Diarra, only Sergeant-Major Diatta is given special emphasis. When Diatta disembarks he is followed by a brief pan towards screen left that ends with his embrace of his uncle, and the uncle's introduction of his wife and daughter to Diatta. On noticing Diatta greeting his relations, Captain Raymond, who had been standing with Major Auguste and Captain Labrousse in the background of screen left, a little distance away from the family, walks across to greet them. Diatta introduces him to the family and then Raymond asks him how they greet in their village in Diola and he is told. But when he stretches out his hand to greet Diatta's uncle, the uncle hesitantly takes his hand. Noticing that his presence is not welcome, Raymond excuses himself. Diatta who is surprised at his uncle's behavior asks if all is well at Effok, their village, and in response to the question, his uncle's wife and her daughter, Bintu, clasp their arms across their shoulders in a mournful gesture and turn their back to Diatta, to signify that all is not well. When he asks his uncle what the problem is, he tells him that he will give him detail information later. The information which is later given to Diatta when he is visited at Thiaroye camp by his uncle's wife and daughter, Bintu, is that in 1942, their village was burnt down by the resident French colonial troops and that his parents were part of the casualties of the massacre. Though the cause of the massacre at Effok is not given in this film, in an earlier one, *Emitai*, Sembène gives the cause of the massacre during the Second World War in the village of Effok, in the Cassamance region of Senegal, as resistance to forced enlistment into the French colonial army and requisition for farm produce by the French military. Even before the outbreak of the Second World War obligatory forced labor was a tool of French colonial administration. For instance, Crowder informs us that

> prior to the Second World War, French West Africa had been economically and politically dominated by the metropolis. In the political sphere, apart from the *Quatre Communes* of Senegal, no African had rights other than a small group of *citoyen*, numbering not more than 2,136 in 1936. The overwhelming majority of the population was classified as *sujets* or subjects, who came under the harsh codes of the *indigenant* or code of administrative justice whereby they could be imprisoned without trial by the administration. It also subjected them to compulsory military service, obligatory forced labor, compulsory cultivation of crops and above all made any form of political activity all but impossible. (Crowder, 1978: 268-269)

As a result of the policy of forced requisition for farm produce, most Senegalese either resisted farming or resorted to hiding their farm produce. The disruption of farming activities in France after the outbreak of the Second World War also further exacerbated this policy. The tradition then was for the troops to raid the villages in search of food. It was during one of such raids, when the people of Effok refused to surrender their farm produce, that the village was sacked. In an interview which Sembène granted Noureddine Ghali in 1976, he makes the point that as far as Africa was concerned there was no major difference in policy towards Africa between the fascist regime of Marshal Petain under whose government the massacre at Effok was carried out, and that of the liberator General de Gaulle whose government sanctioned the massacre at Thiaroye camp in December, 1944. As he puts it,

> for us, who were then the colonized, Petain and De Gaulle were the same thing, even if young people today know there is a difference between them. The story of the soldiers killed in Senegal is De Gaulle; the story of Algeria in 1945 is De Gaulle; the story of Madagascar is De Gaulle: why do people want De Gaulle presented as a hero or super-hero? . . Where I come from, he was a colonialist and he behaved as such. (Ghali: 48)

This theme that bars distinction between Petain and De Gaulle in respect of their African policies is fully exploited by Sembène and Sow in *Camp de Thiaroye*. In the sequence that deals with this argument in some detail, which will be analyzing shortly, Diatta draws an analogy between the Nazi massacre in the French village of Oradour-Sur-Glane and that of the French colonial troops in the Senegalese village of Effok. Captain Raymond, with whom he debates this issue, takes a rather defensive stance by arguing that there is no justification for drawing a comparison between what he calls Nazi barbarism and the dictates of the French Army. Diatta, on his part, counters Raymond's attempts at differentiation by stating that the armies in the cases in question were colonial armies and that they have the same mentality. The opening sequence thus highlights some of the ethical issues related to Franco-African relationship that will be fully exploited later in the film. It also highlights the dilemma of the French liberals like Captain Raymond, caught in the crossfire between the excesses of a fascist colonial regime and the response of the victims of the regime to French people interested in cultivating genuine relationship with Africans.

The next sequence I would like to examine is that which deals with the official reception of the soldiers by the commandant of Thiaroye Camp, Captain Labrousse. The sequence begins with the reception of the soldiers and ends with Pays' subjective flashback. The scenes I will be focusing on are those that deal with Pays' experiences at Buchenwald and the relevance of those experiences to the views later expressed by Labrousse concerning African prisoners of war in German concentration camps. The first scene that gives the spectator an intimate knowledge of the Pays' character begins at the end of the commandant's address to the soldiers at the parade ground. As the soldiers disperse to their various blocks, there is a cut to Pays moving almost in a trance-like state toward screen left, followed by a slow pan, with a mouth organ improvised sound-effect signifying impending danger in the sound track. Towards the end of the pan, we notice that the object of Pays' focus is a watchtower guarded by a sentry. Next there is a cut to Pays as he shifts his attention to the barbwire fence of the camp, followed by a close-up point-of-view shot of him as he moves closer to the fence, looks at it, and at the guards at the watch towers in both off screen left and right. Gradually he begins to turn around at the same position to get a total view of the four guards guarding the watchtowers. With the sound effects, Pays' scrutiny of the security arrangements of the camp gives one a sense of foreboding danger. This is an army demobilization camp fenced by barbwire with a single gate and four strategically located watchtowers guarded regularly around the clock.

We will later be told that Pays was a prisoner of war at Buchenwald, where he lost his power of speech due to torture. As Pays digests the security arrangements of the camp, there is a cut to a group of soldiers carrying their bags from the truck that brought them from the port. This is followed by a cut to Lance-Corporal Diarra and a group of soldiers carrying Sergeant-Major Diatta's belongings to his quarter. As Diatta opens the door for the soldiers, he notices that Diarra is carrying two kits and asks him why he is carrying a double kit. Diarra informs him that one belongs to Pays. Next, there is a cut to Pays moving forward to feel the barbwire fence. As he does this the soldiers in the blocks overlooking where Pays is standing come out of their blocks to watch the scene. Diarra joins him by the fence and tries to comfort him. He bends down, fetches some sand and pours it at the back of Pays' palm, telling him that they are now on African soil and assuring him that they are not in a concentration camp, that Buchenwald is over. While Diarra is comforting him, Pays continues examining the camp like a man in a trance. Next, there is a cut to two soldiers looking at the scene. One of them comments that Pays' experiences at Buchenwald have cracked him up a bit. In a cut back to Diarra and Pays, Diarra continues robbing the sand slowly at the back of Pays' palm while telling him that he should feel the warm soil of Africa, that soon they will go back home to see their mothers and fathers in their village. He gives Pays his kit to carry and leads him gently away from the fence.

The next immediate scene, which also focuses on Pays, begins with an establishing shot of a group of soldiers bathing in a communal bath. A pan follows them from screen left to right, ending in a pullback to a long shot of the bath. Next, there is cut to a medium close-up of a lone soldier bathing under one of the rows of showers, and a cut to a group of soldiers in a single file washing their clothes in washbasins in front of the bath. This is followed by a cut to two soldiers preparing to hang their clothes. As they move toward the barbwire fence to dry the clothes, they are followed by a pan toward screen left. Just as they are about to hang the clothes on the fence, Pays dressed in complete German trooper gear with helmet on, blocks their way since he imagines that the barbwire fence may be connected to live current. He gestures at them to look at the guard on the watchtower. Instead of trying to understand what Pays is communicating to them, they beat a retreat, having misinterpreted his gestures to be antagonistic. One of them comments that Pays spent too long a time in German concentration camps. He advises his colleagues that they should leave Pays alone or he might fight them because he is completely crazy. When Pays notices that they are not taking note of what he is trying to explain to them, he simply stretches out his hands in a crucifix-like fashion to block their path and growls at them.

As they walk away, there is a cut to a medium close up of Pays accompanied by martial drums and the sound of the boots of storm troopers marching. Next, there is a cut to a medium close-up of the side view of him, displaying the "SS" sign on his helmet. As he turns his head slowly to look at the guard at the watchtower in the background towards screen left, there is a cut to a flashback scene full of memories of his days at Buchenwald. The flashback scene, which is shot in black and white, begins with a medium close-up of the side view of a lone German trooper maintaining the same pose as Pays' at the beginning of the transition into the flashback. Next, there is a cut to man hanging on a barbwire fence accompanied by a bust of gunfire. This is followed by a cut to a side view of the man hanging on the fence with the fence stretching out into a vanishing point in the background where we see the silhouettes of parading guards. The flashback scene ends with a cut to a group of prisoners of war sleeping on the bare ground of the camp.

The importance of these two scenes lie in the fact that they totally contradict a statement which Captain Labrousse will later make at a meeting called by the General at army headquarters to discuss the rate at which to exchange the soldiers' money and matters related to payment of their gratuities. At that meeting, Labrousse makes a statement to the effect that he was sure that the soldiers may have been subjected to good treatment and manipulated or even paid by the Nazis or the Bolsheviks to destabilize the Empire, otherwise they would not have survived their stay in the concentration camps. Raymond, who is peeved by the cruel remark, reminds him that as far as Hitler was concerned, Jews, Communists, Freemasons, Gypsies, and Blacks, were all earmarked for elimination. The example of Pays, who lost his speech power due to torture at Buchenwald, makes Labrousse's remark look ridiculously fascist. In this sequence as in many others, he equates any opposition to the policies of French colonial authorities as evidence that the soldiers have been brainwashed to revolt against France by her enemies. The two scenes are also significant for other reasons. First, they privilege Pays' subjectivity because he is shot mostly, in close-ups and medium close-ups, which grant spectatorial accessibility to him. Second, even though he cannot speak, his point of view is put across, through his subjective flashback. In the flashback scenes, the spectator is made to experience the horrors of Buchenwald through his memory recall, thereby making the spectator to empathize with him. Besides, Pays is the only character in the film that is granted narrative authority through subjective flashback. In the case of Diatta, even though the spectator is granted spatial accessibility to him through the use of close-ups and medium close-ups, especially, in the scene where he gives a forceful long speech when they are accused by the French officers of acquiring the money they want to exchange by stripping corpses in the warfront, his internal anxieties are externalized only once in the film, when he writes his wife.

With respect to imagery, one can give several interpretations to Pays' possession and usage of the German army uniform. First, the possession of the uniform can be interpreted as a war memorabilia, and as a sign of bravery. In traditional African societies, the numbers of uniforms and charms of opponents in a warrior's possession measure a warrior's worth. One interpretation could be that Pays' possession of the army uniform is in recognition of this tradition. Second, African Second World War veterans have a lot of respect for the discipline, ruthless efficiency and fighting spirit of German soldiers. Since, Pays always wears the German army uniform or only the helmet in situations requiring vigilance, one interpretation could be that wearing the uniform is a signification for alertness and ruthless efficiency. Third, one could interpret the imagery of the German army uniform as a satire on the barbarism of the Second World War.

With respect to the causes of conflicts in the film, evidence from the film indicates that the soldiers' protests are reactions to the policies of the French colonial authorities. A typical example is the cause of conflict between the soldiers and the authorities in the sequence dealing with the soldiers' protests over the bad meal served them at the camp. The sequence begins with the soldiers rejecting the meal because it contains no meat and it is watery, and ends with a *marabout* slaughtering a sheep for their own meal. The scene, which will be examined, is that which deals with the arrival and inspection of the meal by Captains Labrousse and Raymond, after they have been phoned by Lieutenant Pierre. Before their arrival, the soldiers had protested to the cook, who informs them that portions of meat are given to soldiers in accordance with racial and class gradation, a gradation which has whites at the top and the *tirailleurs* at the bottom. The scene begins with Captains Labrousse and Raymond driving into the camp, followed by a cut to the soldiers at their dining shed. The three officers, Pierre, Labrousse and Raymond, join the soldiers at the shed. As they inspect the food they are followed by a leftward tracking shot. Toward the end of the track, one of the soldiers attempts to show his bowl of meal to Captain Labrousse, who pushes it back onto the table as they move on. Next, they move toward the kitchen at extreme screen left, where Labrousse asks the cook why the soldiers refuse to eat. The cook tells him he does not know because he cooked the usual meal of rice, potatoes and beans. As they converse, one of the soldiers takes a specimen of the meal to Raymond. He inspects the meal closely and asks the cook why it contains no meat. He tells him that he received no meat. Labrousse himself adds that it is the usual ration. Next, there is a cut to a medium close-up of Raymond taking a measure of the meal and smelling it. He then tells the other officers that it is quite bad and inedible. Labrousse, who is embarrassed by Raymond's observation, calls him aside for a tête-à-tête. As they move toward the gate, he tells Raymond that the soldiers are usually given meat once a week, that at their homes they eat just rice and millet. Raymond responds by telling him that even if that were true, it will not be excuse for denying them meat in their meal. He further reminds him that the men are soldiers returning from the war front and that they deserve better meals. What then follows as they are about to drive away after Raymond has borrowed a novel from Diatta is that they find the soldiers who are supposedly brought up on a diet of plain rice and millet returning from the village with chickens, goats and sheep meant for the preparation of their own meal. The good thing, however, about this protest is that after this incident, the authorities from then on supply beef for their meals. This incident, and others that will follow, represent the officers of the Vichy regime in Dakar as fascists.

Another sequence which holds significance for the type of subjectivity constructed in this film with regards to both African and European characters, is that which deals with Diatta's uncle's maneuver to have Diatta marry his daughter, Bintu. The importance of this sequence lies in the fact that it deals with the influence of maternal uncles in the Senegalese family structure. In addition, it also deals with the subtle ways in which uncles apply pressures upon their nephews to have their will done. The sequence begins with the arrival of Diatta's uncle at Thiaroye camp and ends with the debate between Raymond and Diatta over whether there are any differences between the fascist Vichy regime and that of de Gaulle with respect to their colonial policies in Africa. The first scene begins with a close-up of Diatta pouring palm wine. He hands it to his uncle who pours a drink to their ancestors, takes a sip, and then passes it to Diatta. He then asks Diatta what happened to his bandaged arm. Diatta explains it away, saying that he hurt it a while ago. Next, his uncle tactfully asks him if the picture on the shelf is that of his wife and child, and he replies it is. To change the topic, the uncle tells him that they are having a special festival that year because they had a very good rice harvest. Diatta, knowing fully well that it is just a diversion from what brought him, answers that God has been good to them. His uncle then reminds him that his parents worked very hard for their village, and Diatta replies that soon he will be discharged, and that after his discharge he will return home to attend the festival. At that, the uncle asks what will happen to his family in France and Diatta tells him that he will spend a few months in Effok and then go back to complete his studies in France. His uncle asks next whether that is with a view to joining his white wife. Diatta, who all along is aware of what he is driving at, diverts the discussion by telling his uncle that now that he has mentioned her, he has reminded him of his plans to send her some coffee. He then asks him if he can help him buy ten kilograms. His uncle, who notices that he is loosing the battle of wits, collects the money for the coffee from Diatta and tells him point blank that he and his mother have already picked a wife for him and that she is his daughter, Bintu. Knowing fully well that he cannot antagonize his uncle by refusing his demand out-rightly, he pauses for a while and then reminds his uncle that he is a catholic.

His uncle, who is unimpressed by his excuse, informs him that there are Catholics in their village, Effok, and that they go to Mass every Sunday, but most of them have two or three wives. Diatta, who feels defeated, keeps quiet after this. He gives his uncle the packet of chocolate, milk and sugar given to him by the black American military police when he came to apologize to him, to give to the children back home. But before his uncle leaves, he tells Diatta that he will give the presents to Diatta's wife, Bintu. Throughout the sequence, both of them are shot in the dialogue format of shot/reverse shot, with no special emphasis on any of them. The significance of the sequence lies in the representation of maternal uncles' authority over their nephews. To those with little knowledge of the ethics of African family relationship, this short scene might appear to be dealing with only the pressures which Diatta's uncle is applying to make him marry his cousin. It is much more complex than that. What Sembène and Sow display in this scene is the intricate and subtle manner in which sensitive issues are dealt within family circles between uncles and their nephews. The central issue, of course, is the authority of maternal uncles in the relation to their nephews. This authority is affirmed by the fact that in the scene that follows, Diatta's uncle does send Bintu to Thiaroye Camp to attend to the needs of her fiancé.

The next scene is also important in other respects. As I earlier noted, it deals with the dilemma of French liberals caught between the desire for personal friendship and the pull of altruistic nationalism, which renders them blind to, and complicit in, French colonial atrocities in Africa. The scene begins with a long shot of an open field with cattle grazing. Next, there is a cut to Diatta and Bintu walking toward the bottom of a cotton tree. Diatta asks her what brought her to Thiaroye Camp and she replies that she came to see him. At that point, she moves round and sits at a strategic hidden space at the bottom of the cotton tree. Realizing that she is tempting him, Diatta puts on his cap, which he had been holding, and walks away. She herself gets up and walks away in the opposite direction. On the way, she passes Raymond who looks at her as she goes off toward screen left. In the next cut, we see Diatta going toward the camp in screen right.

When he notices footsteps behind him, he stops and waits for Captain Raymond to join him. After exchanging greetings, he gives Diatta the novel, *The Silence of the Sea*, by Vercors, which he borrowed earlier. Diatta then tells him that he has heard that he will soon be going back to France with new recruits; he requests that Raymond should help deliver some coffee to his wife in Paris and Raymond obliges his request. Next, Raymond asks about Bintu and Diatta replies that she is fine. Noticing the change in his uniform, Raymond asks why they bothered to change their uniform when they are about to be demobilized and Diatta replies that they are not French citizens but subjects. When Raymond reminds him that he can apply for French citizenship since he is educated, Diatta replies that he wants to be an educated African. Raymond then asks him if he still intends to carry on with his studies in France, and he replies he does, adding however, that he will do that as soon as he is free to go to see the ruins of his village. When Raymond asks what ruins, he tells him the story of the rice requisition expedition carried out by French soldiers into Effok, which ended in the massacre of the villagers where women refused to surrender their produce. He also informs him that he lost his parents in the incident. Raymond, who is sincerely remorseful about the incident, gives his condolences to Diatta. However, on learning that it occurred in 1942, he rationalizes it by remarking that it was because

France was still under the Vichy regime. He consoles Diatta by telling him that time and attitude change, and also asks Diatta if he had been following the conference in Brazzaville and he replies that he has. Throughout their discussion, both of them are standing beside each other, resting on a cotton tree, and are held in a neutral, fixed camera, in a medium shot. Raymond raises the issue of the Brazzaville conference to assure Diatta that de Gaulle's regime is responsive to African aspirations, but Diatta's ironic smile at the mention of Brazzaville indicates he thinks otherwise.

The Brazzaville conference, which was organized after the establishment of the Free France regime in Paris in 1944, initiated a lot of liberalization in French colonial policy toward Africa, much of it having to do with the building of infrastructures, schools and hospitals, areas in which Francophone Africa lagged behind countries in Anglophone Africa at the time. During the conference, de Gaulle also acknowledged formally the contribution of Africa to the liberation of France. With regards to the conference, Crowder has noted that

> though for the most part Africans had been passively conscripted into support of the Free French regime in French Black Africa, de Gaulle in recognition of the contribution Africa had made to the liberation of France offered them political, social and economic reforms. Without Equatorial Africa as an initial base for his Free France, without Black African troops and the food supplied by African peasants, it is doubtful whether de Gaulle could ever have achieved his goal of the rehabilitation of the defeated France. As de Gaulle put it himself at the Brazzaville conference: France found in Africa 'her refuge and the starting point for her liberation.' (Crowder, 1978: 279)

The conference also adopted a resolution that the Empire should be known as the French Union, that each constituent of the Union should develop in its own way, that loyalty of individuals to the Union should be given through their own units, and that the economic policy of the colonies should be directed toward the advantages of the inhabitants. The conference however stood resolutely against any idea of independence. It has also been noted by Frederick Pedler that when de Gaulle flew into Brazzaville for the conference accompanied by the governor-general and all the governors, there was no single African on his entourage (Pedler: 50). Whatever reforms were adopted at the conference, therefore, precluded Africans from direct participation in the running of their own affairs.

The main point of disagreement between Diatta and Raymond in this scene lies in Diatta's analogy between the French colonial massacre at Effok and that of the Germans at Oradour-Sur-Glane. Raymond objects to the analogy on the ground that he does not feel that there is justification for making such comparisons. Diatta, for his part, argues that they were both massacres by colonial armies with the same mentality. He also reminds Raymond that in 1940, the fascist French officers, resident in Senegal, refused to admit West Africans to the Free France Army that those Senegalese who enlisted were shot by the officers. The importance of Raymond's rationalization lies in the fact that whereas he is prepared to accept what the Germans did at Oradour as a barbaric act, he does not accept the fact that what the French did in Effok in Senegal fits such description. Though the camera is neutral in the scene, Diatta's arguments carry more weight because of the force and anger underlying the delivery of his lines, in contrast to Raymond's gentle attempts at placating him, through rationalization of the atrocities of the French colonial troops.

The major conflict, which builds up into a climax toward the end of the film when the *tirailleurs* take the General hostage and the camp is razed, occurs in the sequence dealing with the refusal by the French military authorities to pay the soldiers the correct exchange rate of 1000 French francs to 500 CFA francs. The most important development in this sequence, however, is the ethical debates between those who fought for the liberation of France like the *tirailleurs* and those troops of the Vichy regime in Senegal who initially honored the armistice imposed on France by the Germans, claimed neutrality in the war in accordance to its terms, and refused to fight. The sequence begins with the arrival of the soldiers at the parade ground, where they were supposed to exchange their money, and ends with Labrousse summoning the camp guards to disperse them. The highlight of the sequence is the accusation by the military authorities that the soldiers stole the money, which they want to exchange, an accusation which makes Diatta to deliver one of the longest and most theatrical speeches in the entire film. I should like to summarize and paraphrase this speech because it bears the bulk of the debate between those who fought and those who did not. In addition, I will respond to Labrousse's reaction to the speech.

The speech begins with Diatta telling the officers that they are insulting the soldiers who fought their battles for them while they remained in Dakar. He also reminds them that they legitimately earned the money, which the offices claimed were stolen from dead colleagues in the battlefield. He reminds them that the soldiers were in the Free France 1st Army that they fought from Fort Lamy, crossed the Tibesti and chased Mussolini's men in Southern Libya, and that they were the first soldiers to enter Tripoli, and again, the first to enter Paris in August, 1944. He then asks them where they were between 1939 and 1940. He reminds them that some of the soldiers were from the Seventh French Army, that together with soldiers from France, England, Holland, Belgium, Luxembourg, they faced the Second Panza Division of the German Army and had to flee to Dunkirk. He further reminds them that though they were part of the allies, the men were not allowed to sail to England on their way home. He also reminds them of the case of Captain Ntchorere. According to Diatta, Captain Ntchorere was taken as a prisoner of war to the concentration camp at Buchenwald, where the Germans tried to separate him from his white colleagues. Upon his refusal to be kept separate from the white French officers, he was shot. The moral of the story is that his white colleagues refused to protest during the incidence and the *tirailleurs* had to risk their lives to bury the captain in an unmarked grave.

Throughout the speech, Diatta stands between the soldiers, standing in the parade ground and the French officers sitting, and he is shot in medium close-ups and medium shots, from behind the officers. As he speaks, he occasionally turns to the soldiers, who lend their support by interjecting with encouraging commentaries. The speech is also delivered with such a force that it is almost unstoppable. For instance, when Diatta says that the soldiers were the first to enter Paris, Major Auguste gestures that it is enough but Diatta replies that he is not done. While Diatta is speaking, there is a cut to a medium close-up of Labrousse, who writes "communist" on a piece of paper and passes it round the table to the other officers. This very long speech, aspects of which I have just paraphrased, deals with the experience of racial discrimination suffered by African soldiers even in the heat of the Second World

War. But most importantly, the speech is an indictment of the French soldiers of the Vichy regime, who initially refused to fight in the war because of the armistice, remained in Dakar from where they committed all sorts of atrocities against a defenseless civilian population, the most often cited in Senegal being the massacre at Effok. The sequence also deals with the tradition of dismissing the arguments of one's opponents by calling them communists, a potent political weapon of the Cold War, which African governments inherited from their colonial masters and used against their political opponents.

The pace of events in *Camp de Thiaroye* does not really pick up until the climax in the last sequence when the General's refusal to pay the *tirailleurs* the correct exchange rate for their money and their discharge entitlements, results in the soldiers taking him hostage and the camp being razed. The most significant events in this sequence are: the display of the African style of popular democracy on the question of whether they should hold the General hostage until he agrees to pay them, the display of the age-old African weakness of credulity, the outcome of which was the massacre of the *tirailleurs*, and lastly, at the level of cinematography, the studied break from the rather hazy formal style of the rest of the film, to a much more naturalistic one in the celebration scene which precedes the bombardment of the camp.

Though historical events in *Camp de Thiaroye* are presented from an African point of view, character-subjectivity and its representation is not premised on a binary Manichean tradition of the sort that one finds in colonialist African cinema, where characterization is rigidly subjected to the classificatory attributes of the races derived from nineteenth century biological theories of race. Characters are not simply good because they are black and bad because they are white. Characterization is approached from the level of individuality, with character attributes firmly anchored in social environment and cultural upbringing. Though in terms of the overall representation of European characters, the majority of them are portrayed as villains, their villainy is attributed to the political character of the regime that they represent. For instance, the French officer corps in the film is represented as composed of two broadly opposed camps — liberal white officers like Captain Raymond whose lack of exposure to the racial politics of colonial societies renders them free to explore the bonds of personal friendship, and utterly fascist ones like Captain Labrousse, Major Auguste, the General, and their simply frightened subordinate, Lieutenant Pierre, who are not only fully steeped in the racial politics of colonial societies but also exercise their authority through the display of excessive militarism of the sort that borders on outright disregard for the humanity of their African subjects. Put simply, this category of officers considers African lives as cheap and expendable commodities.

The film also deals with the dilemma of white liberals like Captain Raymond who are sometimes rebuffed by Africans because of the past betrayal of the bonds of friendship, but who equally suffer rejection from racist French officers for being too sympathetic to the black cause. For instance, in the two scenes set at the Officers' Mess, Captain Raymond is not only put on the defensive over his support for the *tirailleurs*, he is also ostracized by the other officers and of course branded a communist. But if the Raymond character represents an image of white liberalism, then, its major flaw as represented in this film is its inability to come to terms with the atrocities of French colonialism in Africa. As the debate between Diatta and Raymond shows, white liberalism is often constrained by the dictates of ethnocentricism. However, if the Raymond character represents the figure of white liberalism — as indeed I think it does – then, the Captain Labrousse character represents not only its underside but also the very excess of white supremacists. He is essentially contemptuous of his African subjects whom he considers overgrown children. And most importantly, he mistakes his forcible exercise of authority for his claimed knowledge of Africans.

For instance, in the sequence where the *tirailleurs* are forcibly made to surrender their smart American military uniforms for those of colonial cooks, when Lieutenant Pierre exclaims in relief to Labrousse towards the end of the exercise that he did not expect it to be carried out without a major revolt, Labrousse replies that he knew they would not, that he was in Niger, Dahomey (now republic of Benin), and the Congo, that ten years out in Africa has taught him a lot about Africans, who he likens to overgrown children. In the scenes that follow the exercise however, the *tirailleurs* are shown to be thoroughly discontent with the exercise, having been forcibly demoted from the status of a victorious army to the lowly status of colonial cooks. In fact, the exercise was the last straw that soured the already tenuous relationship between the men and the military authorities. Furthermore, the Labrousse character lacks not only the subtleties and paternalistic attitudes of a Commissioner Sanders, of *Sanders of the River*, but also the shrewdness and bureaucratic behavior of the District Officer, E.R. Chadwick, of *Daybreak in Udi*. Finally, though Vichy Dakar has provided Sembène and Sow with the opportunity to detail the characteristic mannerisms of colonial figures such as that of Captain Labrousse, colonial societies were replete with such figures, and the catalogues of colonial atrocities which abound across Africa outside the initial framework of conquest and colonization, owe much to the militaristic excesses of such figures.

Among the African characters, Sergeant-Major Diatta is the only fully drawn character. We know for instance that he was a Law student in Paris before the outbreak of the Second World War made him to suspend his studies. Though we are not told how he joined the Free France 1st Army, it would seem that his was a voluntary enlistment rather than forcible conscription. We do know however, that his period of enlistment was forcibly extended. From his wide knowledge of black diaspora scholarly and artistic works, the Diatta character is shown to be a pan-Africanist to the core, an intellectual whose range of knowledge covers not only works by black writers but also French writers. Indeed, the Diatta character cuts the image of the young Sembène who voluntarily enlisted in the Free France Army and was equally well exposed to works by black diaspora authors as well as French writers even before he began his writing career.

In his personal relationships, Diatta is portrayed to be a faithful and dedicated husband and father. As his letter to his French wife shows, their relationship was one based on love and friendship, one that stood above the bigotry of race and creed. It was above all else a private personal relationship as opposed to his public pan-Africanist obligations. In his relationship with his maternal uncle, he is shown to be a respectful nephew who would not, however, sacrifice his personal happiness on the grounds of some quaint tradition, such as an arranged marriage. However, even though he firmly rejects his uncle's propositions, he does not dismiss him outright; rather, he handles him tactfully but firmly without making the man loose his face. In his relationship with his men, he is shown to be a courageous leader who has earned the respect of the *tirailleurs* through selfless service. Most importantly, as the scenes of consultation about the fate of the General show, he is sensitive enough to know when to bow to public opinion. Finally, as the scenes of his outing in Dakar show, he is respectful towards his elders as well as compassionate towards disabled people.

Apart from Diatta, the next most important African character in the film, who is granted narrative authority, is Pays. Though the cause of his disability is given as torture while he was a prisoner of war at Buchenwald, the Pays character is essentially an African archetype who either because of his or her noted drunkenness or mental instability, enjoys some modicum of license from society to say or do what he or she likes, and in return, society is expected albeit always at its own peril, to disregard the opinions of such characters. It is through this characteristic nature of the archetype that Sembène and Sow explored the theme of gullibility of Africans. For instance, in the scene where the General promises to pay the *tirailleurs* — in desperation after noticing that his officers have failed to secure his release — it is only Pays whose realizes that the General is lying to them in order to regain his freedom. When later he warns his colleagues of the impending bombardment of the camp, as is usual with such characters, his warnings are misinterpreted as the jabbering of a crazed fellow.

Though the single most conspicuous African character in the film is Diatta, the concept of heroism as an individual accomplishment is not linked to this single character, as it would be the case in most Western texts. Rather, heroism is conceived as a collective enterprise with the mantle of leadership falling upon the person with the most visible leadership qualities for the challenge at hand. Such a leadership mantle makes the person so recognized a leader of a collective struggle. This collective definition of heroism is also very much linked to the African tradition of defining the individual through the collective rather than the collective through the individual as is the case in Western societies. Though heroism is a collective concept in African culture, there is however room for the display and acknowledgement of individual leadership qualities, which may be exhibited and collectively acclaimed by society. But such public acclaim does not necessarily bestow upon the person so acknowledged the title of heroism. Rather, what it bestows is the title of leadership. As a result the democratization of the concept of heroism in African society, we find that in many of the scenes in the film, Diarra and Pays assume the mantle of leadership, since they have little to loose, in situations that do not call for the type of leadership that Diatta is expected to provide. For this reason, events in the film do not revolve all the time around the fortunes of a single individual like Diatta.

With regards to the social composition of colonial societies, *Camp de Thiaroye* highlights the racial division of public spaces in colonial societies between the colonizer who is European and lives in the European quarters, and the colonized who in this case is African and lives in the poor and destitute section of the city designated as "native" quarters. Thus when Diatta tries to violate the boundary of these antagonistic spaces without either the sanction of colonial authority or the benefit of being an honorary European like black Americans, the weight of the law is brought to bear upon him. Apart from the racial division of public spaces, the film also highlights the linguistic division which exists in colonial societies, between the colonizer and the educated/illiterate colonized, and on the one hand, and between the educated "native" and the uneducated, on the other. For instance, in *Camp de Thiaroye*, while the French citizens and educated Africans such as Diatta speak French, the *tirailleurs* made up of people of different ethnic backgrounds and countries, with little education, speak Pidgin French, the linguafranca in Francophone Africa among the illiterates, just as Pidgin English is the linguafranca among the illiterates in Anglophone West Africa.

No doubt the directors' choice of pidgin French as language of the illiterate *tirailleurs* is part of the response to the ongoing debates about the continuing linguistic hegemony in Africa of the inherited languages of the erstwhile colonial powers. Since Obi Wali initiated the debate on inherited European languages and African literature in the early sixties, writers and artists alike have had to respond to it in accordance with the nature of materials they are dealing with. Sembène himself is a strong advocate of the Obi Wali position that only works by African writers and artists based on indigenous languages and culture qualifies to be referred to as African literature or art. To this end, he has always used Wolof, the predominant indigenous language in Senegal, as medium of filmic expression. But since *Camp de Thiaroye* deals with a multi-national experience and the *tirailleurs* do not share a multi-national indigenous language, Sembène and Sow have had to employ the next best alternative to such a medium, which is Pidgin French.

With regards to spectatorial textual positioning, since the story is told from an African point of view, the spectator is positioned textually to empathize with the African characters over the injustices committed against them by French colonial rule. In most of the scenes involving Africans and the French officers, the African position is strongly presented, with the result that the French officers look pathetic, since most of their actions are driven solely by racism. However, empathy with Africans in the film has been highly balanced by the process of having the French characters defend and rationalize whatever atrocities they are accused of. It is a colonial situation and people like Labrousse feel that they have nothing to apologize for. Sembène and Sow's handling of foreground/background action in spatial composition is quite an accomplishment but this was almost marred by the rather slow pace of the film. As I earlier noted, the pace of the film does not really pick up until the very last sequence. The only savior in this respect has been the many occasions for laughter provided for by comic relief.

In sum, *Camp de Thiaroye* is an historical recreation of the events that built up to the French colonial massacre on 1st December, 1944, of repatriated Francophone African colonial infantry men, who had just completed their tour of duty. Though the film was meant to be a rehash of the events leading to the actual massacre itself, its main subtext is the disputation of the view that French colonial atrocities in Africa were exclusive products of the Vichy regime. The massacre at Thiaroye Camp, Sembène and Sow seem to point out, was the handiwork of de Gaulle's regime. In this respect, both directors seem to argue that there was little difference between the colonial policies of the Vichy regime and those of de Gualle's.

Summary

In this chapter, the historical background to the emergence of historical colonial encounter films in African cinema has been examined. In addition, the root of this cinematic genre has been traced, with respect to the relation between it and the discursive tradition of colonialist African cinema/discourse. As regards the texts, the argument pursued is that most of them have been produced as a means of both historical documentation and of bringing to African spectators and the larger world cinema audience, an African version of history and of the historical events produced by the encounter between Africans and Europeans, beginning from the era of slave trade, through colonial conquest, colonialism, and the struggles for independence. What stands out in these works is an African version of the history, which has long been suppressed, in European historical documents of the period under study. Of the two films studied in this chapter, *Sarraounia* deals with the era of colonial conquest while *Camp de Thiaroye* deals with the era of colonial rule. *Sarraounia* explores the theme of colonial conquest and resistance, with specific reference to the role of African women in resisting colonial conquest, symbolized by the resistance of the Azna warrior-queen, Sarraounia, to French colonial force. Since the film is set in the era of colonial conquest when European cultural influence had not been established, African religio-cultural practices have been highlighted and textually foregrounded as a means of cultural authentication. The film, like Sembène's *Ceddo*, treats Islam as a foreign religious and cultural practice promoted by traditional African rulers, after their conversion by Arab traders and scholars, at the expense of traditional African religio-cultural practices. With regards to the historical context of colonial conquest, the film explores the nature of the socio-political atmosphere, i.e., that of inter-ethnic struggle for power, within which European colonial conquest took place.

In *Sarraounia*, one finds that even though various forms of spatio-temporal articulations have been exploited to confer narrative authority upon the main protagonist, Sarraounia, her heroic image emerges not so much because of discriminating choices made in the spatio-temporal constitution of her subjectivity but because of the quality and tone of verbal discourse and physical actions, i.e., from the strength and conviction of her exhortation speeches and her war tactics. Her nationalistic speeches, which are richly couched in the imagery and rhetoric of traditional African public discourse, help to historicize the text by placing it within the framework of the epic genre. I have equally argued with respect to the constitution of European characters that the film has been generally faithful in terms of its representation of the historical accounts of the atrocities committed by the Voulet-Chanoine force.

With regards to Captain Voulet himself, one has argued that his characterization as a murderous officer lacking self-discipline, emerges not through forms of spatial distortion of his image or character make-up meant to reflect his deviousness or even spatial distancing of the spectator from his character but through his personal activities such as his derogatory speeches about Africans and his casual summary executions of both his soldiers and prisoners of war which shows that he has no regard whatsoever for African lives.

With respect to *Camp de Thiaroye*, the main argument pursued is that though the film is meant to be an historical documentation of the events leading to the massacre at Thiaroye Camp on 1st December, 1944, its main subtext is the disputation of the view that French colonial atrocities in Africa were exclusive products of the Vichy regime. The massacre at Thiaroye Camp, and so many others which Sembène and Sow cite as inspiration for making the film, were carried out under General de Gaulle's regime. Though events in the film are articulated through the personal experiences of Sergeant-major Diatta and Private Pays, and as such, both characters are granted comparatively more narrative authority, in relation to other characters in the film, the overall sense of tragedy transcends the personal experiences of these two characters. Furthermore, the overall development of character and narrative viewpoint emerge not so much through the application of discriminatory spatio-temporal articulation in respect of both African and European characters but through the quality and tone of verbal discourse and narrative actions. By this I do not mean to infer that character development is not spatio-temporally articulated in both films. Indeed they are, and in certain instances they have been used to foreground the narrative voice of African characters. However, the overall narrative viewpoint of these films does not emerge through the choices made in respect of forms of spatio-temporal narration applied in the representation of characters but through the quality and content of verbal speech and narrative actions. Of course, all the verbal discourses and narrative actions are spatio-temporally articulated but they are not discriminatorily articulated in respect of African and European characters. In Western narrative practice for instance, verbal discourse is subordinated to the spatio-temporal orders of the film, and in the case of colonialist African cinema, it constitutes African subjectivity and space as objects of spectacle ethnographic interest and pleasure. This is not the case in both films. As a result of the spatio-temporal generosity underlying African cinematic practices, the themes of colonial atrocities and resistance, which are treated in the films, emerge, more from the quality and content of verbal speech and narrative actions than through forms of spatio-temporal articulations. In the concluding chapter of this work, a comparative analysis of the cinematic practices, which has been studied, will be undertaken.

SUMMARY AND CONCLUSION

This study has been concerned with examining the nature of modern African subjectivity in African cinema. The study has approached the cinema as a modern institution inherited from European colonialism, and has analyzed its history, to assess how both Europeans and Africans have used the institution to define the emerging modern image of Africa and Africans, from the 15th century, right into the era of globalization and consumer capitalism. In addition, the work has provided a theoretical framework for a proper definition and critical study of African of both colonial and post-colonial African cinema. The main thrust of the work has been to examine the nature of colonial and post-colonial African cinema, with emphasis on how the cinematic practices of the colonial period and post-colonial texts situated in that era, have constructed African subjectivity and culture. The study has been approached by examining the nature of each cinematic practice, the historical background of its emergence, and its generic forms and modes of representation as exemplified in the film texts.

With respect to the colonial period, the argument pursued is that two divergent cinematic practices existed during this era, namely, colonial African instructional cinema and colonialist African cinema. The former was sponsored by governments and non-governmental agencies while the latter was driven by purely commercial interests. The historical context within which colonial African instructional cinema emerged has been examined, with a view to placing in proper perspective, the fundamental drives underlining instructional cinema projects such as the Bantu

Educational Cinema Experiment and those of the Colonial Film Unit (CFU) of the British colonial government, and its Belgian counterparts such as the Film and Photo Bureau and Center for Catholic Action Cinema (CCAC). With regards to the construction of African subjectivity and culture, one has argued that this cinematic practice represents Africa as a developing society, and Africans as backward but intelligent and hardworking people, able and eager to learn from the European colonizers, modern methods of social organization and development. One has equally argued that these films do not represent Africans as lacking their own forms of government, education, agriculture, health care, building construction, etc, but rather represent Africans as doing these things in the old and ineffectual traditional ways, and that once it is proven to them that modern methods of doing things are more effectual, they will eagerly try to adapt to change by learning to master the recommended modern methods of doing things.

As a result of the emphasis on the use of the cinema as a medium of instruction, most of the films are oriented towards assisting Africans to master these modern methods. With respect to the textual positioning of Africans, these films situate Africans at the center of narrative action as subjects in narration, as opposed to the narrative technique in colonialist African cinema which positions Africans as objects in narration. In colonialist African cinema, space and time are defined by the activities of the resident European conquerors. This cinematic tradition therefore stands in contrast to that of instructional cinema, which celebrates the active participation of Africans in the project of modernity. Consequently, it is their struggle for the modernization of their communities that is foregrounded in films such as *Men of Africa* (Alexander Shaw, 1939) and *Daybreak in Udi* (Terry Bishop, 1949), which have chosen as case studies. Though the films also represent British institutions and agencies assisting in the process of modernization, it is not the actions of British colonial officials that are foregrounded in them, rather, it is self-help spirit of Africans that are celebrated, with British colonial institutions providing guidance in ongoing projects of modernity on the continent. The irony underlying the whole colonial enterprise is that while colonial African instructional cinema is celebrating the process of modernization going on in Africa, colonialist African cinema preoccupies itself with the representation of Africa as one huge jungle inhabited by savage and bestial people who have just been "pacified" but are constantly on the verge of relapse into barbarism in the slightest absence of colonial authority.

With regards to colonialist African cinema, I have argued that the roots of the cinematic practice can be traced contextually to the uneven knowledge and power relations underlying Afro-European relationship as a result of European colonial authority, and the superiority complex which it has produced in the European imagination, as the more powerful partner in the relationship. Colonialist African cinema is a product of this uneven knowledge and power relations, and of course, of the intertextual authority of the colonialist canon which, as earlier argued, stretches as far back as the classical era. With respect to the modern era, colonialist African literature, especially travel literature, the adventure novel, memoirs of colonial administrators and missionaries, autobiographies, etc., furnished the materials for filmic representation. The main idea which informs these literary texts and the films adapted from them is that of European racial superiority as propounded in nineteenth century racial theories. Though this idea has been in existence since the classical era, with respect to the representation of Africans, it was codified and scientifically justified through nineteenth century racial theories

With respect to the representation of African subjectivity and culture, the colonialist genre is organized around a comparatist schema which, working from physical outlook, through institutions of governments, to cultural and religious practices, etc., sets up Africans and their institutional and cultural practices as inferior in comparison to those of Europeans. Though these films occasionally acknowledge the underlying uneven knowledge and power relations between Africans and Europeans, through physical display of militarism as in the case of the sequence dealing with the meeting between District Commissioner Sanders and King Mofalaba in *Sanders of the River*, in most cases, the regime of authority of the genre is masked and naturalized so that the basis for European presence on the continent, and for the comparative narrative schema, is made to look as the natural order of things.

The genre employs various metaphors of savagery and bestiality meant to draw associations between Africans and animals or between their behavior and those of animals. Instances of such representations can be found in the pit prison sequence in *Tarzan the Ape Man* where shots of the physical outlook of the giant ape in the pit and its act of strangling its victims, are intercut with those of ecstatic pygmies dancing amidst drumbeats on the stand overlooking the pit. Another example of such a metaphoric representation can be found in *Sanders of the River* where an analogy is drawn between Africans and various animals celebrating the absence of law and order from the district in the sequence dealing with Sanders' departure on leave, where for instance, a shot of a man climbing a coconut tree with bare hands and movements resembling that of a bat crawling up a tree trunk, is intercut with shots of men passing the message of Sanders' absence through drumbeats, to scenes of resumption of slave raids, and of elephants, hippopotami, giraffes, etc., lumbering in and out of water as if in joyful celebration of this absence. Thus the sequences dealing with Sanders' absence from the district are carefully ordered to signify this shared degeneration into a state of savagery. The metaphors of savagery and bestiality also take the form of the mindless and unexplained murders of Europeans and their African collaborators as in the representation of the Mau Mau Movement in Kenya, in films such as *Simba* and *The Kitchen Toto*, or it may take the form of a revenge on an innocent child, France, by Protée in *Chocolat*. In these instances, the idea is to draw sympathy for Europeans who are presented as victims of African barbarism.

In the colonialist genre, the only good African is one who collaborates with European colonial authority while the African villain is one who opposes, in whatever guise, this authority. European villainy or social degeneration, the phenomenon of Europeans going "native," represented in form of sympathy for or fraternization with Africans through marriage or friendship is linked to Europeans of working class background.

In terms of spatio-temporal articulations, space and time are defined in the genre by the presence and actions of European characters, with Africans functioning as the background of actions. Consequently, European characters are positioned in these films as subjects in/of narration while Africans are positioned as objects of spectacle or objects in/of narration. Deviations from this framework are linked either to the comparative schema or to omniscient narration, in which instance, a certain amount of neutrality is established. There is however a tendency in the genre towards regular subjectivization of space and time by anchoring narration through character point-of-view, flashbacks, reflections, etc., as a result of the linkage between space and time, and the relays of looks, gazes, and spectacles, to European characters. This is why the geographic space of Africa and Africans and their cultural practices function in these films as objects of ethnographic interest and spectacle. The subjectivization of space is stretched to the limits in *Chocolat*, for instance, where the main story is anchored through France's flashback, and in this sense, the film can be read as an allegory of French imperialism in Africa. Adult France's return to post-colonial Cameroon and all her memory recalls can be considered as the allegorical return of France to the country, to claim credit for whatever infrastructural development or modernization there are in her erstwhile colony, as product of France's colonial beneficence. In fact, the representation of modern infrastructural development in post-colonial Cameroon such as roads and airport is linked through the narrative emphasis on road construction and airfield, in France's flashback, as products of this colonial heritage. At the bottom line, the film seems to suggest that without French colonialism, Cameroon would not have developed its modern infrastructures. This is also the basic thought projected in the whole genre.

The colonialist genre never deviates from the projection of its central idea of European racial superiority. It may be projected in subtle forms through the framework of institutional, cultural and religious comparative schema; it may even incorporate Africans as tamed and controllable subjects, as in the case of Umbopa in *King Solomon's Mines* and Bosambo in *Sanders of the River*, as an acceptable face of the African, but it does not pretend that the highest acceptable African type is equal to the unacceptable European type. Intelligence, the ability to plan, organize and execute - whether the goal is adventure as in *Tarzan the Ape Man* and *King Solomon's Mines* or the conception and execution of a road project, as in *Mister Johnson* — are represented as biological and hereditary qualities and linked to the idea of race. Since the genre projects Europeans as naturally endowed with these qualities on account of their racial superiority and Africans as lacking them on account of their racial inferiority, the genre, in whatever sub-generic guise it takes, perpetuates the devaluation of African humanity. In this regard, it differs in no small measures from the colonial instructional genre which, as earlier stated, represents Africans as backward but intelligent and hardworking people able and eager to acquire new ideas and knowledge to modernize their society. It is for these reasons that one has argued that of the two cinematic practices of the colonial period or of post-colonial European texts set in the era, it is the colonialist genre, rather than the colonial instructional genre, that motivated the institution of the tradition of colonialist counter-discourse in post-colonial African cinema.

With respect to the post-colonial period, this study has been approached by examining the scope and limitations of works already done in the field as well as proposing a theoretical framework, intended to fill the gap in the existing works, for the criticism of African cinema. Equally examined were colonial and post-colonial film production structures and sponsorship policies in Anglophone and Francophone African countries. This has been done with a view to assessing how colonial production structures and sponsorship policies have affected those of the post-colonial era.

With regards to post-colonial African historical texts situated in the colonial period, though the colonialist counter-discourse genre in African cinema, responds to the whole colonial enterprise, it has been argued that it is motivated, first and foremost, by the desire to refute the images of Africa and Africans identifiable with the discursive tradition of the colonialist genre. The spatio-temporal order of the colonialist counter-discourse genre is not individualized and radicalized as in the colonialist genre. In films of the colonialist counter-discourse, space and time are democratized in relation to the representation of both African and European characters. It is not race that determines how space and time are articulated, and how narrative authority is granted to characters or even spectatorial accessibility granted or denied, but the position of each character in the text, the nature of events represented and the contingencies of plot.

In *Sarraounia*, for instance, Captain Voulet and his camp are granted as much narrative authority, both in terms of the detailed psychological study of characters and of spectatorial accessibility, as Sarraounia and members of her camp. What grants Sarraounia overall narrative authority in the film is the fact that it is her story that is being told, her resistance to French colonialism is what is being celebrated, and so, the dictates of plot management demand that enough space and time be devoted to her background, to explain how she came to acquire her reputation as a sorceress and warrior-queen so that her rise to fame does not seem contrived and unbelievable. On the other hand, Captain Voulet's villainy is not attributed to biological or natural causes, rather, it is treated as a product of French colonization wars and an overriding personal desire for fame and glory. There is no spectatorial distancing from the Voulet character. He is given detailed psychological study, and sometimes, there is even an overt solicitation of the spectator's sympathy for him, as his regretful moments of personal reflection during the withdrawal sequence can attest. What establishes Voulet's villainy in the film is the detailed recounting of historically documented atrocities of the force which he commanded and encouraged, not invented stories. Also, in *Sarraounia*, we are made aware of the fact that the French colonial authorities did not sanction the atrocities of the Voulet force. The attempts made by the French colonial authorities to replace him as the commander of the expedition force, are represented.

In *Camp de Thiaroye* also, the arguments of the French commanders and administrators, are given detailed attention. French characters are granted as much narrative authority, through detailed study of characters' psychology and spectatorial accessibility, as their African counterparts. If the African characters in the film appear to attract more sympathy, then, it is because the film details the historically documented atrocities committed against the force during the Second World War. In addition, the villainy of the French officers is not attributed to biological or natural causes nor is it extended indiscriminately to all French officers in the film, as Africans are often represented in the colonialist genre. In *Camp de Thiaroye*, Captain Raymond is not represented as a racist like the other French officers of the Vichy regime in Dakar.

In the colonialist counter-discourse genre therefore, the desire to document for posterity European colonial atrocities against Africans is not used as an excuse to give an unbalanced accounts of historical events. Though history is not accurately represented with respect to the actual details of historical events – the films do not in any case pretend to be aspiring to the truth and objectivity required of history as a discipline – they nevertheless do not contradict, in broad terms, the historical accounts from which they draw inspiration. The genre celebrates African religious and cultural belief-systems but it does not set them up within a comparative framework with those of Europeans, nor does it uncritically celebrate them. It does project good aspects of African culture such as respect for old age and the elderly, the simplicity and warmth of traditional African society, the care and protection of the extended family system, the hospitality of traditional African society, etc., as valuable aspects of the African heritage, but it does not disregard the need for a balanced plot and story. In this respect, the history represented in the genre is very much a contested history.

BIBLIOGRAPHY

Achebe, Chinua (1988) *Hopes and Impediments: Selected Essays*, 1965-1987, London: Heineman.

Akudinobi, Jude (2000) "Reco(r)ding Reality: Representation and Paradigms in Nonfiction African Cinema," *Social Identities*, Vol. 6, No.3: 245-367.

_____ (2000) "Reel Zones of Ex(Change): An Interview with Mweze Ngangura, *Social Identities*,"Vol. 6, No.3: 369-395.

_____ (1999) "African Cinema and Question of Meaning: An Interview with Jean-Pierre Bekolo, *Third Text*," No. 48 (Autumn): 71-111.

_____ (1995) "Tradition/Modernity and the Discourse of African Cinema," *Iris*, No. 18 (Spring): 26-37.

Andrade-Watkins, Claire (1992) "France's Bureau of Cinema: Financial and Technical Assistance between 1961 and 1977: Operations and Implications for African Cinema," *Framework*, No. 38/39: 27-46.

Anstey, Roger (1976) "The British Slave Trade: A Comment," *Journal of African History*, Vol. XVII (4): 606-607.

_____ (1975) The Atlantic Slave Trade and British Abolition, 1760-1810, London: Macmillan Press Ltd.

Appiah, Kwame A. (1992) *In My Father's House*, London: Methuen.

_____ (1984) "Strictures on Structures: The Prospects for a Structuralist Poetics of African Fiction," in Henry Louis Gates, jr. (ed) (1984) *Black Literature and Literary Theory*, New York: Methuen.

Armes, Roy (1987) *Third World Film Making and the West*, Berkeley: University of California Press.

_____ (1981) "Ousmane Sembène: Questions of Change," *Cine-tract*, Vol. 4 (3/4) (Summer-Fall): 71-77.

Arulogun, Adegboyega (1979) "The Role of Film in Cultural Identity," in Alfred E. Opubor and Onuora E. Nwuneli (eds) (1979) *The Development and Growth of the Film Industry in Nigeria*, Lagos: National Council for Arts and Culture.

Azikiwe, Nnamdi (1968) *Renascent Africa*, New York: Negro University Press.

Bachy, Victor (1987) *To Have an African Cinema*, Brussels: OCIC.

Balogun, Françoise (1987) *The Cinema of Nigeria*, Jos: Nigerian Film Corporation.

Banton, Michael (1987) *Racial Theories*, Cambridge: Cambridge University Press.

Barthes, Roland (1981) "The Death of the Author," in John Caughie (ed) (1981) *Theories of Authorship*, London: Routledge and Kegan Paul.

Baucom, Ian (1991) "Dreams of Home: Colonialism and Postmodernism," *Research in African Literatures*, Vol. 22 (4) (Winter): 5-27.

Beale, Colin (1948) "The Commercial Entertainment Film and Its Effects on Colonial Peoples," in *The Film in Colonial Development: A Report of Conference*, London: The British Film Institute.

Bender, Wolfgang (2001) "Independence, Highlife, Liberation War: Lagos, 1950 and 1960s," in Okwui Enwezor (ed.) (2001) *The Short Century: Independence and Liberation Movements in Africa, 1945-1994*, New York: Prestel Verlag.

Bernal, Martin (1987) *Black Athena*, Vol I, London: Free Association Books.

Bester, Rory (2001) "City and Citizenship," in Okwui Enwezor (ed.) (2001) *The Short Century: Independence and Liberation Movements in Africa, 1945-1994*, New York: Prestel Verlag.

Bhabha, Homi (1986) "Forward: Remembering Fanon: Self, Psyche and the Colonial Condition," in Frantz Fanon (1967) *Black Skin, White Mask*, trans. Charles Lam Markmann, London: Pluto Press.

_____ (1984) "Of Mimicry and Man: The Ambivalence of Colonial Discourse," *October*, 28 (Spring): 125-133.

_____ (1983) "The Other Question," *Screen*, Vol. 24 (November-December): 18-36.

Biri, Fernando (1983) "Cinema and Underdevelopment," trans. Malcolm Coad, in Michael Chanan (ed) (1983) *Twenty-five Years of the New Latin American Cinema*, London: BFI.

Blackburne, K.W. (1948) "Financial Problems and Future Policy in British Colonies," in *The Film in Colonial Development: A Report of a Conference*, London: The British Film Institute.

Blyden, E.W. (1888) *Christianity, Islam and the Negro Race*, London: New edition, 1967, Edinburgh University Press.

Boal, Augusto (179) *Theatre of the Oppressed*, trans. Charles, A. and Maria-Odilia Leal MacBride, London: Pluto Press.

Bogle, Donald (1973/2001) *Toms, Coons, Mulattoes, Mammies and Bucks: An Interpretive History of Blacks in American Films*, Fourth Edition, New York: The Continuum International Publishing Group, Inc.

Bohanan, Paul (1974) "The Myth and the Fact," in Richard Maynard (ed) (1974) *Africa on Film: Myth and Reality*, Rochell Park, New Jersey: Haden Book Company, Inc.

Bordwell, David, Staiger, Janet and Thompson, Kristin (1985) *The Classical Hollywood Cinema: Film Style and Mode of Production to 1960*, London: Routledge.

Bordwell, David and Thompson, Kristin (1979) *Film Art: An Introduction*, New York: McGraw-Hill Publishing Company.

Boughedir, Férid (1982a) "Controlling the Market," in Angela Martin (ed) (1982) *African Films: The Context of Production*, London: BFI.

_____ (1982b) "The Principal Tendencies of African Cinema," in Angela Martin (ed) (1982) *African Films: The Context of Production*, London: BFI.

_____ (1982c) "Aesthetics: The Two Major Schools of African Cinema", in Angela Martin (ed) (1982) *African Films: The Context of Production*, London: BFI.

Bowser, Pearl, Jane Gaines and Charles Musser (eds) (2001) *Oscar Micheaux and his Circle*, Bloomington, Indiana: Indiana University Press.

Branigan, Edward (1992) *Narrative Comprehension and Film*, London: Routledge.

_____ (1984) *Point of View in the Cinema*, Berlin: Mouton Publishers.

_____ (1981) "The Spectator and Film Space - Two Theories," *Screen* Vol. 22 (1): 55-78.

Brantlinger, Patrick (1986) "Victorians and Africans: The Genealogy of the Myth of the Dark Continent," in Henry Louis Gates, jr. (ed) (1986) *"Race," Writing and Difference*, Chicago: The University of Chicago Press.

Brooks, Peter (1976) *The Melodramatic Imagination*, New Haven: Yale University Press.

Browne, Nick (1982) *The Rhetoric of Film Narration*, Ann Arbor: University of Michigan Press.

_____ (1981) "The Rhetoric of the Specular Text with Reference to Stagecoach," in John Caughie (ed) (1981) *Theories of Authorship*, London: Routledge and Kegan Paul.

Burton, Julianne (1985) "Marginal Cinemas and Mainstream Critical Theories," *Screen*, Vol. 26 (3-4) (May-August): 2-21.

Buscombe, Edward (1981) "Ideas of Authorship," in John Caughie (ed) (1981) *Theories of Authorship*, London: Routledge and Kegan Paul.

Butler, Alison (1992) "New Film Histories and the Politics of Location," *Screen*, Vol. 33 (4) (Winter): 418-426.

Caughie, John (ed) (1981) *Theories of Authorship*, London: Routledge and Kegan Paul.

Cham, Mbye (1993) "Official History, Popular Memory: Reconfiguration of the African Past in Films of Ousmane Sembène's Cinema," in Samba Gadjigo, Ralph H. Faulkingham, Thomas Cassirer, and Reinhard Sander (eds) (1993) *Ousmane Sembène: Dialogues with Critics and Writers*, Amherst: University of Massachusetts Press.

Cham, Mbye (ed) (1992) *Ex-iles: Essays on Caribbean Cinema*, Trenton, NJ: Africa World Press, Inc.

———— (1987) "Film Production in West Africa," in J. Dowing (ed) (1987) *Film and Politics in the Third World*, Brooklyn: Autonomedia.

———— (1982) "Ousmane Sembène and the Aesthetics of African Oral Traditions," *Africana Journal*.

Chanan, Michael (ed) (1983) *Twenty-five Years of the New Latin American Cinema*, London: BFI.

Chinweizu (2001) "The Weapon of Culture: Negritude Literature and the Making of Neocolonial Africa," in Okwui Enwezor (ed.) (2001) *The Short Century: Independence and Liberation Movements in Africa, 1945-1994*, New York: Prestel Verlag.

Chinweizu, Jemie, Onwuchekwa and Madubuike, Ihechukwu (1980) *Toward the Decolonization of African Literature*, Enugu: Fourth Dimension Publishers.

Chinweizu (1978) *The West and the Rest of Us*, London: NOK Publishers.

Cowhig, Ruth (1985) "Blacks in English Renaissance Drama and the Role of Shakespeare's Othello," in David Dabydeen (ed) (1985) *The Black Presence in English Literature*, Manchester: Manchester University Press.

Craven, Marie (1990) "Chocolat," *Cinema Papers*, No, 81 (December): 55-56.

Cripps, Thomas (1977) Slow Fade to Black: The Image of Blacks in American Films, 1900-1942, New York: Oxford University Press.

Croft, Stephen (1993) "Reconceptualizing National Cinema/s," *Quaterly Review of Film and Video*, Vol. 14 (3): 49-67.

Crowder, Michael (1978), *Colonial West Africa*, London: Frank Cass.

_____ (1968) *West Africa Under Colonial Rule*, London: Hutchinson and Co. (Publishers) Ltd.

_____ (1962) *The Story of Nigeria*, London: Faber and Faber.

Curtin, Philip (1976) "Measuring the Atlantic Slave Trade Once Again: A Comment," *Journal of African History*, Vol. XVII (4): 595-605.

_____ (1969) *The Atlantic Slave Trade: A Census*, Madison: The University of Wisconsin Press.

_____ (1964) *The Image of Africa: British Ideas and Action, 1780-1850*, Madison: The University of Wisconsin Press.

Dabydeen, David (ed) (1985) *The Black Presence in English Literature*, Manchester: Manchester University Press.

Davis, Merle J. (1937) "Forward," in L. A. Notcutt and G. C. Latham (1937) *The African and the Cinema*, London: The Edinburgh House Press.

Debrix, Jean-René (1982) "French 'Co-operation' ...and England?," in Angela Martin (ed) (1982) *African Films: The Context of Production*, London: BFI.

Diawara, Manthia (2001) "African Cinema and Decolonization," in Okwui Enwezor (ed.) (2001) *The Short Century: Independence and Liberation Movements in Africa, 1945-1994*, New York: Prestel Verlag.

_____ (1998) *In Search of Africa*, Cambridge, Massachusetts: Harvard University Press.

_____ (1992) *African Cinema*, Bloomington and Indianapolis: Indiana University Press.

_____ (1990-91) "The Nature of Mother in Dreaming Rivers," *Third Text*, (Winter): 73-84.

_____ (1990) "Black British Cinema: Spectatorship and Identity Formation in Territories," *Public Culture*, (Fall): 33-47.

_____ (1989) "African Cinema Today," *Framework*, No. 37: 110-128.

_____ (1988a) "Popular Culture and Oral Tradition in African Cinema," *Film Quarterly*, Vol. 41 (3) (Spring): 6-14.

_____ (1988b) "Black Spectatorship: Problems of Identification and Resistance," Screen, Vol. 29 (4) (Autumn): 66-112.

_____ (1986) "Sub-Saharan African Film Production: Technological Paternalism," *Jump Cut*, No. 32 (April): 61-66.

Dickinson, Margaret and Street, Sarah (1985) *Cinema and State*, London: BFI.

Donadey, Anne (2000) *Recasting Postcolonialism*, Portsmouth, NH: Heinemann.

Dyer, Richard (1988) "White," *Screen*, Vol. 29 (4) (Autumn): 44-64.

Dyer, Richard and Vincendeau, Ginette (1992) *Popular European Cinema*, London: Routledge.

Ekwuazi, Hyginus (1987) *Film in Nigeria*, Jos: Nigerian Film Corporation.

Elleh, Nnamdi (2001) "Architecture and Nationalism in Africa, 1945-1994," in Okwui Enwezor (ed.) (2001) *The Short Century: Independence and Liberation Movements in Africa, 1945-1994*, New York: Prestel Verlag.

Enwezor, Okwui (ed.) (2001) "The Short Century: Independence and Liberation Movements in Africa, 1945-1994: An Introduction," in Okwui Enwezor (ed.) (2001) *The Short Century: Independence and Liberation Movements in Africa, 1945-1994*, New York: Prestel Verlag.

Elsaesser, Thomas (1989) *New German Cinema: A History*, London: BFI/Macmillan.

Espinosa, Julio Garcia (1983) "For an Imperfect Cinema," trans. Julianne Burton, in Michael Chanan (ed) (1983) *Twenty-five Years of the New Latin American Cinema*, London: BFI.

Fabre, Geneviève and Feith, Michel (eds.) (2001) "Temples for Tomorrow: Look Back at the Harlem Renaissance: An Introductory Essay," in Geneviève Fabre and Michel Feith (eds.) (2001) *Temples for Tomorrow: Look Back at the Harlem Renaissance*, Bloomington and Indianapolis: Indiana University Press.

Fanon, Frantz (1967a) *Black Skin, White Masks*, trans. Charles Lam Markmann, London: Pluto Press.

_____ (1967b) *The Wretched of the Earth*, trans. Constance Farrington, Harmondsworth: Penguin.

_____ (1967c) *Toward the African Revolution*, trans. Haakon Chevalier, London: Monthly Review Press.

_____ (1967d) *A Dying Colonialism*, trans. Haakon Chevalier, New York: Groove Press.

Feuchtwang, Stephen (1985) "Fanon's Politics of Culture: The Colonial Situation and its Extension," *Echoes of Empire*, London: BFI Summer School.

Foucault, Michel (1977) *Discipline and Punish: The Birth of the Prison*, trans. A. M. Sheridan, New York: Pantheon Books.

_____ (1981) "What is an Author," in John Caughie (ed) (1981) *Theories of Authorship*, London: Routledge and Kegan Paul.

Freire, Paulo (1970) *Pedagogy of the Oppressed*, trans. Myra Bergman, Harmondsworth: Penguin.

Frye, Northrop (1957) *Anatomy of Criticism: Four Essay*, Princeton, New Jersey: Princeton University Press.

Furendi, Frank (1989) *The Mau Mau War in Perspectives*, London: James Currey.

Fusco, Coco (1989) "About Locating Ourselves and Our Representations," *Framework*, No. 36: 7-14.

Gabriel, Teshome H. (1986) "Colonialism and 'Law and Order' Criticism," *Screen*, Vol. 27 (3/4): 140-146.

────── (1985) "Towards a Critical Theory of Third World Films," *Third World Affairs*: 355-369.

────── (1983) "Teaching Third World Films," *Screen*, Vol. 24 (2) (March-April): 60-64.

────── (1979) Third Cinema in the Third World: The Aesthetics of Liberation, Ann Arbor, Michigan: UMI Research Press.

Gadjigo, Samba, Ralph H. Faulkingham, Thomas Cassirer, and Reinhard Sander (eds) (1993) *Ousmane Sembène: Dialogues with Critics and Writers*, Amherst: University of Massachusetts Press.

George, Kathrine (1958) "The Civilized West Looks at Primitive Africa, 1400-1800," *Isis*, Vol. 49: 62-72.

Ghali, Noureddin (1987) "An Interview with Ousmane Sembène," in J. Downing (ed) (1987) *Film and Politics in the Third World*, Brooklyn: Autonomedia.

Gledhill, Christin (ed) (1987) *Home is Where the Heart Is*, London: BFI.

Grierson, John (1948) "The Film and Primitive Peoples," in *The Film in Colonial Development: A Report of a Conference*, London: The British Film Institute.

Grosz, Elizabeth (1990) *Jacques Lacan: A Feminist Introduction*, London: Routledge.

Hammond, Dorothy and Jablow, Alta (1977) *The Myth of Africa*, New York: The Library of Social Sciences.

Harrrow, Kenneth (ed) (1999) *African Cinema*, Trenton, NJ: Africa World Press.

Haynes, Jonathan (ed) *Nigerian Video Films*, Jos: Nigerian Film Corporation.

Heath, Stephen (1981) "Comment on 'The Idea of Authorship,'" in John Caughie (ed) (1981) *Theories of Authorship*, London: Routledge and Kegan Paul.

———— (1976) "Narrative Space," *Screen*, Vol. 17 (3) (Autumn): 68-112.

Higson, Andrew (1989) "The Concept of National Cinema," *Screen*, Vol. 30 (4) (Autumn): 36-46.

Hutcheon, Linda (1985) *A Theory of Parody*, London: Methuen.

Inikori, Joseph (1979) "The Slave Trade and the Atlantic Economies, 1451-1870," in UNESCO Report (1979) *The African Slave Trade: From the Fifteenth Century to Nineteenth Century*, Paris: UNESCO.

———— (1976a) "Measuring the Atlantic Slave Trade: An Assessment of Curtin and Anstey," *Journal of African History*, Vol. XVII (2): 197-223.

———— (1976b) "Measuring the Atlantic Slave Trade: A Rejoinder," *Journal of African History*, Vol. XVII (4): 607-627.

Irele, Abiola F. (2001) *The African Imagination: Literature in Africa and the Black Diaspora*, Oxford: Oxford University Presss.

———— (1990) "The African Imagination," *Research in African Literatures*, Vol. 21 (1) (Spring): 49-155.

———— (1981) *The African Experience in Literature and Ideology,* London: Heinemann.

Izod, Alan (1948) "Some Special Features of Colonial Film Production," in *The Film in Colonial Development: A Report of a Conference*, London: The British Film Institute.

JanMohamed, Abdul R. (1985) "The Economy of Manichean Allegory: The Function of Racial Difference in Colonialist Literature," *Critical Inquiry*, Vol. 12 (1) (Autumn): 59-87.

———— (1983) *Manichean Aesthetics: The Politics of Literature in Colonial Africa*, Amherst: The University of Massachusetts Press.

Jeyifo, 'Biodun (1985) *The Truthful Lie: Essays*, London & Port of Spain: New Beacon.

—— (1984) *The Yoruba Popular Traveling Theatre of Nigeria*, Lagos: A Nigeria Magazine Publication.

Jones, Creech (1948) "Opening Address," in *The Film in Colonial Development: A Report of a Conference*, London: The British Film Institute.

Kabbani, Rana (1986) *Europe's Myth of Orient*, London: Pandora Press.

Kariuki, Josiah Mwangi (1963) *"Mau Mau" Detainee: An Account by a Kenya African of His Experiences in Detention Camps, 1953-1960*, Harmondsworth: Penguin Books.

Kuhn, Annette (1978) "The Camera I: Observations on Documentary," *Screen*, Vol. 19 (2) (Summer): 71-83.

Lazarus, Neil (1993) "Disavowing Decolonization: Fanon, Nationalism, and the Problematic of Representation in Current Theories of Colonial Discourse," *Research in African Literatures*, Vol. 24 (4) (Winter): 67-98.

Leab, Daniel (1975) *From Sambo to Superspade: The Black Experience in Motion Pictures*, London: Secker & Warburg.

Leahy, James (1989) "Camp de Thiaroye," *Monthly Film Bulletin*, Vol. 56 (667) (August): 270-271.

—— (1988a) "Sarraounia," *Monthly Film Bulletin*, Vol. 55 (648) (January): 8-9.

—— (1988b) "CinemaScope South of the Sahara: Med Hondo Talks to James Leahy About Making a New Cinema in Africa," *Monthly Film Bulletin*, Vol. 55 (648) (January): 9-10.

Lovell, Terry (1983) *Pictures of Reality*, London: BFI.

Mackenzie, John M. (1984) *Propaganda and Empire: The Manipulation of British Public Opinion, 1880-1960*, Manchester: Manchester University Press.

Malkmus, Lizbeth and Armes, Roy (1992) *Arab and African Film Making*, London: Zed Books Ltd.

Mamdani, Mahmood (1996) *Citizen and Subject: Contemporary Africa and the Legacy of Late Colonialism*, Princeton: Princeton University Press.

Man, Kristin and Edna G. Bay (eds) (2001) *Rethinking the African Diaspora: The Making of a Black Atlantic World in the Bight of Benin and Brazil*, London: Frank Cass.

Martin, Angela (ed) (1982) *African Films: The Context of Production*, London: BFI.

Mason, Peter (1990) *Deconstructing America: Representations of the Other*, London: Routledge.

Maynard, Richard (ed) (1974) *Africa on Film: Myth and Reality*, Rochell Park, New Jersey: Hayden Book Company, Inc.

Mazrui, Ali A. (2002) "The Study of Africa: Genesis, Substance, and Cultural Boundaries," in Ricardo Rene Laremont and Tracia Leacock Seghatolislami (eds.) (2002) *Africanity Redefined: Collected Essays of Ali A. Mazrui, Vol. 1*, Trenton, NJ: Africa World Press.

Metz, Christian (1981) "History/Discourse: A Note on Two Voyeurism," in John Caughie (ed) (1981) *Theories of Authorship*, London: Routledge and Kegan Paul.

_____ (1974) *Film Language: A Semiotics of the Cinema*, trans. Michael Taylor, New York: Oxford University Press.

Mgbejume, Onyero (1989) *Film in Nigeria: Development, Problems and Promises*, Nairobi: African Council on Communication Education.

Mudimbe, V. Y. (1988) *The Invention of Africa*, London: James Currey.

Mulvey, Laura (1991) "*Xala*, Ousmane Sembène 1976: The Carapace that Failed," *Third Text*, Vol. 16-17 (Autumn-Winter): 19-37.

_____ (1975) "Visual Pleasure and Narrative Cinema," *Screen*, Vol. 16 (3) (Autumn): 6-18.

Naremore, James (1991) "Authorship and the Cultural Politics of Film Criticism," *Film Quarterly*, Vol. 44 (1) (Fall): 14-22.

Nash, Mark (2001) "The Modernity of African Cinema," in Okwui Enwezor (ed.) (2001) *The Short Century: Independence and Liberation Movements in Africa, 1945-1994*, New York: Prestel Verlag.

Neale, Stephen (1983) "Masculinity as Spectacle," *Screen*, Vol. 24 (November-December): 2-16.

_____ (1980) *Genre*, London: BFI.

Nesteby, James (1982) *Black Images in American Films*, Washington D. C.: University Press of America.

Nichols, Bill (1987) "History, Myth and Narrative in Documentary," *Film Quarterly*, Vol. XLI (1) (Fall): 9-20.

_____ (1983) "The Voice of Documentary," *Film Quarterly*, Vol. 36 (3) (Spring): 17-30.

_____ (1976-77) "Documentary Theory and Practice," *Screen*, Vol. 17 (4) (Winter): 34-48.

Nkrumah, Kwame (2001) "Speech by the Prime Minister of Ghana at the Opening Session of the All-African People's Conference, on Monday, December 8, 1958," in Okwui Enwezor (ed.) (2001) *The Short Century: Independence and Liberation Movements in Africa, 1945-1994*, New York: Prestel Verlag.

Noble, Peter (1948) *The Negro in Films*, London: Robinson.

Notcutt, L. A. and Latham, G. C. (1937) *The African and the Cinema*, London: The Edinburgh House Press.

Nowell-Smith, Geoffrey (1981) "A Note on 'History/Discourse,'" in John Caughie (ed) (1981) *Theories of Authorship*, London: Routledge and Kegan Paul.

Nyamnjoh, Francis B. (2002) " 'A Child is One Person's Only in the Womb': Domestication, Agency and Subjectivity in the Cameroonian Grassfields," in Richard Werbner (ed) (2002) *Postcolonial Subjectivities in Africa*, London & New York: Zed Books.

Obiechina, Emmanuel (1975) *Culture, Tradition and Society in the West African Novel*, Cambridge: Cambridge University Press.

Okeke, Chike (2001) "Modern African Art" in Okwui Enwezor (ed.) (2001) *The Short Century: Independence and Liberation Movements in Africa, 1945-1994*, New York: Prestel Verlag.

Okome, Onookome (1990) "The Rise of the Folkloric Cinema in Nigeria," Ph.D Thesis. (Unpublished), Ibadan: University of Ibadan, Nigeria.

Okome, Onookome and Jonathan Hynes (1995) *Cinema and Social Change in West Africa*, Jos: Nigerian Film Corporation.

Okpewho, Isidore (1979) *The Epic in Africa*, New York: Columbia University Press.

Okpewho, Isidore, Carole Boyce and A. Mazrui (eds) (1999) *The African Diaspora: African Origins and New World Identities*, Bloomington, Indiana: Indiana University Press.

Oksiloff, Assenka (2001) *Picturing the Primitive: Visual Culture*, Ethnography, and Early German Cinema, New York: Palgrave.

Opubor, Alfred E. and Nwuneli, Onuora E. (eds) (1979) *The Development and Growth of the Film Industry in Nigeria*, Lagos: National Council for Arts and Culture.

Parry, Benita (1987) "Problems in Current Theories of Colonial Discourse," *Oxford Literary Review*, Vol. 9 (1-2): 27-58.

Pearson, George (1948) "The Making of Films for Illiterates in Africa," in *The Film in Colonial Development: A Report of a Conference*, London: The British Film Institute.

Pedler, Frederick (1979) *Main Currents of West African History, 1940-1978*, London: Macmillan Press.

Pedersen, Carl (2001) "The Tropics in New York: Claude McKay and the New Negro Movement," in Geneviève Fabre and Michel Feith (eds.) (2001) *Temples for Tomorrow:*

Look Back at the Harlem Renaissance, Bloomington and Indianapolis: Indiana University Press.

Pfaff, Françoise (1988) *Twenty-five Black African Filmmakers*, New York: Greenwood Press.

———— (1986) "An African Filmmaker in Paris," *Jump Cut*, No. 31 (March): 44-46.

———— (1984) The Cinema of Ousmane Sembène: A Pioneer of African Film, Westport: Praeger & Greenwood Press.

Pieterse, Cosmos and Duerden, Dennis (1972) *African Writers Talking*, New York: Africana Publishing.

Pieterse, Jan Nederveen (1992) *White on Black: Images of Africa and Blacks in Western Culture*, New Haven: Yale University Press.

Pick, Zuzana M. (1993) *The New Latin American Cinema: A Continental Project*, Austin: University of Texas Press.

Pines, Jim (1975) *Blacks in Films: A Survey of Racial Themes and Images in the American Film*, London: Studio Vista.

Pinto, Françoise Latour de Vega and Carreira, A (1979) "Portuguese Participation in the Slave Trade: Opposing Forces, Trends of Opinions Within Portuguese Society: Effects on Portugal's Socio-Economic Development," in UNESCO Report (1979) *The African Slave Trade: From Fifteenth Century to the Nineteenth Century*, Paris: UNESCO.

Porter, Dennis (1985) "Orientalism and its Problems," *Echoes of Empire*, London: BFI, Summer School: 179-193.

Potts, James (1979) "Is there an International Film Language?," *Sight and Sound*, Vol. 48 (2) (Spring): 74-81.

Povey, John (1972) "The Novels of Chinua Achebe," in Bruce King (ed) (1972) *Introduction to Nigerian Literature*, New York: Africana Publishing Co.

Rahill, Frank (1967) *The World of Melodrama*, University Park & London: The Pennsylvania State University Press.

Ranvaud, Don (1978) "Interview with Med Hondo," *Framework*, Nos. 7-8 (Spring): 28-30.

Regester, Charlene (1998) "Headlines to Highlights: Oscar Micheaux's Exploitation of the Rhinelander Case," *Western Journal of Black Studies*, Vol. 22 No.3 (Fall).

_____ (1998) "The Reading of a Still: The Evocation of Death in Dorothy Dandridge's Photograph," *Art Criticism*, Vol. 13, No. 1 (Spring/Summer).

_____ (1997) "African American Extras in Hollywood during the 1920s and 1930s," *Film History*, Vol. 9, No.1 (Fall).

_____ (1997) "Oscar Micheaux the Entrepreneur: Financing The House Behind the Cedars, " *Journal of Film & Video*, Vol. 49, Nos.1-2 (Spring/Summer).

_____ (1994/1996) "African Americans in the Early Period of Cinema: A Period of Protest and Self-Assertion," Clair Dupre la Tour, Andre Gaudreault and Roberta Pearson (eds) *Cinema at the Turn of the Century: Proceedings of the Third International Conference at Domitor*, New York: New York University Press, Reprint, Quebec: Nuit Blanche Payot-Laussane.

_____ (1996) "Black Films, White Censors: Oscar Micheaux Congronts Censorship in New York, Virginia, and Chicago," in Francis G. Couvares (ed) (1996) *Movie Cencorship and American Culture*, Washington, D.C.: Smithsonian Institution Press.

_____ (1995) "The Misreading and Rereading of African American Filmmaker Oscar Micheaux, " *Film History*, Vol. 7, No. 4 (Winter).

_____ (1995) "Oscar Micheaux's Multifaceted Portrayals of the African American Male: The Good, the Bad, and the Ugly," *Studies in Popular Culture*, Vol. 17, No. 2 (April).

_____ (1994) "Oscar Micheaux's Body and Soul: A Film of Conflicting Themes," in Phyllis Klotman and Gloria Gibson (eds) (1994) *In Touch with the Spirit: Black Religious and Musical Expression in American Cinema*, Bloomington, Indiana: Indiana University Press.

_____ (1994) "Lynched, Assaulted, and Intimidated: Oscar Micheaux's Most Controversial Films," *Popular Culture Review*, Vol. 5, No. 1 (Fall).

Reid, Mark (1986) "Working Abroad," trans. Sylvie Blum, *Jump Cut*, No.31 (March): 48-49.

Richards, Jeffrey (1973) *Visions of Yesterday*, London: Routledge and Kegan Paul.

_____ and Aldgate, Anthony (1983) *Best of British Cinema and Society, 1930-1970*, Oxford: Basil Blackwell Publishers.

Rocha, Glauber (1983a) "The Aesthetics of Hunger," trans. Burnes Hollyman and Randall Johnson, in Michael Chanan (ed) (1983) *Twenty-five Years of the New Latin American Cinema*, London: BFI.

_____ (1983b) "Down with Populism," trans. Julianne Burton, in Michael Chanan (ed) *Twenty-five Years of the New Latin American Cinema*, London: BFI.

Roscoe, Adrian A. (1971) *Mother is Gold: A Study in West Africa Literature*, Cambridge: Cambridge University Press.

Said, Edward (1994) *Culture and Imperialism*, London: Vintage Press.

_____ (1978) *Orientalism*, London: Penguin Books.

Sanjines, Jorges (1983) "Problems of Form and Content in Revolutionary Cinema," trans. Malcolm Coad, in Michael Chanan (ed) (1983) *Twenty-five Years of the New Latin American Cinema*, London: BFI.

Sarris, Andrew (1981) "What is Auteur Theory?," in John Caughie (ed) (1981) *Theories of Authorship*, London: Routledge and Kegan Paul.

Shaka, Femi (2000) "Instructional Cinema in Colonial Africa: A Critical Analysis of Terry Bishop's Daybreak in Udi," *The Literary Griot*, Vol. 12, No. 1. (Spring) 62-86.

_____ (2000) "Parody and The Colonialist Autobiographical Film: A Critical Analysis of Claire Denis's Chocolat," *Journal of Creative Arts*, Vol. No. 1 (April): 19-25.

_____ (1998) "The Effects of British and French Colonial Policies on Film Production in Anglophone and Francophone African Countries," *The Literary Griot*, Vol. 10, No.1 (Spring): 28-42.

_____ (1998) "History and the Historical Play: A Critical Study of Ola Rotimi's Kurunmi, *Ovonramwen Nogbaisi*, and *Hopes of the Living Dead*," *The Ethnographer: A Journal of the Niger Delta Research Association*, Vol. 1, No. 1 (June): 1-15.

_____ (1996) "African Cinema" by Manthia Diawara: A Critical Review, *Africa Studio*, Vol. 1, No.1: 96-97.

_____ (1995) "The Politics of Cultural Conversion in Colonialist African Cinema," *CineAction*, No. 37 (June): 51-67.

_____ (1995) "Vicky Dakar and the Other Story of French Colonial Stewardship in Africa," *Research in African Literatures*, Vol. 26, No. 3 (Fall): 66-77.

Singer, Ben (2001) *Melodrama and Modernity: Early Sensational Cinema and Its Contents*, New York: Columbia University Press.

Smith, James (1973) *Melodrama*, London: Methuen and Co Ltd.

Smyth, Rosaleen (1983) "Movies and Mandarins: The Official Film and British Colonial Africa," in James Curran and Vincent Porter (eds) (1983) *British Cinema History*, London: Weidenfeld and Nicolson.

_____ (1979) "The Development of British Colonial Film Policy, 1927-1939, with Special Reference to East and Central Africa," *Journal of African History*, Vol. 20 (3): 437-450.

Snowden, Frank, jr. (1970) *Blacks in Antiquity*, Cambridge, Massachusetts: The Belknap Press of Harvard University Press.

Sobchack, Thomas (1977) "Genre Film: A Classical Experience," in Barry K. Grant (ed) (1977) *Film Genre: Theory and Criticism*, Metuchen, New Jersey & London: The Scarecrow Press, Inc.

Solanas, Fernando and Getino, Octavio (1983) "Towards a Third Cinema," trans. Julianne Burton and Michael Chanan, in Michael Chanan (ed) (1983) *Twenty-five Years of the New Latin American Cinema*, London: BFI.

Sorenson, M. P. K. (1968) *Origin of European Settlements in Kenya*, Nairobi: Oxford University Press.

Soyinka, Wole (1976) *Myth, Literature and the African World*, Cambridge: Canto.

Stam, Robert, Burgoyne, Robert and Flitterman-Lewis, Sandy (1992) *New Vocabularies in Film Semiotic: Structuralism, Post-Structuralism and Beyond*, London: Routledge.

Stam, Robert (1991) "Eurocentrism, Afrocentrism, Polycentrism: Theories of Third Cinema," *Quarterly Review of Film and Video*, Vol. 13 (1-3): 217-237.

_____ (1982/83) "Slow Fade to Afro: The Black Presence in Brazilian Cinema," *Film Quarterly*, Vol. XXXVI (2) (Winter): 16-32.

_____ and Spence, Louise (1983) "Colonialism, Racism and Representation: An Introduction," *Screen*, Vol. 24 (2) (March-April): 2-20.

Stephan, Nancy (1990) "Race and Gender: The Role of Analogy in Science," in David Theo Goldberg (ed) (1990) *Anatomy of Racism*, Minneapolis: University of Minnesota Press.

_____ (1982) *The Idea of Race in Science: Great Britain, 1800-1960*, London: The Macmillan Press.

Stiller, Nikki (1990) "Chocolat," *Film Quarterly*, Vol. 44 (2) (Winter): 52-56.

Stott, Rebecca (1989) "The Dark Continent: Africa as a Female Body in Haggard's Adventure," *Feminist Review*, No. 32: 69-89.

Street, Brian (1985) "Reading the Novels of Empire: Race and Ideology in the Classic 'Tale of Adventure'," in David Dabydeen (ed) (1985) *The Black Presence in English Literature*, Manchester: Manchester University Press.

Tandina, Ousmane (1993) "Sarraounia, An Epic?," *Research in African Literatures*, Vol. 24 (2) (Summer): 23-32.

Taylor, Clyde R. (1998) *The Mask of Art: Breaking the Aesthetic Contract: Film and Literature*, Bloomington, Indiana: Indiana University Press.

Ukadike, Frank (1994) *Black African Cinema*, Berkeley: University of California Press.

_____ (1991a) "Anglophone African Media," *Jump Cut*, No. 36 (May): 74-80.

_____ (1991b) "Framing Fespaco: Pan-African Film in Context," *Afterimage*, Vol. 19 (4) (November): 6-9.

Vaughan, Kehinde J. (1966) "Africa and the Cinema," *African Statesman*, No. 2 (April-June): 29-31.

Wa Thiong'o, Ngugi (1986) *Decolonizing the Mind: The Politics of Language in African Literature*, London: James Currey.

Wali, Obi (1964) "Polemics: The Dead End of African Literature - A Reply to Critics," *Transition*, Vol. 12 (6-7): 6-7.

_____ (1963) "The Dead End of African Literature?," *Transition*, Vol. 10 (13-15): 13-15.

Walters, Margaret (1989) "Overseas Affairs: Colonial Roots and Primitive Rites," *Listener*, Vol. 122 (3110) (April): 47.

Werbner, Richard (2002) "Introduction: Post-colonial Subjectivities: The Personal, the Political and the Moral," in Richard Werbner (ed) (2002) *Postcolonial Subjectivities in Africa*, London & New York: Zed Books.

Willemen, Paul (1989) "The Third Cinema Question: Notes and Reflections," in Jim Pines and Paul Willemen (eds) (1989) *Questions of Third Cinema*, London: BFI.

Williams, Alan (ed) (2002) *Film and Nationalism*, New Brunswick, NJ: Rutgers University Press.

Wylie, Hal and Bernth Lindfors (eds) (2000) *Multiculturalism and Hybridity in African Literatures*, Trenton, NJ: Africa World Press.

Yearwood, Gladstone (2000) *Black Film as a Signifying Practice*, Trenton, NJ: Africa World Press.

Government Reports

Mass Education in African Society, Colonial Office, Colonial No. 186, London: Her Majesty's Stationary Office.

The Film in Colonial Development: A Report of a Conference, London: The British Film Institute, 1948.

The Instructional Film in the United Kingdom Dependencies, Central Office of Information (COI), No. R. 3161, October, 1955.

INDEX